An English Nationalism

Tony Linsell

Athelney

Published by
Athelney
1 Providence Street
King's Lynn
Norfolk
England

Printed by
Antony Rowe Ltd
Chippenham
Wiltshire
England

Published 2001

Copyright Tony Linsell

ISBN 1 903313015

British Library Cataloguing-in-Publication Data. A catalogue record for this book is available from the British Library.

Vanessa, Stuart, Anthony
Julia & Peter, Jeremy & Anne-Marie
My wife Pearl
My father Cliff
My mother Irene, a woman
of courage and determination
who died 5th February 2000

Contents

Foreword

We live in an age when many English people, and in particular the young, know next to nothing about their history, and are uncertain about their national identity. One of the reasons for this sad state of affairs is that for many years the English have been encouraged to think of themselves as being primarily British and, more recently, as Europeans or even as *citizens of the world*; a term that reveals the confused thinking of those who use it. In schools, English history has been replaced with British and World history, and any promotion of an English national identity is treated as subversive of an *inclusive* state ideology. Those righteous individuals who promote the official creed are so convinced of the universal application, and everlasting nature of their ideology that they feel no need to defend it with rational argument. Instead, unbelievers who openly question the assumptions that underlie the modern liberal world-view are treated either as evil heretics or as fools.

A simple illustration of the propaganda used to promote a *correct* view of the world is to be found in the experience I had early in the 1990's when I visited a school and saw a large poster which proclaimed, *We British are a rich mixture*. It listed in a random manner many national and other groups including: Bangladeshi, Jamaican, Welsh, Nigerian, Somali, Turkish, Scots, Indian, Cypriot, Irish. When I asked a teacher why there was no mention of the English, I received a blank look and a shrug of the shoulders. His surprise at being asked such a question changed to suspicion, and it became obvious that I was seen as a troublemaker. No answer was given and I left the school puzzled as to whether the teacher really believed that there is no English nation or he simply preferred its existence to be downplayed or denied. Perhaps he was confused about the difference between being English and being British or maybe he found the notion of an English nation distasteful or ideologically inconvenient. Whatever the reason, it made me wonder what justification there could be for displaying that poster in a school. The motives of those who produce such propaganda are clearly ideological but to question their right to introduce it into schools, or to suggest that Englishness and English history be presented in a positive way, is to invite facile insults. A more hostile response can be expected to the suggestion that there is more to being English than being born in England or living there.

The school poster has given rise to this book, which has been written on and off, mostly off, from 1993 until 2000. The delay means that many of the events referred to in the text were happening at the time of writing but are now history. The great speed with which attitudes have changed over recent years became apparent during the process of revising and updating the text for publication. For instance, when I started I found it difficult to understand why English football supporters waved Union flags and sang the UK state anthem. Since then, the Euro 96 football championship and the creation of a Scottish Parliament has helped to

11

change perceptions. The Union flag and the Britishness it represents has suddenly become a relic of the past. Perhaps by the time Euro 2004 arrives, the English will have a national anthem and England will be nearer to regaining a Parliament of its own.

My thanks go to those who encouraged me to *say what needs to be said*, and to the many people who in various ways give their time and energy to awakening the English from their communal sleep. Guy Green and Cyning Meadowcroft are two on a long list of determined and dedicated campaigners. I am grateful to David P for his advice and to Tim Bragg for his encouragement and help in bringing back to life a manuscript that had been gathering dust for nearly three years. Thanks also to my wife Pearl for her forbearance and practical help. This would not have been possible without her.

Introduction

One of the aims of this book is to encourage the English to shake off the crippling burden of guilt and shame that has been unfairly heaped on them during the past forty years. The English are a nation with the same right as other nations to assert their identity in a confident and dignified manner, and to preserve their way of life.

Another aim is to encourage members of the Anglo-Saxon diaspora to take an interest in their shared early history. It belongs to all of them and is an important part of their individual and communal identity. Those who have firm roots in the past have a sense of time and place that makes them better able to resist the ideological, economic and cultural uniformity being foisted on them by contemporary globalism.

The early sections of **Part One** may at first seem irrelevant to English nationalism but the intent is to put flesh on the early English and give a feel for what they believed and how they lived. Taken as a whole, it gives a brief outline of early English history and will, I hope, counter the idea that the English appeared out of thin air sometime after the arrival of the Normans in England. In an attempt to overcome that common misconception, attention is given to the arrival of the English in Britain about 600 years before the Battle of Hastings. Some readers may prefer to skip Part One and return when its relevance is better appreciated.

Very little contemporary documentary information is available for the early period of English history so to a large extent we have to rely on archaeological and later documentary evidence. In recent times, genetics has provided an additional means of helping us gain a better understanding of where various groups of people came from and where they settled.

Old English texts give a valuable insight into the values and outlook of the English in the early period. The maxims, charms and tales of heroism, such as *Beowulf* and the *Battle of Maldon*, give a feel for the period and make it clear that attitudes, perceptions and values can endure even though much else is short-lived.

A useful foreign text is the *Prose Edda* of Snorri Sturluson (1179–1241), an Icelandic Christian. The *Prose Edda* tells us much about Norse mythology, which had been a vigorous and evolving collection of stories and wisdom. The problem is that the myths recorded in the 13th century are unlikely to be a reliable guide to the beliefs of 5th–8th century Scandinavians let alone those of the English, whose culture took a similar but different evolutionary path. However, despite reservations, the *Edda* is an important source of information which gives the flavour of pre-Christian ways and beliefs. The values and attitudes it promotes are rooted in a folklore that was known in some shape or form throughout Northern Europe. Stories and customs differ in detail from place to place and from time to time but the values and perceptions they promote are fairly constant. Because of that, the *Edda* gives an insight into how the early English lived and viewed the world. Also, parts of the creation story told in the *Edda* come from a much earlier period and were probably known to the early English. For that reason a creation story based on the Norse account opens Part One. It is presented in a way that is sympathetic to the beliefs of the time. English names, particularly those for the gods, have been used in place of Norse names.

The English generally know little about the beliefs and customs of their early ancestors. One reason for that is that the Church did its best to destroy, suppress or disguise traces of the Old Ways. Another is that with a few notable exceptions, academics have adopted a wholly hostile and dismissive view of indigenous Northern European beliefs and customs, believing them to be inferior to those that have their origins around the Mediterranean and Near East.[1] They suppose that the people of Northern Europe were barbarians with no wisdom or culture of their own, and that everything that was sophisticated and clever was borrowed from the South. The Romans are deemed to have introduced the Germanic tribes to *civilisation*, while Christianity brought them spiritual enlightenment.[2] Many adopt this view without question and overlook the fact that much of the old culture and way of life was lost during the *conversion*, a period when many traditional communal institutions were destroyed and the old gods demonised.

Classicists prefer stone buildings and the written word. They tend to view the Roman Empire as a font of civilisation rather than as a bureaucratic and military imperial power. The colonised people lost the power to govern themselves and became trapped in an economic and political system over which they had no control – a form of globalisation. But now we are supposed to regard such things as immense good fortune, a view that perhaps reflects current liberal dogma. Similarly, we are encouraged to see the arrival in England of Augustine in 597 and Duke William in 1066 as *a good thing*. A different interpretation, which probably better represents the feelings of the English of that time, is that the arrival of Augustine started a process of cultural imperialism that made possible William's conquest and the misery it caused. None of this is meant to suggest that the Christian cultural invasion marked a complete break with the past. A more realistic view is that there was a Germanisation of Christianity. Although the Church dominated the *official culture*, many of the old practices and beliefs were

---

[1] A book that played an important part in stirring an interest in the subject was Brian Branson's *The Lost Gods of England* (Thames and Hudson, reprinted by Constable). Following on were Kathleen Herbert's, *Looking for the Lost Gods of England*, and *English Heroic Legends* (Anglo-Saxon Books). Also *The Way of Wyrd* by Brian Bates.

[2] It can be argued that the knowledge and forms of administration commonly attributed to the Church were in fact the product of the heathen Greek and Roman civilisations. The Church adopted skills and knowledge it found useful and suppressed learning that conflicted with Christian doctrine. As a result, much of what the Greeks and Romans contributed to European civilisation was for many centuries lost to Europe, being re-introduced, with additions, by the Arabs. That re-introduction marked the end of the intellectual Dark Ages and a re-awakening, or renaissance, that made possible rationalism and the scientific method which gradually undermined the position of the Church as the font of all knowledge and wisdom.

absorbed into Christianity and continue to this day. For example, the heathen celebration of birth and rebirth (Mothers' Night and the god Ing – the Green Man) and the turning of the year (Yuletide) became Christmas. If the Christian and Norman veneers are peeled back, traces can be found of the indigenous culture and the threads that link the English of that time with this. To assist in that, and help counter the idea that civilisation was unknown to the English until it was kindly bestowed on them, the focus of Part One is on the pre-Christian period of early English history. This approach suggests that many of our modern-day institutions and attitudes have their origins in early English and Northern European culture and are not imported from the Mediterranean or Middle East. It would be silly to take this too far and dismiss Christianity as an irrelevance. That is certainly not the intention because Christianity has clearly played an important part in the evolution of both the English way of life and a wider European civilisation.

It is worth restating that the early history of the English and England belongs not just to the English in England but to all those of English descent in North America, Australia, Canada, New Zealand and elsewhere who together form the Anglo-Saxon diaspora.

Parts Two and Three are concerned with issues that are important to all nations but which cannot be discussed in a sensible and open way in many Western states. In working through the various topics it has been necessary to use some of the shorthand commonly used when discussing or reporting *international* events. However, an attempt has been made to avoid shorthand that alters the meaning of words that are essential to a proper understanding of world politics. For example, a report in a newspaper which proclaims that the United States and China have reached agreement in their negotiations on trade, means that the governments of the USA and China have reached an agreement, or the political elites or even individuals have reached an agreement. The use of shorthand does little harm provided we are aware it is being used.

One of the problems with the study of nationalism is that the literature is dominated by those who view the subject from the outside and with great disdain. Even at the highest level, we find academics treating nationalism as if it were like plutonium in a reprocessing plant. Those engaged in the work have to make it clear that they understand that the material is dangerous and might contaminate them. They wear a protective dogma and run an ideological Geiger counter over their colleagues from time to time to make sure they have not been contaminated. Any academic who admits to being a nationalist has at the very least to claim to be a *liberal* nationalist, although that gives rise to difficulties and does not absolve them from suspicion. The result is an approach to nationalism that is no more neutral than would be expected if study of the Roman Catholic Church was dominated by Moslems, or worse still, Protestants. Only the naive believe that the work of social scientists is free from ideological bias.

The English nationalism presented here is just one variant. There is no pretence that the English are superior to other nations or more deserving of special treatment. Like other nationalisms, this one is inspired primarily by the need to protect and defend. But that does not mean it is passive. Those who attack and seek to destroy a nation should expect a vigorous defence and counter attack.

Many of the points and complaints made here are commonplace but they need to be made again because they are an essential part of a nationalist world-view. For instance, attacks on consumerism and materialism are far from new (going back to the ancient Greeks) but those *isms* are at the heart of the new globalism to which nationalists are opposed.

There is some repetition and overlap between sections but that is to some extent unavoidable in book like this where some sections need to stand alone.

Much of what follows is dismissive of liberals and their propaganda. It should therefore be made clear from the start that *liberal* is used in the way defined in the text. What is meant by *liberals* is *social-liberals* and *economic-liberals*, and not those people who display qualities that are sometimes claimed by modern ideological liberals as their exclusive property. I mean by this that being easygoing, tolerant, open-minded, and generous has little to do with being an ideological liberal. Those qualities often spring from community and the sense of security it gives. Ideological liberals often lack any of those qualities and their societies do little to promote them, although liberals pretend otherwise. If we judge them by their actions rather than their words, it can be seen that ideological liberals are no more tolerant or open-minded than any other group of people.

For the great amusement of liberals everywhere, I would like to mention that some of the nicest people I know are ideological liberals. However, none of them are so wedded to their creed that they would risk life or limb to defend my right to freely express my views, although I think that most liberals expect others to put themselves at risk to defend free expression for liberals.

All readers will disagree with some or all of the definitions given here, and much else besides, but that is inevitable and to be expected. If it is thought that the terms have been misunderstood or misused then the reply is that an attempt has been made to use them *properly*. If there has been a failure to do so, it is at least reasonably clear what the terms have been taken to mean. It is an impossible task to arrive at *ideology-free* definitions. Liberals have for a very long time assumed the right to define terms in ways that suit their convenience and to impose those definitions and their terminology on others. An attempt has been made here to define and use certain terms in a way that suits a non-liberal view of the world. If liberals dislike the result that is regrettable but it cannot be helped.

Part One   The Origins of the English

The Creation

Allfather is very strong and full of might. He lives through all time and governs all things. He is the father of the heavens and the earth and all that is in them. When he made man he gave him a soul that can live on and need never die though the body will drop to dust or burn to ashes.

Night is the greatest of mysteries; she is the past and the future.
All of creation came from her womb and to her embrace it will return.

Allfather took on the form of Twilight and had a child by Night;
it was a son named Space.

Allfather had a second child by Night; it was a daughter named Earth.

Allfather took on the form of Dawn and had a third child by Night;
it was a son named Day.

The first world was one of great heat and great cold. The north was full of ice and frost and gusts of wind. The south was full of fire and sparks and glowing embers. Where the soft air of the heat met the harsh frost of the cold the air was mild and windless. The ice began to sweat, and life appeared in the running drops. From out of the ice and mud there came a giant called Clay and while he slept there grew under his left arm a man and a woman, and from them came the first race of men that was given the Earth to live in. Then one of the giant's legs had a son with the other and that is where the family of frost giants came from.

Next to appear from the ice was a cow called Nourisher. Four rivers of milk sprang from her teats and from these the giant fed. Nourisher licked the salty ice and by the evening she had uncovered some hair. On the second day she uncovered a head and on the third day the whole being in the form of a man was revealed. His name was Tuist and he was handsome, tall and strong. He had a son named Mann, who had three sons by the daughter of a frost giant. The first son was Wisdom; the second Will; the third Holiness.

The three sons fell out with Clay and killed him. So vast was his size, and so great were the torrents of blood that poured from his wounds, that all the Frost giants were drowned; all except one who escaped with his wife in a boat.

The three sons of Mann made the world from the corpse of the giant. From his blood came the sea and the lakes; from his flesh, the earth; from his bones, the mountains; from his jaws, teeth and broken bones came rocks and pebbles; from his hair, the trees. Maggots came to life in his flesh and the gods gave them the appearance of men and human understanding. This was the origin of the dwarfs who live in the earth and rocks. They are the wisest and most skilful of craftsmen.

17

From the giant's skull the sky was formed. It was placed over the earth and under each corner the three sons placed a dwarf. These are known as North, East, South and West. The brains of the giant were flung into the sky and formed clouds. Higher than the clouds were flung sparks and embers and these became the heavenly lights. The position of the stars was fixed and the lights that wandered at will were given paths on which to travel.

Night, and her son Day, ride around the earth on two horses. Night rides first on a horse called Frosty-mane and every morning the foam from his bit covers the earth as dew. Day rides on a horse called Shining-mane and the sunlight glistens on his golden hair.

When Wisdom, Will and Holiness had finished making the world they travelled about it to inspect their work. While they were walking together by the sea they found two trees that had been washed ashore. The brothers made a man from one tree, and a woman from the other. Wisdom gave them each a soul and life. Will gave them understanding and movement. Holiness gave them the power of speech and the senses of sight, touch, smell, taste and hearing. From that man and woman came the people of Allfather and the Gods looked on them with favour.

The Gods

Sunnandæg. The first day is for Sun the fiery light that is drawn through the heavens by a team of horses. Sun rises in the East, turning frost giants into stone, then hurries across the sky chased by a snarling wolf that catches her at the edge of the western sky and swallows her whole. Then Night rides out and covers the Earth until Sun, the companion of Day, escapes and once again casts her bright light over the earth. By Sun we measure a year.

Monandæg. The second day is for Moon the silver sphere that lights the night sky with its ghostly gleam. Moon, the companion of Night, waxes and wanes, and we call this time a month.

Tiwesdæg. The third day is for Tiw.

Allfather created the gods of the shining stronghold that is Heaven, and bestowed on each of them great powers. Tiw was the first of the gods of Heaven; the Sky Father, the God of Brightness. It is from Tiw the great warrior and God of Battle, that warriors seek courage and strength. He is protector and provider; the God of Order, Law and Justice. Tiw watches over the assembly of the people that is called the Moot or Thing.

Wodnesdæg. The fourth day is for Woden.

Woden is the God of Wisdom, the God of Magic, and God of the Dead. He is a healer and has the power of prophecy. In his quest for knowledge and understanding he gave an eye and hung from Irminsul the Pillar of the Universe, for nine days and nights, wounded by a spear.[3] His powers are beyond the understanding of men and from Woden, the one-eyed god, came the runes. It is to Woden that the wise look for truth and knowledge. It is to Woden, God of the Slain, that the dying look for comfort. In his search for lost souls he comes to the Middle Enclosure, the world of men, and moves stealthily across the earth in cloak and hood. On dark and stormy nights he rides across the sky with the Valkyries, the Daughters of Night.

Þunresdæg. The fifth day is for Thunor.[4]

Thunor is very strong and full of vigour. The dwarfs made him a mighty hammer called Crusher, and a pair of iron gloves with which to hold it. They also made him a belt of power with which he can double his strength. Thunor uses these gifts to help him protect Heaven and the world of men. He is God of the Weather and the Seasons. He drives his chariot over the storm clouds and throws thunderbolts from the mountaintops. From his chariot he can hurl Crusher to earth, fell an oak, and have the hammer return to his hand.

Thunor cares for the wellbeing of men and helps them build and cultivate. He is at the rite for the naming of children, and at weddings, cremations and burials. His emblem is the hammer and he is with those who wear it.

Frigedæg. The sixth day is for Freo, known to many as Frig.

Earth is the daughter of Night. She cares for us and provides us with all that we need for a full and happy life, just as she provided for those who went before. It is for us to use her ample harvest wisely. We are wardens of Earth and we must care for her so that she can care for us and those who come after us.

Freo is Earth and of Earth. She is her own daughter and is known by many names. Freo is Mother Earth, the Goddess of Fertility and Love. She brings us the fruits of the earth and of our loins. She is Goddess of the Harvest and the Mother of Men. The Wise seek her help in many things. Freo, like her companion Woden, has the power of prophecy.

Sæternesdæg. The seventh day is for our ancestors.

Many have gone before and many will follow. Those who went before live on in our bodies and our memories. Those who will follow live in our bodies and our hopes. We are the meeting place for past and future. We must keep alive the memory of the dead, so that the unborn can know and remember them. Remember their names and their deeds and yours in turn will be remembered.

---

[3] Irminsul, was associated with Tiw, the sky god, and was represented by massive wooden pillars that were erected in the woods that served as places of worship.

[4] The letter þ (lower case thorn) and Þ (upper case thorn) represent the sound *th* as in thin.

Allfather has no form but that of the universe, the emblem of his existence. The emblem of the universe is Irminsul the great Yew, the pillar of the universe; its roots and branches reach into all the worlds of creation.

The emblem of Tiw is the sword.

The emblems of Woden are the ring and the spear.

The emblem of Thunor is the hammer.

The emblems of Freo are the sheaf of corn and the amber necklace.

The emblems of our forebears are our bodies.

Irminsul and the Seven Worlds

Around the earth in a ring are four seas, two fresh and two salt. Along the outer shores of the seas the gods gave the giants a land to live in but not all the giants are to be found there; some live in the depths of the earth, while others can be found in caves high in the mountains, or beneath the waves in the deep sea.

Away from the ring of sea the gods built a stronghold from the eyebrows of the dead giant, and they called it Middangeard, (the Middle Enclosure). This is Earth the land of men. It is midway between the world of the gods and Hel, the realm of death and darkness. Then the gods created Heaven and built many fine halls there for themselves and their kindred. The route from earth to Heaven is over a very strong bridge made with great skill and cunning. It is called Shimmering Rainbow and it is guarded by Hama, the White God, who never sleeps. He sits at the edge of Heaven watching like a hawk, both night and day, and listens for the smallest sound. If Hama detects the faintest threat to Heaven he will blow Echoing Horn, which will be heard in every part of every one of the seven worlds.

Each day those gods who are not travelling in other worlds ride over Shimmering Rainbow and meet by Irminsul, the great yew, that is the pillar of the universe. It has very strong roots and its branches tower into the sky. Irminsul stretches into every part of the universe and connects the worlds of the Gods, Light Elves, Dark Elves, Men, Dwarfs, Giants, and the Dead. Beyond the Realm of the Dead there is fire and heat. Beyond Heaven there is ice and cold.

Irminsul has three long roots. One passes into the World of the Dead, another into the World of Frost Giants and the third into the World of the Gods. Under the root that goes down to the World of the Dead is the spring called Roaring Cauldron and nearby lives a dragon called Devourer of Corpses. Under the root that turns towards the World of Frost Giants is the spring that is guarded by the god Mimir. Those who drink its waters are given great wisdom and understanding. Such was Woden's thirst for knowledge that he gave an eye for a drink from that spring.

Under the root that rises into Heaven is the spring of Destiny. It is by this water that the gods meet each day. Near by live the three Daughters of Night called Wyrd, Metod and Sculd. They are the Spinner, Measurer and Cutter of the threads of life that are woven into the Web of Wyrd. The first sister, Wyrd, spins the thread and it is she who determines its quality. Metod measures the thread and determines its length. Sculd cuts the thread and by the nature of the cut, be it clean or ragged, she determines the manner of each death. We know these midnight women, the Wyrd Sisters, as Past, Present and Future. Each day they draw water from the Spring of Destiny and return to their dark cave where they spin and weave the destinies of men. On the night of a full moon they gather round the pool and call down the shimmering light into the sparkling water. Wyrd is everywhere and all the inhabitants of all the worlds are within her power.

The Valkyries, the fierce Daughters of Night, ride across the dark and stormy skies on their black steeds, and present a dreadful sight to those who see their staring, hideous eyes, and hear the din of their hunt. They are able to bring defeat or victory in battle and they weave the Web of Victory from the guts of men on a bloodstained frame of spears. An arrow is the shuttle and the warp is weighted with human skulls. These mighty women ride to the field of battle and select those who are to die. When the fury of battle is spent, they appear on the crimson field among the dead as wolves and ravens. Then, blotched with blood, and with sparks flashing from their spear points, they ride away with the souls of the dead.

Fiercewolf, the World Serpent, and Hel

Deep in the great forest, to the east of the land of men, lived giant women with magical powers. One of those women, who was very old, gave birth to the two wolves who chase Sun and Moon across the sky. Many years later the woman had three more children by a giant. The first was called Fiercewolf; he grew larger and more ferocious with each day that passed. The second was a monstrous serpent which grew more ugly and venomous. The third was a daughter, named Hel, and she was black in parts and looked grim and shadowy.

The gods knew of these children and the threat they posed to Heaven and Earth so they went to the forest in search of them. When they found the serpent they threw it into the deep sea where it grew so large it circled the earth, and its head touched its tail. Hel was sent to the seventh world, the realm of the dead, and there she rules a world surrounded by high walls and secured by heavy gates, so that those who enter never return. She lives in a damp hall called Chill Wind, where Glimmering Misfortune hangs from the walls. Her plate is called Starvation; her knife Famine; her door Ruin; her bed Pestilence.

The gods attempted to capture Fiercewolf, but he was very large and strong, and all the fetters they put on him were easily broken. They went away and made a very strong chain, and when they returned they asked the wolf to test his strength against it. Fiercewolf looked at the chain carefully and accepted the challenge. At his very first attempt he easily broke free. The gods went away and made a chain twice as strong as the one before, and asked the wolf to test his strength again. They told him he would gain great fame if he could break free from such a strong fetter. The wolf thought about it carefully and decided that, if he were to achieve fame, he would have to face danger. The chain looked very strong, but he had grown in size and strength since the last challenge, so he agreed to have the chain put on him. The wolf struggled and strained so hard that the chain shattered and flew off. The gods were worried that they might never be able to restrain the wolf, so they sent a messenger to the Dwarfs who live deep underground. Those most excellent craftsmen made a fetter from six things: the roots of a mountain; the breath of a fish; the noise of a cat's footstep; the beard of a woman; the sinews of a bear; the spittle of a bird.

The messenger returned with a fetter that looked like the web of a spider. The gods challenged the wolf to be bound once more, but Fiercewolf thought it must be a trick and snarled at them, and said there was no fame to be gained from breaking such a flimsy fetter. The gods said that if he were afraid they would promise to free him if he could not do so himself. Fiercewolf did not believe them, but he did not want to be thought a coward, so he agreed to the challenge provided one of them, as a token of good faith, placed a hand in his (the wolf's) mouth. The gods looked at each other wondering what to do. Tiw stepped forward and placed his hand between the wolf's powerful jaws. The other gods bound the wolf, who then began to struggle, but the more he struggled the tighter the fetter became. All the gods laughed; all except Tiw who lost his hand. The gods pulled the fetter tight and fastened its end to a large rock. Fiercewolf snarled and frothed at the mouth but the gods forced a large sword upright between his jaws and left him howling as a warning to others who might threaten them.

Migration

The people of Allfather lived in the Middle Enclosure by the waters of the Black Sea. Their language and mythology had a common root but with the passing of time they became many tribes and each developed its own customs and dialect. As they moved into new lands, some to the east and some to the west, the differences grew greater and their languages evolved in different ways according to their different circumstances, needs and customs.

Two main language groups formed. From one came the Germans, Greeks, Latins (Romans), Celts, Tocharians, Hittites and Albanians. From the other came the Balts, Indics, Iranians, Armenians and Slavs. They came to call the Gods by different names and worship them in different ways but they all gave praise to Sun and Moon, and the Sky Father, and the Earth Mother.

One of the tribes, the Aesir, migrated to the north-west and followed great rivers and passed through vast forests and marshes. They wandered for many generations and faced testing challenges and dangers together, and in doing so they became a more tightly knit community with a strengthened sense of common purpose. In the North they came to the land of the Vanir, a people who worshipped gods of the sea and of the earth. The Aesir found land for themselves and built houses, grew crops and raised cattle. After a long war between the two tribes a truce was agreed. The people prospered, had many children and became many tribes. Scania, the name of the land in which they lived, became the womb of nations.

Over three thousand years ago, some of the people of Scania moved south across the sea to Jutland and then further south to the great northern plain that stretches from beyond the Rhine in the west to beyond the Vistula in the east. They spread across the plain, along the coasts and up the rivers. When they settled their way of life changed to suit their new surroundings. Despite the resulting differences in custom and dialect the many tribes retained a wider common identity founded on shared cultural and linguistic traits. An awareness of their common roots was kept alive by the tales embedded in their cultures. They were oral societies that recorded their communal history and individual heroic deeds in verse. Storytellers travelled widely and spread news about the goings on in far-off places.

As periodic waves of migration brought more tribes south from Scania, so the fertile lands near to the northern seas became more heavily populated. Some communities cleared forest, while others moved south-west along the river valleys. The great advance of the Northern people towards the central uplands took many generations to complete and as they went they displaced and pushed before them other peoples.

Around 250BC, after a long period of consolidation and a growth in population, Northern tribes advanced into the Central Uplands and another wave of migration began. The early movement was, as before, mostly south-east along rivers that flowed from the uplands to the northern seas. When the tribes crossed the watershed, they travelled down rivers flowing south-east to the Danube and the Black Sea. During the following 200 years the Northern peoples occupied, and took control of, most of the land between the Rhine and the Vistula, and the Danube and the Baltic. As they spread out across this vast territory they came to be described as Germans of the Sea, Germans of the Forest, and Germans of the Steppes. The Germans of the Sea gave praise to Ing, from whom they were descended, and among their number were the Engle, Friese, Eote and Seaxe (English, Frisians, Jutes, and Saxons).

Language

The differences in dialect between the widespread Germanic peoples became great enough for three distinct language groups to be discerned; the Northern, Eastern and Western Germanic groups. The dialects of the people of the north developed through Norse into Danish, Icelandic, Norwegian, Swedish and Faroese. The dialects of the Eastern group, which were very similar to those of the Northern group, became Gothic, Vandalic, and Burgundian, and are now extinct. The dialects of the Western group became Frisian, English, Scots, Dutch, and German. The first four of these are *Ingraeonic* or North Sea Germanic.

Some Western tribes moved south, and their language evolved in a different way to that of the lowland Germans they left behind. Members of the southern group, who lived in the central uplands, called themselves *Duesche* (modern Deutsch), which means *Men of the People*. They are the people that the modern English call Germans.

The People

Cultures and religions vary over time to suit the needs of the communities they serve. Sometimes the gods of war are dominant and at other times the gods of fertility and the harvest come to the fore. Whether war or peace prevailed, there were always farmers, warriors, and priests. Tacitus described the customs and appearance of the first century Germanic tribes in *Germania*. They were a warrior society made up of self-sufficient communities which at first had little contact with non-Germanic peoples except as enemies in war. These Northern Europeans had blue eyes, fair skin, fair or reddish hair, and they were taller and bigger than the people of the south. The men wore long woollen cloaks fastened with a brooch or thorn. In some tribes, women wore loose, sleeveless, outer garments, made from linen, which exposed part of their breasts. Boys and girls were brought up together and young women were able to match the strength of young men of their own age. Children were not pampered and grew up able to endure cold, damp and hardship. In some places, sexual activity before the age of twenty was considered scandalous and harmful to the development of a tall stature and fine physique. Once married no attempt was made to restrict the number of children and it was not their custom, as it was in many other places, to kill girls at birth. A large number of kin gave one authority and social standing.[5]

Houses and Settlements

The Northern people tended to live in small self-sufficient settlements. Houses and farm buildings were constructed from timber and some had walls that were

---

[5] Tacitus, *Germania*, written about 98AD, contains descriptions of various Germanic tribes and their customs.

smeared with a clay that gave them a bright appearance.[6] Although all buildings were made from timber, the layout and method of construction varied according to the climate and the nature of the land. Some settlements started as single farmsteads consisting of a small two-post building and assorted shelters. Successful families built a larger house close to the first, which was often taken down and the timber re-used. As the size of the family increased so additional houses and sheds for use as workshops or food stores were built nearby. If the land was well drained, wood-lined pits were built for the storage of grain but in other places it was stored in buildings with raised floors. Where the climate was mild, cattle and other animals were left in the open during the winter, but if it was very cold or wet the houses were made longer to provide a home for the family at one end, and shelter for the livestock at the other. These buildings are known as longhouses.

A common type of small building was the *Grubenhauser* or *sunken building*. These were built on well-drained land around a flat-bottomed pit of two feet, or more, in depth. Their turf or thatch roofs were supported at the high point by two upright posts and a ridge-pole, while the bottom edge rested on the ground, or on a turf wall. The buildings were used as small houses or workshops and offered greater protection against cold winds and snow than ground-level structures. The floors were mostly of chalk, clay or compressed gravel. The hearth in earthen-floored houses was situated either in the centre of the floor or in one corner.

Some of the sites on which the Germanic peoples built their settlements had seen earlier occupation. It was usual for migrating people to make use of, and modify, the economic and military resources and structures of earlier inhabitants. In the frontier regions use was often made of old unoccupied hill-forts. The addition of a fence of wooden stakes to a ditch-and-mound defence-work could quickly provide a secure place of settlement. Good military positions often remain as such despite the passing of time and changes in technology and tactics. Likewise settlements tend to grow up near mountain passes, river fords and where tracks converge. Newcomers often find a settlement site as attractive as earlier occupants and for the same reasons.

Settlements founded by a large group of people were more likely to be planned and laid out around a central open space or along a street whereas settlements that grew gradually, perhaps from a single homestead, had buildings and animal pens arranged in a less systematic way. Most buildings were constructed on an east-west axis so that one of the long walls faced south towards the sun and allowed more light to enter through the doorway and small shuttered windows.

Some settlements failed and became deserted while others thrived and were populated by several hundred people. Successful settlements became the focal

---

[6] Possibly wattle and daub with a lime wash.

point of stable farming communities, and some became centres for the manufacture of various artefacts such as pottery and iron products. Many have developed into the present-day towns and villages of Northern Europe.

Land

Much of Northern Europe was covered with forest and marshland. Clearing a new area for farming was by necessity a communal effort so, when the clearance was completed, the land tended to be held in common by those who had helped clear it and shared out by a means that was fair and agreeable to everyone. The sharing of land, conditions, and problems helped promote community spirit. Status within the group was achieved not by accumulating land but by demonstrating loyalty, generosity and courage. Some display of material wealth was possible through the acquisition and breeding of livestock, which was not held in common. It was probably for this reason that cattle (Old English (O.E.) *feoh*) came to represent wealth and why wealth is represented by the rune *feoh* ᚠ.

It seems that the yearly allocation of arable land was made to families, each being allocated strips from several different parts of the common arable land to ensure that all shared similar rewards and hardships. In some places the kin worked the land together and shared the produce while in others they sub-divided the land amongst themselves with the size of the allotments being adjusted to reflect the needs and social rank of the individuals concerned.

Crops and Husbandry

Settlements were generally situated in a central and/or raised location so that the arable and pastureland encircled it and gave a clear view of the surrounding countryside and a good warning of the approach of strangers. Such a layout was also the most economical in terms of travelling time between house and field. It enabled a team of oxen to be driven to the furthest field each morning and back each evening, which was especially useful during the early part of the year when the days were short.

The boundaries of fields were often marked by ditches and earth mounds. To these were added the stones that were gradually cleared from the field during preparation of the soil for sowing. On sloping ground the long fields or strips ran lengthways across the slope to lessen soil erosion from running water.

As the territory of the Germanic peoples advanced south they took possession of existing field systems. Where fields had physical boundaries, such as ditches or piles of stones, they where retained and modified only slowly but new fields were laid out in a way that was traditional to the new occupants.

The distribution of land between arable, meadow, and pasture varied, as did the size and shape of the fields, from place to place according to climate and the nature of the land. A single family farmstead in North-West Germany with fields totalling thirty-five acres, might have only seven to ten acres of arable with the remainder being a mixture of pasture and hay meadow.

Two main types of plough were used to prepare the ground for sowing. The first, an *ard*, used a wooden or iron share to scratch or dig a furrow and push the displaced soil to each side. The other type of plough had a share that pushed the soil to one side and turned it over. A piece of timber known as a mould-board was sometimes fitted to the plough to assist the turning of the soil. The ploughs were drawn by teams of oxen and it was found to be more economical in time and effort to plough long furrows to reduce the number of times the animals had to be turned. As a result the fields tended to be long and narrow. Such a system also reduced the amount of unploughed land required at the end of each field for turning the oxen.

The main cereal crop was barley, which was used to make bread and beer. Oats and rye were also harvested but in much smaller quantities. There were vegetable crops such as cabbage, carrots, beans, and peas. Apples, pears, cherries and plums were grown, and in the south there were apricots and peaches. Bilberries, blackberries, elderberries, raspberries and strawberries were cultivated and gathered, as were many herbs for use in cooking and medicines. Common herbs included caraway, dill, garlic, and parsley. Some plants were grown for use as dyes. Flax was grown for linseed oil and the fibre used to make linen.

There was no division of pasture-land but there may have been restrictions on the number of sheep or cattle which could be grazed there. Pigs fed at the forest edges where they ate acorns and beech-mast in winter. The farm animals provided, in addition to meat: milk for cheese and yoghurt; wool and hide for clothing, blankets, belts and shoes; fat for burning in lamps; bone for making combs, needles and other implements. Most utensils and artefacts were made from wood, leather or clay.

Spinning and weaving were highly developed skills and each settlement or family produced cloth for its own use. The quality varied according to the use to which it was to be put but it was possible to produce fine cloth on a simple loom. Pottery for everyday use was simple in material, technique and design, and most of it was made by members of the household as and when it was required.

Government

The kindred groups were mostly independent and self-governing in time of peace but in war they joined together and elected a leader (king) for the duration of the conflict. Practices varied and sometimes it was necessary to have a joint leadership. At first it was the custom for all warriors to be eligible for election but among some tribes it became the practice to select the leader from one family and eventually the king remained as such for life. Whatever the method of selection, the chieftain did not have absolute power. He could be overruled by a council of leading men among whom there would probably have been a holy man of some kind, possibly a shaman.[7] As the chieftain had no power to compel warriors to fight he had to lead by example and show skill and courage in battle.

The council of leading men had the power to make decisions on many matters affecting the community, but on important issues the council discussed the matter before putting a recommendation before an assembly of warriors who were able to discuss the proposal and then adopt or reject it. The assembly came to be known as a *Thing* or *Moot*. The meeting took place just before the full moon or shortly after the new moon, these being considered the best times to make decisions or start new ventures. All warriors, with the exception of those who had shown cowardice in battle, were entitled to attend the moot and did so fully armed to show their right to carry arms and their ability to fight if necessary. When a matter had to be decided those opposed to the proposal shouted their disapproval and those in favour clashed their spears. A warrior who gave his support to a proposal was honour bound to act in support of it. Thus if he voted for war he was expected to fight.

The moot dealt with the criminal offences of treachery, desertion, cowardice and sodomy. Those found guilty of any of the first three offences were hung from a tree but sodomites and oath-breakers were bound and pushed face down into the waters of a bog or pool under a wicker hurdle or branches weighed down with stones. The executions were probably carried out as part of a religious ritual.

Other criminal offences were punished by a fine called *wergild*, part of which was paid to the community and part to the victim or his kin. Murder, wounding and theft were, where possible, avenged by the victim or his kin. It was therefore desirable to have a large number of kin who could exact vengeance on an offender. It was known that retribution from a victim or his kin would be more swift and certain than that from a remote and disinterested third party.

Compensation and retribution were allowed only to those of the rank of freeman or above. Many bondsmen (slaves) were captives or debtors. It is probable that some bondsmen performed household duties but most were like tenants tied to rendering services to their masters (owners) who in return provided them with a house and land. The bondsman's service may have taken the form of an obligation to either provide a certain number of days labour at ploughing, sowing and harvest times, or make a payment in grain, livestock, cloth or other produce each year.

---

[7] The origin of *shaman* can be traced back through Russian to Sanskrit *srama* meaning *religious practice*. Given that Sanskrit is an Indo-European language, it is likely that there is a more direct link that has been lost.

Bondsmen could not carry arms or participate in the political life of the community. If they were killed, compensation was paid to the master and not to the bondsman's family, which had no right of retribution.

The moot elected a law officer and one hundred respected advisers for the settlement of civil disputes. The law officer visited settlements at regular intervals to hear disputes and make judgements. Some of the advisers accompanied him to the hearings and lent weight to his decisions. They probably also witnessed the proper conduct of the proceedings, the verdict reached, the compensation awarded and the punishment given. Perhaps just twelve of the advisers were employed on such duties at any one time. Such an arrangement may have been a forerunner of the jury system.

When a young man was competent in the use of weapons and had reached a given age he attended a moot and was presented with a spear and shield by his leader, or his father, or one of his kin. Only warriors were allowed to carry arms and all business, public or private, was conducted with both parties armed. The presentation of the spear and shield therefore had a civil as well as a military significance as it marked the acceptance of the young man as a freeman and a warrior.

If the moot decided on a course of military action, all freemen were duty bound to fight. However not all armed conflict was between nations. A warrior might put forward plans for a venture of his own. He could call on the others for support and those who gave it were bound to take part. Warlords led their followers on raids into enemy territory or they fought as mercenaries. Young warriors joined such ventures in order to prove their worth, both to themselves and others. They also sought fellowship and fame.

Runes, Divination and Prophecy

Northern Europeans used symbols to represent the mysterious forces of nature, the blessing of life, and the curse of death. It seems likely that some of the ancient indigenous signs were mixed with signs borrowed from the people of the South, to make a runic alphabet or *futhorc*. Whatever the origin of individual runes, their original purpose, and however great or few their number, it is probable that they were used for magic, divination and writing. As the language and the requirements of those skilled in magic changed and evolved so new runes were devised and old ones modified to suit the new needs.

Runes were cut into pieces of wood and marked on objects to denote the maker or owner. Sometimes the purpose was to invoke a god, as with victory-runes used to summon Tiw, the god of courage and glory. Runic charms were marked on possessions to protect them from theft, and craftsmen inscribed them on pieces of bone, wood or other material that they were about to work, in order to guard against mistakes or prevent breakage.

Women were recognized as having greater powers of prophecy than men. The fame of some seeresses was widespread and their power and influence very great. Such women, called *Alrynia*, were skilled in the use of runes and the casting of lots. They and their followers were accorded privileges and high status when they visited those who sought their services. Alrynia were often consulted before wars and other enterprises were undertaken.

Many decisions were taken by the casting of lots. The fate of enemy prisoners could be determined in this way and it is recorded that lots were cast on three successive days to decide whether a captive should be killed by fire, and on each occasion it was decreed that he should live. Important leadership decisions were sometimes taken in the same way. The Continental, or Old Saxons, continued at a late date to be ruled by regional kings who, when war threatened, met to decide by the casting of lots which of them should lead the whole Saxon nation for the duration of the conflict.

Battlefield tactics were sometimes determined by the casting of lots. When Ariovist, the leader of the Sueb was confronted by a Roman army he followed the customary procedure and let the matrons of the tribe decide by means of lots and divinations when it would be best to attack the enemy.

One of the early procedures for the casting of lots was to cut a branch from a nut-bearing tree and split the wood into strips. Symbols were marked on the pieces of wood which were then thrown on to a white cloth. A prayer was offered to the Gods by the person conducting the ceremony and then, with eyes looking to the sky, three strips were picked up, one at a time, and their meaning read out. If the signs were unfavourable, the matter was put off to another day. If the signs were good a favourable omen might be sought from the observation of the flight and song of birds, or from the movements and noises of sacred horses which were kept for that special purpose. In the latter case a holy man (shaman?) and the leader of the council of elders, or the king, hitched the horses to a sacred wagon and walked beside them listening to their snorts and neighs. If the matter being considered was war and the omens for battle were good, the holy man brought emblems from the sacred grove and prepared them for carriage into battle. A ceremony was held to invoke the help of the gods. War leaders often pledged the spoils of war to the gods (e.g. Tiw and Woden) if they gave the warriors victory. A special spear was prepared and marked with the runes of victory. The enemy was promised as a sacrifice to the gods and before the battle began a chosen warrior hurled the spear over the heads of the enemy in order to seal the bargain.

If the battle was won, all weapons and war-coats of the foe were bent and broken and thrown into a lake or bog. Their bodies were hung from trees. The sacrifice was great because much of the war-gear consisted of swords, helmets and war-coats of great value. When the Cimbre defeated a large Roman army in 105 BC they captured a huge amount of equipment and valuables. Orosius tells how the Romans and all their possessions were destroyed in order to honour a pledge that in return for being granted victory the enemy would be sacrificed to the gods. All clothing was ripped to pieces; gold and silver was flung into the river; the war-coats were hacked to pieces; horses drowned and their harnesses destroyed; prisoners hung from the trees by their necks, and nothing was left for the victors and no mercy shown to the defeated. Much the same happened when Hermann drew a Roman army of three legions into an ambush in the Teutoburger Forest. Shortly before the battle started a thunderstorm broke and continued for two days. In that time the entire Roman army and all its equipment was destroyed. The bodies of Roman soldiers were hung from trees and their shields, swords, spears and other equipment bent and broken and thrown into rivers and swamps.

Tacitus records how in 58 AD two German tribes, the Chatti and the Hermunduri, fought a great battle over possession of a rich salt-producing river. Each side dedicated the other to Tiw and Woden. The Chatti were defeated, and all survivors, equipment and horses were destroyed.

Funerals

In some places and at some times bodies were buried and at others burnt. Usually only one body was burnt on each pyre but after a battle the victors collected the bodies of their dead comrades and placed them together on the bed of wood. The weapons of the dead warriors were thrown into the fire and sometimes the bodies of their horses were burnt with them. Special timbers were used for the pyres of great people. Their remains were buried under mounds of earth, the size and location of which depended upon their status.

The mourners ate seeds which symbolized rebirth, and handfuls of grain, herbs and potions were thrown into the flames. Burning the body may have been seen as a way of releasing the soul from the body and allowing it to rise with the heat and smoke into Heaven but there is no evidence of a belief in a heavenly after-life until the much later Norse period. Ceremonies appear to have been simple and although women were able to express their grief men were not expected to do so other than in their words of praise for the dead. For some it was the custom to place the ashes of the dead in patterned clay pots which were sometimes marked with symbols, including runes, and buried in shallow graves. Personal possessions of the dead were often placed in the grave which was marked only by a raised mound of turf. In those places where it was the custom to bury bodies in the ground, the rites accompanying the burials were similar to those used at cremations. For example grain was burned in a dish and then placed in the grave.

Evidence from later English cemeteries shows that fires were sometimes lit in the grave, perhaps to harden or purify the soil, before the unburned body was placed in it. Burials were sometimes sprinkled with charcoal, which could have been the remains of a fire lit next to the grave as part of the burial ritual. When wooden coffins were introduced, their surface was sometimes burned before the body was placed in them. The purpose of this practice may have been to harden the wood to help preserve it. Large pieces of burned timber were sometimes placed beside the coffin and might have had the same symbolic meaning as the Yule log which represented continuity. Small fire pits were made near the graves, presumably for use during the ceremony. They may have been used to burn personal possessions of the deceased. Personal items placed in the grave were often broken or damaged in some way perhaps as a symbolic gesture to end their life, or possibly to deter grave robbers or to symbolize a spiritual break with the deceased and discourage their recovery and use for magical purposes. When the grave was closed large stones were sometimes placed on the grave, perhaps as a memorial or, as has been suggested, to prevent the body rising from the grave. A more practical explanation for the stones is that they prevented animals digging up the corpse.

Much of the ritual accompanying burials seems to have been carried over from cremation ceremonies. For example the custom of throwing corn on to the funeral pyre probably gave rise to the practice of burning corn in a dish and placing it in the grave. Later burials sometimes contained joints of meat and may have been the deceased persons share of a last meal, which was perhaps cooked and eaten at the graveside.

The usual explanation for the placing of items in a grave is that they were for use in the next life. This is the standard explanation when there is no evidence of any other reason. We do not know why items were placed in graves. One explanation for the deposits is that the gifts were committed to the ground by individuals and communities as a sacrifice, a demonstration of the high regard in which the deceased was held. The building of a monument is another way of demonstrating that regard. Burying valuable items with the dead may have been a form of sacrifice, a way of showing high regard for the deceased that can be compared with the modern practice of spending vast sums on a coffin and ceremony. Placing personal items with the dead seems a natural thing to do, that is where they belong. Unfortunately, it was one of the practices prohibited by the Church.

There is little, if any, direct evidence to suggest that the heathen English believed in a life after death, other in the memory of those that came after them. Physical death gave the opportunity to win fame but otherwise it seems to have been regarded as a curse. If it is accepted that this worldly life is short, it suggests that it should be lived to the full. We should strive to do deeds that will live on in the communal memory, which is a higher level of existence than this worldly life. Something of it might have prompted Bede to write, *It has ever been my wish to live honourably while alive, and after my death to leave to them that come after me my memory in good works*. Bede's good works were suited to his skills and circumstances. Others took a different path to winning fame.

The Early English

The Engle

In the fourth century of the first millennium, in the lands of Southern Jutland north of the Elbe, there lived seven tribes united in their worship of Mother Earth. One of those peoples was the Engle and their country was called Angeln. Nerthus was the name by which they called the Earth Mother. Her presence was symbolized by an idol which was kept in a covered waggon, in a small wood, on an island in the sea. It was covered with a cloth and cared for by holymen, who acted as wardens. When the time was right, the waggon, accompanied by a warden, was drawn by cows from settlement to settlement and everywhere it went there followed days of celebration and merry-making. During the travels, all iron objects were locked away and no one took up arms or went to war. When the travels were ended, the warden returned the waggon to its island where it and its contents were washed in a secret lake by slaves who were drowned when the cleansing had been completed.

The chief place of worship for each of the seven tribes was situated near the middle of their territory. They followed the example of the gods and made their places of congregation and worship by lakes, springs and pools. In some places wooden idols were placed on piles of stones in the middle of bogs, and tall poles were set up, either singly or in groups. Sacrificial items were placed in the waters around the idols. The gifts reflected what was being sought from the gods, the importance of the place of worship, the nature of the community and the needs of the time. At first, sacrifices were mostly animals, household items and agricultural tools, but later, manufactured ornaments, clothing, wooden vessels, war-gear and even ships were placed in the bogs.

The ritual slaughter of animals was carried out by a holy man, who killed many of the animals with a blow to their forehead. The head, feet, tail and skin of each animal were removed and prepared for burial. Sometimes the severed parts were placed in the earth together, at other times apart. Sacrifices might be buried in the earthen floor of a newly-built house or put into the waters of a sacred pool or bog. The entrails were sometimes placed in pots and left at a shrine, while the flesh was cooked and served at a feast held in honour of the god to whom the sacrifice had been made.

Most of the sacrificed animals were ordinary farm animals but some were horses or dogs. The sacrifice of a good horse was a great loss because they were expensive animals that conferred status on their owners and were considered sacred. Horse-gear, such as bridles, saddles and spurs, was sometimes thrown into a bog as a sacrifice or buried with the remains of its owner. Dogs were not eaten but killed on the death of their master and buried with his remains.

Warriors sometimes drew lots before battle to decide which of them would be sacrificed to Woden, but most human sacrifices were probably criminals who had been sentenced to death. Tacitus tells of such victims being taken to a holy place where they were stripped, bound and blindfolded before having a woollen thread tied round one of their ankles. Then, at the appropriate stage in the ritual, the victim was hanged with a hide noose or strangled with a cord or hazel branch. The feet, the hands, or the head were sometimes removed from the corpse and buried separately before the remnant was put into a bog or pool.

As the influence and power of warriors in society became greater so the number, and extent, of the sacrifices to the war gods increased, but many sacrifices were still made to Thunor and the gods and goddesses of fertility and the sea. Wooden idols with clearly defined male and female sexual parts were cast into the pools and bogs as part of a ritual to invoke the favour of the gods, and fertility idols were stood upright in the bogs. Male fertility figures, sometimes ten feet high, were more common and generally much larger than the female figures. In areas where there were no bogs, the people dug pits and shafts, and the sacrifices, some in pots, were placed in them. The holes were refilled and sometimes a pile of stones was placed over them.

The waters of the North Sea were abundant with fish. The people living at the edge of the ocean took much of their food from it and, in recognition of its importance to them, a shrine dedicated to Nehalennia, a goddess of the sea's fertility, was established on an island off the coast. Sea fishing helped the people to become expert boat builders and sailors. Those skills were made use of by those who sought adventure and fame, on land and at sea. At first the warbands raided nearby coastal and river settlements, but as their skills and the need for new targets increased so they sailed further, sometimes reaching the coast of Spain. Before setting out the warriors sought a safe passage from the gods and goddesses of the sea and the giants and giantesses who lived in it. They asked for favourable winds and currents, and vowed that in exchange for a safe journey they would cast gifts to the mighty spearman that is the sea. A letter written by Sidonius, about the year 470, reveals the form those gifts might have taken. He described how the Saxons, after raiding the lands to the south, performed a rite on the eve of their setting sail.[8] One tenth of the prisoners they had with them were selected, by the casting of lots, for sacrifice by crucifixion or drowning.

Offa King of the Engle

In the time before the English came to Britain they lived in the land between the seas north of the river Eider. They were known as the Engle and their country was called Angeln.[9] In the fourth century Wermund, son of Wihtlæg, was their king and his domain stretched from the Baltic coast in the east to the North Sea coast in

---

[8] This, incidentally, is evidence that the North Sea Germanic tribes had sailing ships long before the Scandinavian *Vikings*.

[9] *Engle*, with time, became *English* and *Angeln* became *England*.

the west. To the north were the Jutes and beyond the river Eider to the south were the Myrgings and Saxons.

Wermund had three sons by his first wife but one son died in a riding accident; another in battle; the third, and his mother, were taken in the same year by fever. Wermund married again and had one son Offa. As was customary, the boy was sent to live in the household of one of the king's companions. Freawine had been appointed by Wermund to govern and defend Slesvig, the southern district of his kingdom, and it was to him that the honour of preparing Offa for manhood and kingship was given. Freawine had two sons of his own, Cedd and Wiga, who, although much older than Offa, became his close companions. They, and their chief warrior Falco, helped train him in the ways and arts of war and prepared him for his initiation as a warrior. Offa, being gifted with a powerful body, sharp wits and quick reflexes, became a formidable swordsman and was well liked by all who knew him.

When Offa was thirteen, Eadgils, lord of the Myrgings, landed with a large force and surrounded Freawine's hall. Eadgils sent a messenger to inform Freawine that he had come to demand tribute and that if Freawine refused to pay he could either fight Eadgils in single combat or face a bloody battle in which everyone in the hall was certain to die. Freawine agreed to fight and was killed by Eadgils who announced that he would return later to collect his tribute.

Wermund, upon hearing of Freawine's death, appointed Cedd and Wiga as joint rulers in his place. The brothers set about preparing for the return of Eadgils and although Offa stayed with them it was arranged that he should be sent to a place of safety before the king of the Myrgings returned. However, the king outwitted them and reappeared earlier than expected. He surrounded their enclosure, and demanded the tribute due to him. He also demanded that the Engle evacuate the northern bank of the Eider to remove any threat they might pose to the Myrgings. The brothers refused to yield to the demand and gave Falco the task of escaping, at night, through the enemy lines to tell Wermund of their plight. Falco managed to reach the king, who was at Jællinge in the north. In gratitude for his bravery Wermund presented Falco with a golden cup and provided him with a host of warriors. Falco swore that he would, if necessary, fight to the death in defence of Offa and Angeln, and said that if Wyrd gave him victory he would drink as much blood as the cup would hold. The blood would be either his own or that of his foe, Eadgils.

Falco went quickly south with the warriors and confronted Eadgils, who was still laying siege to the hall in which the companions were sheltering. After a ferocious battle the Myrgings were forced to flee to their ships, and despite the bravery of Falco, Eadgils escaped. Falco was true to his oath and as he stood on the shore watching Eadgils's ships sail into the distance he opened a wound received in the fighting and trickled blood into his helmet and drank from it.

Cedd and Wiga were eager to avenge the death of their father. They hatched a plan that involved leaving Falco in charge of the district while they set sail for the land of the Myrgings disguised as Frisian merchants. Late in the voyage, they discovered Offa hidden among the cargo but, as the winds were favourable, they sailed on and soon arrived in the domain of King Eadgils. They were taken with a sample of their wares to the king's hall and shown in to see him. After inspecting the goods Eadgils offered them his hospitality. After giving them a meal they were provided with lodgings. During the following few days samples of the ship's cargo were transported to the king's hall and much of it was to his liking. After several days the threesome gained the confidence of Eadgils who entertained them alone at night in the high hall, drinking, playing dice and talking. When it was late, and after Eadgils had sampled a large amount of drink, Wiga took a concealed sword from his belongings and revealed his true identity. He challenged Eadgils to fight but the king, believing Wiga to be no match for him, tried to persuade him to desist from the challenge and go on his way. However, when Eadgils was attacked he had no choice but to fight. Despite the vast amount drunk by the king he still had the beating of his challenger. Eadgils warded off several attacks and urged Wiga to leave. Cedd, seeing that his brother could not defeat the king, attempted to do so himself. While Eadgils was distracted, a blow from Wiga's sword killed him. When the infamous deed had been done Wiga and Cedd grabbed Offa and made their escape.

When the brothers arrived back in Angeln they told how Wiga had, with skill and courage, fought and killed Eadgils to avenge his fathers death. On the strength of that tale Wermund and all the people welcomed them as heroes. However a different story was put about by the kindred of Eadgils and soon it reached Angeln. It was not one of bravery but of treachery and cowardice. The Engle sensed the truth of the account and, being an honourable people, the matter was regarded as a national disgrace.

From the day of the killing Offa didn't speak a word and could not be induced to confirm or deny the story told by his companions. He felt bound by a bond of loyalty to them and could not deny their account of events, but honour prevented him from confirming it. He decided to pay a penance of silence for the cowardly deed.

Offa's friendship with Wiga and Cedd quickly faded. He returned to live with Wermund and became solitary, withdrawing to a hall where he lived with some of the king's old and trusted warriors. Within a year or two word got round that he was dull and foolish, and his early promise as a warrior was soon forgotten.

Following the death of their king, the fortunes of the Myrgings waned and they were compelled to pay tribute to the powerful Swabians on their southern border. The King of the Swabians, knowing that Wermund was old, almost blind, and believing him to have an idiot son, ordered the leader of the Myrgings, Meaca, to go to Wermund and demand tribute of him. Meaca, a great warrior never beaten in combat, went to the hall of Wermund and demanded land and tribute. If the terms were not acceptable the king was to send a champion of royal blood to meet him in combat in seven days time. The king decided it would be better for him to die with honour in combat than surrender or see his simple-minded son butchered. He refused the terms and accepted the challenge.

At this point Offa stepped forward and spoke his first words since the killing of King Eadgils many years before. He declared that he would not only fight Meaca but also any other warrior he cared to bring with him. If Offa lost, the land and tribute demanded would be given in full but if he won, the Engle would take equivalent tribute and land from the Myrgings. It was agreed that the combat would take place at Rendsburg on an island in the river Eider that separated the two kingdoms. Offa believed that this arrangement would wipe out the disgrace that had been brought on the Engle by Wiga and Cedd.

Wermund was surprised to hear Offa speak the challenge. Knowing the fighting skills of Meaca, Wermund feared that his son would be unable to defeat one opponent let alone two. Despite concern about the outcome, everyone drew comfort from Offa's strength of mind and the quietly determined way he went about preparing for the fight. Wermund presented Offa with the sword called Steadfast, a much-prized weapon crafted like no other. It matched Offa's size and strength. Thus equipped, Offa set about practising his swordcraft and sharpening his reflexes. He also spent many hours alone making his mind firm and his belief in victory absolute. Above all, he wished to restore the good name of the Engle.

Offa travelled to Rendsburg and at the appointed time went to the place of combat. All those who met him were impressed by his sense of purpose and destiny. However, Wermund was still certain that his son would be slain by his experienced opponents. At the time of the combat he stood on a high bridge ready, on receipt of news of his son's death, to throw himself into the torrent below.

Offa, with his shield and the sword Steadfast, met Meaca and his companion in combat. Offa used only his shield to fend off their rain of blows. It was hard work for him and for them. The longer it went on like that the more his foes and their supporters became frustrated and thought Offa a lucky half-wit who should be quickly cut down. Meaca and his companion stood back and goaded Offa with insults in the expectation that he would anger and lash out at them. He stood silent; the tip of Steadfast resting on the ground and his steady piercing gaze resting on Meaca. The Myrgings were the first to anger and rushed forward to strike Offa down. He fended off their blows with his shield then swung Steadfast with such power that he sliced halfway through Meaca's body with one blow. The companion faltered for the blink of an eye before Steadfast cleaved through his helmet and into his skull. The crowd was shocked into silence by the sudden ending, then a great roar went up from the Engle. The Myrgings looked pale. Offa had single-handedly restored the honour of the Engle, won land to the south of the Eider and gained everlasting fame. Upon the death of Wermund, Offa became king of Angeln.

Later, when the Engle sailed over the sea to Britain, two of the greatest kings of Mercia, Penda (c.577–655) and Offa II (d.796) were proud to claim descent from Offa the son of Wermund.

The Migration to Britain

Breakthrough in 406

By the end of the fourth century Germanic tribes were spread far and wide across Northern Europe. Their societies had developed in different ways and they often fought each other, but they had much in common. The migrations and wars of that time resulted in the break-up of some tribal alliances and the creation of others, with the result that new loyalties and new elites were formed. For example, at the end of the first century there is no record of the Saxons and Franks but by the fifth century they were two of the most powerful confederations of tribes in Northern Europe.[10]

The early fifth century was a time of great importance for the Germanic tribes who had by that time taken control of nearly all the territory on the east bank of the Rhine and held most of the north bank of the Danube. There had been several military successes against the Romans in the east but in the west there had been no recent breakthrough. Now, however, there was a new wave of migration and invasion from the east. The ripple effect reached the west and created the need for new land to settle. It became apparent that some degree of co-operation between the tribes would be necessary if a major defeat was to be inflicted on the Romans. Such an alliance came into being in 406 when a force of Vandals, Swabians, Burgundians and Alans gathered on the east bank of the Rhine. It is probable that omens were sought, runes read, and lots cast, before they launched their attack across that powerful river. They fought their way through the enemy defences and broke them so that when the fighting was done they had the whole of Gaul before them. In an attempt to re-establish control the Romans withdrew troops from Britain but they were unable to recover their position in Gaul.

---

[10] In *Germania*, 98AD, Tacitus mentioned the tribes that later became part of the Saxon confederation but not the Saxons as such. Ptolemy mentions them in his Geography, c.150 AD, and is thought to have based much of his work on information from a Roman naval expedition 150 years earlier. In other words, it is not known when the confederation began but it is probable that it started with a small group of tribes, including the Aviones and Reudingi, and was situated between the southern end of the Jutland peninsula and the Elbe. Saxon expansion after that was probably due to a mixture of voluntary membership and conquest. Certainly by the time of Offa, the Saxons were a powerful southern neighbour of the Engle.

During the breakthrough the Asding, King Godegisel, was killed but his son took command and led the Vandals into Gaul and then into Spain. In 429 they crossed to North Africa and captured Carthage and forced the Romans to formally cede a large part of that territory to them. The Vandals landed in Sicily and forced further concessions from the Romans. After a period of peace, a new wave of activity began around the year 455 with the capture of Corsica, Sardinia and the Balearic Islands. Raids were made on the coast of Spain and Greece, and a landing in Italy culminated in the capture and sacking of Rome.

The Swabians, like the Vandals, moved across Gaul to the Iberian Peninsula where they established their own kingdom. The Burgundians remained in the east of Gaul and eventually created a kingdom with two capitals; one at Lyons and the other at Geneva. The Alans went to Spain and North Africa but gradually lost their identity and became merged with the Vandals who in turn became absorbed into the populations of the conquered territories.

The Alamans and Franks made less spectacular advances into Gaul than the Vandals and other tribes but their gains were to be more long-lasting because they captured and settled land lying next to their existing territory. The Alamans, which means 'all men', were a confederation of several Germanic peoples, the largest group being Swabians.

The Franks were also a mixture, or confederation, of peoples who lived near the Rhine. They did not take part in the events of 406 but were able to take advantage of the disintegration of Roman power in northern Gaul and move into territory adjacent to their own. Their advance was mostly by means of steady migration and settlement rather than sweeping military conquest. Towards the end of the fifth century the Franks became a powerful people and much later one of their kings, Charles the Great (Charlemagne) 742–814, created a great empire. The Frankish population was small compared with that of the Empire they created, and although they gave their name, and much else to France, their separate identity was eventually lost in the large Gallic population.

The victory of 406 dealt a great blow to the Roman position in Gaul and to the Empire as a whole, and it was one from which it never recovered. In the east the Goths moved into Italy and took Rome in 410, and in the extreme west the seaborne expansion of the North Sea tribes, known collectively to their enemies as Saxons, contributed to the Roman abandonment of Britain.

The success of the various Germanic tribes in following up the victory depended mainly on the size of their population and the extent of the new territory they controlled. The Vandals travelled great distances and made a powerful impact before disappearing almost without trace. The Franks moved into territory adjoining their own and survived as a distinct people for many generations.

A lesson to be learnt from this turbulent period is that there is no long-term survival for a small nation that conquers and lives among a larger nation. A native people who remain on the land, and are more numerous than the invaders, can survive many defeats and long periods of foreign rule. Elites can be overthrown or absorbed into the native population.

When invasion and defeat of the enemy is followed by tribal migration and displacement of the earlier population, the future of the victors is assured. Those who take land, live on it, produce children and govern themselves, are well placed to remain united and strong both in arms and culture.

The Saxons and Frisians

The empathy and loyalty that bind people together as a community varies from time to time and place to place. The Saxons were a mixture of peoples united by a family of warrior kings while the unity of the Frisians was based primarily on their long history and comparative isolation. The unity of the Engle was in part based on common religious practices. All of these tribes had contact with Britain, the Frisians primarily as traders, the Saxons and the Engle as raiders and as mercenaries fighting for Rome.

The Saxons were a confederation of peoples living in the lands between the lower Rhine and Jutland. When faced with an external threat they united under a family of warrior kings, but in times of peace their unity was not great and many warlords took independent military action. The Saxons took to piracy and coastal raids in much the same way as the Franks. The seafaring exploits of the Franks, and others, during the third and fourth centuries are far more extensive than is commonly believed, and are largely overlooked by those who enthuse about Scandinavian Vikings. Franks, Saxons, Engle and other North Sea and Baltic people had well-designed and built sailing ships which enabled them to make long-range coastal and river raids, and attack Roman shipping. Eutropius reported that by the mid-280s, the coasts of Belgica and Armorica were infested with Frankish and Saxon pirates.[11] A Roman writer reported that the courage of the Saxons was so great and their seamanship so expert that they welcomed a storm because of the opportunity it gave them to take their enemy by surprise. Saxon and Frankish attacks on the coasts of Gaul and Britain, and on Roman, Gallic and British ships, became so frequent and troublesome that the Romans tried to sweep them from the sea. Despite the considerable resources devoted to the task they were unsuccessful and the attacks continued. The Romans also built strongholds at strategic points on those parts of the coast of Britain and Gaul known as the Saxon Shore.

After the victory of the Germanic tribes in 406 and the withdrawal of Roman forces from Britain, the Saxon war bands increased the frequency and duration of

---

[11] *Dark Age Naval Power*, John Haywood (Anglo-Saxon Books, 1999)

their raids on Britain which in 408 were on such a large scale that they amounted to an invasion. The British leaders appealed to the Romans for help but none was given because the Romans were trying to regain control of Gaul. It is probable that most of the North Sea tribes took part in the raids on Britain but they became known collectively, by foreigners, after the name of the largest and probably most active group of raiders, the Saxons.

The Frisians were among the first of the North Sea peoples to cross to Britain and settle there. They went as traders and farmers, and settled in the east of Britain between the Thames and The Wash. Frisian merchants traded with the Britons and some lived in the ports and other towns of eastern Britain where they were able to acquire information about the happenings in that land. The merchants' cargo ships, knowledge of Britain, and trade routes across the North Sea, drew them into the movement of settlers to Britain. Frisian cargo ships were better suited than Saxon or Engle warships and coastal traders to the task of carrying baggage and cattle. The early Frisian involvement in seaborne trade and settlement led to their language becoming known beyond their own land and Frisian played a part in the development of the English language, to which it is closely related.

North of the Frisians and Saxons, across the Eider, were the Engle who, as we have seen, were united in their worship of Nerthus. They too had considerable seaborne power but it was mostly projected into the Baltic. To the north of the Engle were the Eote (Jutes).

Britain

It is evident from history that those with the greatest power take the best land while the weak have to be content with poorer soils. In the distant past Britain was inhabited by a people we call the *Ivernians* or *Hibernians*, most of whom lived on the fertile and easily cultivated lands of the south and east. They were driven off that land by invading Gaels (*Goidels*) a people who came to Britain from the continent. The Gaels were better armed, motivated and organized than the Hibernians, many of whom moved to high ground or into the forests that covered much of Britain. The Gaels were greatly influenced by Druidism, the religion of the Ivernians, and some of them adapted and developed it for their own purposes.

After the Gaels came the Britons (*Brythons*) who in turn drove out many Gaels and took the best districts. As Gaels migrated to the north and west, they conquered, or pushed before them, the Ivernians and Hibernians who were only able to be free in Ireland and the north of Britain. The power of the Britons increased and their control of much of the island that was to be given their name became firmer. As it did so the Gaels moved further north and west, many crossing the sea to Ireland where they occupied the eastern districts while the Ivernians and Hibernians lived in the west. In those parts of western Britain where the two peoples had little choice but to live together the population became mixed and it was only in the north of Britain and the west of Ireland that the Ivernians and Hibernians were able to preserve their separate identities.

Many of the migrants to Britain from the continent were part of the Celtic language group. There is little to suggest that they were part of the Celtic tribe that had sacked Rome and then spread across Southwest Europe. It is more likely their ancestors had been ruled by Celts or been subject to them, and had absorbed, to varying degrees, elements of Celtic culture. Like the Vandals and Normans, Celts made a great impact for a relatively short period then disappeared from history having spread themselves thinly, and expended their military and cultural energy. They were absorbed into the much larger populations amongst whom they settled.

Tribes from Belgica, some of whom were Germanic, crossed the sea to Britain during the period of German and Roman expansion and there were also migrations of other people. The most unusual journey was that made by North African Berbers who arrived in Spain and then sailed to the west coast of Britain where they settled and created a kingdom on the western shore of what is now Wales.[12]

In the north of Britain lived tribes to whom the Romans gave the collective name Caledonians. The most powerful of those people were the Picts. Little is known about them but it has been suggested that they may have been either one of the earliest tribes to migrate to Britain, having entered from the south, or possibly to have been of Germanic origin and to have migrated from Norway via the Shetland Islands.

Like many people of that time the Picts painted their bodies when they went to war but they seem to have developed that custom more than most and had unique tattoo designs. They also had distinctive forms of writing and patterns, both of which they marked on rocks.

The population of Britain consisted of an assortment of tribes who, as far as possible, sought to settle, control and defend territory in a collective way. Sometimes the incoming population was a comparatively small but effective military elite which defeated and ruled a long established population. At other times whole tribes migrated. Once established, they increased their territory and power by increasing their population and number of settlements. They wanted land for their own use, not as a way of ruling others. Displaced people were forced to move on and perish or displace others. Thus, a succession of migrations produced a ripple effect across Europe and Britain.

During the periods of migration a very large number of people and tribes were on the move seeking land for settlement. A people, or tribe, might number one hundred thousand individuals or more. The migrations gave rise to widespread disturbance and conflict. Some tribes were powerful enough to resist such pressures and to hold their territory but others were driven from their land and

---

[12] The Berbers also settled in Ireland and influenced the development of the Gaelic (Irish) language.

sought more elsewhere. It was the custom at that time for individuals to migrate as part of a large group as it made them stronger in defence and attack. It also enabled them to retain their communal and cultural identity.

As we have seen earlier, it was the custom of the Germanic peoples to sacrifice captives to the gods but sometimes prisoners were taken, either to ransom or to keep as bondsmen (slaves). Presumably any skills the bondsmen had were made use of but most were probably put to work as labourers. The extent to which slaves were absorbed into the societies they served is not clear but evidence from other places and times suggests that much probably depended upon the extent to which they were physically and culturally similar to their captors.

Surplus captives and criminals unable to pay their wergild, were sold to traders and transported to Roman slave markets where demand was high.

The English and Welsh

The people of the North Sea tribes (Jutes, Frisians, Saxons and Engle) were collectively known as Saxons to the people of Britain. Yet when those North Sea migrants settled in Britain they became absorbed into a common core English identity. Their country became England and their language English. Hereafter they will be referred to as English or Anglo-Saxon.

The non-English population of what is now England and Wales were known to the English as Welsh (Old English *wealh*, meaning *foreigner* or *slave*). The Welsh were a mixture of peoples, many of whom had adopted various aspects of Celtic culture, especially language. In order to simplify matters this population will be referred to as the Welsh, and the inhabitants of Ireland will be called Gaels. The homeland of the Picts was known to the English as Pictland and roughly corresponded with what is now Scotland.

Roman Britain

The Romans conquered Britain for the purpose of absorbing it into their empire, extracting minerals and exacting taxes. They sought land to rule rather than settle. Many of the troops employed in the conquest and later defence of Britain were Germanic and their camps were usually in strategic defensive positions either close to, or inside, Roman fortifications. The Roman forts at Brancaster, Burgh, Bradwell, Reculver, Richborough, Dover, Lympne, Pevensey and Portchester were strategic strong points in the Saxon Shore defences, which stretched from The Wash to the Isle of Wight. Norwich and York were important garrison towns and there were German camps guarding the lower Thames (Mucking) and the southern approaches to London (Croydon and Mitcham). Germanic mercenaries were also stationed along the Middle Thames to provide protection for the heartland of Southern Britain.

Some Germanic warriors stayed on in Britain after their term of service as Roman mercenaries ended. They continued to live in or near the settlements that had grown up by the camps and were able to obtain there the goods and services that were being provided locally for the garrisons. They also benefited from the security that such settlements offered. It was in this way that small Germanic communities were created in Britain even before the Romans abandoned it in 410. Many of those communities survived the economic upheaval of the Roman withdrawal and were strengthened by the arrival of settlers who were seeking new land. The settlement of Britain by North Sea Germans was not a sudden or swift occurrence. It started slowly and carried on for many years at a low level. Then later, when the circumstances where right, it became a great surge.

When the Romans abandoned Britain, those Welsh who had benefited from the Roman occupation naturally wished to preserve Roman customs and forms of administration. They had grown accustomed to living in towns and wanted to maintain the economic and political system that made the Roman way of life possible. They believed the Roman withdrawal was only temporary and that once the legions had re-established the boundaries of the empire on the Continent they would return to Britain and restore the position of their allies and the Church. Their response to Saxon and Pictish raids was to appeal to the Romans for help rather than to attempt to unite and provide their own defence.

Without the Romans the political and economic structures they had created started to decay, as did the towns, churches and estates that were a part of that society. The partially suppressed culture and way of life of the Welsh was able to re-emerge, as were the ancient hostilities. As is common when an imperial power declines, there was a struggle for power. Various tribes, local leaders and factions fought each other for political dominance.

The Welsh managed to unite for the purpose of repelling an invasion of Picts in 410 but after that there was little unity. Many years later a Welsh king named Vortigern achieved a position of dominance and became an overlord.[13] The Welsh continued to fight amongst themselves and while they did so Engle, Frisians, and Saxons crossed the sea to Britain and steadily strengthened their position in the East and, possibly, in the Thames valley. The lack of unity among the Welsh suggests that tribal and ethnic divisions were much greater than is often thought.

The twenty years following the Roman withdrawal were not all ones of war. There were times of peace and prosperity but that comparatively tranquil period came to an end about the year 430 with an outbreak of plague and renewed Pictish attacks. After suffering several defeats at the hands of the Picts, the Welsh decided to seek help from abroad. Some still wanted to re-introduce Roman power but Vortigern was opposed to that policy, probably because he thought it would undermine his

---

[13] *Vortigern* might be a personal name or a title.

own position. Instead, he obtained support and promises of funding from Welsh leaders to recruit mercenaries to fight against the Picts. The natural thing to do was to employ the warriors that the Romans had used, so Vortigern sent a messenger across the sea with an appeal for help.

Hengest and Horsa

The messenger from Vortigern arrived at the hall of Hengest and his twin brother Horsa. They were invited to Britain with their companions to protect the Welsh and drive out the Picts. The payment would be land and provisions. The offer was accepted and a host of warriors set sail in three longships and landed at a place called Ypwinesfleot (Ebbsfleet, Kent). They took possession of the land that had been given them (Isle of Thanet) and then went north in their ships to fight the Picts who had been attacking the Welsh on land and from the sea. Hengest and Horsa were victorious wherever they went and drove out the Picts and brought peace to the land.

The warriors served Vortigern well for many years and there was peace and prosperity in Britain. Each year they received the food, and other provisions promised them. Their success, and the economic and political stability it helped bring, encouraged more of their fellow countrymen to cross the sea and their number in the east of Britain increased. As the English population in the East increased, so the Welsh began to move away. The movement need not have been far or in all places. A continuing trend involving a few people at any one time can, after a decade or two, have a marked effect. The need for people to live with those of their own kind is very strong. The Welsh preferred to withdraw and seek new land rather than live in areas being increasingly populated by people who could not be absorbed into Welsh society and culture, and had no wish to do so. In those early years of settlement, the English gained control of territory in the east by a gradual and steady increase in their numbers and expansion of their settlements. The taking of land by one people from another is more often achieved in this way than by military conquest. When the process is gradual, and the will to organize and resist is low, the point eventually comes when the settlers have control of the land and effective resistance by the earlier population is impossible. They are sometimes provoked to fight for their independence but usually their position is by that time too weak. More often they drift away to another part of their country and abandon increasingly large parts of it to the settlers who come to regard it as their own and use it as a base for further expansion.

One of the reasons for people to want to move from Northwest Europe to Britain was the rising sea level, which caused flooding and salt contamination of low-lying arable land along seacoasts and river mouths.

Shortly after 440, following a long period of peace, many Welsh leaders complained about the levy being raised to pay Hengest and Horsa. It was felt that there was no longer a need to pay for protection and they refused to make any further contributions – they *welshed on the deal*, which was not something the cheated warriors could be expected to take lightly. Just as in the heat of summer it is hard to recall the biting cold of winter, so in the calm of peace it is hard to recall the turmoil and suffering of war. An assembly of representatives from the Welsh kingdoms withdrew their support for Vortigern and his policy. He had no choice but to inform Hengest that the agreement was ended and the payments would stop.

When Hengest heard that the Welsh were refusing to supply his warriors with the food and other provisions they were due, he went to Britain to assess the situation and to talk with Vortigern, who was facing increasing internal opposition. Hengest offered to fight for the King against his opponents and a deal was struck by which Hengest would receive additional land in Kent in return for his support. Word was sent back across the sea to Angeln ordering them to send more men. When reinforcements arrived Hengest and his twin Horsa led the rebellion and drove away those who wished to overthrow Vortigern. But Vortigern, concerned at his increasing reliance on Hengest and fearing that he was losing the support of his countrymen, turned on Hengest who again sent for more men and told them of the worthlessness of the Welsh and of the excellence of the land. A large force of picked men was assembled and sent across the sea in nineteen ships to help the others.

Hengest and Horsa were said to be the sons of Wihtgils, the son of Witta, the son of Wecta, the son of Woden. Many of the southern kings and all the Northumbrian royal family claimed descent from Woden. Hengest and Horsa fought Vortigern in the place called Aegelsthrep (Aylesford, Kent). Hengest was victorious but Horsa was killed and Oisc succeeded to the kingdom and ruled with Hengest. Two years later Hengest and Oisc fought the Welsh at a place called Crecganforf (Crayford, Kent) and killed four thousand of the enemy. The Welsh abandoned Kent and fled to London in great terror.[14]

Hengest fought in many battles in the south and the north of Britain and he put the Welsh to flight through fire and the sword's edge. Hengest and Oisc fought them near Wippedesfleot and killed twelve Welsh lords. One of their own thanes, Wipped, was also slain there. Eight years later the Anglo-Saxons again fought the Welsh and captured innumerable spoils, and the Welsh fled as one flees from fire. The Anglo-Saxons became rulers of their own lands in Britain and the dominant political and military force.

Migration

The warriors who sailed to Britain to fight for Hengest came from three powerful nations of Germany; the Engle, the Saxons and the Jutes. From the Jutes came the people of Kent and the people of the Isle of Wight and the mainland opposite

---

[14] An account of the early conquest is given in *The English Chronicle*, otherwise known as *The Anglo-Saxon Chronicle*.

Wight. From the Saxons came the East Saxons and the South Saxons and the West Saxons. From the Engle came the East Engle, Middle Engle, Mercians and all the Northumbrians. Such was the extent of the migration from Angeln to Britain that when it was finished, the country of Angeln stood empty.[15]

Behind the warriors went settlers, who farmed the new land as they had the old. The king of the Engle, his family, companions, and all his people went to Britain. Some went to the lands to the south of the River Humber (Southumbrians) while some went to the lands north of the Humber (Northumbrians). They eventually occupied the East Coast of Britain as far north as the Firth of Forth. Many of the Lowland Scots are descended from the Engle, and their language, Scots, is a dialect of English.

Saxons, Jutes, Frisians and Franks[16] also settled in Britain but the bulk of those groups remained on the Continent. The Engle were probably the most numerous of all the Germanic nations that crossed the sea to Britain. Whatever their numbers may have been, theirs was certainly the core community, culture and identity into which other settlers merged. The English nation spoke English and their country was England.

It was not unusual at that time for migrations to take place on a very large scale with whole nations moving together as an organised group. For example, in Caesar's *Gallic War* there is an account of how the Helvetii, who numbered about 263,000, set about preparing for migration. They lived in a large territory north of the Alps between the Rhine and the Rhone but they decided it was no longer suitable for them because, despite its large size, the geographical and political conditions were unfavourable to their aspirations. It seems that several other tribes in the area were persuaded to join the migration.[17]

A common feature of migrations was massive baggage trains. The Helvetii prepared by buying all the draught cattle and wagons they could get hold of. They sowed as much of their land as they could with corn so that they would have a good supply for their journey. In addition to grain, each family was instructed to take with it three months' supply of flour for its own use. It was all highly organised and followed a two-year plan. In the third year they burnt to the ground all twelve of their towns and four hundred villages. All isolated buildings were also destroyed, as was all the grain they were unable to take with them. They then set off with the other tribes on a migration. The total number of people on the move was 360,000, of which 92,000 were warriors.

---

[15] Bede's, *Ecclesiastical History of the English People.*

[16] Franks settled in Kent and their kings had some influence there.

[17] The other tribes were the Tulingi, Latovici, Rauraci, and Boii. This and other information is from *Caesar: The Conquest of Gaul*, Translated by S. A. Handford. (The Penguin Classics, 1951).

It is not being suggested that the English did the same as the Helvetii but it is clear that whole nations did migrate in a planned and well-ordered manner. Instead of buying waggons, the English may have bought cargo ships to supplement their own or chartered ships from trading nations such as the Frisians. A well-organised migration could have moved a lot of people, livestock, and baggage in a relatively short time. Perhaps it took place in stages over a number of good sailing seasons. Whatever the method, the idea that the seagoing Germanic tribes of that time did not have sailing ships or were unable to navigate across open sea and had to hug the coast, is outdated.[18]

Another fallacy, and one commonly promoted in schools, is that Anglo-Saxon migration was small-scale and of no special importance, being just another of many similar migrations. This view is promoted primarily for ideological reasons that are dealt with later. For the time being, it is worth noting that the evidence for the migration being very large and very important is overwhelming. It brought a deep and lasting change in the population, culture and language of lowland Britain. It was probably the most important event in English history.

The Settlement

In the time of Hengest, new territory was opened up to English domination and eventual settlement. In later times, the threat of force was often there and sometimes used as advances were periodically made in a general east to west direction. As the English population increased it began to displace the Welsh who gradually migrated to areas where they were still dominant. The English advance was marked by changes to place names. The Welsh names for settlements and local features of the landscape were either Anglicised or given new English names. Woods, streams and settlements became known to the English by names derived from the names of the tribe or family who owned the land, or lived on it, or to the use to which it was put, or its physical description. Some woods, hills, and springs were given names that linked them with the Gods, for example, Tuesley (Tiw) and Thursley (Thunor) in Surrey, Wednesfield and Wednesbury (Woden) in Staffordshire. Harrow-on-the-Hill in its earliest form means *the holy place of the Gumeningas*, the Gumeningas being a tribe.

The names of Romano-British towns and the Welsh names for geographical features, such as large rivers, were retained because they had been learned from the Welsh by the early English settlers. While it is easy to change a local name, it

---

[18] John Haywood (*Dark Age Naval Power*, Anglo-Saxon Books, 2000) and others have advanced a convincing and widely accepted argument that the shipbuilding and seamanship skills of the North Sea Germans were far in advance of those with which they were formerly credited.

The First

England

(the land of the Engle)
at the end of 4th century

Jutes

North Sea

E
n
g
l
e

Jællinge

Rendsburg

Eider

Myrgings

Weser

Elbe

Ems

Saxons

England

Late 5th century

The West Engle were called Mercians
which means 'borderers' or
'dwellers on the march'.

North Engle

Mercians

Lindesey

East Engle

Middle Engle

East Saxons

West Saxons

Jutes

South Saxons

Jutes

ENGLAND

9th Century

Strathclyde

Bernicia

Northumberland

Welsh

Deira

Gwynedd

Mercia

East Anglia

Northfolk

Southfolk

Powys

Dyfed

Welsh

Essex

Middlesex

Kent

Wessex

Sussex

Welsh

is more difficult to change the name of something known to many people over a wide area. A similar process occurred when the English settled in North America. Indian names were retained for mountains and large rivers but smaller geographical features and settlements were, generally, given English names. More North American Indian words entered the English language during the conquest of North America than Welsh words entered the English language during the conquest and settlement of much of Britain.

The extent to which words from one language enter another during periods of migration and settlement is a good indication as to whether populations became mixed or remained separate. Other than place-names, very few Welsh words have entered the English language. The flow from English to Welsh is also small. This suggests little cultural or other interchange between the two groups.

With the exception of large towns, the place names of a country rarely change while the indigenous population remains on the land. For example, Wales, Scotland, and Ireland were later absorbed into the English state, and the population of those countries now speak English but there are few English place names. The exceptions being mostly in areas where the English settled. For instance, in Scotland, English place names are mostly found in areas of Anglo-Saxons settlement, which are mainly in the lowlands, particularly in the east.

An important issue is the extent to which the Anglo-Saxon population drove out and replaced the Welsh, or Romano-British, population. Those who can best be described as *Celtic* nationalists, tend to be drawn to one of two opposing views on this matter. The first argues that the English drove the Welsh from their land, burning and looting towns and churches as they spread destruction across Britain from one sea to the other. This *barbarian approach* has little to support it because it seems that buildings and parts of towns fell into disuse and disrepair, and did not meet a swift end by fire. The evidence suggests that the Roman way of life and economy started to decay shortly after the Romans left. That process was well under way by the time of Hengest. However, the barbarian approach appeals to those modern day Celtic nationalists who use it to justify the view that the English are a nasty lot deserving the wrath of the gallant Celtic peoples who were defeated by the treachery and savagery of the English. In other words, we are justified in using every means possible in our modern-day fight against the English (e.g. bombs in shops and pubs) because they did the same to us.

The second view takes a different and subtler approach. It suggests that the Welsh population, which they mistakenly refer to as Celts, remained in place and absorbed the Saxon invaders who were small in number and only constituted local ruling elites. In other words, there are no such people as the English, just a mostly Celtic people living in a place called England. Just how a small *Saxon* elite was able to bring about such profound and rapid change in every aspect of society, and at all levels, is never adequately explained. How, for example, do they explain the absence in England during the relevant period of Welsh cemeteries and the large number of Early English cemeteries? It seems that the small ruling elite was able to get the *Celts* to not only change their place names and language but also to build and farm like the English, use English artefacts and in every way adopt an English way of life. The graves and their contents where not English at all, merely *Celts* who were buried wearing English dress and accompanied by artefacts in the English style. Likewise, buildings, weapons, literature, etc. were not English but in the style of the small English elite. This line of argument shows the desperately low levels to which some will go in trying to construct a Celtic heritage.

Many of those advocating the absorption theory are engaged in a form of cultural warfare in which history is rewritten. Such propaganda has had much success in recent years amongst young romantics who like to see the *Celts* as nice peace-loving people who lived in harmony with nature. Celts are also often incorrectly credited with being the founders of Druidism and having constructed the ancient earthworks and stone circles of Britain. The need to believe this nonsense springs in part from a search for roots. Celtic mania has been rolling along unopposed for such a long time that criticism of it is much resented.

Also linked to the absorption theory are those who, for ideological reasons, favour the *continuous waves of migrants* integration and absorption *cultural enrichment* interpretation of English history, which they like to call British history. This approach attempts to demonstrate that the population of Britain has always been ethnically and culturally mixed, and that is something undeniably good, to be welcomed and encouraged.

The population of Britain has indeed been varied but that does not mean that the different groups lived happily together in multi-cultural communities. The various groups were not organised in a way that could cater for people of different cultures. The ethnic groups in Britain, including the English, lived apart and defended their territory and way of life.

A third and more realistic approach is that the creation of the English kingdoms took many generations to complete and took different forms in different places at different times. At some times and in some places the Welsh were defeated and put to flight, in others they went overseas or gradually migrated westwards. During the later western conquests, it is probable that quite a large number of Welsh remained on the land but were gradually absorbed into English society. With the exception of Wales and some western regions (such as Cornwall, Dorset and Cumbria), the Welsh only survived as self-governing communities for a short while in small enclaves situated in forested or hilly areas, e.g. parts of the Chiltern Hills. In most of England, and especially in the lowland areas, the changes were very deep and widespread. The English brought with them a system of law and administration that formed the foundations of the institutions that are still found in Anglo-Saxon societies. The type of agriculture, holding of land, shape of fields, construction of buildings, methods of burial, type of grave goods, place names, religion, trade routes, and language, all changed with their arrival. The evidence for a profound break is overwhelming, whereas the evidence for ethnic, social and cultural continuity in Britain from before the Germanic migration until the formation of England is very slight and not at all convincing. To see continuity takes the determination and blindness of those who wish it were true.

Research based on the distribution of ABO blood groups supports a large-scale Anglo-Saxon migration. Blood group O is more common in Ireland and the west of Great Britain, while A is more frequent in East Anglia. A blood-type map produced by Kopec (1970) from the records of half a million blood donors, showed a very high incidence of A, and a very low incidence of O, in East Anglia. It also showed the incidence of A decreasing and that of O increasing from east to west and from south to north.

Another study (Roberts et al., 1981) showed that if the gradient is looked at closely it is seen to contain within it a patchwork of gene pools that are, or were, separated by geographical barriers such as mountains, rivers marshes or forests. Where geographical factors were not the cause of the enclaves it must be presumed that they were due to cultural barriers. For example in Cumbria, where there is a high incidence of group O, it is possible to identify areas high in group A which corresponded with Norwegian place names. That such a gradient and patchwork still exist would seem to indicate that one wave of migrants tended to displace an earlier wave who tended to move west or north-west and that the mixing of the population was not so great as to produce an even distribution of blood groups.[19]

For the most part the Welsh and English lived apart and retained their own languages and customs. The English and the Welsh were proud of their history, achievements and way of life. They did not praise all gods but their own or tell of the deeds of all heroes but their own or see the worth of any culture but their own. They were confident and noble peoples who had no wish or need to adopt the customs of others.

It is highly likely that there was some trade between them and later, during the period of the separate English kingdoms, there were occasions when English and Welsh leaders formed alliances for the purpose of confronting a common Welsh or English enemy. However, most English trade was with their fellow countrymen in

---

[19] Some of those who are keen to demonstrate that the population of Britain is homogeneous and has been much the same since the last Ice Age, like to produce genetic maps based on *mitochondrial* DNA, which is passed on through the female line. Such maps do the job intended and show an almost common genetic inheritance for the whole *indigenous* population of the British Isles. But, they also show much the same thing for most of Europe because they reveal common female ancestors from very ancient times. A lesson to learn from this is that genetics is increasingly becoming a battlefield, and caution is needed in interpreting DNA evidence. Much depends on what a particular form of genetic evidence is able to prove and how it is used.

England and with the Germanic peoples across the North Sea.[20] Likewise, the Welsh traded mainly with their fellow countrymen in Britain, and with Ireland, Brittany and the lands that had been part of the Roman Empire.

Brief Outline of the Period 400–1100

Anglo-Saxon settlement and the creation of England occurred in several stages. Their settlements grew up close to Roman garrison towns during the Roman occupation of Britain and most of those settlements remained after the withdrawal of Roman forces from Britain and acted as focal points for later migration. After the withdrawal of the Romans there was a gradual peaceful settlement of the coastal areas of what is now East Anglia by various Germanic peoples. The second half of the fifth century was a period of steady military conquest and migration, in which the early settlements formed a base and secure bridgehead. The Welsh either migrated from, or were driven from, most of Eastern, Southern, and South-eastern Britain, and at the end of the fifth century the land east of a line from The Wash to the Isle of Wight was in English hands, as were lowland areas north of the Humber. The Welsh managed to halt the advance for a generation at the Battle (or Siege) of Mount Badon where they enjoyed a rare but significant victory over the English and may as a result have recaptured some territory. Where and when the battle took place is unknown but two of several suggested locations are a hill just east of Bath and Bradbury, south-east of Swindon. Suggested dates for the battle range from 490 to 516.

After a generation of stability, in which the Anglo-Saxons were able to consolidate their position, they advanced once again, but more quickly than before, and drove many of the Welsh into the inhospitable lands on the western fringe of Britain. That last advance, which may have followed an outbreak of plague in the west, was carried out in a series of rapid campaigns that captured large territories. It is likely that a greater number of the Welsh population remained than had been the case in earlier campaigns but those that stayed were gradually absorbed into the advancing English population and their culture.

The Anglo-Saxons went to Britain as heathens and took with them their institutions, their Gods, and the confident and positive outlook on life that their beliefs fostered. More than 150 years after that migration began, Augustine landed in Kent (597) and set in motion the process which saw the nominal conversion of the English people to Christianity. The strategy employed by the Church was top down, which meant they converted kings first, usually by offering a political advantage of some kind, and then using the influence of the Church at the heart of the state to impose conformity to its ways on the whole population. That process did not involve an abrupt end to one system of belief and the beginning of another,

---

[20] Baltic trade was still of great economic importance to England 1,000 years later. Indeed it was the search for trade routes beyond the Baltic that led to the creation of the English Empire.

it was instead a gradual take-over of the existing institutions and the adoption and modification of many heathen customs and the suppression of others. The success of the Church was in part due to its ability to adapt to local conditions and to assimilate local customs, folklore and beliefs. In this way the Church preserved and promoted as Christian much that had its roots in the heathen past. This is not to say that the Church was not hostile to the Old Religion or that it did not discriminate against or punish those who indulged in practices which the Church deemed un-Christian. However, it would seem that nothing like the witch burning of later times or the practices popularly attributed to the Spanish inquisition occurred in England during the first millennium.

The Anglo-Saxon migrants were able to merge into one nation because of their similarities. For the same reason, the Danes and other Scandinavian settlers were absorbed into the English population, culture, and identity. Many parts of Eastern England saw Danish settlement but there was not a mass migration on a scale comparable with that of the English. The Danes in England were comparatively small in number but of considerable significance, although it is often overstated. For example, some would have us believe that *Vikings* founded York. It was in fact a Roman town that had a large English population when the Danes and other Scandinavians arrived. The later migrants built their own settlement on the edge of York.

An important consequence of the Danish invasions was that it led to the unification of the English under one king. England existed before the time of the Dane Guthrum and King Alfred but it was divided into several kingdoms. After the lowest point in the fortunes of the English and Alfred (849–899) at Athelney (878), the creation of one English kingdom for the whole of England began. All of the fighting, clever planning, and hard work were rewarded when under King Athelstan (893–939), England became a united and powerful kingdom.

The assimilation of the Danes led to changes in the English way of life and some Danish words were introduced into the English vocabulary. The most important consequence of the linguistic compromises that took place during that period of assimilation was that English was simplified. For example, word endings were dropped and word order was changed. These fundamental changes were far more important than the comparatively few additions to English vocabulary.

The Norman invasion, which left its mark on the English language, also had other far-reaching consequences for the English. Whereas Danes eventually joined and fitted in with what they found, the Normans imposed themselves on the English.

The Normans were *Northmen* who, under the leadership of Rolf Ganger, a Norwegian, went to Northwest Gaul in 911 and, after an initial defeat and conversion to Christianity, established the Duchy of Normandy. It might have been because they were so different in appearance from the native population that the Northmen felt able to assimilate Frankish culture and language without it threatening their group identity. When the Normans, lead by Wilhelm, invaded England 155 years later, they formed a comparatively small ruling elite. It was perhaps because of their similarity to the English in appearance that they used their adopted Frankish culture and language as a way of preserving their separate identity. The main influence they had on the English language was to greatly expand its vocabulary by introducing foreign (Norman-French) words. It was this that gave rise to much of the confusion we have in Modern English with, for example, different rules for spelling different foreign loan words. Much is often made of the introduction of new words and *the enrichment of the language* but the other side of it was the loss of many English words.

Because Norman-French was used by the political, administrative, legal and religious elites, it became entrenched in those areas of activity and among certain classes. However, the English language continued to be spoken and written by the English. In the fourteenth century, Chaucer and others wrote in English instead of French or Latin. The English they used was that of the English people. This suggests an evolving language and literary tradition. There was not a sudden change from Old English to Middle English; one flowed into the other.

Since 1066 there has been no successful military invasion of England, and until the twentieth century there was no significant migration of peoples into England that could not be absorbed into an English identity.

During the late sixteenth and early seventeenth centuries, English adventurers, explorers and colonists laid the foundations of the English Empire which was to later become known as the British Empire. For the next three hundred years the English migrated overseas and created new communities with institutions rooted in England. The way of life and the outlook of those people remained that of English men and women. Even after independence, the political and legal systems of the new states remained, at least for a while, for the most part English in character.

It was natural that the different English communities evolved in different ways and that the descendants of those settlers should identify with their new homeland. However, they are still Anglo-Saxon, a term used in modern times for people of English origin wherever they might live in the world, and whatever their attachment to the country in which they live. This means primarily the Anglo-Saxon people of Australia, Canada, England, New Zealand and the USA. It also includes others of English ancestry wherever they might be. The early period of English history belongs to them all because it is the early history of the Anglo-Saxon diaspora.

Some ask why the English should look to the Continent for their origins and early history. The answer is, because the Engle provided the core identity into which others were absorbed. It is with them that the origins and early history of the English are to be found.

I am English, my language is English, and my homeland is England. It is therefore not unreasonable for me to trace my communal English identity back through that group of people who have called themselves English and spoken English. That journey takes me back to Offa and Nerthus, not to the Britons or pseudo-Celts. This is not to deny that some Britons, Danes, Normans and others have been absorbed into the English community and influenced the way it has evolved. The point though is that I am English, not Danish or Norman.

Afterword

The name of the Engle was recorded in Latin as *Anglii*, which later became *Angle*. As their own language evolved the Engle became the Englisc and then the English. The Engle, along with the Jutes and Frisians, were known collectively to the people in Britain and to the south of the Rhine as Saxons. The Saxons were in fact a confederation of tribes that lived to the south of the Engle. They were widely known for their seaborne raids along the East coast of Britain and the Atlantic coast of Europe. Because the Germanic tribes of north-west Europe shared a similar appearance, culture and language, they were all known to outsiders as Saxons.

The reason for the much later introduction of the term Anglo-Saxon is uncertain but it may have been used to distinguish the English-Saxons (Engle, Jutes, Frisians, and Saxons) who migrated to Britain from those who stayed behind and were called Old Saxons. Another possibility is that *Anglo-Saxon* recognised the mixed origins of the migrants. In more recent times, *Anglo-Saxon* has been used as a name for members of the English diaspora.

For whatever reason, (e.g. large population, cultural dominance) all of the Germanic migrants to Britain became absorbed into a core English (Engle) identity. They lived in England (Englalond) and spoke English. That language, now called Old English, has evolved through Middle English into the English we speak today (Modern or New English).

During its history, English has absorbed many foreign loan words. Some are very useful, sit well with English and enrich it. Many others are unnecessary and ugly misfits. For example, the English *town rubbish dump* is more direct than the Latin *civic waste-disposal facility*; *near miss* is better than the ugly *aircraft proximity incident*; *rat catcher* is better than *rodent exterminator*.

One of the consequences of adopting foreign words is that English words are lost and the orderliness of the language is disturbed. It is all very well to repeat the oft-heard claim that importing foreign words enriches the English language but that does not happen if a word gained means a word lost.

Old English is a beautiful language, as is Latin, and it can say much with few words. Mixing the two together spoils them both. The King James Bible is written in simple English with very few foreign loan words and is the better for it. The Lord's Prayer says much with few words and is memorable. The English used by Shakespeare stems almost wholly from Old English roots. The novels of Jane Austen owe much of their beauty to the use of plain English. Fill any of these works with Latinisms and they would become the ugly mess known to social scientists and the military, e.g. *interdiction* and *collateral damage*. The great political speeches in the English language have for the most part been in plain English, which is a form of English containing a mix of mostly English root words and commonly used and understood loan words.

There is a link between language and culture and the way people view the world. A language is shaped by the communal, cultural and physical environments of those who use it. It affects the way we think and the way we see the world. It helps unite a nation and provide a sense of communal and cultural continuity. The French understand that and rightly feel protective about their language.

English is tight and thrifty. It promotes clear thought and encourages people to say what they really mean. English is more modern and simple than Latin, a flowery language that encourages wooliness. Latinisms are the resort of the vague and the lazy. *Facility* is a word commonly used by such people. There is no longer a need to, for instance, distinguish a factory from an office from a hospital from a warehouse; just call it a *facility*. *Functionality* is another word of this ilk. Ask the user what it means and see the struggle start. One of the difficulties associated with the use of Latinisms is that they change the way sentences are put together, thus it is not always easy to simply replace a Latin word with an English equivalent.

We have lost so much of our English word-hoard that it is near impossible to write or speak on most matters without using Latinisms. But that is not a good reason for encouraging the further colonisation of our language. If we are to preserve our language, which is an important part of our identity, we should use English words whenever we can.

It is certain that someone will point out that this particular messenger fails in many ways to do as he bids others. That is quite true but it does not disprove the argument. Those of us who lack skill as wordsmiths have as much right as the gifted to put our point of view. What is being suggested is that each of us should do the best we can, given our ability, to use a suitable English word when one is available. This plea is most certainly not a call to purge the language of Greek and Latin root words, which would be a silly and impossible task. It is merely a plea that where possible we use the plain English that is available to us, and, when new words are needed, we try to make them from English roots. In that way our language will be more easily understood by the whole English nation. Those who came up with the name *Consignia*, and others like it, would do well to remember that new words can enrich a language but they need not have foreign roots to do so.

We are often told that it is impossible to control the use and development of a language and we should not waste the effort trying. It is true that the evolution of a language cannot be controlled but it can be guided this way or that, as can other aspects of culture. It is our duty to try to keep the shape of English so that it is an effective tool for the job.

If the English were aware of the history of their language they would perhaps be encouraged to preserve its simplicity and directness. It might also enable them to see that words with Greek and Latin roots are not superior to English words, although the pretentious and pompous think they are.

Part Two   A World View

To fully understand why nationalism is made to appear bad, and Englishness is ridiculed and denied, it is necessary to step back from the fray in England and take a wider view of the forces that are intent on shaping our perceptions.

What is a Nation?

The word nation is commonly used in the following three ways:

1. As a synonym for *state*. For example, when the European Union is discussed, mention is often made of its member nations pooling and sharing their sovereignty. The members of the EU are in fact states.

2. As a term for the citizens of a state. For example, reference is often made to the British nation when what is meant is citizens of the UK or the British people. Also, at the time of the coming to power of Nelson Mandela there was much talk of the people of South Africa being one nation; a rainbow nation. What was meant was that the people of many nations shared the same citizenship.

3. As a term for a group of people who share a common descent, culture, history and language. For example, the Kurds, Zulus, Palestinians and Tibetans are all nations, as indeed are the English.

Those who are careless with their terminology, which includes many journalists, tend to use the words *state* and *nation* as if they are interchangeable. Those who study global society (International Relations) or are involved in inter-state relations have to be more precise with their terms and better appreciate the need to distinguish a state from a nation.

The misuse of the terms is mostly due to ignorance but sometimes it is a deliberate act by those who wish to promote an inclusive civic identity in place of an exclusive national identity. They believe that the state should be central to the identity and loyalty of those who live in it. They further that aim by merging national identity into a civic or state identity. Thus, *nation* and *nationality* are used in a way that implies that they are political rather than cultural terms. *Nationality* is equated with *citizenship*, which can be constitutionally defined and bestowed by the state. For example, if a person is a citizen of France they are deemed to be French and to owe loyalty to the French state.

A very different view is that a nation is a community of people with a communal name, ancestry, culture, history and language. Those who take this stance believe that nations exist independently of states, and that nationality is determined by membership of and loyalty to a cultural and kinship community; a nation. For

61

example, an Algerian who becomes a French citizen remains an Algerian. It is this fundamental difference in outlook that is explored below.

It is widely recognised that it is difficult to define a nation but that does not mean that nations do not exist. A fairly simple definition, or collection of guidelines, as to what constitutes a nation is that it is a group of people who share all or most of the following: a collective name; a perceived or real common ancestry; a history; a culture; a language; and sometimes a common religion. There is nearly always an association between a nation and a specific territory that is regarded as its homeland. A nation has myths, legends, heroes and loyalties. It is a community with a sense of solidarity and common identity; there is a *we* sentiment and a *they* sentiment; *insiders* and *outsiders*. A greater degree of empathy and sympathy exists among insiders than between insiders and outsiders. Indeed, the notion of *insiders* and *outsiders* derives from the concept of a community living closely together within a physical boundary, e.g. an encampment or settlement enclosed by a fence or ditch. A nation's boundary markers are more often cultural and perceptual than physical.

One of the most important things that binds a nation together is the fact or perception of insiders sharing a common history and ancestry. The members of a nation usually have real ancestral links, but even in those instances where the links are weak, the illusion of common ancestry is possible because insiders share certain physical characteristics that make it possible for them to believe in a shared ancestry. As is so often the case, perception is more important than fact but pretence has its limits. For example, it would be difficult for a Japanese to pretend to be a Zulu because whatever clothes that person wore or the language they spoke, their appearance would remain so different from that of Zulus that any claim to share a common ancestry would obviously be doubtful.

That we have mental images of Zulus, Swedes and Japanese indicates that the linked factors of common physical characteristics and common ancestry are important considerations in determining membership of national communities. Despite the instinctive links we make, some ideologues are outraged by the idea that common ancestry has any part in determining nationality, not because it is untrue but because it is ideologically inconvenient. The very people who deny a link between kinship and nationality when defining, for example, Swedish nationality, nevertheless think it relevant when, for example, determining membership of North American Indian nations. An instance of this is the procedure used when the US government granted the remnants of certain Indian nations various land rights in a belated attempt to compensate them for the loss of their homelands. The financial benefits for members of those nations can sometimes be great, and there are many claimants. The method used to establish membership of an Indian nation is ancestry, which has to be proved.[21] In other words, that which determines membership of a North American Indian nation is judged to be *in the blood*, hence, for example, the term full-blooded Navajo. A similar blood-line procedure is used by the US government for determining who are indigenous Hawaiians. Place of residence or birth or the expression of a firmly held belief by the applicant that they are a member of the appropriate tribe/nation counts for little. Nationality is not, therefore, taken to be a matter of personal choice.[22]

Other factors that help identify a nation are myths and folklore that throw light on its origins and ancestry. Mythology is important even when it is only loosely based on fact or is a complete invention, as is the case with the various legends of King Arthur.[23] Folklore and history help to unite a nation and give it a distinct identity but it need not be one hundred percent *true* in order to fulfil that function.

Religions and political ideologies are powerful bonding factors that sometimes cut across national identity but they more often compliment and re-enforce national identities and promote alliances of nations and their states. For example, the conflict in Bosnia re-enforced various alliances of states based on common religion. Turkey and other Moslem states supported the Bosnian Moslems, and the Greeks supported their fellow Orthodox Christians, the Serbs. States with large Catholic populations supported the Catholic Croats. Another feature of the war was the way Moslems in Bosnia used, or had imposed on them, a religious identity as an ethnic identity.

Individuals tend to feel more secure when they are in the company of persons with whom they have much in common; birds of a feather flock together. Common values, experiences, attitudes and perceptions help make up the glue that bind together both small, face-to-face, local communities and large national communities. A nation is organic; it lives; it is more than the sum of its parts; it repairs and renews itself; it has a memory; it evolves. Its personality is to be found in its culture, its institutions and the attitudes and behaviour of its parts. Each member of a nation is a link between its past and its future. As with all living

---

[21] North American Indian nations find the process acceptable because blood ties play an important part in their cultures.

[22] It is to be noted that states sometimes take the line that citizenship is in the blood and not conferred by place of birth. If a US citizen gives birth to a child while on a visit to another state, the child is deemed to be a US citizen by both the US and the other state.

[23] The invented tales of a King Arthur were promoted by the Normans and Plantagenets in place of English history. It was part of a policy that can be called cultural genocide. The aim was to impose on the English a history of Britain in which the English played little part except as villains. This fictional account served the dual purpose of providing the Britons with a glorious history that made them feel better about themselves, and undermining English national identity, thus making the English more accepting of Norman rule. The legends took on a life of their own and as they developed they came to represent an ideal of chivalrous behaviour which influenced real knights and kings.

things a nation has to renew itself if it is to survive. It is the communal duty of each generation to preserve and renew the national culture. In doing so, it in turn becomes part of the nation's present, past, and future.

When a nation ceases to renew itself it dies and the memory of those that have gone before and the culture they helped to weave dies with it: it is a loss to all mankind. A dead nation leaves behind it artefacts, buildings, a history, language and culture but nothing to bind those things together and give them life. The parts remain as curiosities, the preservation and interpretation of which lies with outsiders. Nationalism is the expression of a will to avoid communal extinction.

A nation is a reference point for individuals, it is a community where individuals can feel comfortable and at ease. A nation provides physical and cultural surroundings that are familiar and unthreatening. A nation is a home, and for many individuals it is such an important part of their being that they are prepared to endure hardships and to fight and die in its defence.

A Tribe

A tribe is a community consisting of one or more extended families. It is sometimes not easy to distinguish between a tribe and a nation but relevant factors, other than kinship, include population size and the distinctiveness of the culture. There is a Zulu nation that has a homeland but it is usually described as a tribe. Such a group of people living in Europe would almost certainly be called a nation but the use of the term tribe in Africa is a hangover from early colonial times when the long histories and rich cultures of African nations was not widely recognised by outsiders.

Nations are sometimes made up of tribes that can be distinguished one from another by small differences in, for example, dialect and material culture. However, these sub-national identities are united within a wider national identity that shares cultural, communal, political and territorial boundaries.

A People

The term *people* is used in many ways but for our purposes a precise definition is not important. It is used here to describe a group of persons who share one or more common characteristic such as culture, political institutions, race or place. A people are at a lesser stage of integration and unity than a nation and generally come within one or more of the following groups:

1. a community or a society, possibly made up of tribes or nations, which is either not large enough or sufficiently homogeneous, to be a nation. For instance, the Nigerian people consist of several nations, as do the British people;

2. the remnants of a nation that has disintegrated;

3. persons who have common national roots but now form separate national communities, e.g. the Anglo-Saxon people (Anglo-Saxon diaspora);

4. a race or sub-race, e.g. the Arab people;

5. a religious group, e.g. the Islamic people;

6. inhabitants of a continent or other defined geographical area, e.g. the African people, Scandinavian people;

7. persons of similar skin pigmentation, e.g. Black people and White people;

8. a group of individuals or nations who share common political institutions, and are usually citizens of one state, e.g. the British people or the American people;

9. a language group, e.g. the English-speaking people.

It can be seen that the members of one group are often also members of other groups. For example, the Anglo-Saxon people are part of the English-speaking people but the two groups are not identical.

Sometimes a people adopt a name which is misleading but serves a political purpose. For example, Black-Americans have taken to calling themselves Afro-Americans or African-Americans. They are free to do so but not all Africans are Black or Negroid and North African people (Arabs) living in the USA are not generally described as African-Americans and most would probably not include themselves in that group because it is seen as a label for Black-Americans. The term African-American has been adopted by many Black-Americans in order to create the notion of a long shared history and common ancestry. They are in the business of trying to merge many African identities into one to provide Black-Americans with common roots. The aim is also to bolster the self-esteem of Black-Americans by laying claim to the cultural achievements of all African civilisations; including that of ancient Egypt. Those Black-American intellectuals who wish to promote the view that Black-Africans were responsible for the great achievements of Egyptian civilisation and that Western civilisation was built on those achievements, are free to do so but others should not feel inhibited about contesting the validity of the claims.

Nations – Community and Communication

A nation is a community. One of the key elements of community is an exchange of information, hence the level of communication technology available at any time or place is an important factor in determining the numerical and geographical size of communities. The dramatic improvements made in travel and communication technology during the past two hundred years have enabled communities to become bigger by making it possible for larger groups of people to be aware that they share common myths, memories, symbols, folklore, values and perceptions.

Developments in engineering skills, scientific knowledge and political organization have all played a part in expanding the boundaries of community. Sailing ships, roads, bridges, printing, railways, the telephone, aircraft, television, satellites and computers, have contributed to faster and wider communication and have enabled individuals to be in physical, visual and intellectual contact with many more members of their own national community, and of other national communities.

One of the consequences of improved communication is that a sense of community is no longer as dependent as it once was on individuals being geographically close to one another in face-to-face relationships. Thus, the importance of local communities has generally lessened, while national communities have become more important in establishing identity and loyalties.[24]

The development of communication technology has not only enabled nations to grow in size and cohesion, but has also provided governing elites with the means to make their states more powerful and exercise control over ever larger numbers of people by means of increasingly sophisticated techniques of persuasion. In other words, those things that have made possible greater national cohesion have also enabled states to become more powerful.

Developments in technology and organization have made it possible for national communities to become wider and deeper but those factors did not create nations and nationalism. Nations and nationalism have existed for thousands of years and are not, as is sometimes suggested, products of the industrial revolution or capitalism, although these things have influenced the way nationalism has evolved. The sentiment itself is much the same as it has always been, but what has changed is the way governing elites have manipulated national loyalties so as to use them for the benefit of the state and elite interests. The Black African nations that are commonly called tribes, existed long before the advent of modern capitalism and industrialisation. A tribe such as the Ndebeli (Matabele), whose language is part of the Bantu group, meets the definition of a nation but it was not invented by intellectuals or conjured out of thin air by capitalists. It is the modern sub-Saharan states of Africa that were invented. European outsiders drew lines on maps with disregard for national homelands and little consideration for the interests of those living there. It is that history and the continuing denial of the importance of national boundaries (geographical, cultural and political) by the current governing elites of those states that is responsible for much of the turmoil in Africa. In states such as Uganda, the governing elite is engaged in what is called a policy of *nation building*. What they are really trying to do is weaken or destroy nations in order to create allegiance to a state. They face a difficult task because the communal instincts that bind nations together have evolved over millions of

---

[24] It is sometimes argued that the Internet has led to the growth of new small communities spread over a wide geographical area. However, such groups are interest groups rather than communities because the common point of contact is typically limited to one area of interest or activity.

years and are deep within us all; they will not evaporate in order to satisfy the wish of an elite to maintain artificial political boundaries, and destroy natural cultural and communal boundaries. A better long-term approach would be to abandon the recently created state boundaries and instead, as far as is possible, map national boundaries and put into effect a policy of national self-government. The creation of real nation-states would remove from domestic politics the wasteful and time-consuming distraction of internal national rivalries. A nation with its own state is relatively well placed to enjoy the internal consensus and cohesion that a nation needs if it is to effectively pursue its external interests. Nation-states are also better able to provide the communal conditions that enable citizens to enjoy individual freedoms.

Nations and States

During the eighteenth and nineteenth centuries capitalism and industrialisation greatly increased the power of states and made it possible for those who controlled them to mobilise more resources for the purpose of pursuing policy goals that were said to be in *the national interest*.[25] Governing elites set about identifying the interests of the nation with those of the state. The two quite distinct concepts were merged into one and the confusion it caused continues today. The purpose of that deliberate policy is the same now as it was then, to harness the communal strength of a nation and use it to pursue the interests of the state and those who control it. What is commonly seen as the rise of modern nationalism would be better viewed as the rise of modern statism.[26] Little has changed since then in that the state is still presented as the embodiment of the nation, and the loyalty that is instinctively given to the nation is still demanded by the state.

The tactic used to promote the preferred perception of a nation was to redefine *nation* in a way that stripped away all the inconvenient cultural attributes and made it into something that suited liberal political theory. Two commonly used nineteenth century definitions of a nation are given below.

> A nation is a grand solidarity constituted by the sentiments of sacrifices which one has made and those that one is disposed to make again. It supposes a past, it renews itself especially in the present by a tangible deed: the approval, the desire, clearly expressed, to continue the communal life. The existence of a nation is an everyday plebiscite.

> Ernest Renan, French historian, in *Qu'est-ce qu'une nation?* (1882)

Ernest Renan's definition is one that is often quoted and is in many respects valid. However, its popularity among liberals is due to the fact that it describes a civic

---

[25] States rarely pursue the *national* interest. It is more usual for them to pursue *state* interests, which are usually the same as the interests of a state's governing elite.

[26] *Statism* is the theory or practise of centralising economic and political power in the state.

society and conveniently lacks any reference to kinship, language, history and a homeland.

Another definition, which is more easily recognised for what it is, comes from John Stuart Mill. Again, it gives a flavour of what constitutes a real nation and real nationalism but omits any mention of culture and a perceived common ancestry.

> A portion of mankind may be said to constitute a nationality if they are united among themselves by common sympathies which do not exist between them and any others – which make them co-operate with each other more willingly than with other people, desire to be under the same government, and desire that it should be government by themselves or a portion of themselves exclusively.

John Stuart Mill, *Considerations on Representative Government* (1861)

The increasing ability of states to mobilise resources (technological and human) and the congruence, more or less, of national and state boundaries, made it easier for the idea to gain hold that state and nation were the same thing. Where several nations were incorporated into one state, the governing elite set about creating and promoting a new *national* identity. For example, the creation of the United Kingdom led to the invention of a British identity. So, instead of a state being created to serve the interests of a nation, a nation was constructed to serve the needs of a state.

In recent times, and especially since WWII, the interests of governing elites and the states they control have become even more remote from the interests of the nations they once claimed to represent. Indeed the distance is now so great that some governing elites no longer justify the existence of the state on the grounds that it pursues the interest of its core-nation. Instead, they deny the relevance or even the existence of nations and see only civic societies and *civic-nationalism*, which amounts to loyalty and devotion to the state. The existence of modern states, and our supposed obligation to obey their rules, has long been rationalised by an argument based on a clearly fictional account of a *natural order* and a binding *social contract* that we are all deemed to have entered into. According to this model, which attempts to make states and constitutions look natural and necessary, states are a collection of neutral institutions that arbitrate between the competing interests of their citizens. In return for providing that service, states are deemed to have the right to demand the loyalty of their citizens. To attempt to overthrow the state and its governing elite is treated as the worst of crimes (treason) and deserving of the most severe penalty (death).

The social contact justification for states completely ignores the fact that real nations are bound together by threads spun from kinship, culture and interests. It is true that nations have a political dimension but it is not the only one. Nationalists argue that the loyalty a community owes to its political institutions is conditional on those institutions pursuing the interests of the community, as determined by the community. And those communal interests include cultural interests.

Nationalists see states as merely a means to a communal end, but liberals see them as things that exist in their own right, apart from and above their individual citizens. Nationalists believe that each nation is best served by its own state, and that loyalty is only owed to a state if it is serving the interests of the nation. Liberals maintain that one state can serve many nations, and that all citizens owe loyalty to the state. This fundamental difference of view is central to the dislike that liberal-statists and liberal-globalists have for nations, nationalists and nationalism, and it is the reason for the campaign of vilification that has been directed against them for many years. Such has been the success of the campaign that *nationalist* is commonly used as a term of abuse, and nationalism is equated with demonic forces.

The perceptual battle has become more intense and wide-ranging in recent times due to the emergence of a global-elite that is detached from nations and has only a logistical interest in the preservation of states.[27] Like other elites, it has common interests, values, perceptions and goals. Unlike other elites, it does not claim to be the guardian of a nation or a state but a global village. The Global Elite, in the guise of the *International Community*, does its best to present itself as a village policeman sorting out criminals and troublemakers for the good of all. The global village is bound together by a non-sexist equivalent of the brotherhood of man, a much higher and purer basis for unity than nations and nationality, which are regarded as primitive. Even states and civic-identity are seen as increasingly outdated. We must look instead to a regional identity and a wider global identity. We are to become citizens of the world. We will unite around our common belief that liberal globalism is the one true way that will bring us peace and prosperity. The only drawback is that you must not ask about democracy.

The world-view of the Global Elite is different from that promoted by state elites but it serves the same purpose, which is to enable the Global Elite to better pursue its own interests while claiming to be acting in pursuit of a noble ideal. Thus, the Global Elite deploys military force and economic sanctions in the name of peace, democracy and human rights, and in accordance with the wishes of the *International Community*.

What some call the *International Community*, others call the *New World Order* or the *Global Elite*. In order to discover what the term *International Community* actually means, those who use it should be asked the following questions. Who are the members of the *International Community* and who has the right to speak for it? How is it known what the wishes of the *International Community* are? Whose interests are being served? Is *peace-keeping* being used as a cover for acts of

---

[27] States raise taxes, provide basic services, keep order and maintain the politico-economic conditions favourable to a particular type of global economy.

aggression, including war? Is the slogan "Freedom and Democracy" a war cry for those who favour an ideological tyranny? Are human rights being used as an excuse for effecting their denial? In short, what is the pay-off and for whom?

On close examination, the *International Community* will be seen to be a global-elite that has the roots of its power anchored in a relatively small group of very powerful states, corporations and institutions. It is through those agencies that elite power is exercised and its interests pursued. The wellbeing of nations plays no part whatsoever in the Global Elite's assessment of its interests. In fact, it is openly hostile to the idea of nations because it sees a world containing many cultures, identities and loyalties as a hindrance to the worldwide acceptance of its values and perceptions. The Global Elite wants to destroy and sweep away what it cannot use to its advantage. In the place of nations it is promoting new civic and institutional identities.

The Global Elite realises that there is a limit to the elasticity of national loyalty, which has been stretched to near breaking-point by states. In its place, the *International Community* is promoting loyalty to something far more distant and vague than a state; it is loyalty to a global society, a global culture, and a universal ideology. In return for supplying an abundance of goods and services, the Global Elite demands acceptance of its values and perceptions and the right to root out or render ineffective those who reject them. Unsurprisingly, despite its immense power, it finds it difficult to compete with or destroy national loyalties, which are founded on considerations other than the need to maximise the consumption of goods and services.

Like all centralists, of whatever political hue, the Global Elite prefers an atomised society of individuals who are powerless before the might of a relatively small co-ordinated ruling group. When national communities and their interests and loyalties persist, what better way to counter them than to create multi-nation-states, denigrate national identity, and promote civic societies. These strands are brought together in a particular form of globalism that is deemed to be both desirable and inevitable. The strategy for defeating opposition within liberal states is to demoralise the enemy by convincing it that it cannot win; it is standing in the path of an inevitable development in the history of mankind. *Progress* will sweep away all who try to resist it.

In its effort to manipulate our communal instincts for the purpose of creating a communal global identity and making us see ourselves as citizens of the world, the Global Elite is undermining the economic, political and military independence of the very states that are the foundation of its power. The increasing unwillingness and inability of states to challenge *global forces* and *progress*, prevents them from performing their traditional functions. The liberal justification for the existence of states is undermined because liberal globalism prevents them from effectively arbitrating between the conflicting interests of their citizens, and defending those citizens and their civic society from outside forces. The waning of citizens' confidence in the ability of states to influence events is made worse by globalists who insist that states *as we know them* are no longer functional and need to be replaced by super-states, regional trading blocs, and global institutions.

In such circumstances it is difficult to understand why a national community or an individual citizen should be expected to be loyal to a political structure (a state) that has diminishing power and does not represent communal or individual interests. Even more puzzling, why should a nation be loyal to remote organizations that are even less concerned than states to pursue national interests? Why should the English be loyal to a dying British state that is continually ceding powers to a newborn European state? Why should the English willingly sacrifice anything, especially their lives, to defend a structure like the EU, which is even less inclined than the UK to represent English communal interests or even recognise the English as a nation?[28]

National Character

National character can be defined as a collection of tendencies that causes a nation (both the community as a whole and its individual members) to act in certain ways in certain situations.

There is little popular opposition to the view that certain national communities have certain behavioural characteristics. For example, funeral processions, burials and public grieving are conducted differently in England and the Middle East. In England it is considered appropriate to be as dignified as possible while in the Middle East it is thought appropriate to demonstrate grief in a public manner. One approach is not inherently *better* than the other they are just different. The people involved share similar feelings of loss and sadness but they are expressed in different ways. Culture to a large extent determines the expected behaviour in such situations but so does the personality of the individuals concerned. Whatever the reasons for the differences, they exist.

A problem that often arises when we try to explain why members of different groups behave in different ways is that the argument becomes centred on whether different behavioural characteristics are innate or cultural. That leads to a polarised either/or approach rather than one that sees both factors as important. What is often overlooked is that instincts and culture are part of the environment that

---

[28] The EU promotes a common European identity by various means including literature distributed in schools. The emphasis tends to be on a supposed common Celtic and Christian heritage. The aim is to promote a sense of common identity, culture, and belonging. In furtherance of that aim, it has been suggested that the school history syllabus in England should place greater emphasis on Britain's Norman heritage and the link it provides to the continent. Running parallel with this is the view that nations and nationalism are problems that need to be overcome so that we can all live happily together in peace and prosperity.

influences the evolution of instincts and culture. It is a circular process. Thus, nature and nurture are intertwined. Man is a communal animal with communal instincts shaped by the cultural and physical environments of our ancestors.

The collection of behavioural characteristics that is called national character has been shaped by many generations of exposure to a given culture, geography, climate, religion and language. Italians are widely thought to be more excitable and temperamental than Swedes. That view makes use of stereotypes but stereotypes are usually based on observation and contain a large kernel of truth. Anyway, it is enough that such differences are widely perceived to exist, and they form part of a nation's identity. Behavioural characteristics, like physical characteristics, help distinguish an insider from an outsider.

Those common characteristics that help promote unity within a community can be a source of conflict between communities. The behaviour of one group might be unintentionally offensive or irritating to the members of another group and give rise to all sorts of problems, the least being that they do not get along together.

Some characteristics are common to all humans; some are more commonly found in men and others in women; some are more common to one nation than another. This is not to suggest that one sex is superior to the other or that some nations are superior or inferior to others, only that they are different in all sorts of subtle ways that are due, at least in part, to their evolutionary history. People who live in places where survival is difficult evolve physical, behavioural, communal and cultural characteristics suited to those harsh conditions. People living in easier surroundings evolve characteristics appropriate to their situation. The behavioural characteristics that help define an Eskimo differ from those that help define a Zulu.

Summary

Communities are exclusive in that membership is open only to those who meet informal and often indefinable conditions. All communities have boundary markers and all communities, be they nuclear families or nations, discriminate between insiders and outsiders. Even African, Asian and North American Indian nations discriminate because without discrimination there can be no boundaries and no community. Nations are not something that one can choose to join like a club. Membership is not open to all and sundry. Nationality is not a commodity, a fashion accessory or lifestyle that can be adopted and discarded at will.

The communal loyalties that naturally exist within nations were stretched to serve the interests of states and then wider to help further the interests of economic and ideological blocs. It was too much; there is a limit to how far communal instincts can be stretched and manipulated. Having found *community* unsuited to the task, the Global Elite wishes to be rid of it and has instead turned to *society*, the more atomised and individualistic the better. To that end, it seeks the destruction of national cultures and identities. In place of *us-cultures* it promotes a global *me-culture* that values individualism, image and immediate self-gratification; all of which are bound up with consumption and status. In place of cultural and ideological diversity, we are force-fed cultural and ideological conformity. The individualism they offer is that of sheep in a flock.

Like a Pied Piper, the Global Elite divorces new generations from the old. Communities are being broken and discarded to make way for civic societies and a citizen-of-the-world-identity. It is an unrealistic and unsustainable policy because there is no adequate substitute for communal glue. The grand new ideological creations will fracture and fall apart. The Global Elite will be unable to satisfy the communal instincts that combine and encourage insiders to:

> *co-operate with each other more willingly than with other people, desire to be under the same government, and desire that it should be government by themselves or a portion of themselves exclusively.*

Nationality and Citizenship

Nationality

Nationality is the condition, or fact, of belonging to a body of people sharing a common descent, culture, history and language. Nationality is normally acquired at birth; individuals are normally born into a community. It is the <u>perception</u> of a common ancestry and shared communal experiences that binds a nation together.

At the heart of nationality is a feeling of belonging and oneness that marks out a communal boundary. The *we sentiment* is not, as many wish us to believe, evil and deserving of eradication. On the contrary, it is at the heart of any community anywhere in the world, and gives rise to positive communal thoughts and deeds.

It is difficult to frame exact rules for determining who is a member of a given nation but a useful guide, which can be used for any nation, is as follows: I am English if I believe[29] that I am English <u>and</u> if I am accepted as being English by the members of that group of people who are commonly recognised as being English. It is a two-way instinctive relationship between individual and community. I could, for example, assert that I am Japanese but if I have physical and cultural characteristics that are not Japanese, as determined by the Japanese, I will not be accepted as part of the Japanese community. No amount of law-making, sulking or haranguing will alter that.

The two-way process of selection for inclusion or exclusion helps provide an answer to the question often thrown at nationalists, "What does it mean [for

---

[29] The word *believe* is hardly adequate to convey the emotional feeling of identity with and concern for a nation that is at the heart of nationality.

example] to be English?" The aim of the questioner is to draw out a list of characteristics that identify the English. Those asked are usually stumped for an answer, which is not surprising because the process of inclusion and exclusion is not a conscious one and does not work in the way implied by the question. The English, like all other nations, first see characteristics that exclude people because that is a more efficient way of working when analysing vast amounts of information.[30] Most of the Earth's population can be quickly excluded from membership of any given nation on the basis of appearance and language. If necessary, other tests of varying degrees of sophistication can be used until we are satisfied that the person is either an *insider* or an *outsider*.

If the person is accepted as an insider, the instinctive assessment process goes on and makes other judgements about the person, including such things as their social class. At this *insider* level of assessment, the filtering process can make finer distinctions because we have far more experience of dealing with insiders and can make better use of small amounts of information. For example, if a Russian gives me his home address it will tell me little, if anything, about him because my knowledge of Russia and things Russian is poor. An address in my hometown will tell me far more about the person who lives there.

Nationality is a total experience that starts in the family, which is the smallest community. Children are born into both a family and the wider communities of which that family is part. They are immersed in and soak up like a sponge the language, culture and history of the communities to which they belong.[31] That experience helps mould children and gives them an identity and sense of belonging. They pick up habits of behaviour and thought that are part of what is meant by national character. That character-building process, if that is what it can properly be called, works best when there is cultural immersion and socialisation from a very early age. Once a national identity has been absorbed, it is embedded for life. It shapes values and perceptions in a way that makes it impossible for a member of one nation to completely shake off that identity and take on another.

---

[30] It is usual when processing a large amount of information to set markers, and exclude information that falls outside the set boundaries. Alan Turin applied this principle when devising the system known as the Bombe, which automated and speeded up the daily processing of information for the purpose of breaking the German Enigma code during World War II.

[31] Young children naturally absorb cultural information from those around them. This instinct enables them to learn up-to-date survival strategies that can be laid over their long-term survival instincts. This ability to quickly adapt to the requirements of the immediate environment has evolved over millions of years, and under conditions where cultural information and skills helped individuals and communities survive and reproduce. We now have conditions where children are subject to the influence of a culture which promotes values and perceptions that are harmful to both individual and communal survival and reproduction. The result is a high proportion of young adults with attitudes and behavioural habits that make them well suited for life in the virtual-reality world promoted by the global me-culture but ill-equipped for survival in the real world. Natural selection ruthlessly weeds out those with unsuitable survival strategies.

Learning another nation's customs, history and language is not enough because the new information is laid on old foundations.

The link between kinship, identity and loyalty can be illustrated as follows. An adopted child reared from a baby by loving adopted parents is likely to feel love and affection for those parents. When the child learns of its adoption it will normally want to seek out its biological parents.[32] If they are found, the child is likely to feel an attachment to them that is different from that felt for the adopted parents, who it will probably continue to love as before. This need to know our origins is instinctive and essential to our sense of identity and belonging. It is therefore understandable that when a child learns that its real parents belong to a nation different from the one it has been raised in, it is likely to be drawn to that other nation's culture, and identify with it. This can cause difficulties that are made worse when differences of race are added to those of nationality. The experience of many children involved in cross-race adoptions is one of confusion in adulthood due to conflicting communal identities and loyalties. Having been immersed in one culture from birth and having had that identity imprinted on them they find it difficult, if not impossible, to feel totally part of another culture to which they are subsequently drawn. They cannot overcome the fact that the first all-important immersion in a communal identity is a one-off experience.

In a similar way, children with parents of the same race but different nationality have to deal with conflicting attractions and loyalties. However, the problem is usually not so great for them because they are generally drawn to, and accepted by, at least one of the nations to which they are linked by kinship. A child raised in the national homeland, culture and language of one parent is likely to be drawn to that nation and be accepted by it. However, physical appearance can sometimes play a more important part than upbringing in determining which community a person is drawn to and which community accepts them. If a person's physical or cultural characteristics differ greatly from the norm for a particular nation, that person is unlikely to seek acceptance in it or to be accepted by it.

Liberals feel the need to put a positive slant on these things and suggest that children with parents of different nationality or race have the advantage of two identities and two cultures.[33] But is it really possible to immerse oneself in two cultures, identify with two histories, feel an insider in two communities, and, more difficult still, be accepted as a full member of two communities? The answer is probably, no. To feel an insider and be accepted as an insider it is usually necessary for a person to be immersed in the culture of that community from birth and to be free of traits that would cause that person to be seen as an outsider.

---

[32] Children who learn that they are the product of an arrangement involving an anonymous sperm donor also feel the need to find their roots and establish their identity.

[33] Multi-culturalism is an ideology (a very recent one) and should be subject to the same tests as any other. It is not, as many of its followers believe, derived from an unchallengeable universal truth.

A nation is an extended family and like a family it has a life greater than that of any single member. Nations, like families, are bound together by the bonds of empathy and loyalty that come from a shared identity. Those bonds are not only with the living but also with those who have gone before and those who are yet to come. That link between past, present and future encourages the living members of a national community to protect the memory of earlier generations and safeguard the position of future generations. That sentiment is not something that can be learned or feigned.

Citizenship

Using *nationality* as a synonym for *citizenship* can cause confusion and misunderstanding. Nationality denotes membership of a particular community, while citizenship denotes membership of a civic-society. The two identities are sometimes complementary (in nation-states) and sometimes they conflict or have no close association (in multi-nation-states).

A civic identity is like a national identity in that it is usually acquired at birth with no opportunity available for opting out or negotiating terms. Those who were born in the Soviet Union usually acquired Soviet citizenship and, like other Soviet citizens, became a part of Soviet society and were subject to the rules of the Soviet state, which like other states deemed that it had the right to demand obedience and loyalty in certain things. Soviet citizens also belonged to a nation (e.g. Russian, Latvian, Armenian) and a family, both of which are communities that endure despite the coming and going of states. In a similar way, a British citizen (more properly called a British subject[34]) might be English, Scottish, Welsh, Nigerian, Bangladeshi, Jamaican, Italian or a member of any nation you care to mention.[35] Citizenship indicates a person's relationship with a state (political structure) and is usually defined in a legalistic form of words that is embodied in the state's constitution. Nationality indicates a person's relationship with a nation (community and its culture) and cannot be formally defined.

Each state determines who are its citizens and how non-citizens can qualify for citizenship. The acquisition of citizenship is a legal formality that gives an individual civic rights and obligations. It is a legal procedure and because of that it is possible to be a citizen of two or more states and have dual citizenship, which is

---

[34] A subject is a person who lives under (is subject to) the rule of a monarch. The term is technically correct but will cease to be so if the UK is absorbed into the European Union. *Subject* is probably no longer appropriate in the UK because although the monarch is Head of State he or she does not rule in any real sense and, in effect, acts as an unelected president. *Citizen* is the more appropriate term.

[35] British subjects in the province of Northern Ireland who are Republicans or members of the *Nationalist Community*, consider themselves to be Irish. The position of the *Loyalist Community* is more complex but they can, with justification, claim to be a nation with a homeland called Ulster. They are Ulstermen. *Protestant* describes their religion and *Loyalist* is a political stance.

often inaccurately termed, dual-nationality. Some states permit their citizens to hold dual citizenship but others do not.

Britishness and UK Citizenship v Englishness

With the union of England and Scotland came the need for a new inclusive identity. The remedy was to make all those living in the United Kingdom and the colonies, British. This sleight of hand was born of the imperialistic fashion of the nineteenth century. The idea that all were equally British was clearly a fiction but it met the needs of the time. Thus, the English Empire became the British Empire.

Nearly all of the nations that were once within that empire have freed themselves from their fake British identity. The English who, with Ulstermen, are the last to begin that process, can make a start by demanding the creation of an English parliament on a par with that so freely granted to Scotland. It is not something that will be easily achieved because the UK government (in year 2000) and politicians in Scotland and Wales have a vested interest in maintaining a relationship that places England at a disadvantage. In other words, most of them want to preserve the Union but to take from it as much power and independence as they can without breaking the link that channels money from England.

An English Parliament will have limited powers and will not solve all of England's problems but it will act as a focal point for the expression of English interests and aspirations. It will also cause many to reflect on what government is for and ask whose interests it should pursue. The campaign for an English Parliament and its creation should be seen as a stage in the recovery of English sovereignty.

The British Empire has long gone and the UK looks to be heading in the same direction. Now, just as Britishness is entering its death throes, the liberals/leftists who were so scornful of Britishness and the Union flag are eager to revive both. They prefer an inclusive British identity to the exclusive English, Scottish, and Welsh identities. They also need a living British identity because without it there cannot be a British responsibility for the people and places that were once part of the Empire. This outlook is an essential part of their ideas concerning globalism; the free movement of peoples; and a preferential right of access to the UK. It is also at the root of their guilt complex.

The desire to promote Britishness carries with it the desire to suppress competing identities such as Englishness. An example of the denial of Englishness is to be found in the various central and local government forms that ask for details of ethnic identity but exclude the option of an English identity. Instead, the English are submerged in a racial *White European* identity This despite the fact that the Irish, Turks, and others are often able to state their *ethnic* identity.

Another example of a reluctance to use the *E* word, is to be seen in a report in the *Daily Telegraph*, 12th June 1997, where, in what appeared to be a quotation from a Commission for Racial Equality investigation, mention is made of "white, Irish and Chinese school-leavers" and "white and Irish applicants". The Irish are apparently not *white*. From the context it seems that by *white* they mean English, Scottish and Welsh. This illustrates the difficulties that multi-culturalists get themselves into when they mix racial and national categories, and try to create bureaucratic and ideological pigeonholes that recognise some nations but not others.

While the English appear to accept without complaint their non-recognition in their own country, it seems that foreigners are not prepared to be invisible. The convoluted categorisation used by multi-culturalists is being challenged by an increasing number of settlers who wish to have their separate nationalities officially recognized. A letter in *The Voice*, 19th May 1997, carried the complaint that, "Asians were quite rightly referred to by their ethnic origin while Africans were referred to by their colour". The correspondent suggested that, "If the BBC and other media are interested in promoting good race relations in Britain and the world, they should begin by referring to African people by their racial origin instead of their colour."

An article in *The Voice*, 26th May 1997, with the headline, "AFRICANS SNUBBED BY NEW RACE SURVEY" dealt with complaints from a Nigerian, Bala Sanusi, President of the Nigerian National Union in Britain, that a government-sponsored report made "no mention of the burgeoning African community". According to Bala Sanusi, "There are over a quarter of a million Nigerians alone. We should have been consulted."

The English community should also be consulted on such matters and recognized as an ethnic group. Why are Turks and Irish accorded that privilege but not the English? The Scots and Welsh also face discrimination but they have the freedom to make known, and assert, their separate national identities without condemnation.

It is not unusual for settlers living in Britain as British citizens, to pick and choose when they will be British. Sometimes they claim to be *as British as anyone else*, at other times they condemn the British for their history of imperialism. In recent years, some settlers have demanded that *the British* compensate people from former British colonies for the hardships and losses that occurred under British rule. In this way they set themselves apart from the British when it suits them and give the distinct impression of not seeing a British identity and history as part of their own identity and history. This suggests that they are not as British as some would have us believe.

The British People

The members of the English, Scottish and Welsh nations are linked together by the fact of being citizens of a state known as the United Kingdom of Great Britain and Northern Ireland. The *people* of the province of Northern Ireland are for the most part divided into two groups known as Unionists and Republicans, or Protestants and Catholics, or Loyalists and Nationalists, or Ulstermen and Irish. Ulstermen can with some justice claim to be a nation as they are a community with their own history, religion and culture. Most do not think of themselves as Irish and wish to remain citizens of the United Kingdom because they believe their identity is less threatened by being part of the United Kingdom than by being absorbed into the Irish Republic. Many, if not most, Catholics in Northern Ireland regard themselves as part of the Irish nation and would prefer to be citizens of the Irish Republic. They believe that the island of Ireland is one country, and the whole of that country should be included in one Irish state. The Protestants are seen as the agents of British imperialism, most of them being descended from Calvinists who in the seventeenth century were encouraged to move to Ireland by King James VI of Scotland – James I of England – a Scottish king. It was a colonisation that involved confiscating land from the Irish and giving it to the immigrants. The purpose was to block the shortest sea crossing and neutralise the threat of Irish Catholics crossing to Scotland and England for the purpose of supporting a Catholic revolution in England. The Irish did not want the immigrants, have never accepted them and have never forgiven those involved in the matter. [36]

An English nationalist can understand and sympathise with Irish nationalists on this and many other matters. The Irish have undoubtedly suffered greatly over the centuries, as have the Scots and Welsh, but it must be remembered that the English also suffered under the a governing elite that saw itself as above and apart from the people it governed. However, the intention is not to enter into a competition over victimisation. The English would not stand a chance because there are several well-practised contestants who are masters of the art. The English grumble a lot (and take little action) but it is usually about current rather than historical events.

A little background information would not go amiss here as it serves as an introduction to some of the problems to be considered later.

---

[36] It is curious that the English tend to regard the Irish as being generally good natured and friendly, while not appreciating the level of dislike, even hatred, that a very large number of Irish people have for the English, who they blame for all their misfortunes. The English would perhaps have more sympathy for Ulstermen if their leaders over the past twenty-five years had not been such unsympathetic characters, especially when compared with Gerry Adams, an intelligent and shrewd propagandist.

When the English came to Britain they conquered and settled much of lowland Pictland (Scotland) and held the land to the south of the Firth of Forth. At that time Britons were in the kingdom of Strathclyde and the Scots, a Gaelic speaking people from Ireland, were conquering and settling that part of the west of Pictland that came to be called Argyll, meaning *the land of the Gaels*. The Picts, who were divided into northern and southern groups, occupied the remaining territory. The fortunes of the different groups waxed and waned but it is probable that it was the Gaels who finally defeated the Picts and destroyed them as a nation.[37]

The descendants of the invaders from Ireland still have a distinct identity in Scotland, as do the Anglo-Saxon settlers of the central and eastern lowlands.[38] That division has continued over the centuries and is evident today in the tendency of the Gaels to be Catholics and the Anglo-Saxons to be Protestant. Hence, Protestants tend to support Rangers and Catholics tend to support Celtic[39]. Scottish Protestants also have a literary heritage (e.g. Robert Burns) based on the Scots language, an English dialect that is close to Northumbrian and has developed from Old English.[40] It retains Old English words which are no longer used in Standard English. Many Scottish Catholics consider Gaelic to be their language and are attempting to revive it. In doing so, they attract far more attention from English liberals than do the far more numerous speakers of Scots. The reason seems to be that liberals mistakenly regard the whole of Scotland as part of *the Celtic fringe* and mistakenly believe that Gaelic is the only ancient language of that land.[41]

---

[37] The destruction of the Picts by the Gaels probably took place over a relatively short period and might have been entirely physical, involving wholesale slaughter. If not, it is likely to have involved sufficient slaughter and scattering of the population as to make those communities that survived too small and isolated to act as carriers of a language and national culture. Today this would be called genocide.

[38] (a) The eastern lowlands of Scotland have been described as, 'that part of Northumberland that lies over the border'. (b) There have been many Scandinavian settlers in mainland Scotland but they did not establish a separate identity. (c) When William the Norman ravaged much of Northern England, many Englanders migrated north to join and swell the population of Lowland Scots/Anglo-Saxons.

[39] Some will need to be told that Rangers and Celtic are Scottish football teams which are identified respectively with the Protestant/Anglo-Saxon/Scots, and the Catholic/Irish communities in Scotland. Celtic supporters often display the Irish tricolour, and Union flags are to be seen in the ranks of Rangers supporters. Until fairly recently both teams showed a distinct preference for players of the *correct* religion.

[40] *Scots* when used in relation to language refers to all the indigenous languages of Scotland, which includes Gaelic. However, Scots is more usually applied in a narrower way to the English dialects spoken by the Lowland Scots.

[41] Cornwall, Wales, Ireland and Scotland are sometimes referred to as the 'Celtic fringe' despite the fact that it is difficult to detect anything Celtic about the people living there or their culture. The claim of Cornish nationalists that the Cornish are a distinct nation descended from the Britons is perhaps true but there are now so few of them, due to population movement that any demand for independence on the basis of national self-determination cannot be taken seriously. It is perhaps for that reason that those who call themselves Cornish Nationalists were opposed to a genetic sampling

Members of *the Celtic fringe* are not, as the term implies, one nation but several. The people of Scotland have much that unites them but there are underlying divisions that present problems for Scottish nationalists, whether they are described as civic or cultural nationalists. Many Scottish Catholics feel that they have more in common with Irish Catholics than with their Protestant countrymen. Likewise many Scottish Protestants support or sympathise with the Ulster Protestants. The division in Scotland is not just one of religion but of identity and is made more complex by the fact that some Catholic Scots would prefer to retain the union with England rather than live in a Scotland dominated by Protestants. The task that confronts the Scottish Nationalist Party (SNP) in bringing these strands together is more difficult than many English people appreciate.

Returning to the problems of modern Ulster, it is sometimes argued that the members of both communities in that land are Irish but divided by religion and history. That is one of those fine-sounding phrases which in reality is meaningless because religion and history are so central to their respective identities that to pretend that they are one nation is a fiction. Those Irish nationalists who claim that they accept Ulstermen as fellow Irishmen do so in order to deny the validity of a separate identity for Ulstermen and their homeland. It is evident from their literature that Irish nationalists do not subscribe to a civic-nationalism. The Irish are rightly seen as a national community linked by kinship, culture and the shared experiences of their history. The claim that Ulstermen are Irish is merely a device to justify absorbing them into the Irish Republic, where it is certain that their separate identity and culture would be lost.

The Irish, quite understandably, fought for the freedom to determine their own future but now deny Ulstermen the same right and oppose any move by them to set up an independent sovereign state in Northern Ireland.[42] This gives rise to the question of how long is it necessary for a nation to live in a defined territory for it to be commonly recognised by other nations as its homeland? The answer seems to be that there is no rule for this other than it being a matter of custom and

common acceptance. It is usually the use of force, the establishment of a majority population and the will to prevail that brings this acceptance. The last people to accept the creation of a new homeland are members of the nation from which the territory was taken. It is only when the dispossessed accept the loss as permanent that the new homeland can be regarded as secure. The North American Indian nations have, for example, been dispossessed of their homelands and that is accepted by all concerned as a fact which cannot be reversed, even though many think it is a tragic outcome.

---

survey in Cornwall. They perhaps anticipated the result, which was that the population of Cornwall is almost wholly Anglo-Saxon.

[42] An English nationalist can understand why Irish nationalists take that view. The Irish perspective is looked at briefly later.

In addition to the refusal of the Irish to accept the loss of part of their national homeland, Ulstermen face the problem of convincing others that the territory they claim as theirs is viable as a political and economic entity. That is not easy because Ulster (six counties) is not economically viable due to a shortage of strategic resources for which they are dependent upon the Republic. It would take a very large injection of capital to overcome that dependency. The construction of a gas pipeline from Scotland to Northern Ireland was perhaps a step in that direction.

It is because Ulster would find it difficult to survive as an independent state that Ulstermen have emphasised their British civic identity. By being part of the United Kingdom, they are better able to preserve their communal identity. A big problem for them is that the Union is breaking up rather in the manner of a foundering ship and a British civic identity is likely to go down with it. In addition, all Ulstermen must by now be able to see that the British government intends to leave them to a slow communal death. Their best hope of survival is to adopt an *ethnic politics* strategy and look to their real communal, cultural and ancestral roots. They will then be better placed to make the same demands of the Irish government that Republicans have made of Unionists and the British government. Another option is the Republican strategy of using extreme violence that sends the message, we will never give up however long it takes and whatever the cost to us – you cannot defeat us – the cost to you in blood and wealth will be high and enduring. This approach was successful against the British government but would it deter the Irish government from wanting to absorb a hostile community into a *united* Ireland?

An argument sometimes used against self-determination for Ulstermen is that they have no country and no national name, and cannot therefore be properly called a nation. The insistence of Unionists that their country is Ulster and that they are Ulstermen is often dismissed on the grounds that the boundaries of Northern Ireland include only six of the nine counties of that ancient kingdom and therefore do not accord with the boundaries of Ulster. However, that is not a valid reason for denying the legitimacy of calling the country Ulster and recognising Ulstermen as a national community. The borders of most national homelands have varied over time but that does not mean they are not homelands or that the nation living there is any less a nation. Parts of Germany were lost to Poland as a result of the post World War II settlement but Germany is still a country and the Germans still a nation. If the ancient boundaries of the land of the English were re-established, Edinburgh would be an English city. England is no less a country for being smaller in size than it once was.

Citizens of the UK are, whatever their nationality, the British people. During the days of the British Empire and probably up to the 1960s there was a much stronger sense of British identity (especially among the English) than there is now. The

British people had to a large extent shared a recent history, including the experience of industrialisation and two world wars. They shared a language and political institutions within one state. It seemed that as time went by the sense of being British might become a habit and grow stronger until it became greater than the separate national identities. Being British meant being identified with the achievements of the British Empire and the United Kingdom. The demise of the empire and the decline of the UK as an economic and world power lessened the attraction of being British. The influx of large numbers of immigrants who where given British citizenship further undermined the already faltering perception of a British community. The immigrants became part of the British people but they had little in common with the English, Scottish or Welsh and their arrival, often in large numbers, was generally resented by the indigenous population. It became clear that to be British meant little more than being a UK subject/citizen.

Summary

A nation is a group of people who share a communal name, history, culture, ancestry, and language. Nations have a homeland that often bears their name. Some nations share a religion.

Citizens are members of a political society; a geopolitical entity; a state. They are subject to the laws of a common political authority.

A nation is an extended community whose members share a complex web of relationships, perceptions and emotions. Membership does not depend on meeting conditions on a formal checklist. Kinship, language, history and culture are all factors that help determine who belongs to which nation but there is no system of measurement that can be applied to them. Many of the *signifiers* we use to distinguish insiders from outsiders are noted subconsciously and the decisions are made instinctively. Insiders are able to recognise each other in informal ways that vary according to the needs of the time. To ask someone to describe the process by which they decide who is and is not a member of their nation is similar to asking a group of friends to explain how they decide who is and who is not a friend. It is not something we consciously think about and it is not something that is easy to describe. It is a process that is guided by a instincts that are deep within all of us and which cannot be eliminated by ideological conditioning, even though there are some who wish it were so.

Nationalists and Nationalism

Those who confuse *nation* with *state* get into difficulties when they come to use and define the words *nationalism* and *nationalist*. A definition of nationalism which suggested that it is *loyalty or devotion to one's state* clearly conflicts with reality because, for example, Kurds living in Turkey, Iraq and Iran are citizens of those states but they do not feel loyalty and devotion to them. Kurdish nationalists feel loyalty and devotion to the Kurdish nation, which has no state of its own. The existence of a Kurdish nation, Kurdish nationalism, and Kurdish nationalists are therefore not dependent upon there being a Kurdish state. Scottish nationalists provide an example of those whose loyalty and identity is with a nation ·in the proper sense of the word, and not with the state (UK) of which they are citizens. Nationalism precedes and gives rise to the demand for a state.

Nationalists

Nationalists are concerned for the wellbeing of their nation. The vast majority of people feel an instinctive attachment to a nation and are concerned to see it survive and prosper. In that sense most people are nationalists. Beyond that there are those who give political expression to their feelings and are commonly labelled as nationalists, either by themselves or others. Political nationalists see nations and national identity as central to their political thinking and outlook on life. Gender, class and race are all secondary considerations because nationality is greater than all of those things. For a nationalist, nationality is the widest communal identity, and the one that is central to any valid claim for the right to self-government. The primary concerns of nationalists are the attainment or preservation of national unity, national identity, national independence, national self-government and the general wellbeing of their nation. A nationalist need not be of any particular political persuasion.

National communities evolve as they wind their way across the landscape of history. Their flow is sometimes hidden beneath the surface of events but all the while they are adapting and evolving so that when the nation re-emerges into the light it appears to outsiders as something new and different. It is often suggested that nationalists invent or reinvent nations but there is no magic formula that can make a nation from nothing. Nationalist intellectuals can help make their nation visible but if they are to be effective in reawakening an outward expression and assertion of nationhood they need to tap into real, but often submerged, national sentiments and loyalties. Their task is to reveal the threads of national identity in a way that meets the needs of the time. If a revivalist nationalist is proclaiming a bogus sense of nationhood, he or she will fail to achieve the aim because it is not possible to create a nation out of thin air.

Some nationalists and nationalisms are seen as more threatening than others to the dogma of the governing elite. One of the main reasons for hostility to English nationalism is that its opponents believe that if the English develop and express a strong national identity they will drop their British identity; Britishness without the English will be dead. That will create the problem of finding an identity for the non-English population of England. It will also remove the glue that holds the Union together, and the UK will fall apart. That process of disintegration will speed up when it eventually dawns on the English that the distribution of UK government resources greatly favours Scotland, Wales and Northern Ireland. The end of the Union in its present form will then be widely seen as a good thing, not least because it will free England from the financial burden of keeping the UK together. It follows that the various parts of the British governing elite have a common interest in maintaining the illusion of Britishness and of denigrating English nationalism. They do that by using phrases such as the sinister *dark forces of English nationalism* and the insulting *Little Englander*. Irish, Scottish and Welsh nationalists are treated far more kindly.

The Welshman, R. S. Thomas, revealed, in his concern to preserve Welsh culture and identity, much of what motivates and drives a nationalist. English liberals found him acceptable and patronised him because he was an elderly Welsh poet, and Welsh nationalism is not seen as a threat. R. S. Thomas was regarded as a *character* with romantic notions about a dying culture. His words are quoted, almost with affection, by liberals who would condemn him and the words if he were English. He said, "To me the average Englishman is a nationalist and England comes first. I'm not against this. When I am questioned I say I love Wales and I hope you love England. But in any free-for-all people are going to fight for their own country. So any Englishman worth his salt wants to keep England together. We know that the UK is only a euphemism for England. The Scots, the Irish, the Welsh are just appendages." He believed that a Welsh Assembly would be better than nothing, despite it being inspired by English imperialism rather than concern for Welsh rights.[43] He was greatly saddened by the colonisation of Wales

---

[43] This is not altogether true because the Welsh Assembly was promoted by a predominantly Scottish Labour government. It made provision for a Scottish parliament and felt it necessary to offer the Welsh an assembly in an attempt to show that the constitutional arrangements had not been devised solely for the benefit of the Scots or for the purpose of protecting the position of the Labour Party in Scotland. Devolution is clearly a device to cut the ground from beneath the Scottish National Party and its demand for independence. Instead of following through the logic of devolution and creating an English parliament, the government has set in motion a process of administrative change aimed at weakening England by dismembering it into nine regions. Such an outcome will rid the Scots of a powerful southern neighbour and prevent effective opposition to the unfair system that gives them a disproportionately large allocation of central government funds. That all this can be done without consulting the people of England and giving them the same opportunity as other parts of the UK to determine their own constitutional future, shows the contempt the governing elite have for the English.

by the English and his belief that only 22 percent of Wales remained Welsh. He wanted Wales to have complete independence so that the Welsh would have the power to determine their own affairs. He looked with envy at the Irish free state when he saw its flag flying and was greatly saddened by the materialism of many Welsh people who would rather enjoy a monetary advantage than enjoy the freedom to govern themselves. Thomas's frustration was such that he wished the Welsh would rise in armed resistance and fight for their independence but he feared that it was too late and the Welsh will never be free.[44]

R. S. Thomas died in his eighties but even in old age he had more fire in him than most of his countrymen, many of whom know little about their history, are unaware of the frailty of their culture and apathetic about the future of their nation. If sport and soap operas are available on television, and supermarkets are open at convenient times, what need is there for a national culture and identity? The situation is even worse in England where watching and consuming help keep most of the population docile.

Fellow nationalists of whatever nation can understand the sadness and frustration that R. S. Thomas felt at the willingness of his countrymen to trade their culture and independence for strings of beads. His burning desire to protect and regenerate his nation is to be found in the hearts of nationalists everywhere.

Nationalism

Nationalism is loyalty or devotion to one's nation, and a desire for national self-government, which in the modern world can only be obtained through the creation of a state. Where a nation does not enjoy self-government, nationalism often expresses itself in the form of a political campaign (by nationalists) to achieve that end. The Kurds want to establish a state so that they can govern themselves and better protect their way of life. In other words they seek the self-determination that is deemed the right of *a people* by the UN Charter, Article 1(1). On establishing a state, Kurds will be able to engage in formal inter-state relationships for the purpose of pursuing their national interests. For example, they will be able to enter into treaty obligations, trade agreements and military and economic alliances with

---

Regions also serve the interests of the European Union, the power of which will increase with the weakening of the larger nations and member states. The EU policy of encouraging regionalism is necessary because the creation of a long-lasting European state will require the creation of a European identity among its citizens. To that end there is an attempt to replace national and state identities with regional and European identities. Sometimes it is convenient for the EU to use the nationalism of small nations to promote regional policy but that is felt to be a price worth paying if it leads to the weakening or break-up of large member states. The aim of the EU political elite is to create a civic society in which no part is able to challenge the central governing authority. EU institutions will then justify their existence by claiming to be neutral arbiters in disputes between citizens and between regions.

[44] These sentiments were expressed in an article by Louise Jury published in *The Independent on Sunday*, 14th September 1997.

states. The creation of real nation-states, like that sought by the Kurds, greatly increases the likelihood of national and state interests coinciding.

Nationalism is a natural, healthy, inborn, tenacious communal sentiment, the expression of which is sometimes suppressed or buried before flowering again in unexpected ways. Nationalism is a sentiment based on common cultural characteristics, customs, traditions, ancestry, history, values and perceptions. It is an emotion that binds a large community together in a way that improves its opportunities for survival, security and cultural achievements. Nationalism is the soul of a community; a force that gives it shape and an identity. Nationalism is an instinct and an emotion; it is like love in that it has to be experienced before there can be any real understanding of it. It is not something that can be reduced to a formula or understood by academics probing it from the outside as if it were a laboratory specimen. No two samples are alike and each is constantly evolving. If academics of the ideological establishment escaped from their dogmatic straitjacket and looked within themselves, they would better understand the thing they are studying. Nationalism is energy and movement; it is always changing and never takes the same shape twice. It appears before each observer in a different form and the values and expectations of the observer colour the observations made. This explains why, with a few notable exceptions, the vast majority of an ever-increasing number of books and papers from the ideological establishment on the subject of nationalism treat it in a wholly unsympathetic and hostile manner. The common lines of attack are to dismiss nationalism as an irrelevant relic of a bygone age or to portray it as a dangerous state of mind found among those who are inadequate or evil. But what other response could realistically be expected of those who wish to make us think and act in the unnatural way their ideology demands?

Nationalism is a communal sentiment. Each member of a community has the right to exercise the maximum freedom that is compatible with being a member of a community and meeting the obligations that such membership brings. One of those obligations is for individuals to behave in a way that does not needlessly cause either them or others to be a burden on their fellows. That means showing consideration for others. From that comes common politeness and good manners. In return, the community offers its members help and protection when they need it. A community has no obligation to help or protect those who flout communal rules.

Nationalism is not a passive sentiment, it is a communal sentiment that draws people together in an active defence of their collective sovereignty, culture and identity. All nationalisms are brewed from similar ingredients but each nation has a unique recipe that is constantly evolving in response to the needs of the time. This process of adaptation and evolution does not mean that the communal sentiment changes, just that it is expressed in different ways in different times. When this is understood, it can be seen that there is little point in making a close examination of a particular nationalism at one time and then declaring it to be invented because it differs from an earlier expression of nationalism by the same group of people. Even more absurd is the suggestion that *nations* and *nationalism* only came into existence with the first use of those words. The English word *folk* (O.E. *folc*) is an excellent alternative to *nation* and better conveys its essence.

Three Levels of Nation and Nationalism

Nationalism consists of many layers of sentiment, each of which merges with and is inseparable from the other layers. Despite the mingling, it is possible to detect three broad levels, each of which has its roots in different types of communal experience.

Level One – Day-to-Day Living

The first level is the physical one of place and kinship, and the instincts that are attached to them. This is the world of reproduction, families, territory and landscape; it is where the physical environment shapes the way kindred groups acquire the necessities of life, such as food, water and shelter. It also plays a part in determining how those assets are shared and how the community defends its territorial boundaries.

A traditional face-to-face community is one where its members live close together in a manner that, on the whole, benefits them all by satisfying basic needs such as food, shelter, defence, and the opportunity for reproduction. Improvements over the years in communications technology has altered the meaning of *living closely together* and has enabled communities to exist where members have little, if any, direct face-to-face contact. The problem with relying on some types of sophisticated communication is that they can be used by those who own and manage them to shape the way a community sees itself or, if the communal identity is ignored, does not see itself. For example, in the UK, the broadcasting media, which is the most powerful medium for shaping perceptions of community and identity, promotes the values and perceptions of a governing elite that favours civic identity over national identity. Hence, Sir Isaac Newton, Sir Francis Drake, William Shakespeare, Lord Nelson, Jane Austen, Joseph Turner, Charles Darwin, and many other great people, cease to be English and are labelled (rebadged) British. When in certain situations Englishness cannot be ignored, and the institutionalised hostility to it has to be overcome, it is presented as an inclusive identity; if you live in England you are deemed to be English, unless of course you are Irish, Scottish or Welsh.

Nations should not allow their communications web to be dominated by organisations that either have no interest in preserving communal ties or are actively bent on destroying them. Nationalists need to constantly strive to ensure that communal needs are recognised and served by those who control the spread of information. If that proves impossible, nationalists must spin new webs and constantly repair and add to them. Even a small or flimsy communal web can spark a spontaneous regeneration of communal identity, solidarity, and empathy.

Level Two – Culture

All communities have to solve similar problems but they do so in different ways according to their experience, resources and environment. The different circumstances and solutions give rise to different cultures, each of which is a store of knowledge that succeeding generations add to and pass on to the next. Cultures are blueprints for survival; some are more sophisticated than others but all are successful if they enable a community to adapt to its physical and social environment, and continually regenerate itself.

Nations exist in the minds of insiders and outsiders. Each nation is a unique mix of shared values and perceptions, of accumulated knowledge, experience and achievement expressed in such everyday things as what is eaten and how it is cooked. Architecture, crafts, art, myths, literature, music, dance, and much more, are part of a culture and give expression to it. Thus, the second level of community is a world of custom, culture, religion, law, science and all the things that spring from communal relationships and the struggle for survival. In all of these areas there are communal and cultural boundary markers that can be detected by insiders but are mostly invisible to outsiders who can see only the broad outline. Insiders and outsiders know that a community exists but neither are able to define its many-layered constantly changing boundaries. Thus the question, what does it mean to be English or Irish or French, has no adequate answer.

Some nations have a strong culture and communal identity that enables them to survive periods of misfortune and decline. After the loss of their state and their homeland they appear to outsiders to be dead and gone forever, but then, after many generations they emerge in an evolved and invigorated form. Other nations, in similar circumstances, collapse and perish because they are either too small to sustain their way of life or their culture has become so diluted that they are unable to maintain communal boundaries.

Level Three – Imagination

If a nation is to survive territorial invasion, the loss of self-government, and a campaign of cultural genocide, it is essential that it inhabits a communal world of the imagination. This third level of community is one that outsiders can never see or gain access to; it is a communal virtual reality in which every member of a nation, past, present and future is linked. The physical deaths of those who have gone before do not prevent them inspiring and motivating those who come after them. Offa, Alfred, Athelflæd, Athelstan, and Hereward are some of the names from the distant past that live on in the web that is the communal memory and imagination of the English nation. There are also a long list of big names from more recent times and the many other individuals who have contributed something special to English culture and identity. Last but not least is the influence of all those who in having children and living their ordinary lives have played their part in keeping the communal identity alive and passing it from one generation to the next.

The world of the imagination is one of empathy, identity, loyalty and emotion. It is here that individuals are able to see beyond their immediate physical world and appreciate that they are, and will continue to be, part of something that has a life far larger than their own. This wider vision is at the heart of freedom because it takes us beyond our solitary human life and releases us from the constraints of time and space; it gives each of us a larger identity and a greater willingness to face hardship, danger and death.

Outsiders may enter and share a nation's physical environment (homeland) and even go out of their way to adopt its customs and culture but they will never be able to enter the world of another nation's imagination because it is impossible for them to escape their own communal identity, which is moulded by their ancestry, upbringing and communal experiences. We carry with us through life the mark of the community into which we are born.

It is possible to chart some of the physical and cultural boundary markers of a nation but it is not possible to map mental boundary markers, which is why they are not only difficult to find but impossible to cross. Thus, the boundaries that exist in the communal mind are easier to defend than territory, provided of course that there is the resolve to do so. It is for political nationalists to maintain that resolve by defending the national culture (e.g. history and language) and promoting a way of life that complements the communal instincts to reproduce and survive.

Political Nationalism

Nations usually identify with a particular territory; their homeland. Political nationalism is the force that strives to defend or create the conditions whereby the members of a nation are able to exercise their sovereign powers through their own political institutions (a state) within the secure boundaries of their homeland. The underlying assumption is that the greatest freedom and security for a nation is to be found when the nation has its own state (nation-state) which it manages and defends. For example, Japan is the homeland of the Japanese, and the Japanese believe that the territory is theirs and that they have the right to defend it and live in it according to their customs. They have the right to govern themselves within that territory in any way they choose, and they have the right to determine who enters their country and on what conditions. They make their own laws, police their own country, and dispense their own justice. Nationalists recognise that all nations have those rights and that pursuing them is a proper expression of nationalism. This is not to deny that nations are often unable to exercise those rights as they would wish due to outside influences.

Political nationalism has a side to it that is often ignored, which is the belief that self-governing communities provide the secure and free environment in which democracy can best flourish and individuals fulfil their potential. Communal freedom creates the conditions for individual freedom, contentment, and happiness. It produces rounded people with a sense of identity and a feeling of belonging that helps them fully develop and bloom. Individual freedom outside of a community tends to be selfish and leads to conflict because there are no communally agreed and enforced limits to the expression of that freedom. Community provides a channel for the expression of individual freedom, and enables it to thrive in a way that benefits both the individual and the community.

The best environment for a democratic civic-society is one where citizens share a wide range of common values and perceptions. In other words, where there is congruence between cultural community and political society.[45] A political society that includes two or more communities with separate cultural identities, histories and values will fracture along communal fault lines. The result will be either the domination of one group over others or a power-sharing arrangement that undermines the ideal of a civic-society in which citizens behave and vote as individuals rather than as members of competing communities.

One of the consequences of bringing people with very different cultural values and perceptions together in one political society is that it stimulates defensive communal instincts. Communal competition and conflict leads to communal insecurity and pressure for greater internal conformity, which in turn leads to a reduction in the scope for personal choice, not an increase. This can often be seen when the members of one nation settle in another nation's homeland. The settler community is usually more conservative and less tolerant of 'deviant' behaviour than it would otherwise have been because, if it is to survive, it has to work harder to maintain its boundaries and its identity.

In addition to the internal pressures that limit personal freedom, there are the external pressures brought by other communities when certain types of behaviour offend them. What is an individual to do if the behaviour deemed offensive to other communities is thought acceptable, or even desirable, by his own community? If the personal freedom of individuals is restrained not only by the norms of their community but also by the norms of other communities, there is less individual freedom than there might otherwise be.

---

[45] The American Constitution was written for just that sort of homogeneous community, which perhaps explains why it is unsuited to the divided political and cultural society that the US has become.

The behaviour of others is usually not a problem for those who have no experience of it in their everyday life. Such a happy position is enjoyed by nations that have their own state (nation-state) and are able to live as they wish without pressure from outsiders to change their ways.

Early English National Identity

Before the English (Engle) came to Britain they lived in the Jutland peninsular and their homeland was called Angeln. During the first century, Tacitus recorded the existence of a tribe, which in Latin he called the Anglii.[46] It was one of seven tribes, safe behind defences of rivers and forests, who worshipped Nerthus, Mother Earth. The next we learn of the early English is from the Old English poem, *Widsið*, which tells us of the first King Offa, king of the English. After naming thirty-three kings the poem goes on:

> Offa rules Angeln, Alewih the Danes
> – he was the bravest of all –
> yet he did not better Offa in heroic feats
> for of these men Offa, while still a boy,
> won the greater kingdom.
> In his time no other won greater fame
> in battle. With his lone sword
> he fixed the border with the Myrgings
> at Fifeldor. Since then the
> English and the Swabians have kept it as Offa made it.[47]

During the century following Offa's death the English crossed the North Sea to Britain and conquered and settled large tracts of land. The migration was so complete that by the time it was finished the old country of Angeln (England) stood empty.[48]

The many small kingdoms the English established in Britain gradually merged into several larger ones which are known today as Northumberland (*Norðhymbre* – land north of the River Humber), Mercia (*Mercie* – the frontier lands – central England and the area to its west), and East Anglia (*Eastengle*). To the south, warriors and settlers from the federation of tribes known as the Saxons (*Seaxe*) conquered and settled the lands that came to be known as Essex, Sussex, Wessex, and Middlesex (*Eastseaxe* – East Saxons, *Suð Seaxe* – South Saxons, *West Seaxe* –

---

[46] The early name of the English was recorded by Roman writers, such as Tacitus, using the Latinised form *Anglii* which later became *Angle*. In English the name evolved from Engle into *Englisc* and *English*. In Old English *sc* is pronounced *sh*.

[47] There are two versions of the story. Details and background information can be found in *English Heroic Legends* by Kathleen Herbert (Anglo-Saxon Books, 2000).

[48] Bede's, *Ecclesiastical History of the English People*.

West Saxons, and *Middelseaxan* – Middle Saxons[49]). There were also Jutes (Kent and the Isle of Wight) and Frisians, a people much involved in trade who seem to have settled in towns and near ports throughout the land.

The Anglo-Saxons (Engle-Seaxe) were able to merge into one national community because their appearance, language, mythology and way of life were very similar. In all those respects they differed from the Welsh who were regarded as foreigners. Looks and language were then, as now, generally the easiest and quickest ways of telling an insider from an outsider. Language is a particularly important boundary marker because it is shaped by and reflects the values, attitudes, history, geographical location, world-view, and everyday life of those to whom it belongs.[50]

Like other nations, the English in Britain were defined by what they had in common with other *insiders* and how they differed from *outsiders* with whom they came into contact. The high level of cultural and linguistic unity among the North Sea Germanic tribes that migrated to Britain was strengthened by the political unity which grew out of the custom of recognising one of their kings as an over-lord or *Bretwalder*.[51] The gradual merging of Engle, Saxon, Jute and Frisian communities did not destroy local loyalties. The men of Wessex and Mercia fought as Englishman and as West Saxons and Mercians when, under King Æthelstan and his brother Edmund, they defeated a combined force of Norsemen and Scots at the Battle of Brunanburh in the tenth century.[52]

The merging of peripheral identities into the core English identity gathered pace during the ninth century, when Danish raids on England grew in frequency, size and duration until they amounted to an invasion before which all of the English kingdoms fell one by one.[53] Alfred became king of Wessex upon the death of his brother in 871. After several battles with the Danes, Alfred paid them tribute and managed to secure peace for a short period. In January 878 Alfred was defeated by

---

[49] There is no evidence for an early Middle Saxon kingdom and it is probable that the name was given to the territory west of, and including London, long after the Anglo-Saxon conquest and settlement had taken place.

[50] For that reason Esperanto, an artificial language, is unlikely to ever amount to much. It is not part of a national culture and is sterile despite the attempts of some of its supporters to breathe life into it and give it a soul.

[51] Bretwalder perhaps means *Britain ruler* or *sole ruler*.

[52] For details of the battle see the Old English verse, *The Battle of Brunanburh*.
The organization of English soldiers into regiments recruited from districts continues today and is said to foster a greater sense of comradeship, community and resolve than is evident among soldiers who have no regional or communal ties.

[53] *Viking* from Old English *wicing* meaning *sea pirate*. It is probable that *viking* was not used in the modern sense until the nineteenth century when it was applied to all 9th–11th century Scandinavian invaders in much the same way that the term Saxon had been used for the Germanic North Sea tribes. To refer to all Scandinavians of that time as Vikings is to suggest a uniformity in culture, allegiance and purpose that did not exist.

the Danes at Chippenham. He took refuge at Athelney, in the Somerset marshes, from where he organised the formation of a new army.

Alfred emerged from hiding in May 878 and successfully lead the English against the Danes at Edington. That was followed by a series of battles and agreements

that enabled the English to first recover Wessex then much of Mercia. The coming together of men from many parts of England to fight against a common enemy increased the sense of unity and national identity. Alfred assisted that process in many ways, including the promotion of English as a language of record, thus ending the exclusive use of Latin. He also created a system of national defence in depth based on burhs (fortified towns) that enabled him to fight successful military campaigns and create the foundations of a well-organized state.

About the year 886[54] Alfred and the Dane, Guthrum, entered into a treaty which divided England along a line running roughly from Chester to Bedford to London. Alfred was recognized as overlord of the territory to the south and west and Guthrum ruled that part of England that lay to the north and east. The treaty protected the interests of the English living in the Danelaw by ensuring that they enjoyed the same compensation rights as Danes of equal social rank.[55] Danes living in Alfred's kingdom enjoyed reciprocal rights. The arrangement demonstrates that Alfred did not believe that all within his kingdom were English, and it supports the view that Englishness, then as now, was determined by ancestry, culture and loyalty; not by place of birth or residence. That view is unacceptable to the modern-day ideologues who are eager to project their civic-society and an inclusive English identity back into a rewritten history. They are uncomfortable with the idea that all who lived in Alfred's kingdom were his subjects but not all were English.

Alfred set about building an English nation-state and in doing so he gave hope to the English that they and England would one day be united under an English king, which they were. Alfred was an English nationalist who acted in the interests of all the English whether they were in his kingdom or that of the Dane, Guthrum. In showing concern for the interests of those of his countrymen who were not and had never been his subjects, he demonstrated a sense of identification and empathy that is indicative of nationalism and a community of the imagination. The English Chronicle (Anglo-Saxon Chronicle) records that a treaty with Guthrum and all the people of East Anglia was concluded by *King Alfred and the councillors of all the English nation*. The entry for the year 900 records the death of Alfred (in 899) and states that he was *king over all the English, except for that part which was under Danish rule*. In other words, the English, who formed by far the greater part of the population ruled by Guthrum, continued to be recognised by both sides as English.

---

[54] The date is uncertain. See Alfred P. Smyth, *King Alfred the Great*, OUP, 1995, p. 92.

[55] The Danelaw was the territory in which the law of the Danes was applied.

That population provided the core culture and identity into which the Danes where absorbed.

Alfred strengthened all the elements of national identity. In addition to updating the Law Codes and putting in place a network of burhs, he also encouraged the creation of centres of learning, and was responsible for the writing of an English history that was regularly added to for the next 200 years. He translated, or had translated, many texts, religious and secular, from Latin into English. The measures that Alfred took to defend, strengthen and preserve the English nation, its culture and way of life, were such that he deserves to be remembered as a great Englishman.[56]

It is a cause for sadness that in our time the English are for the most part unaware of Alfred's achievements or even of his existence. Those modern day institutions that should be passing on English history to English children seem to believe that Alfred is irrelevant to contemporary life. He is not an icon for those who wish to denigrate and deny Englishness.

The English of Alfred's time would view with dismay and disbelief the English of today, so many of whom are timid and apologetic about their history and ignorant of the deeds of their ancestors. Fortunately, there are still English men and women who carry within them the courage and energy of their forebears.

Afterword

Nationalism is the name given to a natural sentiment that is essential to the wellbeing of all communities. It is entirely natural and healthy for individuals to act together for the purpose of keeping alive their communal identity and imagination. That does not mean that they are filled with a fear and hatred of outsiders or wish to harm them. The assertion of national identity is not an act of aggression and it does not imply a belief that one culture or way of life is superior to another. Neither does it imply that the members of one community are superior or inferior to others. What it does mean is that the members of all national communities have an interest in their communal achievements and shared experiences because those achievements and experiences have helped shape them as individuals and as a group. The English, like all other nations, naturally have an emotional as well as an intellectual interest in their communal history because it

---

[56] It can be argued that Alfred, through his support of the Church, assisted the import into England of an alien Mediterranean culture and religion that weakened an essentially North European English culture. However, that process had been under way for nearly three hundred years, with the result that most of the governing elite was under the influence of a foreign power (the Church) and used a foreign language (Latin) for the business of the kingdom (state). As with the later but bloodier arrival of the Normans and their Norman-French language, the English survived as a nation. Alfred in effect Anglicised the Church and used it to strengthen an English identity. He borrowed and made English those things that he believed were useful.

uncovers the beginnings of a fascinating journey they have travelled together; it reveals the roots of their Englishness.

States

A State

A state is similar to a corporation in being a legal entity. It is able to enter into agreements with other states and endures through time even though its citizens and governors come and go.

A state can be defined as a political and legal entity that has a government which is in effective control of a territory and its population. Another, similar definition, is that a state is a geographical territory within which a political community has supreme power. These definitions accord with the external view of states that is often used in the discipline of International Relations. Up until the 1970s it was common to compare states with billiard balls of differing size and weight. Strike a ball in a certain way and it will behave in a certain way, rather as Newtonian theory predicts. This approach regards the internal workings of states as being largely unimportant because their business is conducted by and through governments, which, given similar circumstances, behave in mostly similar predictable ways. States are seen as the main actors in a global system that works according to rules that endure despite changes in ideological fashion and internal political structure. For example, the Cold War conflict between the USSR and the USA would have occurred whatever the stated ideology of the governing elites of those super-powers because those states have interests which are shaped by geopolitical, economic and power considerations that remain remarkably constant regardless of the ideology of the governing elite. Power and interests are seen as the key to an understanding of the global state system.

A shift away from what was essentially a Machiavellian outlook, helped to avoid the implication that the states of *The Free World* behaved in the same way as the states of *The Evil Empire*. The central idea of the new view was that the importance of the state was declining due to the increasing power of supranational organisations, global corporations, non-governmental organisations and other non-state actors. It was felt that not enough attention had been paid to the internal working of states and the fact that economic and financial power was increasingly within the control of non-state actors. As is usual in such things, the pendulum has swung much too far the other way and now we are asked to believe that states are outdated and virtually powerless. Instead of being encouraged to look critically at who has power and how it is used, we are encouraged to think of globalism, interdependence, free markets and the free movement of capital as factors in a natural and irreversible progression that puts *real power* beyond the reach of states. Global capitalism and its values are deemed to be inevitable and to herald the best of all possible worlds. Perhaps it will take a war, global economic and financial meltdown or natural catastrophe that directly affects the populations of liberal democracies for there to be a widespread realisation that states are still focal points for marshalling economic and military resources, and managing the welfare of large populations. It might take the collapse of health insurance companies and pension schemes to bring this message home to those who think they can provide for themselves and have no need of the state. When the bubble bursts, there will be a lot of people who suddenly realise that they have little, if any, democratic control over the institutions that affect their lives. It will be found that *real power* has indeed passed beyond the state and beyond its electorate. Liberal Representative Democracy will be seen to be a sham because like everything else about it, liberal democracy is market-driven, and politics is increasingly conducted as if it were a marketing exercise. Eventually the point will be reached when communal loyalties and political structures independent of the state will once again be recognised as essential to a long-term survival strategy.

Believers in the new orthodoxy tend to overstate the extent to which the billiard ball model was ever anything other than a useful method for illustrating a point. However, in response to criticism, a neo-realist school has evolved which takes account of non-state actors, the internal affairs of states, and the ideology of governing elites. The realist approach has adapted to the new globalism but it still emphasises the importance of states, war, power and territory and provides a fairly authentic model of global society.

The State

Another definition of a state is, *a set of administrative, policing and military organizations headed, and more or less well co-ordinated, by an executive authority*.[57] That definition results from an internal view and is less concerned with territory than with the internal coercive nature of states. Depending on how the term *executive authority* is defined, a state, any state, might be seen not as a neutral entity but as an organization controlled by a governing elite and used for the purpose of furthering and defending the interests of that elite. It uses the state to promote its values and perceptions both inside and outside the political space that is the state. If, despite the use of techniques of persuasion, citizens fail to see the world as the elite would like, the institutions of the state are used to make them behave in a way that is not harmful to the elite. The degree to which coercion is used, and the subtlety with which it is used, depends on how threatened the governing elite feels and how effective their non-coercive options are.

Governing elites in general, and liberal governing elites in particular, are keen to promote the perception that the states they control and manage are for the most part free of physical or ideological coercion. Liberal states are portrayed as being merely a collection of neutral institutions controlled by a representative

---

[57] Theda Skocpol, *States and Social Revolutions*, CUP, 1979.

government elected to act in the best interests of the electorate. The system is deemed to contain checks and balances that prevent an abuse of power. Those who collectively govern the state and manage its institutions are deemed to be free of shared values and interests that are separate from and sometimes incompatible with those of the citizens.[58] It is considered unsavoury to suggest that *elites*, *coercion* and *state ideology* exist in liberal states. Such things, so liberals tell us, only exist in non-liberal states, which have *regimes* rather than *governments*.

Sceptics are doubtful about the altruism of those with wealth and power and tend to see great similarities between all states. Many argue that all governing elites, to a greater or lesser extent, control the ideological agenda, do their best to prevent effective opposition developing, and, where there are elections, *the representative is not elected by the voters but, as a rule, has himself elected by them ... or .... his allies have him elected.*[59] One faction of the governing elite is replaced from time to time by another faction to maintain the pretence that there is meaningful choice and that elections can bring fundamental change.

The definitions of a *state* and *the state* can be combined and reformulated as follows. A state is a legal, political, coercive and territorial entity that manifests itself in the internal and external projection of power.

What is the Purpose of States?

Why should we obey the laws and demands of the state? One answer might be that if we do not comply with the rules we will be punished, ultimately with imprisonment or execution. But by what right does a state and those who control it direct and coerce those people who are deemed to be the property/chattels/citizens of the state? What is the purpose of, or justification for, the existence of states? Why do states exist and whose interests do they serve? These are old questions and there are a lot of old answers.

There are many social contract theories but they seem to be primarily concerned with the relationship between the individual and the state – an unequal power relationship if ever there was one. A liberal state is seen as a collection of institutions that exist to:

a) pursue the greatest happiness of the greater number;[60]

b) arbitrate between the sometimes conflicting interests of its citizens.

---

[58] In republican Venice it was thought prudent to ensure that the chief magistrate, the doge, neither owned property nor engaged in commerce.

[59] *Sulla Teorica dei governie sul governo parlamentare: Studi storici e sociali*, Gaetano Mosca (Turin, 884).

[60] Even if we accept the proclaimed liberal goal of the greatest happiness of the greater number, can it really be said that people living in liberal societies are happier than those in, say, Islamic societies?

The more conflict that exists within a state, the more the existence of the state is seen to be necessary. This suggests that state governing elites may have an interest in fermenting conflict from time to time to justify the existence of the state. Leaving that aside, liberal theory follows on from the Hobbesian idea that without the state mankind can endure only a brutish existence. Individuals are obliged to be loyal to the state and abide by its rules because they are deemed to be party to a social contract that protects them from barbarism. It is a neat idea but it bears no relationship to reality.

The interests arbitrated by the state are seen by liberals as being primarily those concerned with property and business. They adopt a utilitarian view in which the welfare of the group is dependent upon individuals pursuing their self-interest in an enlightened way.[61] It is unfortunate that those best able to pursue their own interests, whether due to inherent skill, inherited wealth or luck, are mostly unenlightened and see their interests in narrow economic terms. Those who are successful, in terms laid down by a governing elite, tend to support or join the governing elite and live under the delusion that they and their like are more worthy of positions of power than are the rest of the population. Not only do they convince themselves that they are more deserving but, stranger still, they also manage to convince others. When addressing political and moral issues they tend to use economic and financial arguments which make it clear that they see the primary purpose of life as wealth maximisation through the production and consumption of goods and services.[62] The state is seen as a device for creating the conditions in which all citizens can pursue their economic self-interest with as few restrictions as possible. The best system of government is thought to be that which enables those who are best able to make money to make more and those who have great wealth to keep it. National culture and national identity are not things they give much thought to or show much interest in. Neither do they appreciate that some people have neither the desire nor the ability to pursue their own best

---

[61] Jeremy Bentham saw morality and 'good' in terms of the individual pursuit of enlightened self-interest. It was for the government of a state to adopt policies that produced the greatest happiness for the greatest number of its citizens. Just how happiness is to be measured is not clear but material wellbeing seems to be the preferred indicator. It is easy when one is comfortably off to sneer at the goal of raising the economic standard of living of the masses but when one is poor such an ideal is attractive. However, once the material basics of life have been secured, factors such as culture, history, security, identity and 'way of life' become more important in the pursuit of happiness. Unfortunately, enlightened self-interest is not something that can be relied on. Many people are neither enlightened nor able to determine what their best interests are. John Stuart Mill saw the danger of relying on enlightened self-interest but his suggestion that we should judge actions by the social good they produce does not take us much further forward because we still need to recognise good when we see it and have a means of measuring it.

[62] Former Prime Minister John Major suggested that it is virtuous to do those things that favour the working of a market economy. By this reasoning, the economic and fiscal policies being followed by his government were more moral than the policies put forward by the opposition Labour Party.

economic self-interest but nevertheless have skills and aptitudes that are essential to a successful community.

Nationalists see a state as a device for furthering the interests of a nation. The political and administrative boundary of a nation-state should coincide with the country/national homeland of the core-nation occupying it. The executive authority should be recruited from the core-nation and be able to more or less control and co-ordinate a set of administrative, democratic, diplomatic, policing and military organizations on behalf of and in pursuit of the interest of the core-nation. A state is the means by which a nation organises itself for the purpose of best pursuing its internal and external interests. Those who are lent the power to govern a nation-state should strive to ensure that all members and sections of that nation are able, as far as is possible, to pursue their self-interest while also furthering the interests of the nation as a whole. Enlightenment means showing concern for communal interests and the interests of individuals within it. The matter of deciding what is in the national interests is a matter of judgement to be made by members of the nation through democratic procedures. The state exists to protect the members of the nation it represents from internal as well as external attack and exploitation.

Marxists and liberals do not make any significant link between state and nation other than to confuse the two. Liberals do not recognise nations as communities with rights but instead see nationalism, the sentiment that binds nations together, as a hindrance in the quest for a civic society where loyalty is owed to the state. Marxists have traditionally held the view that capitalism gave rise to the state and to nationalism. States are seen as a device employed by an economic class (capitalists) to further their interests.[63] Nationalism is seen as something invented by the ruling class for the purpose of manipulating the masses and getting them to fight wars that are, at base, about the control and exploitation of economic resources. The Marxist solution is for the state to own and control property and wealth, and manage it in a way that benefits the state and its citizens, in that order. Marxists and liberals are similar in that they believe loyalty to the state stands above loyalty to national communities.

Many nationalists agree wholeheartedly that nationalist sentiment is exploited by governing elites and that modern states are a device for the manipulation of individuals and the pursuit of elite interests. However, nationalists argue that nations and states existed long before the advent of capitalism.[64] Nationalists also

---

[63] The terms *capitalist* and *capitalism* are unfashionable and have been replaced by *free marketeer* and the *free market system*. We are told to *let the market decide*, i.e. let the supply of goods and services be determined by demand from those with the means to pay. The logical outcome of such an approach is an economic and political system geared to the needs and interests of the wealthy. The more you spend, the more you influence the allocation of resources.

[64] For an excellent discussion on the origins of nations see Anthony D. Smith, *The Ethnic Origins of Nations* (Basil Blackwell, 1986).

reject the view that loyalty to an artificial and temporary political structure can ever stand above the natural loyalty owed to communities founded on ties of culture, language, history and kinship. Loyalty is divisible and conditional but it is given naturally to the layers of community to which we belong. The layer deserving the greater loyalty depends upon the circumstances prevailing at any given time, which usually means the degree of perceived threat.

An often-used example of a nation with a long history is the Jewish nation. For most of its life it has survived without formal state institutions even though states have existed from the beginning of recorded history. Indeed, it was the existence of states that made possible much of the recording of human history.

A few religious Jews are opposed to the existence of a Jewish state because they feel that allegiance to a state and its secular institutions will undermine allegiance to religious institutions and weaken them. Dependence on formal state institutions is considered a weakness because they are more easily destroyed than community-based religious institutions. For that reason the state of Israel is seen by some Jews as a threat to the long-term survival of the Jewish nation. They believe that the state of Israel will encourage an increase in secularisation and the religious side of Jewish life will become a less important part of a national survival strategy. Members of the Jewish religious establishment may be motivated in part by concern about their own loss of power within the Jewish nation but there is sense in their argument despite the fact that a state is the most efficient way of mobilising and concentrating the resources of a nation for the protection of its national homeland and its people.

The Armenians are another ancient nation that has used religion as a unifying force. Christianity helped Armenians retain a strong national identity which has prevented them from being absorbed into neighbouring nations. The Moslems of Bosnia have also used religion as the core of their national identity. Catholicism helped bind the Polish nation together during the period when the Polish state ceased to exist and their country was absorbed into the Russian state. Roman Catholicism is also an important part of Irish national identity, which is one important reason why Ulster Protestants find an Irish identity repellent.

State Recognition of States

States need the official recognition of other states if they are to participate in normal diplomatic activity within the global state system and become members of the United Nations. Widespread formal recognition by other states usually indicates that the necessary conditions for statehood have been met but sometimes recognition is given or denied for political ends. For example, in the case of Bosnia recognition was given even though the necessary condition had not been met, which in short is a government in effective control of a territory and its population. A settlement was imposed on the Croats and Serbs because their territory was needed to create a state of viable size. Another reason was that it met the strategic interests of those enforcing the arrangement. Such beginnings do not bode well for the future of Bosnia. In the long term, it is difficult to see how the Catholic Croats and Orthodox Serbs can be prevented from withdrawing themselves and their territory from a mainly Moslem Bosnia. They do not want to be part of that state and feel no sense of common identity with those who call themselves Bosnians. Thus, the Daytona Agreement has sown the seeds of its own destruction.

It is perhaps to avoid a nearby precedent for withdrawal on the basis of national self-determination, that the *International Community* maintains the fiction that Kosovo is an integral part of Serbia. It cannot be admitted otherwise because what is good for Albanians in Kosovo is good for Serbs and Croats in Bosnia.

Kingdom

A kingdom is a geographical area within which a king, or queen, has supreme political and legal power. Monarchs (sovereigns) are sovereign; which means they are subject to no higher worldly authority. The institutions of government through which a monarch rules are, in effect, the state. Many modern states vest the sovereign powers (i.e. those powers formerly held by a sovereign) in separate political and legal institutions. In the UK the monarch is Head of State but sovereign powers are *held by the monarch in parliament* (the House of Commons, and the House of Lords) which until recent times recognised no higher legal authority.[65]

Country

A country is a territory, generally within defined borders, that is or was the homeland of a nation. The border between one country and another is often marked by geographical features such as rivers and mountains. The physical boundary usually also marks a cultural boundary, e.g. language and religion. The name of a country is generally derived from the name of the nation that lives in it or created it. Most of the countries of Europe have been named in that way. For example, England was created by the English and is their homeland. A country is not the same as a state; the terms are not interchangeable.

Province

A province is a territory that forms part of a country, state or empire. Canada, for example, is divided into administrative units called provinces. The term *province* is sometimes used for a territory that is in some way marked off from, and treated

---

[65] The European Court of Justice (the court of the EU) is now the highest legal authority.

differently to, the state or empire of which it is a part. A province is sometimes regarded as something less than an integral part of a state or empire. The obvious example is Northern Ireland.

States, Nations and Countries

Some states include two or more countries. Others are formed from part of one or more countries. A state might have within its borders several nations or part of one nation. For example, the Soviet Union contained many countries and nations while the German Democratic Republic (East Germany) contained only part of one country and part of one nation. France has deemed that its overseas territories, which other states would call colonies, are part of France. Presumably they mean part of the French state. The claim that Guadeloupe is as much a part of France as Bordeaux is clearly a fiction but it enables the French government to deny that there are French colonies and to reject calls for the independence of the colonies and to use military force to retain control of them.

Tahiti is another example of a French colony where it is obvious that the indigenous population, which is Polynesian, is not part of the French nation. For that reason, many of them seek independence from France and the opportunity to govern themselves. The United States has a similar relationship with Hawaii, which in reality is a colony. The Irish regard Ulster/Northern Ireland as a British colony. The Spanish see Gibraltar in the same way. It has been suggested that if the people of Gibraltar agree, it should become part of the UK, thus undermining the charge that it is a colony. These examples raise the question, what territory can be properly included in a state? Does it depend on geography or the will of the indigenous population? Why is it easy to accept the Isle of Wight as part of the UK but not the Falkland Islands? The answers to these questions is that states recognise acquisition by right of conquest, occupation (squatters' rights), sale (Alaska), transfer by treaty (Gibraltar).

Non-State Actors

States are the main actors in the *International Community* but there are others. Some are state sponsored such as the United Nations (UN) and the European Union (EU). Others, such as the International Monetary Fund (IMF) and the World Bank for Reconstruction and Development (World Bank), are created by and run for states. There are also non-state actors such as global corporations (multi-national corporations). Many global corporations have far greater financial and economic power than many states and for this reason there was much discussion in the 1960's and 1970's about states losing their independence and being increasingly subject to the power of corporations and other non-state actors. In other words, the existing state system and theories of International Relations were seen by some as being out of date and unable to cope with modern global conditions.

While it is true that many global corporations are larger and financially more powerful than many states, much of their power comes from a working relationship with states that are able to mobilise and co-ordinate massive economic, diplomatic and military power. It is states not corporations that are recognised as having the right to maintain and deploy armed forces in certain circumstances.

The major oil companies are, for the most part, run as businesses independent of direct state control but they serve the interests of industrialised states by supplying them with the oil they need to function. When the Iraqi army invaded and occupied Kuwait it was not the oil companies that drove the Iraqis out but the armed forces of states, principally the USA. It is therefore a mistake to equate the power of corporations with that of states on the basis of some measure of wealth, such as comparing corporate turnover with Gross Domestic Product (GDP). The ability of states to call on citizens to take up arms is a form of power that often counts for more than GDP.

One view of the relationship between powerful states and global corporations is that states control and use corporations in pursuit of state interests. Another is that corporations control and use states in pursuit of corporate interests. A third view is that global corporations and states are interdependent parts of a web that has at its centre a global governing elite which uses both to pursue its own interests. At the heart of the Global Elite is the US governing elite. What is at the heart of the US governing elite? Well, it certainly is not the President, who is largely a figurehead working within unofficial limits determined by others. The US governing elite consists of sub-elites, which include the news media, entertainment, military, business, banking, politics. Linking many of those groups are other sub-elites, one of which is *organised crime*, a powerful force with *interests* in business, banking, and entertainment. The various sub-elites provide the advisors and policy-makers who advise the president.

The sub-elites, and the easy movement of individuals from one to another, were at one time called the military-industrial complex. That model is now, and perhaps always was, too narrow.

The Global Elite's web is three dimensional and added to at every opportunity. The primary interest of its sub-elites, including the business elite and the corporations it controls, is to expand and preserve the web that benefits them all. Corporations and banks spin a trading and financial web that is protected by the political and military elites.

Global financial and economic institutions may be technically independent of states but that means little if the most powerful corporations, states and institutions are controlled by the Global Elite. All of the parties are able to play a part in promoting and defending political, economic, fiscal, and social conditions that suit their common interests and goals. Those conditions include a *free market economy* and a *global marketplace*.

It is in the interest of the Global Elite to promote an image of independent global institutions and a global market place. Among other things, it makes it possible for state governing elites to justify giving priority to corporate interests over those of the state or its citizens by claiming to be powerless before the forces of the very global system they strive so hard to strengthen and protect. The World Bank and IMF are institutions that restrain non-elite states by tying them into a web of economic relationships (usually involving debt) from which it is difficult, if not impossible, for any one state to break free. The Multilateral Agreement on Investment (MAI), is a budding organisation awaiting the right conditions to bloom.[66] If or when it does so, it will prevent states hindering the activities of corporations. It will make it necessary, and possible, for governments to argue that they have no choice but to give in to the demands of corporations, and to repeat even more frequently than at present the mantra, "We have to operate in a global economy."

What is being suggested here is that it serves little purpose to distinguish between states, suprastate organisations, and non-state actors as if state involvement is the key to a proper understanding of how the global political system works. What is important is that for the most part they are all controlled by the same group of people. Therefore, if we are to distinguish between global actors it would be better to do it on the basis of who has ultimate control rather than the technicalities of their creation or structure.

Even some apparently entirely innocent charitable organisations play a part in propping up and preserving a global system that suits the interests of the strong and ruthless.

Suprastate Organisations

A suprastate organisation is one that has been created by two or more states for the purpose of performing specific functions, and which has the power to make decisions, within a defined area, which are binding on its member states whether

---

[66] The Multilateral Agreement on Investment was scheduled to be signed in spring 1998 but nearly everything about the agreement was so ambitious and extreme that it proved difficult, for the time being, to get states to accept its terms. The aim of MAI is to institutionalise the view that corporations should be beyond the bounds of democratic accountability or the control of states. If MAI or an agreement like it ever comes into effect, it will make corporations the legal equal of states. Corporations will be able to move capital and plant around the world as they please and sue any state that interferes. The intention is that MAI or something like it should be an institution with an appointed body rather than an elected one that will enforce the treaty. Like other institutions of its kind, it will be controlled by the Global Elite. Small states will have little choice but to become parties to the treaty and abide by the judgement of its enforcers.

or not they have participated in the decision making process. Examples of supranational institutions are: the European Court of Justice; the World Trade Organization; the proposed Multilateral Agreement on Investment (MAI).

Non-Governmental Organizations (NGOs) and other Non-State Actors

Trans-state organizations are global actors that are not controlled by states, at least not officially or directly. Some of these organisations are known as Non-Governmental Organizations (NGOs). They exist for the purpose of advancing the particular interests or concerns of their members, which might, for example, be scientific, business, trades union, educational, cultural, environmental or political. One of the oldest NGOs is the International Red Cross. There are also charities (e.g. Oxfam), human rights organizations (e.g. Amnesty International), and environmental organisations (e.g. Greenpeace). Other non-state actors include corporations and, rarely, individuals with great influence – e.g. Julius Nyerere, Mahatma Gandhi, and Bertrand Russell.

Some organisations hide their links with, and dependency on states and are in effect *front organisations*. For example, the Soviet Union set up supposedly independent trades union and peace organisations solely for the purpose of promoting Soviet interests. In a similar way, states create and maintain hidden links with news agencies.

Global corporations, such as those in the oil and aerospace industries, are linked with and serve the interests of certain states. Some corporations receive state funding indirectly through contracts for equipment or grants for research. The funding of defence projects can be seen as a form of subsidy. Corporations also benefit from other forms of state help which include, for instance, an education system geared to corporate labour needs; export promotion and funding; the furthering of corporate interests in other states through diplomatic channels.

Business corporations with essential parts of their structure in two or more states are trans-state actors (usually called multi-nationals or trans-nationals). For example, a motor vehicle manufacturer that makes parts of a vehicle in two or more states and assembles it in another, is a trans-state corporation. A corporation that makes its product in one state and sells it in another is not, on those facts, a trans-state corporation. The major oil companies are an example of trans-state businesses that operate in many states and can be called global corporations.

Nation-States

A nation-state is commonly defined as one where state boundaries and national boundaries coincide; in other words the territory of the state is populated by one nation. A widely accepted rule among nationalists is that the prospect of peaceful relations between states is greatly improved when the whole of each nation lives in its own state. When part of one nation lives as a minority in another nation's state, there is a greater likelihood of conflict within that state and between states.

Peaceful relations between nation-states are enhanced when state borders coincide with a nations historical and spiritual homeland. An ideal world for nationalists would be one where all states are nation-states. Such an arrangement would reduce the possibility of territorial disputes between states and lessen the likelihood of conflict and civil war within them. Nation-states are generally more stable and long-lasting than multi-nation-states.

A world of nation-states is an ideal that cannot be completely achieved but it serves as a model and guide in the resolution of disputes. For example, instead of trying to make Tutsis and Hutus live together in one state, it would be better in the long term to use incentives to encourage people to move so that state boundaries can be redrawn in a way that enables each of those nations to live in their own nation-state. There are obvious problems concerning agreement over boundaries and it would require a wider settlement including Rwanda and Burundi. Another difficulty in that dispute and others like it is that nations are reluctant to leave the land they have occupied for generations. However, generous financial incentives and, more importantly, the prize of a nation-state, would offer a better chance of a successful long-term settlement than the present policy which merely controls inter-communal tensions. Giving grants to encourage people to move and secure a lasting peace is surely preferable to bearing the cost of perpetual conflict. The major obstacle to putting into effect such a commonsense arrangement is the dogma that would condemn it as ethnic cleansing.

Core-Nations

Most state boundaries do not contain the whole of a nation but it is generally recognised that some states, such as Japan, come very near to meeting the definition of a nation-state. What is needed is a definition that enables us to distinguish between a state that is within striking distance of the ideal and one that has no dominant core-nation.

For practical purposes, a nation-state is a state where:

1. an indigenous nation forms a majority of the population of the state;

2. the territory of the state coincides more or less with that of the national homeland of the core-nation;

3. the governing elite is recruited from the indigenous or core national community.

4. the culture, values and perceptions of the core-nation underlie the public culture of the state.

The Republic of Ireland is fortunate in nearly meeting the definition of a nation-state despite the fact that a large number of Irish people do not live in that state. In other words, state boundaries do not coincide with national boundaries. Some states, such as France, contain substantial parts of one or more other nations, e.g. Algerians. If the foreign population is small and unable to demand and gain political or cultural concessions from the host nation, the state can be deemed to be a nation-state. The slippery slope starts with power-sharing and quota arrangements based on *ethnicity*. It does not matter whether they are formal or informal arrangements; they are a sign that a nation-state is becoming a multi-nation-state.

The republics of Ireland and France fail to meet the ideal for a nation-state but are nonetheless regarded as such. The Republic of Ireland does not include either the whole Irish nation or the whole of what it claims as its homeland. France does not include the whole French nation (French in Switzerland and Belgium, and Quebec?) and it contains parts of other nations. However, both have a dominant core indigenous nation that controls the institutions of the state. If it were not for the need to bow to ideological restraint, the French would be using their position to pursue their primary interests, which are those of any nation and include the welfare of its population and the defence of its territory, culture, sovereignty and way of life. To openly pursue such goals in the present ideological climate would be deemed discriminatory and unacceptable.

If a nation-state is to remain as such, the indigenous core-nation has to defend its position and ensure that its culture, values and perceptions continue to underlie those of the state. One of the principal means of defence is to ensure that the public education system passes on the core culture from generation to generation. Many European nations are hindered in this because their state education systems are in most cases managed and controlled by those who do not regard the pursuit of the indigenous nation's interests as a role for education. Instead, they see it as the unquestionable duty of teachers to promote an inclusive civic identity. The unstated aim is to break the thread of communal memory and to deny the whole population, starting with the children, a communal history and identity.

The methods employed in education and elsewhere to promote an inclusive identity are many and of varying degrees of subtlety. Whatever form they take, they have a cumulative effect that shapes perceptions. For instance, Ely Museum seems unwilling to use the E-word. St Etheldreda is described not as an English saint but as a "British saint". Hereward was not an English resistance fighter but a "British resistance fighter". It may be reasonable to suggest that Cromwell lived during "a turbulent period in British history" but it was an even more turbulent period in English history. Another example is that of the *Oxford Nursery Storybook* which in its *inclusive* version of *Jack and the Beanstalk*, has the giant saying, "Fee fi fo fum! I smell the blood of a Britishman." It is through an accumulation of these many small and apparently unimportant things that the moulding of perceptions takes place.

Multi-Nation-States: Internal and External Weakness

Nation-states enjoy many advantages over multi-nation-states because within the latter there is usually either conflict born of competition for power between national communities or, more often, resentment by smaller nations of a large dominant nation. The result is underlying friction and instability. Lebanon is an example of a multi-nation-state which, despite constitutional arrangements designed to protect the interests of all its communities, has been plagued by instability. Such power-sharing arrangements are bound to fail in the long term because rigid constitutional directives cannot anticipate and deal with every eventuality. For example, the size and economic power of the various national communities will vary over time due to their different cultures giving rise to different fertility rates and different attitudes to commerce. The resultant changes in population size and relative economic power can quickly make a constitutional power-sharing arrangement outdated. One community may feel aggrieved because it does not have the formal political power that it feels its size and wealth merit. Another community may feel threatened by the growing physical presence and economic power of another community. There can never be peace and security while one or more communities, and in particular the indigenous community, feel that their position is being undermined. For example, Fijians are on the whole as nice a group of people as you could wish to meet. They have a very relaxed attitude to life and a culture that does not encourage an obsession with the desire to run a business or accumulate private wealth. The Indians in Fiji have a higher fertility rate and place much greater importance on making money and succeeding in business. As a result, Indians dominate and control Fiji's economy, and Fijians make up less than fifty percent of Fiji's population. The capital of Fiji, Suva, has become an Indian colony. Under a system of government based on majority rule, Fijians will increasingly find themselves governed by foreigners, a situation that most people will instinctively feel to be wrong. However, liberals prefer to be guided by dogma rather than instinct so, according to them, Fijians should think themselves lucky that such enterprising people have settled in Fiji. Perhaps they should encourage even more Indians to settle for the purpose of filling skills shortages. In reality, the vast majority of Fijians wish the Indians had never come to Fiji and that most of them would return to India. Fijians could then govern themselves and enjoy their way of life in their own homeland.

The Soviet Union was a multi-nation-state; the UK and USA are multi-nation-states. Such states are generally stable while one nation (the core-nation) forms the majority of the population, dominates the other nations, and provides the governing elite. The stability that is sometimes enjoyed by a powerful multi-nation-state can be undermined when its economic, military or diplomatic power

109

declines. Decline usually brings with it the need for internal reforms and the need to revise expectations and perceptions. In such circumstances, the authority of the dominant nation is often weakened and its ability to provide the governing elite is challenged by one or more *counter-elites,* which represent the interests of one or more other internal nations. If the values and perceptions of the competing elites are very different, the resulting conflict can easily become violent and result in either the replacement of one governing elite by another or the break up of the state into two or more states.

Friction can also arise in multi-nation-states where the political elite is recruited almost exclusively from one nation and the military elite from another. Recent examples are Rwanda, Burundi, Nigeria and Sudan. In Sudan the divisions are deep because the governing elite consists of people from the north who are mostly Arab and Moslem while those in the south are mostly Negro and Christian. The Negroes of the south are exploited in many ways and, unsurprisingly, they have expressed the wish to govern themselves.

Where two or more nations living in their homelands share one state, and one or more of them finds the arrangement unacceptable, there is likely to be communal conflict and a competition for power and resources. The weaker nation will probably want to withdraw from the state and the dominant nation will try to prevent it. Such a situation invariably brings war. The sensible solution would be for each nation to form a nation-state in its homeland, thus making one state into two or more states. In places like Sudan and Iraq that solution would be possible but the governing elites have an interest in preserving the existing state.

In other places separation would not be so easy because:

(a) populations are spread amongst many scattered, disconnected territories, as for example in the Balkans;

(b) homelands are too small, poorly placed or lacking in natural resources to make a state viable.

In the Balkans, many of the problems could be solved if the outside enforcing powers accepted that populations need to be moved. In some other places, small nations just have to face the fact that, however regrettable it might be, their homeland is not suited to being a state.

In rare cases, it is possible to create a stable constitutional arrangement which meets the needs of all parties. The usual example given of a successful multi-nation-state is Switzerland but Switzerland is an alliance of convenience. None of the national groups claim the whole of Switzerland as their homeland, each has a bloc of territory which they are content to hold.

The institutions and laws of a nation-state reflect the history and culture of the core-nation. It is not possible to absorb into those institutions and laws, the conflicting values of other cultures. For example, there are fundamental differences between Islamic law and the law of Western states. Those Moslems who live in Western states and wish to observe Islamic law are unable to do so and that causes tension and resentment. Moslems are drawn closer together and an Islamic community is formed that develops political and other institutions of its own. Leaders of that community emerge and voice its aspirations and frustrations.

In liberal states, the larger a non-core-nation becomes, the more concessions it is able to win from the governing elite. It therefore pays to have a higher birth-rate than the core-nation, thereby increasing electoral power and occupying more territory. Some settler communities use public disorder, or the threat of it, to extract political and economic concessions. The usual way for threats to be issued is for *a community leader* to set out the concerns of *the community* and suggest that if they are not addressed there will be trouble. While this tactic is often successful in liberal states, in other places it can have disastrous results for those issuing the threats.

The English are handicapped in the process of winning concessions from the government because there is no formal process by which leaders of the English community can emerge and as a result they do not have community leaders who are able to voice concerns, make demands and get something from it. The English are heading down a one-way street where they continually make concessions that undermine their core position and gain nothing in return. The English are always on the defensive because the English are made to bear the burden of a British identity. This is due to the common but mistaken belief that the British governing elite pursues English national interests. The governing elite is a British governing elite that pursues its own interests, which it believes it can best serve as part of a European and global-elite. The British governing elite clearly does not pursue the interests of the English community, indeed it does not even recognise an English community.

The way for the English to escape from the trap they find themselves in is for them to view the British government in the same way that all the other national communities in the UK do, as something apart from them; something to make demands of and extract concessions from. The British governing elite deems that we live in a multi-cultural civic society where the government arbitrates between the competing interests of individual citizens and ethnic groups. The English should take them at their word and adopt the stratagems and tactics of other ethnic groups. The English have been headless, voiceless, and walked on for far too long.

It is common practice for minority foreign national communities to retain their homogeneity, institutions and links with the homelands but when they are strong enough to do so they demand that their members be admitted to the institutions of the host nation. Thus, foreign communities retain their boundaries and exclusiveness while the boundaries of the host nation are breached and its identity deemed to be inclusive. The aim is to create multi-nation institutions that no longer pursue the interests of one or more indigenous nations but seek to represent, or arbitrate between, the interests of all. The host nation is handicapped in its ability to discuss and publicly articulate its interests because it has no institutions of its own for that purpose. It suffers a loss of privacy and is placed in a position of always having demands made of it but being unable to make demands of others. If the institutions of the host nation are closed to outsiders it is deemed to be discriminatory (racist) and undesirable despite the fact that those who seek entry are able to discriminate when they recruit people for their institutions. One has only to look at the membership of cultural, religious and political organizations that represent the interests of foreign national groups in the UK to see that they recruit people of their own kind. It is quite natural and understandable for communities to do that because outsiders are generally considered to be less committed, reliable and trustworthy than insiders. In times of conflict, the loyalties of an outsider might lie elsewhere.

The issues of recruitment, loyalty, and unity create problems not only for host nations but also for states. If a government is to enjoy the maximum freedom in formulating and pursuing foreign policy goals, it needs a strong domestic base with citizens and government united in a common cultural and political identity. That unity will not exist if a large number of citizens do not identify with either the core-nation or the public culture of the state. Outsiders are likely to have a greater sense of identity and empathy with their national homeland and its inhabitants than with the citizens of the state they live in. A state is weakened in dealings with other states if a large section of its population is likely to support the aims and policies of other states.

In matters of loyalty, states face the same problems as other organisations. They try to ensure the loyalty of those entrusted with confidential or secret information, much of which concerns policies and capabilities. The usual practice is to ensure that the institutions of the state are controlled and managed at the highest and most sensitive levels by those who are sympathetic to the ideology of the governing elite and likely to be loyal. For this reason, recruitment is usually from the core-nation, or in the case of the UK from the core-nations. Persons within that core group who support ideologies incompatible with that of the governing elite are by one means or another denied employment in key governmental departments and administrative levels. For example, during the Cold War it was widely accepted as prudent to exclude communists from positions in the command structure, and posts that gave access to secret information. Likewise when there was open warfare between the northern European Protestant states and the southern European Catholic states, Catholics were excluded from positions of power in the English state and laws were introduced to prevent the monarch marrying a Catholic. The Vatican was seen as a foreign power, and allegiance to the Pope was seen to conflict with allegiance to the state. In much the same way, it is probably now thought sensible to exclude Moslems and others with foreign connections or sympathies from the highest positions in the UK that are directly linked to state security. The difficulty for the governing elite is that it cannot admit to such a discriminatory policy because it conflicts with the notion that we are all equal British citizens of a multi-cultural state.

The formal system of control and exclusion is supervised by the security services, which are managed by individuals recruited from the governing elite and those loyal to it. There is nothing unusual or surprising about this because it is exactly what one would expect of any state. In the UK, the usual practice has been to recruit graduates from universities that have a high proportion of students who attended the major public schools.[67] The recruitment net is now cast wider but it still ensures that members of the governing elite have privileged access to positions of power. A system based on class can comfortably exclude the large number of British citizens with overseas links and allegiances. It cannot be long before the Commission for Racial Equality asks why there are not more members of Moslem ethnic groups in the Ministry of Defence, the security services and the Foreign Office.

Whether a state is a nation-state or a multi-nation-state it can only operate according to one set of values and perceptions. In a multi-nation state there will always be conflict over what the common working values and perceptions should be. Those who do not share the values and perceptions of the state will always feel excluded and will of necessity need to be excluded because it is not in the best interests of any state for individuals of doubtful loyalty to hold positions of power in state institutions or have access to valuable information, be it military, economic, political, scientific or technological. When those who are excluded belong to sizeable politicised religious, racial or national groups within the state, the difficulties become much greater and give rise to resentments that invariably generate conflict. Nation-states are not faced with such acute problems of divided loyalty.

The English Nation and the English State

Northern European kings during the period 200–500AD, were the symbolic heads of tribes or nations. The kings of the Saxon federation were elected or appointed for the duration of a war from among the leaders of the federated tribes. The Saxon kings were an emblem of unity and provided the leadership necessary for the conduct of efficient and effective warfare. A council of tribal leaders decided the wartime goals. When the war was over, the kingship ended and all involved returned to their former pursuits. This system had the advantage of preventing kings from becoming too powerful and using their position to pursue their own

---

[67] North American readers should appreciate that in the UK, schools known as public schools are in fact private schools.

interests to the detriment of others. Whether or not the system was designed to prevent the formation of a dominant central power, it seems to have had that effect. It bears some resemblance to the system seen later in England whereby the various kingdoms united under a *Bretwalder*, or over-king.

In the early days of kingship, the relationship between a king and those he led was similar to the traditional one between a warlord and his followers.[68] The companions swore an oath to uphold the interests and good name of the lord, to be loyal to him, to fight with him in battle and if necessary die in his defence. The lord, in return, was duty bound to be loyal to his companions, to reward them for their service and to further their honour and welfare.[69] The relationship between lord and companions involved rights and duties for both parties.[70] If the lord did not meet his side of the bargain there was no duty on the companions to observe theirs, and that principle underlay the relationship between the king and his subjects. That the king was seen as separate from the embryonic state is indicated by the fact that the king's title to land was the same, in principle, as any other. When he rewarded his followers, and later the Church, with grants of land it was from his own estate.

When relationships are based on loyalty, it is necessary to maintain a balance of power between the parties. Without it, the relationship is likely, if it continues, to become one where the more powerful side demands loyalty as of right but does not give it. As communal institutions become more sophisticated and turn into state institutions (a form of specialisation of labour) so the relationship between rulers and ruled becomes unbalanced and the notion of mutuality fades. Communal rules and conventions usually need little formal enforcement because they are seen to be fair and for the overall benefit of all members of the community. But when *community* degenerates into *society*, the laws and conventions of a state tend to be observed not so much out of a sense of enlightened self-interest but because the state enforces it.

The early English system of justice, democracy and administration evolved from the Northern European tradition of which it was a part. The early English state was as decentralised and democratic as one could reasonably expect for its time. The general principle underlying the structure of government in Northern Europe was that administration and justice should be dealt with locally. Although it is unlikely

---

[68] *Lord* is an Old English word meaning *loaf giver* or *bread giver*.

[69] In this two-way relationship of loyalty, a warrior who took loaves and rings from his lord but failed when the time came to honour his boasts, faced shame and disgrace. It was perhaps considered to be more a matter of dishonesty than cowardice. Those who profess loyalty and take the rewards should live up to their boasts.

[70] The comradeship within a companion group is revealed in the Old English poem *The Wanderer*. It tells of the sadness of a warrior who has survived the death in battle of his lord and companions. He wanders middle-earth friendless, recalling their memory and the companionship they enjoyed, which has gone forever.

that early English democracy ever took the idealised form attributed to it by Thomas Jefferson or the seventeenth century Levellers, it is certain that the structure of the early English state made possible a higher level of democracy, freedom and national unity than was evident for many centuries after 1066.[71]

An individual's survival and wellbeing often depended on living and working with people who could be trusted and relied upon for support in times of trouble. It is trust and enlightened self-interest that are at the heart of community. The first among communities is the family, to which the first natural loyalty is owed. From family ties come the threads of kinship and loyalty that bind wider communities together. For that reason, kindred relationships were and are seen to be important in all aspects of communal life.

Families have many functions, one of which is as a self-sustaining economic community within a network of economic communities. In early times, when most families were engaged in farming, the survival of a family (the whole and parts) required more co-operation and trust than is necessary today. All able-bodied members of the family, including children, had a job to do and all had to work well together. The death or injury of a family member affected the family in many ways. Early English law recognised that relationship and the need, right, and duty, of individuals to seek redress for harm done to their kin. It was for the victim or victim's kin to start proceedings for compensation from the wrongdoer. The principles that underlay that system of justice are those upon which English Common Law is based. Communal or customary law is concerned with the settlement of disputes in a fair and equitable manner with reference to the principles of natural justice and natural morality. Common Law seeks commonsense solutions to disputes.

---

[71] The Levellers were English radicals who believed that sovereignty lay with the people and that the structure of the state and its system of government should reflect that. They were opposed to a form of government that perpetuated the rule of a governing elite which saw itself as being above and apart from the English people. In other words, their model of democracy was inspired by that existing in England before 1066.

The Levellers have been adopted by Marxists and labelled as members of the 'petty bourgeoisie' and early socialists, even though they were unaware of it because "they had no concept of the workings of early capitalism". Having been recruited to the Marxist cause, the Levellers are then stripped of their inconvenient core beliefs, which are dismissed as, "a romantic idea that William the Conqueror had brought the Norman Yoke". It can be seen from this that the Marxists and socialists who meet in Burford each May have very little in common with the Levellers and next to no sympathy with their outlook. The Levellers were English and that identity was very important to them. They were radical democrats who would today be dismissed by socialists as populists who wanted the will of the people to prevail. The Levellers favoured bottom-up democracy and would have opposed the European Union and the top-down power structures that Marxists prefer. Today they would be campaigning for an English parliament and the retention of English Law and trial by jury. The Levellers believed that it was for those to whom the people lent the power of government to listen to the people not lecture and deceive them. John Lilburne and his fellow Levellers were English radicals to whom we owe a great deal.

Beyond the immediate family, there was a wider face-to-face community to which family members belonged. The members of such communities lived a public life that made it difficult to do wrong and remain undetected. If you have two cows one day, and three the next, someone will want to know where the new one came from. The interest would be greater if somebody else had a cow missing. A public life and extended kindred ties tend to reduce criminal activity if only for the reason that individuals are less likely to harm those they have to deal with on a daily basis. In addition, there is a greater likelihood of detection and a wider knowledge of those involved in a dispute, and the sort of people they are. Because of that knowledge, insiders are often better able than outsiders to devise a suitable solution to a dispute, or punishment for a crime.

Extended kinship ties helped promote lawfulness by engendering empathy among members of a community and public shame and humiliation for wrongdoers who were caught. Individuals could not be anonymous and unconcerned about what others thought of them because there was a high level of contact with and dependency upon other members of the community. Wrongdoing quickly became public knowledge and affected the way individuals and families were treated by others. Because the family was central to identity and economic wellbeing, it was difficult for individuals to ignore the displeasure of others. Moving from one place to another to make a fresh start was not a practical option.

Beyond the local community there was a district identity founded on, among other things, the co-operation required for defence against outside attack. A mutual interest in maintaining internal peace and good order also drew small communities together. This web of interests and relationships spread outwards and upwards linking local communities with the king who represented the national community and acted as a leader and figurehead around which the nation could unite in times of trouble.

Entry in the English Chronicle for the Year 1066

1066 In this year King Harold came from York to Westminster at the Easter after the Christmas the king died; Easter was on 16th April. Then all through England a sign was seen in the heavens such as no man had seen before. Some men said that it was the star 'comet', which some men call the long-haired star; it appeared first on the eve of the Greater Litany, 24th April, and shone for seven nights. Soon after that eorl Tostig came from across the sea into the Isle of Wight with as large a force as he could gather, and was given money and provisions. And King Harold his brother gathered a shipforce and a landforce greater than any king had gathered before in this land, because he had been told that William the Bastard would come here and strive for the land, just as it happened afterwards. Meanwhile eorl Tostig came into the Humber with sixty ships, and eorl Edwin came with a landforce and drove him out. The shipmen deserted him and he went to Scotland with twelve small vessels. Harold, king of Norway, met him there with three hundred ships, and Tostig bowed to him and became his man. They both went up the Humber until they came to York, and there eorl Edwin and eorl Morkere his brother fought with them but the Norwegians had the victory. Harold, king of the English, was informed of the event; and the fight was on the Vigil of St. Matthew. Then Harold our king Harold came on the Norwegians unawares, and met them beyond York at Stamford with a great host of English folk; and that day a very fierce fight was fought on both sides. Harold Hardrada and eorl Tostig were killed, and the Norwegians that were left were put to flight, and the English fiercely struck them from behind as they chased them to their ships. Some drowned, some were burnt, some perished in various ways, so that there were few left, and the English had control of the battlefield. The king made terms with Olaf, son of the Norwegian king, and the bishop and the eorl of Orkney, and all those on the ships. They went up to our king and swore oaths that they would ever keep peace and friendship with this land, and the king let them go home with twenty-four ships. These two pitched battles were fought within five nights. Then William, eorl of Normandy, came to Pevensey on Michaelmas eve, and as soon as they were prepared, they moved on and built a stronghold at the town of Hastings. This was made known to king Harold and he gathered a great army and came against them at the hoary apple-tree. William came upon them unawares, before they had all gathered ready for the fight. The king, nevertheless, fought very hard against them with those men who stayed with him, and there were many killed on both sides. There king Harold was killed and eorl Leofwine his brother and eorl Gyrth his brother, and many good men. The French held the field of the dead as God granted them because of the sins of the people. Archbishop Aidred and the townspeople of London wanted the child Edgar for king, as was his natural right; and Edwin and Morkere promised that they would fight on his side. But though haste was needed, it was put off and grew worse from day to day, just as it all happened in the end. The battle was fought on pope Calixtus' Day, 14th October. Afterwards, eorl William went back to Hastings and waited there to see whether men would submit to him. When he saw that no one would come to him, he went inland with all his army that was left to him, and those who came to him from over the sea, and ravaged all the parts he went over, until he came to Berkhamsted. There he was met by archbishop Aldred, child Edgar, eorl Edwin, eorl Morkere and all the leading men of London. They went, out of need, to submit to him when most harm had been done; and it was most unwise that none had gone before, since God would not change things because of our sins. They gave him hostages and swore oaths to him, and he promised them that he would be a faithful lord to them, yet at the same time he and his men plundered all that they could. On Christmas Day, archbishop Aldred consecrated him king at Westminster. Before Aldred placed the crown on his head William promised Aldred on the book of Christ that if they would be loyal to him he would rule all this people as well as the best of kings before him. Yet he taxed the people very severely. And in the spring he went over the sea to Normandy and took with him archbishop Stigand and abbot Æthelnoth of Glastonbury and the child Edgar and eorl Edwin and eorl Morcar and eorl Waltheof and many other good men from England. Bishop Odo and eorl William stayed behind and had castles built across this land and much distressed the wretched folk and always it became much worse. May the end be good when God wills it.

The arrival of the Normans brought an end to what remained of the unity between king and nation. William swore at his coronation to rule all his people as well as the best kings had done before him but, as the English Chronicle reports, this did not prevent him taxing the people heavily and generally causing them much distress. Property law was changed so that the king owned all the land in his kingdom and title to it was derived from him. The Normans ruled and the English were ruled. The English paid taxes and the Norman governing elite spent the revenue in England and abroad on projects that served their interests. It was clear that the Normans loathed the English and cared nothing for their interests.

The Death-Bed Confessions of William of Normandy

as recorded by Orderic Vitalis.

I have persecuted the English beyond all reason. Whether gentle or simple I have cruelly oppressed them; many I unjustly disinherited; innumerable multitudes perished through me by famine or the sword . . . I fell upon the English of the Northern shire like a ravening lion. I commanded their houses and corn, with all their implements and chattels to be burnt without distinction, and great herds of cattle and beasts of burden to be butchered wherever they were found. In this way I took revenge upon multitudes of both sexes by subjecting them to the calamity of a cruel famine, and so became the barbarous murderer of many thousands, both young and old of that fine race of people. Having gained the throne of that kingdom by so many crimes, I dare not leave it to anyone but God . . .

It cannot truthfully be claimed that there was a golden age of English democracy and statecraft in the century before the arrival of the Normans. The power of the state had increased, as had the burdens on the people. The two-way loyalty of the early period was moving towards the one-way upward loyalty of an infant feudalism. The qualifications for kingship had, over the centuries, become more restrictive, making it necessary for a candidate to be a member of a royal family. The witan (Council of wise men) originally had the right to select from among the members of the royal family the person thought most suitable to be king but by the eleventh century succession of the eldest son had became normal and the task of the witan was merely to confirm that the proper rules of succession had been observed. The arrival of William rapidly accelerated the trend towards a centralisation of power but the transfer of all land into his ownership probably took the process far beyond anything that would have occurred under an English king.

The alliance between the Norman monarchy and the Roman Church helped to further strengthen the state and enabled a vast amount of wealth to be wrung from the English in the form of taxes and theft. That wealth financed the building of castles, churches and cathedrals in England and Normandy. It also financed costly wars in the British Isles and on the Continent. The Crusades, like other wars of the time, were not in the English national interest but were fought to further the interests and glory of the Norman governing elite. England, a once rich country was reduced to poverty and exhaustion.

The divorce of the state from the nation was stark and readily apparent in the fact that the language of the state, both written and spoken, became Norman French. As a result, English men and women who went to law, or were put on trial, had their cases dealt with in a foreign language. Instead of being able to speak for themselves in court and make their own case they had to pay a lawyer to do it for them. Trials continued to be conducted in French for many centuries.

The Normans set about destroying English culture and national identity to undermine resistance to foreign rule. Six hundred years of English history in Britain was dismissed and replaced with an invented history in which the English were portrayed as barbarian Saxon pirates and invaders, who were defeated by a Christian King Arthur, the saviour of a Romano-British civilisation. Little changed for the English when the Norman kings gave way to the equally foreign Plantagenets.[72] St Edmund, the patron saint of England, was replaced by St George, who if he existed at all was probably a Syrian who had no connection with England. For the English, 1066 was to be year zero.

The Britons, including those called Bretons, who had been allies of the Normans, were treated differently. They were given a manufactured glorious past to substitute for the reality of defeats and decline. The aim was to bolster the self-esteem of the Britons and deny the English a national identity. Political and cultural propaganda is not new and it is a testimony to the effectiveness of Norman propaganda that even now we have misguided Englanders who believe that the King Arthur of legend actually existed and that he was English.[73] There was no King Arthur and the Arthurian fables are nothing more than layers of myth that reflect political needs and literary fashion. At one stage in the evolution of the

---

[72] Plantagenet period is from the crowning of Henry II, 1154, to the death of Richard III, 1485.

[73] The following quotation is an example of the mistake and how it is passed on as fact. "The story of this English king and his Knights of the Round Table has inspired a mass of films, novels, and poetry." *The Week*, 15th August 1998.

myth, Arthur was a heathen king, in another a Christian king, and in yet another his importance is secondary to that of Lancelot and Guinevere.

It is understandable that some members of the *Celtic-fringe* should promote the Arthurian myths because it forms part of the anti-English strand that runs through much of their culture and in large part helps define them as nations. In recent times, they have cultivated the myth that they are Celts and have basked in the glory of the cultural and technological achievements of the Celts. It needs to be made clear, once again, that members of the *Celtic-fringe* are not Celts; they are neither ethnic Celts nor cultural Celts. Any trace of Celtic culture that might exist among those people is due to some of their remote ancestors having absorbed elements, including language, of a successful and dominant culture. It is not difficult to argue that the Irish, Scottish and Welsh cultures contain far more that is English than Celtic.

The device of claiming greatness by association is common throughout history but those doing so reveal ignorance of, or dissatisfaction with, their own real history. Many modern Irish, Scottish and Welsh nationalists know that their history and culture is rich enough without a fake Celtic inheritance. In fact many of them are embarrassed by those of their countrymen who perpetuate a bogus Celtic identity and Arthurian history.

In modern times, the English are once again having their history and culture denied. We have a liberal governing elite that is hostile to the idea of an English national identity rooted in history, culture, and ancestry. It seeks to undermine Englishness in two ways. One the one hand it does its best to discredit and mock the idea of an English nation. On the other, it tries to *redefine* Englishness in a way that suits its ideological and political needs. Resistance to this moulding of perceptions is handicapped by the fact that early English history and culture is an area of knowledge that is for the most part preserved in our universities, where most academics treat it as something remote and unconnected with the present.

The final indignity that takes us back to the eleventh century is the process that is transferring to the EU the power to make and enforce law. Once again we will be taxed, judged, punished and ruled by foreigners who have no interest whatsoever in preserving English culture and national identity. Indeed they have an interest in destroying it and replacing it with a concocted European identity that will serve much the same purpose as the legend of King Arthur.

The English nation survived the Normans and the attempt by the Norman military dictatorship to destroy it. That governing elite crumbled because despite its massive power, it was a small minority of the population and it needed to speak English more than the mass of English people needed to speak Norman French. After several generations of interbreeding between Norman and English, the ancestry of the governing elite was more English than Norman. English eventually became the language of the state but due to snobbery and force of habit French and Latin continued to be regarded as high status languages in government and education, and served as a means of setting the governing elite apart from the masses. One of the demands of the Levellers, made in the *Agreement of the People*, 1647, was that proceedings in law courts be conducted in English, not French.

Throughout the period of its banishment, the English language continued to be spoken and written, and to evolve. Layamon in the twelfth century wrote in almost pure English.[74] Unfortunately, a large number of French words displaced English ones, and much of the Norman official and technical vocabulary used by the ruling elite remained when spoken and written English were officially re-introduced. As a result, many English words were lost from what was to become Standard English but much of the Old English vocabulary was retained in regional dialects such as Dorset.[75] Another loss was the English style of alliterative verse, which was replaced with the French rhyming style.

Summary

It is easy to deride those who attach importance to military and political events that occurred nine hundred years ago but criticism usually comes from those who are either ignorant of the importance of those times and the hardships that were suffered or simply could not care less. The Normans took control of a highly developed and sophisticated English state and used it to subjugate and exploit the English people. It was the English state that made possible the Doomsday Book which, although it may not have been specifically made for the purpose, better enabled the Normans to tax the English and raise revenue for the purpose of building castles from which they were able to rule over a hostile population. They destroyed English churches and cathedrals and put up Norman buildings in their place. The larger English towns and their people were soon dominated both physically and psychologically by large buildings that were powerful symbols of foreign rule. The great wealth needed to finance the vast building programme, both in England and abroad, came from the English people. Much wealth was moved to the continent where the Normans involved the English in very long and costly foreign wars that were of no relevance or benefit to the English national interest.

---

[74] Layamon, a poet and priest, helped promote an invented history of Britain in *Brut* but at least he did so in English and in an English style. He and others subverted the mythical British history by giving it an English gloss.

[75] William Barnes, the Dorset poet, was very keen on re-introducing Old English words into everyday use and to that end he produced word lists giving English (Saxon-English) equivalents to foreign words. Where he could not find appropriate English words he re-created them, using English root words. If he were alive today he would be promoting the use of plain English. See *The Rebirth of England and English: The Vision of William Barnes*, Andrew Phillips (Anglo-Saxon Books, 1996).

Many of the changes that occurred as a result of Norman rule can be summarised as follows.

1. The nature of kingship changed from one where the king was a symbol of national unity and a protector of the people and their rights, to one where the king was divorced from the English nation, its interests and wellbeing. The monarch became an absolute ruler and head of state, guided only by his own interests and those of his allies, nearly all of whom were foreign.

2. The king did not just own a private estate but all the land in his kingdom.[76]

3. The rights attached to the ownership of all the land of the kingdom (payments and the provision of services) were transferred to the king and then from him to those of his allies he wished to reward.

4. The state finally changed from one that had originally been created to serve the interests of the nation to one that served the interests of the ruling elite. The English people were treated as an enemy of that elite and had few rights and many duties.

5. The language of the rulers became the language of the state and its courts. English was treated as a low status language.

6. The Church in England lost much of its independence. The pre-Norman English Church, which had enjoyed a considerable degree of independence from Rome, came more directly under papal authority and Norman management.

7. The history of the English nation was suppressed and in its place was put a mythical history of Britain in which the Britons played a glorious part and the English became the wicked Saxon enemy.[77]

8. The history of England was deemed to start in the eleventh century with William being treated as though he were the first king of England. This had the effect of furthering the process, begun when Christianity was introduced into England, of distancing English traditions, culture and learning from Northern Europe and linking them with the Mediterranean world. The attack that took place on English culture and national identity would today be called cultural genocide.

It is evident that many of the changes introduced by the Normans, and much of their propaganda, have endured down the ages. The use of foreign words and phrases are still mistakenly thought to demonstrate intelligence, sophistication and education. As a result, stupid people believe that using long words with foreign roots, instead of shorter English words, will make them seem clever. Clear, simple

---

[76] Title to land is still derived from the Crown and reverts to it when title is lost.

[77] According to *The Cambridge Guide to Literature in English*, Ian Ousby, CUP 1995, some of Geoffrey of Monmouth's *Historia regum Britanniae* (c. 1135) "bears a remote resemblance to actual events" but "the majority is pure invention".

language usually indicates clarity of thought and is generally more pleasant to the English ear and mind. Saying much with few words is in the tradition of the Old English wordsmiths but the fashion now is to say very little with as many words as possible, and the longer the word the better it is deemed to be.

The English survived the rule of the Normans and other hardships but what happened to the Normans? The only trace to be found of them in England is in the remnants of the landed aristocracy where there are still those who express pride in the belief that their ancestors came over with The Conqueror.[78] That they think such a connection reflects well on them says much about them and the teaching of history. The class system in England has been kept alive by those who mistakenly believe that they have Norman blood coursing through their veins.[79] That group of misguided people provided good reason for the reform of the House of Lords, which is in effect the remnant of a Norman institution. This is not to deny that there are many current and former members of the House of Lords who have a very strong sense of Englishness and are concerned to preserve England and English political and cultural identity. That is more than can be said of a Scottish-dominated British government that is as contemptuous of English rights as were the Normans.

It is unwise to claim too much for early English society but it is probably true that in that time, and especially before the introduction of Christianity, freemen (and women) were freer, and individual and communal rights were greater than after the Norman invasion. The system of justice and the settlement of disputes was built around the idea that an individual belonged to a family and a wider community and was obliged to act in the best interests of both. Kinship brought with it an obligation to protect and assist others in times of need; the closer the relationship, the greater the obligation.

Liberals are given to ridiculing Englishness but in response to one such attack in *New Statesman and Society* (NSS), Sir Richard Body, Conservative MP for Holland-with-Boston, replied in a way that expressed the situation rather nicely, even though some might agree with it more in spirit than in detail. After pointing to the libertarian nature of Anglo-Saxon society he went on as follows:

> The Englishness mocked in *NSS* columns belongs to the Normans. Snobbish, conformist, pageant-adoring and hard of heart, the Normans introduced a contrast, which has given England two distinct streams which have mingled uneasily. The civil war saw them clash. The Roundheads were very English; the Cavaliers very Norman. Three

---

[78] Duke Wilhelm of Normandy was once better known to the English as William the Tanner or William the Bastard.

[79] The widely-held belief that it is a good thing to have *come over with the Normans* is made use of by those who peddle completely bogus family trees and coats of arms. Everyone it seems can be connected to a line of Norman aristocrats and sold a coat of arms with a Latin motto.

centuries on, and the distinction is becoming blurred, but we can discern the true Englishness still. It is not in the City of London, the armed services, the House of Lords, the established church or any other allegedly English institution, for they are in the Norman tradition – conformist, regulated and authoritarian. For true Englishness, we turn to the millions of self-employed businessmen, our public services, the chapels and meeting-houses, the House of Commons and a vibrant, variegated press. The caricature of Englishness is pure Norman.

For a true specimen of Englishness, I will nominate Michael Foot. It would have been Kingsley Martin if he were still around.

Many more names could be added to the list, including the following MPs: Tony Benn, Dennis Skinner, Frank Field, Barbara Castle, the late Alan Clark and, of course, Sir Richard Body.

Great Britain and the United Kingdom

Despite all that has been written and said about devolution in recent years, there is still widespread confusion about the meaning of *Great Britain* and *United Kingdom*. Great Britain is the largest European island. It is the geographical area that includes England, Scotland and Wales. The inhabitants of Britain are known as the British. The inhabitants of Northern Ireland are not, by this definition, British. However, states are able to apply whatever label they wish to their citizenship and *British* is used to denote both citizenship and place of residence.[80]

Wales was conquered by King Edward I in 1284 and became part of the Anglo-Norman state. Scotland was united with England by treaty in 1707 thus creating the United Kingdom of Great Britain.[81] The 1801 Act of Union with Ireland created the United Kingdom of Great Britain and Ireland. Following the Easter rebellion, or revolution, of 1916 the Irish Free State, consisting of 26 southern counties, gained its independence. The northern six counties remained a part of the United Kingdom, which now consists of Great Britain (England, Scotland and Wales) and Northern Ireland.

That the English are confused about their identity and that of the UK can be found in simple things. It has been pointed out many times during the past few years that the English have at last realised that their flag is the red cross of St George. However, there are still many, mostly middle-class Englanders, who still feel

---

[80] *The British Isles* is a term that includes Ireland but it is not liked by the Irish who do not want any association with Britishness.

[81] The union between England and Scotland was effected by a treaty between the two states. Queen Anne acted as both the Scottish and English monarch (Head of State) when she signed the treaty that merged the states, each of which had a parliament. Anne became Queen of Great Britain and Ireland. It has been argued that the recent creation of a Scottish Parliament was a breach of the Treaty of Union and invalidates the whole thing. Thus, they argue, the UK no longer exists.

attached to the UK and the Union flag (invented by a Scottish king), which perhaps explains why the Union flag and the word *English* can still be found together on labels stuck on apples. Butchers are also prone to that mistake when displaying English lamb. The Scots and Welsh usually think the misuse of the Union flag is due to English arrogance but it is probably due more to ignorance or plain stupidity. There is a similar problem with *national* anthems. *God Save the Queen* (words written by a Scotsman) is not the national anthem of the English but the state anthem of the UK. The English national anthem is probably, by popular choice, *Land of Hope and Glory,* although some would prefer revised words.[82] Despite this, unionists still ensure that English sports teams have *God Save the Queen* played as their national anthem, which suggests that England is the last colony of the Norman British state. Fortunately, Scottish and Welsh teams have their own anthems. The Welsh anthem is one of the very best. As for *Flower of Scotland,* the Scottish national anthem, it is no business of an Englishman to comment. What is the business of the English is that those who are in charge of English national sports associations, and especially the "Old Farts" of Rugby Union, should be shaken out of their stupor and made to learn the difference between a state anthem and a national anthem. Fortunately, the people who run Rugby League are far more enlightened.

English Nationality

The matter of who is and who isn't English came to the fore in July 1995 when an article by Robert Henderson was published in *Wisden Cricket Monthly.* Mr Henderson drew attention to the fact that many individuals get an emotional charge when they play for their national team and it boosts their performance. When the whole team enjoys that emotional charge the performance of the parts and the whole is raised to a new level. In other words, he suggested that a higher level of individual and team performance is likely to be attained if all members of an England team are English. This is seen as a general rule that applies to all national teams.

The following extracts are from Robert Henderson's article.

"At the very least, it is difficult to see how playing for England could be anything more than a means of personal enhancement and achievement for players of West Indian ancestry."

"The common experience of mixed groups makes it immensely difficult to accept that a changing room comprising say six Englishmen, two West Indians, two

---

[82] Those who suggest *Jerusalem* would do well to look closely at Blake's words (e.g. arrows of desire), and also to consider the wisdom of having a national anthem named after a foreign city claimed by two other nations as their first city.

South Africans and a New Zealander is going to develop the same camaraderie as 11 unequivocal Englishmen."

"All the England players who I would describe as foreigners might well be trying at a conscious level, but is that desire to succeed instinctive, a matter of biology? There lies the heart of the matter."

Matthew Engel, the editor of Wisden's Cricket Annual was quoted as saying, "There is a vast difference between wanting to play Test cricket and wanting to play for England."

Mr Henderson expressed in his own way an opinion that is shared by many others. He explained why he felt as he did but he nonetheless offended liberal sentiment by casting doubt on the unjustified assumptions that underlie their ideology. Shortly after publication of the article it was reported that two cricketers were consulting their lawyers about its implications.[83] The general manager of Derbyshire Cricket Club, Reg Taylor, said that the club was consulting lawyers with a view to taking legal action against the magazine.

An article by Robert Winder in the *Independent*, 4th July 1995, took a somewhat muddled approach to the issue and included the statement that Graham Hick had applied for *English citizenship* and then, after dismissing Mr Henderson's argument, went on to affirm it by stating that when the South African team beat the All Blacks in the 1995 Rugby World Cup final it was clearly harnessing some ferocious national willpower. Mr Henderson was then condemned for having produced a sad and thin piece of work which implied that national identity is something that can be conferred only by birth and not by choice. This was said to run counter to just about every democratic principle in the land. What, we might ask, has democracy to do with nationality, and which democratic principles were infringed?

This *democratic* approach to the issue of nationality reveals underlying liberal assumptions. The first is that democracy is a synonym for liberalism, and the second, that democracy involves the freedom of individuals to choose an identity for themselves and others to accept that choice. It follows that because liberals believe nationality is a matter of personal choice, those who reject that assertion are opposed to democracy, which is clearly absurd. It is not necessary to be a liberal to be a democrat, and democracy is not a liberal invention, and neither is it their ideological property, although they behave as if it were.

The Independent, 5th July 1995, carried a letter which mentioned the "xenophobic" and "spurious reasoning" of Mr Henderson. It then went on to suggest that if ancestry is an important factor in national identity then the current White players be examined and so-called Englishmen with Norman-French,

---

[83] *The Independent* 3rd July 1995

Germanic-Saxon, Roman-Italian and Celtic origins be rooted out. Readers were then informed that as *Homo Sapiens* had not originated in "the land of the Union Jack" it would be logical to reject anyone who claimed to have passed the Tebbit test of pure Englishness. The letter ended with one of the best-loved of liberal clichés, "there is only one race, the human race."

If we overlook the fact that the correspondent completely avoided the point Mr Henderson had made and is unaware that the English flag is the cross of St George, we can note the *xenophobic* and *land of the Union Jack* and *so-called Englishmen* slurs. Had similar statements been made by an Englishman about a non-European nation the writer would have been condemned, probably as a racist. Is the point about *so-called Englishmen* and their ancestry supposed to demonstrate that there is no such person as an Englishman? And is the completely spurious point about *Homo Sapiens* meant to show that because *so-called Englishmen* are the descendants of immigrants that this somehow proves that nobody is English? Or is it supposed to demonstrate that everyone living in England is English whether their ancestors migrated here fifteen-hundred years ago or five years ago? As for the dismissal of *Germanic Saxons*, perhaps the writer knows nothing at all about the origins of the English. He apparently does not understand the meaning of xenophobic because there is nothing in the article to suggest that Mr Henderson hates or even dislikes foreigners or things foreign.

The *Tebbit Test* refers to an observation by Norman Tebbit (now Lord Tebbit) and many before and since. It is a fact that at cricket matches between, for example, England and Pakistan, Pakistanis living in England, who liberals claim to be as English as anyone else, support the Pakistan team. Norman Tebbit did not say that they should not do so or that it was undesirable or unnatural, he was merely pointing to the fact that by supporting Pakistan they showed their lack of identification with England and the English. This statement of the obvious brought down on Norman Tebbit the scorn of liberals who proclaimed the remark to be racist and offensive. The truth of the statement was not, as far as is known, denied. Indeed, it would be difficult to do so because it is obvious that the people cheering the Pakistan team and waving the Pakistan flag are not English. Among other things, if they were English they would be likely to support the England team. It is equally likely that if any of those supporters were invited to play in the England team they would feel as much part of it as would an Englishman playing for Pakistan.

It is common for multi-culturalists to mockingly refer to the *Tebbit Test* but there is little else that they can do because they see the truth of it and have no effective argument against it. Instead, they fall back on their usual tactic of ridiculing and dismissing issues and ideas that they find difficult to cope with. Their guffawing at those who make a telling observation says much about their vulnerability and the frailty of the ideological illusion they are promoting.

Very few Pakistanis or other foreigners living in England claim to be English or want to be English. They have their own nationality and culture to which they are deeply attached and rightly proud. It tends to be patronising liberals who wish to confer English nationality upon Black and Asian people living in England as if they want it and will be grateful for the favour bestowed.

The last point is that of there being one race, the human race. This is presumably meant to be an incredibly clever thing to say because liberals never tire of saying it. If there is only one race, why do liberals complain endlessly about racism, race relations and, in the UK, support the existence of a Race Relations Act? If there is only one race, what is meant by a multi-racial society?

Another correspondent, in a letter also published in the *Independent*, 5th July 1995, said how depressing the sentiments expressed by Mr Henderson were and that by describing Black Englishmen as foreigners he might incite others to racial hatred, which is an offence under the Public Order Act 1986. Mr Henderson was then accused of attempting to recycle the pseudo-science on which the Nazis based their creed. Then the editor of *Wisden Cricket Monthly* was criticised for his attempt to start a serious debate and for his appalling ignorance, *not least when 'ethnic cleansing' takes place daily in the Balkans*. Again, there is no attempt to address the point at issue. Instead, Mr Henderson and others were warned that in making their views known they could be committing a criminal act and might be punished for it. Mr Henderson and the editor were then unjustifiably linked with the Nazis and ethnic cleansing. This type of liberal propaganda and intimidation is often used and continues to work despite its crude and obvious nature. The technique is simply to repeatedly associate ideological enemies with icons of evil. The aim is guilt by association even when the association is merely asserted and not proven. The technique of the writer who managed to link Mr Henderson with the Nazis and ethnic cleansing is, to use that person's method, worthy of Dr Josef Goebbels.

A few days after the appearance of the article, David Frith, the Editor of *Wisden Cricket Monthly*, apologised for having published the piece. As on other similar occasions, it was reminiscent of the Chinese Cultural Revolution when those who expressed views that did not accord with the ideological orthodoxy of the time were made to apologise and suffer public humiliation. David Frith's apology may have been prompted by advice from the publisher's lawyers that the writer, editor and publisher could be prosecuted under the Public Order Act 1986 or be subject to action in the civil court. The publisher was subsequently sued and made to pay damages.

The point made by Mr Henderson, and ignored by all those who attacked him, except Robert Winder, is that nationality can in certain circumstances affect sporting performance. An example of this can be found in Grand Prix motor racing where it is widely recognized that a driver competing in his own country instinctively tries a little harder to win and is also *lifted* by the support of the home crowd. This even applies to Michael Schumacher who is very competitive and consciously drives as well as he can in every race. If it can be widely accepted that emotional and psychological factors, which are not subject to will or choice, are able to improve the performance of an individual sportsman why should they not also improve the performance of a team.

This is not to suggest that sportsmen do not try their hardest when representing a community to which they do not belong. Successful sportsmen are generally very competitive people who have a very strong will to win but the emotion being considered is something different and beyond the will to win. In the same way it can be seen that someone fighting in a war to defend their own community will take greater risks and endure greater hardships than a person fighting for another community. The principle can be easily understood by those who apply common sense to the issue rather than dogma.

The special fellowship that comes from the feeling of belonging to a group and being comfortable in it is greatly enhanced by links of kinship. That applies whether it be the close kinship of a nuclear family or the wider kinship of a nation. As we shall see later, communities are a collection of individuals with shared interests, perceptions and memories. Insiders empathise with and feel protective towards one another in a way that they do not with outsiders. Formal and informal bonds and webs of communication give insiders the will and the means to co-operate and put communal interest above self-interest.

Community fosters trust, loyalty and empathy and a willingness to defend collective interests and reputations. It is not the professionalism and will to win of the individual but the sense of communal honour and the need to uphold it that is central to the collective *lift* that a national team enjoys. Added to that is the feeling of being supported and willed on to win by a large group of people who identify with the team and share that sense of honour. If an England football team (note – *England* not an *English* team) were to consist of eleven foreigners who happened to live in England, whether born there or not, it would not be thought of by the English or other nations as a proper England team. For nationalists, a football or rugby match between England and France means a match between English and French players. A football match between a team of eleven West Indians living in England and a team of eleven North Africans living in France would not be regarded as an England v France international.

The Great Britain ice hockey team is ahead of the rest in that it does not contain a single British player. The players and management care if they win or lose but frankly, could anyone else give a damn.

The events surrounding the *Wisden* article can be contrasted with those that followed the statement by Diane Abbott, a Black Member of Parliament, who was

129

reported as being "surprised" that a hospital in her constituency had chosen to employ, "...blonde, blue-eyed girls from Finland, instead of nurses from the Caribbean who know the language and understand British culture and institutions." "And are Finnish girls, who may never have met a Black person before, let alone touched one, best suited to nursing in multi-cultural Hackney?"[84] There were no letters or articles in *The Independent* condemning Miss Abbott as a racist and no mention of ethnic cleansing or the Nazis. Instead, on the following day there was a picture of a smiling Diane Abbott above an article that was less than hostile. It was headed with the misleading words, "Diane Abbott says she is sorry (For the record Miss Finland is Black)" All that Ms Abbott had said was that she was sorry and upset that her words had been interpreted as racist. In other words she was not sorry for what she had said; the fuss was the fault of those who had *misunderstood* her. It is difficult to see what could be misunderstood. Those involved in the publication of the *Wisden* article were no doubt sorry that their words had been misinterpreted as racist but that did not seem to be a mitigating factor for them.

It is for each of us to examine the words used by those involved in such events and make up our own minds as to whether double standards exist. In addition, we should also consider the reported comments of fellow Black MP the late Bernie Grant, which reveal even more: "She is quite right. Bringing someone here from Finland who has never seen a Black person before and expecting them to have some empathy with Black people is nonsense. Scandinavian people don't know Black people – they probably don't know how to take their temperature." Other than point out that Finns are not Scandinavians, it must be asked what the reaction of Black people and liberals would have been if a White person had suggested that Black nurses where unsuited to nurse Whites because they were unable to empathise or know how to take their temperature.

The issue raises the following points:

1. Miss Abbott was not concerned that the Finns might never have met or touched an *English* person; her concern was for *Black* people. Presumably that concern was to do with the feelings of empathy that one Black person has for another due to shared interests, perceptions, and experiences? The way in which she expressed her concern for Black patients who feel uncomfortable being nursed by people so obviously different from themselves, suggests the following to be true:

   a) Black people feel uncomfortable being nursed by White nurses whether Finnish or English; [85]

---

[84] *The Independent*, 28th November 1996

[85] There is a widespread belief among multi-racialists and multi-culturalists that it is understandable for the members of minority ethnic communities to prefer to confide in and be cared for by members of their own community, i.e. by those who are *sensitive to their cultural needs*. For example, an

b) White people, including English and Finns, feel uncomfortable being nursed by Black nurses;

c) the English do not feel uncomfortable being nursed by Finns – fellow Whites;

The logic of Diane Abbott's argument is that both White and Black people, regard race and colour as being an important factor in determining whom they feel comfortable with.

2. The *Independent* article mentioned that Marc Wadsworth, executive member of the Anti-Racist Alliance, is himself half-Finnish. – *he pointed out, that the present Miss Finland, Lola Odusoga, is Black, of Nigerian and Finnish descent. "She's a Black Finn like me", he said.*[86] Why should Marc Wadsworth be described as half Finnish, and why is it common for social-liberals to boast that they are, for example, one quarter Irish or half Spanish? They cannot have it both ways, either nationality is determined by parentage or it is determined by place of birth and residence. If, as liberals would have us believe, nationality is determined by where you were born or where you live, it is nonsensical to claim to be half one nationality and half another. Such statements only make sense if there is an underlying belief that nationality is, at least in part, *in the blood*. In a similar way, the liberal craze for nations apologising for past wrongs is recognition of the existence of a nation as a group of people linked by kinship and sharing a common identity from generation to generation.

3. Marc Wadsworth's words, *"She's a Black Finn like me"*, – *Black, of Nigerian and Finnish descent,* imply that it is self-evident that her Finnish parent is White and her Nigerian parent is Black. But the point to be made is that if Lola Odusoga is part White and part Black, why should she be described as Black and not as White?

---

advertisement in *The Voice*, 28th April 1997: *African-Caribbean Development Worker... Applicants should have groupwork experience and good knowledge of living and working with the African-Caribbean community. They should have the ability to support and communicate effectively with African-Caribbean women, and be sensitive to individual cultural needs. The post is reserved for an African-Caribbean woman...*
Other advertisements of a similar kind in the same edition include:
Community Development Co-ordinator for African Caribbean Elders Organisations... The successful candidate will have· – at least two years experience of working within the African-Caribbean community with knowledge of the needs of this client group.
All well and good but have you ever seen an advertisement that mentions the English community and English cultural needs?
[86] *The Independent* 29th November 1996

131

4. Marc Wadsworth criticised Diane Abbott, but not in the hostile way used by members of the Anti-Racist Alliance when challenging those they regard as racists. He was *sympathetic* with Ms Abbott's comments, but they were based on ignorance. *In a Borough like Hackney, black people are disproportionately unemployed, and they are discriminated against in the NHS. But to attack people for having blue eyes and blonde hair is nonsense and ill-informed. It is the kind of stereotyping in a way that Diane would strongly oppose if a white person applied it to a black person.*[87] He did not go on to attack *Diane* for being a racist but instead defended Finns by saying that because of the treatment they had received from their neighbours throughout their history they would understand the sense of exclusion and difference felt by Black people and were potential allies not enemies. This stance makes it possible for someone who is half Black and half Finnish to be 100% a victim.

5. Diane Abbott thinks Finns unsuited to multi-cultural Hackney but if Hackney is multi-cultural why should Finns be denied the pleasure of living there? Surely, Finns can be as much a part of *vibrant* Hackney as Black people.

The hostility shown by liberals to the comments of Robert Henderson and Matthew Engel, contrasts with the muted response to the comments of Diane Abbott and Bernie Grant. The matter raises the tangled issue of how words like *foreigner, ethnicity, nationality, race* and *racism* are defined.

Ethnicity and Race

Over the years there has been a deliberate and largely successful attempt to link nationalism with racism. The purpose is clearly ideological and political. Race has been used as a political cosh, a weapon with which to intimidate people and beat opponents into submission. The success of the strategy has been such that multi-culturalists, and those who use multi-culturalism as a cover for advancing their own ethnic interests, have been given the freedom to invent, define and redefine the terms that form part of their perceptual and ethical landscape; a virtual reality in which they make and enforce the rules. To challenge that *reality* is to risk provoking the wrath of its inhabitants and invite a barrage of accusations and abuse. Despite the risks, an increasing number of people are willing to openly deny the validity of the liberal model and start pulling it apart. Part of that process of deconstruction involves defining terms in a way that frees them from liberal distortions.

---

[87] *The Independent* 29th November 1996

Native

It is enough to be born in a place to be a native of that place. A child born in Rhode Island is a native of Rhode Island and a native of North America. Being a native says nothing about citizenship or nationality.

For a long period *native* was used in a way that implied much more than just birth. It was used as a term for a person, or group of people, who belonged naturally to a place, and it is meant in that way in the phrase, *The natives are friendly*. Those who were called natives, were in fact indigenous peoples, but in a time when there was comparatively little movement of population, native meant much the same as indigenous.

Indigenous

Indigenous is a term that is increasingly used as an alternative to native because it means more than just being born in a place. Indigenous means originating or produced or occurring naturally in a country; not imported.

Problems arise here with a definition of *naturally* but commonsense tells us that a person born in a country during a visit there by his or her mother, can be said to be native to that place but not indigenous. If a Japanese woman gives birth to a child while on a visit to China, that child is, in the true sense of the word, a native of China but on returning to Japan the child would be considered to be an indigenous inhabitant of Japan.

There are many examples of organisms that have moved from one place to another and have lived in their new surroundings for many generations but are not considered to be indigenous to their new home. Sometimes the newcomers are eventually regarded as indigenous in the same way that the oak tree is considered to be indigenous to the British Isles despite it at one time being a newcomer or foreign. For something or someone to be regarded as indigenous, it is necessary for it or them to have had many generations of their ancestors living in that place and to have become assimilated into the environment to such an extent that they are perceived as being a natural part of it. It is a matter of perception and judgement. North American Indians regard themselves as indigenous to North America and do not think of European and African settlers, and their descendants, as indigenous. North American Indians have for many years been labelled as *Native Americans* but recently they have been deemed to be aboriginal. This despite evidence that they were not the first people to live in North America.

Aborigine

An aborigine is an original or indigenous inhabitant of a country or place. Aboriginal implies a belonging that goes beyond indigenous. An aboriginal people have lived in their homeland *since the beginning of time*; there is no record of

133

earlier inhabitants. Aborigine is the name by which the aboriginal people of Australia are known to outsiders.

The terms indigenous and aboriginal are not ones that liberals apply to Europeans because they are deemed to be an assortment of immigrants with no valid claim to a national identity and national homeland. Non-Europeans are treated less harshly. Their creation mythologies, folk-traditions, and sense of place and belonging are accorded due reverence. When their real history includes instances of migration, colonisation, imperialism, slavery, or genocide, there is a reluctance to draw attention to it. Knowledge of such shortcomings is generally ignored or even suppressed, so as not to cause offence. This difference in approach enables liberals to deny preferential treatment to Europeans living in Europe but makes it possible to grant special land rights and other privileges to certain non-European aboriginal nations. Thus, for example, North American Indian tribes are deemed to have communal land rights but the English are not.

Foreigner

A foreigner is a person from a foreign country; an outsider; a stranger. A foreigner can be a native of a place but not indigenous to it.

Ethnic

Ethnic means relating to or characteristic of a group of humans who have racial, cultural, linguistic, and certain other traits in common. In other words an ethnic group is the same as a national group. *Ethnic* is from the Greek *ethnos* meaning *race* or *nation*. In the past, the words *race* and *nation* where so closely linked as to be interchangeable. They have in common the notion of a common ancestry. Nation has the added dimension of common culture.

That there is little difference between an ethnic group and a nation is evident from the fact that national names and ethnic names are generally the same. For example, Somalis, Irish and Turks are all national and ethnic groups. *Afro-Caribbean*, *Asian* or *White European* are not strictly ethnic groups though the terms are often used as ethnic categories in UK local and central government monitoring schemes.

Liberals have linked nationalism almost exclusively with the Nazis and have blamed nationalists for wars and just about every ill that afflicts mankind. This demonisation posed difficulties for multi-culturalists when during the period of post WWII decolonisation and migration they wanted to recognize and accommodate the needs and interests of non-European nations. Even liberals could see that it was hypocritical to lecture Europeans about the evils of nationalism while campaigning for the rights and interests of non-European nations. Their solution was to substitute *ethnic group* for *nation*. As a result, nationalism is bad but ethnisism is good; Europeans are nationalists but others are ethnisists; nations are a thing of the past but ethnic groups and their rich vibrant cultures are to be preserved and promoted. To be a member of an ethnic group is to have rights and a proper concern for communal interests, survival, culture, history, identity and wellbeing. In addition to all those things, to be a member of an ethnic group is to be a victim. To add weight to the image of victim status, ethnic groups are invariably called *ethnic minorities*. This helps promote the image of a small oppressed group struggling against the might of a majority; the weak against the strong; good against evil. But should the Chinese living in England really be considered to be members of an ethnic minority when there are more than one billion Chinese but fewer than forty million English. Who are the colonisers, who the ethnic minority, who the victims?

Unfortunately, the English and other European nations are not deemed worthy of an ethnic identity, even as an *ethnic majority*. It seems that the *ethnic* label is reserved for national groups that are foreign to the country in which they live. Instead of having the group rights and privileges of ethnic minorities, Europeans have only individual civic rights.

The English and other Europeans are not only denied recognition as ethnic groups but also as communities. The reason is clearly that ethnic groups and communities are exclusive, something forbidden to Europeans. Yet liberals freely refer to ethnic groups as communities. For example, in the UK we have, among others, the Bengali community, the Sikh community, the Irish community. In addition to their own exclusive ethnic communal identity, members of these groups in England are also deemed to have an inclusive English identity. Thus they are English but, for example, of Bengali *origin* or Irish *descent* or Jamaican *born* or of Iranian *ancestry*. The intention is to make outsiders feel like insiders but it is a forlorn hope because playing with words will not, for example, prevent a Bangladeshi living in England from feeling an outsider. The aggressiveness of multi-culturalists in their assertion that people with a hyphenated identity are as English as anyone else and naturally belong in England, is a sure sign that they do not. Members of the Bengali community are no more likely to feel part of the English community than the English are to feel part of the Bengali community. Each has a distinct and separate identity.

The many years of propaganda and playing with language has not altered the fact that the English are ethnically English, belong to the English community, are of English origin, English descent and English ancestry. The English are not a hyphenated nation.

The constant assertion of the *right* of settlers in England to their own ethnic identity and a non-ethnic English identity gives the settlers something at the expense of the English, whose communal identity is denied. Englishness is made something without substance – a mere geographical identity. The problem for multi-culturalists is that the vast majority of settlers in England know that the

135

English are a nation – an ethnic group – and the settlers know that they are not part of the English nation, do not want to be English, and feel embarrassed by those liberal Ladies Bountiful who believe they have the power to bestow an English identity on anyone they wish.

There are a few outsiders who assert in an aggressive and unpleasant way that they are English. "I am English and you had better accept me and others like me as English or there will be trouble."[88] Hectoring of that kind only serves to demonstrate that outsiders are often unable to judge the fine distinctions between what the English regard as acceptable and unacceptable behaviour. Only an outsider would make such a crass demand of the English community, which regards such behaviour as ill mannered and offensive, as would any other community.

Thanks to liberals and their use of *ethnic* we also have *ethnie, ethnisism* and *ethnicity* in place of more easily understood words. *Ethnie* (ethnic community) means *nation; ethnisism* is difficult to distinguish from *nationalism; ethnicity* means the same as *nationality*. This ploy of tinkering with our language has led to the affliction of *deconstructionalism*, a sort of cultural revolution in which liberal Red Guards have, among other things, set about purging language (especially English) of words and expressions that promote *unacceptable values and perceptions*. This is not done in the interests of seeking neutrality but to impose liberal values and perceptions in place of those they despise. They disfigure the English language in an attempt to make it ideologically correct. Those responsible are often the very same people who tell us that it is foolish and reactionary to try to control the use of language – it will take us wherever it goes. It seems that the simple, no nonsense, pithy nature of English is too sharp and direct for them. Instead, they prefer foreign root words which have a wooliness that enables them to fit into a woolly frame of mind. Clearly, nothing must be left for the English to call their own.

The true feelings of liberals and others for the English can be found in the disparaging clichés they use, such as, *The English are a bastard race* or *The English are a nation of immigrants*. Their purpose is to create the impression that the English are merely a hotchpotch of unrelated immigrant groups who live in England, and that a few more will make no difference. That propaganda is clearly having some success when we have simple-minded people saying, "There is always room for one more potato in the stew." They probably also believe that the camel can always take one more straw.

---

[88] This approach was once taken by Darcus Howe (a Trinidadian) but he now seems to accept that he is not English. Instead he calls himself an Englander, i.e. someone who lives in England, which is a reasonable position to take.

The hatred that some settlers have for the English is combined with the communal self-hatred and guilt of English liberals to produce a steady flow of anti-English propaganda. The English are mostly ignored but they have to be mentioned from time to time for the purpose of maintaining the tarnished image. Among the many insults there is always the allegation of innate English racism. We are all racists and there is no point denying it. The English are not and cannot be victims; they can only be oppressors. Ethnic good – English bad. These attacks are curious because they produce the following logic.

a) The English are inherently racist and responsible for the ills afflicting ethnic minorities.

b) The members of ethnic minorities living in England are English.

c) The members of ethnic minorities are racist and responsible for the ills afflicting ethnic minorities.

Despite the best endeavours of liberals, a real English national identity exists and grows stronger. A low point was reached a few years ago but the unrelenting attack of the liberal storm troopers has helped to bring about a revival. Their constant harping about the hardships suffered by various ethnic groups and their mocking condemnation of the English make it only too clear that the English exist. They are the people who do not qualify as members of the Turkish, Black, Bengali, Irish, or any of the many other ethnic communities that are deemed to have special interests and problems. The leftovers are, in a sense, English by default.

Race

Our natural history museums are a testament to the patience and diligence of those Victorians who enthusiastically classified things. Botanists classified plants; zoologists classified animals; ethnologists classified the human species. In each of those fields of study, a *race* is a sub-group of a *species*. Homo Sapiens are a species, and within it there are races made up of individuals who share a set of common physical characteristics such as hair type, colour of eyes and skin, stature, skull shape, etc. There are three or more races, depending on how sophisticated and subtle the distinction between physical characteristics becomes. The principal races are Caucasoid, Mongoloid, and Negroid.

It should be noted that the classification of humans by race is concerned only with physical characteristics. Apparently some people find such categorisation objectionable but it is difficult to understand why that should be. Perhaps they mistakenly believe that race says something about the worth of a person. Or, is the concept of race unwelcome because it draws attention to the fact that humans are not the same, and their appearance cannot be manipulated by social engineering.

Maybe race is seen as an infringement of human and democratic rights (the right to choose) in the same way that nationality is.

Those who are the most fanatical in claiming that race is unimportant, usually attach the greatest importance to it. They often use the very simplest form of racial classification and see only a Black race and a White race. Unfortunately, this ignores the fact that many of those who are neither Caucasoid or Negroid do not easily fit into the Black – White scheme. This leaves the problem of how to label *the others*.

Although the terms *Black* and *White* are used as synonyms for *Negro* and *Caucasian*, many consider it racist to refer to Mongoloids as, for example, *Yellow*.[89] The term *Oriental* was once used instead of *Mongoloid* but that is also considered to have racist overtones, so *Asian* tends to be used instead even though it is not a good substitute because it involves mixing terms: Blacks and Whites are labelled by appearance while Asians are labelled by place.

Another drawback to using a term such as *Asian* or *African* is that it is not sufficiently specific. It is not helpful to label someone an African when what you mean is Black or Negroid because most North African Arabs do not regard themselves as Black and have a greater sense of identity with Asian Arabs than African Negroes. Neither is it helpful to use the term Asian when you mean an Arab.[90] Those people who live in England and are commonly called Asians usually dislike being called Black and do not think of themselves as being part of *the Black community* even though multi-culturalists and some politicians have tried to impose that label on them so as to create a larger and more powerful political grouping.[91]

Despite the difficulties associated with using the races and sub-races of mankind defined by Victorian ethnologists, they are usually more helpful and precise labels than *Black, White, Asian* or *African,* although this is not to deny that those labels are sometimes useful as a form of shorthand. By far the most helpful and informative label for a person is national identity, which says far more about them

---

[89] It is curious that *Mongoloid, Mongol, Negroid* and *Negro* are thought by some to be offensive but no objection is made to *Caucasoid* and *Caucasian*. David Frith, the editor of *Wisden Cricket Monthly*, felt it necessary, presumably due to complaints, to apologise for using the word *Negro* in an article he published. If *Negro* was acceptable to Malcolm X it should be acceptable to liberals and everyone else, and if not, frankly that is their problem.

[90] *Arab* is an abbreviation of *Arabic*. An Arab is an inhabitant of Arabia or a person related by descent to an inhabitant. Arabic is also the language of the Arabs. Arabic is a Semitic language and Arabs are Semites. A Semite is a member of the Semitic language group.

[91] Most Asians from the Indian sub-continent who live in the UK refer to themselves as Asian, and then within that category they have their national identity. They seem happy with the terminology because for the most part they wish to retain their separate identities. Why, for example, would Sikhs or Bangladeshis who have rich national cultures wish to give up their national identities in order to adopt a crude racial identity?

than race, place or colour. For example, the English, Irish, Scots and Welsh are all nations but each of them fits into the categories White, European, and Caucasian. To say someone is English is more informative than to say they live in England.

One of the many dilemmas faced by liberals is that on the one hand they use race as a political weapon but on the other they wish to downplay the importance of race and even deny its existence. In an attempt to get over the difficulty, their ideologues have resorted to the following argument.

1. The term race "has dubious descriptive value" because there has "always been so much interbreeding between human populations" and "the distribution of hereditary physical traits does not follow clear boundaries".[92] In other words, the boundaries are so blurred that it is no longer possible to distinguish one race from another.

2. Although we know the term race is of dubious descriptive value, it is nonetheless a concept that exists and it affects the perceptions and behaviour of the general population. In other words, it is of sociological importance even though it does not exist.

Are racial boundaries so indistinct that we are unable to distinguish Caucasoid, Mongoloid, and Negroid? The same argument about the lack of clear boundaries can be applied to Black and White but that does not stop liberals using them.

Despite the argument that the term race has dubious descriptive value because of the lack of clear boundaries, multi-culturalists have no problem in distinguishing one group from another when it suits them. For example, if an organization awards grants or advertises a job, and invites applications from Asians or Blacks and I go along and say I am Black I will be told that I am White. If I then say the boundaries between White and Black are so indistinct due to interbreeding that the terms have dubious descriptive value, I think it likely that I would be told I was talking nonsense and my application would be refused, or ignored.

When such advertisements appear, as they often do in the UK, the advertisers should be asked how they define *Asian* or *Black*, or whatever term they use. For example, *The Voice* (*Britain's Best Black Paper*) regularly carries advertisements asking for ethnic minority and Black job candidates. In the edition of 24th February 1997 there were vacancies on a "Production Training Scheme for People from Ethnic Minority Groups". (Should Welsh people apply? Probably not.) Sheffield Health wanted a "Black Health Strategy Co-ordinator" and NACRO wanted a "Black Project Worker". These advertisements, and many like them in every edition, do not indicate that Black people or social-liberals think that *Black* has a dubious descriptive value because there are no clear boundaries. If there are clear boundaries then perhaps they would define them. How Black do you have to

---

[92] Text in quotes is from *Ethnicity and Nationalism*, Thomas H. Eriksen, London, Pluto Press, 1993.

be to get a job reserved for Black people? Perhaps skin colour is not decisive and it could be argued by an applicant that, "I have white skin but one of my grandmothers was Black". If one grandparent is not enough how many are needed? Or would those who determine who is Black disregard skin colour if other physical characteristics indicated Blackness? Perhaps a person with some Negroid characteristics would be accepted as Black even if that person had a white skin. Is it necessary to be black to be Black? The answer seems to be no according to a report in *The Voice*, 22nd September 1997, where, in a short piece on Black talent in Wales, a few well-known people are mentioned including "Ryan (looks white) Giggs". Is this some sort of *outing* borrowed from homosexual groups? If so perhaps we will see references to Malcolm (looked Black) X and Martin Luther (looked Black) King.

An example of physical appearance and ancestry determining group membership is to be found in Australia. If Australian Aborigines are granted land rights on the scale proposed early in 1998, it will be necessary, as with North American Indians, to determine who is an Aborigine. Ancestry is likely to be the formal test but insiders and outsiders will judge informally on the basis of physical appearance. Victorian ethnologists were able to distinguish Australian Aborigines as a race, and it is likely that a modern day assessor will reach a decision in much the same way. Most of us have a mental image of what an Aborigine looks like, and we compare it to what we see.

Black groups use physical characteristics to determine who is and who is not a member and skin colour is obviously one of them, as is indicated by the name they give themselves, i.e. Black. When they are presented with a person of mixed race, who is neither black nor white-skinned, they make fine judgements in deciding whether that person is an insider or an outsider. There are no hard and fast rules when it comes to borderline cases but that does not mean there is no border, or that it cannot be seen, or that it is unimportant.

Another consideration to be borne in mind is that the informal rules for inclusion and exclusion vary from culture to culture. In North America, *Black* is an inclusive identity in that the boundaries are widely drawn. The situation is different in sub-Saharan Africa where many people who are labelled Black in the US would be excluded from that identity because they are not black enough. When the vast majority of the population is Black there is no political advantage to be gained from diluting the boundaries, as the mixed race *coloured* citizens of South Africa know only too well. When everyone in a society is the same race, it ceases to be an important issue within that society. The more people look alike, the more important cultural differences become.

An example of blurred boundaries of a different sort can be found in languages. English is a Germanic language but it contains many words from Latin, Greek and other languages. Are we to believe that references to the English language are of dubious descriptive value and the English language does not exist merely because it is not *pure*?

The second stage of the argument – *we know that race is meaningless but others attach importance to it* – denies the fact that it is social-liberals and Black political activists who are obsessed by race and instead puts the blame for that obsession on the wider population. It is those who argue that race is unimportant who are the most fanatical about introducing it into just about every sociological and political issue. At the root of their paranoia and anguish is an unwillingness to accept that in appropriate circumstances all humans use physical appearance as a boundary marker. They cannot understand that, for example, Swedes do not exclude Black and Asian people from the Swedish community because they are Black or Asian but because they are not Swedes. The Swedes also exclude the English, as indeed do the Japanese and Kikuyu communities, but that is not due to racism. Race is just one of very many characteristics that help distinguish an insider from an outsider.

Over many hundreds of thousand years of human existence, the process of natural selection has enabled us to instinctively distinguish an insider from an outsider. For obvious reasons there has been an evolutionary advantage in being able to distinguish at a distance a likely friend from a possible foe.[93] We do this by sight and sound, and over thousands of generations our species has learnt to recognise many subtle signs in the appearance and language of someone we meet for the first time. Hence a reply to the demand, *Who goes there?* gives many clues. We listen and look for the obvious clues first and compare them with a stereotypical image of the communal norm. The closer the match between the two the more likely it is the person is an insider.

Some distinguishing characteristics are due to the influence of culture, some are innate, e.g. facial features. Racial characteristics are important because they provide information that can be easily seen at a distance. When there is an obvious difference, such as skin pigmentation, between groups there is little need to look further. This can give rise to the situation where through lack of need and practice, outsiders find it more difficult than insiders to distinguish one insider from another. With closer and longer contact it becomes easier for the members of each group to improve their recognition skills. It can be argued that appearance should not matter but it does and it is often an important factor in being accepted into a social class, a caste, or a nation.

If I were to visit Nigeria I would be perceived and treated as a foreigner, someone who does not belong there. If I lived there for fifty years I would still be a foreigner. If I had a tantrum and accused the people I was living amongst of being racists they would, rightly, tell me where to go and regard me as even more of an

---

[93] This reasoning is applied to sports teams who wear some form of team uniform so that they can be identified by insiders and outsiders.

outsider than before. As a guest in their homeland, I would be expected to behave like a guest and not make demands or issue threats.

A Libyan in Nigeria would also be seen as a foreigner but if, as is probable, he were a Moslem and he visited the part of Nigeria that is mainly Moslem he would be seen as less foreign than me because his appearance and his culture would almost certainly be seen as less different from that of the local community than would mine. This does not mean that I would necessarily be made unwelcome but it would mean that I would be more obviously a foreigner. Despite the great physical differences, I might be treated far better than a person from a neighbouring community who was in nearly every respect very much like the hosts. The reason being that outsiders who are nearby and large in number are often seen as a greater threat than those who are very different but live far away.

Another way of tackling the liberal rejection of the concept of race is to point out that, as with many other forms of categorisation, it is based on *ideal types*. Even if racial ideal types did not exist in reality they could still serve as a standard by which to categorise people, which is something the human brain does well and as a matter of routine. We are able to draw together and compare a complex mix of physical characteristics in order to determine if a stranger is or is not a member of a kindred group. In other words, we can detect family, and wider kinship resemblances. Where natural physical differences are slight, cultural differences help recognition. Some cultural attributes are deliberately cultivated for just that purpose.

Racial classifications are based on physical characteristics, many of which are obvious to one and all. Physical characteristics have served as community boundary markers for many thousands of generations. For liberals to dismiss such discrimination as unnatural or evil or outdated or unimportant or racist is nothing less than nonsense. Even within communities where members look alike, there is a tendency for sub-groups to form and for members of those sub-groups to make their existence known through obvious visual signals, such as clothing, hair-style, tattoos.

Another argument used by liberals for the purpose of showing that race should be of little importance as a boundary marker is that there are greater genetic differences within races than between them and therefore racial classifications are meaningless. Great significance is attached to the suggestion that *only* 6% of a persons genes decide the various physical characteristics that are used to determine race. The response that comes to mind is, so what does that prove? What is important is the number and type of observable significant differences and not the percentage of genes producing those differences. The figure of 6% may well be right but it would not matter if it were 99% or 0·01%. The figure of 6% is used in a way that suggests it is a small and almost insignificant percentage. But, what are we to make of the information that there is a 7% genetic difference between humans and chimpanzees.[94] If someone argued that classification by species is meaningless because there is only a 7% genetic difference between some species, we would think they had missed the point. It does not matter how many similarities and differences there are between groups, what matters is the instinctive and cultural importance attached to those similarities and differences.

Yet another of the arguments frequently used by liberals, and one that contradicts much else that they say, is that an infusion of fresh racial blood is needed from time to time in order to widen the gene pool and keep a race, nation, or society vital. This despite the claim that the inhabitants of England are a mongrel population with, presumably, an already wide gene pool which is not in need of *new* genes. An example of the advocacy of this liberal theory of genetic injection was to be seen in *The Independent* of 28th March 1995 where, in an article by Andrew Marr entitled, *Keep the mix salty and strong,* it was argued that *Britain* would be a dreary dump today if it had been left to the Anglo-Saxons[95] [i.e. the English] and that *Britain* has needed regular *floodings* of outsiders to keep it fertile. He advocated that the Hong Kong Chinese should be encouraged to migrate to Britain before the colony was handed back to China to improve Britain's economic performance. This from a Scot who must be aware that most of those who migrate to Britain settle in England. If an influx of immigrants were an aid to improved economic performance, England would be near the top of the economic league having been subject to massive immigration during the past forty years.

It is certain that if the theory of genetic diversification were applied in a different way it would be condemned. For example, if it were suggested that Negroes needed some Caucasian genes to improve their genetic inheritance or that Zulus would benefit from interbreeding with Afrikaners, such remarks would be condemned as outrageous and racist but the suggestion that the English need an injection of foreign genes is considered by some to be liberal, progressive and acceptable. The Japanese have done very well considering their alleged genetic handicap but perhaps they would do even better if they were to invite large numbers of Jamaicans, Bangladeshis, Irish, Somalis and many others to their country. It has become apparent over the years that the Japanese regard such immigration policies as foolish and view multi-culturalism as something to be avoided at all costs.

---

[94] The estimated percentage difference is in a constant state of flux and may well be much less than 7%. What matters is that an apparently small difference can have a very great effect.

[95] Being rude about Anglo-Saxons is always good sport and never considered racist. Jacques Delors, and others, were able to condemn the Anglo-Saxons as being responsible for the trouble the European monetary system got into but when, during that period, Nicholas Ridley suggested that there was a danger of the Germans dominating Europe he was severely criticised for being anti-German and he eventually resigned.

In summary, most communities make lone strangers welcome if for no other reason than that strangers can be a source of information and satisfy a natural curiosity about strange people and places. In nearly all cultures it is a moral imperative to show hospitality to strangers. A few strangers can be a benefit but communities in all parts of the world view a large number of strangers within the communal boundary as a physical and cultural threat.

Hostility is directed against foreigners because they pose a threat, and race is just one factor in what it is to be foreign. The more foreigners there are, the greater the perceived threat and the greater the hostility. It is not race in itself that promotes hostility and exclusion; it is the fact of being an outsider. The Zulus, and other African nations, did not fight European settlers because they were White but because they were outsiders who were moving into the communal territory of the Zulu nation and in doing so posed a threat. It was easy for Zulus to identify their enemy by very many characteristics including the colour of their skin but it did not make the Zulus racists. Likewise, North American Indians fought against the *pale-faces*. Race was not the cause of these conflicts it was merely one means of identifying intruders. If those who use race to explain every ill and misfortune would understand this simple fact, they could perhaps escape from their one-track racist reasoning process.

Although many of those who use race for political ends understand only too well that all communities discriminate, they are unwilling to give up racial politics and the powerful weapons it gives them. Those weapons, are the pointing finger that says *you are a racist*, and the cosh that punishes offenders. Neither of them poses any threat to the user but both render the enemy helpless. It causes division in enemy ranks and suppresses opposition to the dismantling of national institutions and national identity. Those who use the pointing finger and the cosh are unable to abandon racial politics because it is all they have. Their lack of options is a problem they are going to have to face because the bludgeoning of dissidents has gone on for so long and so freely that the weapon is losing its effectiveness. There are more and more English who are not afraid to speak out. Fear is the most powerful enemy but that evaporates when the ideological tyrants are seen for what they are, bullies who lack substance. We are not confronted by a Grendal but another kind of monster, a spoilt child with a big stick.

Racism and Racist

Some definitions of racism:

1. Racism is the belief that human attributes other that physical characteristics are linked to race and that a particular race is superior to or inferior to another race.

2. Racism is discrimination or prejudice based on race and might take the form of aggressive or abusive behaviour towards members of another race.

3. Racism in general terms consists of conduct or words or practices which advantage or disadvantage people because of their colour, culture or ethnic origin. (A definition given in *The Lawrence Report, 1999*.) The inclusion of 'culture' and 'ethnic origin' in this definition makes it possible to be a racist even when the issue of race is irrelevant to the offending conduct or words or practices.

4. Racism is ill feeling or hatred between races. – *racism/racialism–racist/racialist.*

5. Racism is the belief that race is the most important factor in human identity. Racists are people who above all else define themselves, and others, in terms of race. There are as many types of racist as there are perceived races, and that includes White racists and Black racists. This last definition of racism reflects a form of racism that is largely ignored but often underlies all other forms of racism.

Racism in all its forms is based on the belief that the boundaries between races are of profound importance. Racial boundaries are now usually drawn more widely than they once were. For example, only forty or so years ago it was common for people to refer to the English, Irish, Scottish, and Welsh races. That was probably a carry over from the early part of the twentieth century, when the attempt to make finer and more sophisticated physical distinctions between groups had been taken to extremes. Few are now willing to argue that the English, Irish, Scottish, and Welsh can be distinguished as separate races.

During the second half of the twentieth century race came to mean little more than skin colour. The primary reason was that Black-Americans needed to forge a common political identity. They had lost their national identities and saw race as a unifying factor that gave them not only a political identity but also the foundations of a new cultural identity. What Black-Americans call Black culture is in reality a Black-American culture with which Negroes in Africa have only a tenuous connection. *Blackness* is probably of far greater importance to Negroes in the US than it is to Negroes in Africa, who still have a national or tribal culture, language and identity. Thus, for the Kikuyu, their national identity is more important to them than being Black or African.

Perhaps in response to the building of a Black identity, many Caucasian-Americans adopted a White-American identity. Caucasians in Europe were less inclined to do that because, like Negroes in Africa, they had a national identity that was of more relevance to them than a racial identity. Thus, being English is more important than being White. However, the positions of English and Ibo are not as similar as they might be because there are very few Europeans in Nigeria and race, in the crude sense of Black and White, is not an important factor in everyday life. Instead, greater importance is attached to the distinction between Ibo, Yoruba, Hausa and the other nations within the Nigerian state.

For the English, racial identity has become more important than it was, mostly because it has been forced on them. In England, unlike Nigeria, there has been a large inflow of people who are racially different from the indigenous population. Many of the outsiders emphasise the racial difference by defining themselves in racial rather than national terms. They also pursue a political agenda that promotes racial identities and focuses almost exclusively on demanding and negotiating rights for racial groups. This politicisation of race, and the moral perspective that goes with it – White oppressors, Black victims, Asian neutrality – breeds resentment and conflict. After several decades of liberals promoting racial politics, and continually telling the English they have a White racial identity, it is hardly surprising that a growing number of English people see race as an important part of their identity. This tendency is already noticeable among the young English who, having been through an education system that denies their national identity, have adopted the only identity open to them – White. The likely outcome is that they will believe they have more in common with Irish, Scots, Welsh, and other Europeans throughout the world than with the Black and Asian people they see around them. In doing that they would be no different from Black people in England who feel a greater affinity with other Black people – especially Black-Americans – than with the English.

Those liberals who promote a racial rather than a national identity must live with the consequences. A racial identity, coupled with the belief that politics is a battle between races, encourages discrimination or prejudice based on race, which takes the form of aggressive, or abusive behaviour towards members of another race. The liberal politics of race and ethnicity is encouraging the very thing that they claim to be fighting against.

Racists have a view of the world that is similar in many ways to the outlook of genderists, Marxists, nationalists and statists.

For feminists and masculinists, gender is all-important; nationality, race and social class are all a long way behind. Feminists are concerned with women's history, achievements, misfortunes, and the like. They promote the interests of women, and gender is the most important part of their identity. Their rallying call is oppression. Social evolution is seen as a power struggle between men and women. Men acquired privileges through the oppression of women. Women are struggling to win equality of rights and opportunities. Not all feminists are women but men who call themselves feminists are often scorned for being patronising outsiders. Not all feminists think women to be superior to men but many of them do. For them, the most important single part of a person's identity is their gender.

Marxists see everywhere class conflict and economic exploitation. The working class has been exploited, and the ruling class has benefited from that exploitation. Marxists believe in the idea of *progress*. Evolution has a goal; the future will bring the inevitable collapse of capitalism and put us on the road to communism. (Even the most fervent of today's Marxists have little faith in the inevitability of communism.) Marxists dislike the notion of nations (a capitalist plot / false consciousness) and instead believe that people throughout the world are united by class interests. Workers of the world unite! The most important single part of a person's identity is their social class. Curiously, it is usually the most middle-class of Marxists who claim to believe in the superiority of the working class. That superiority does not belong to the working class as it is but how it would be in a Marxist society where the working class has become middle class.

Nationalists are concerned with communal identity and the wellbeing and survival of their nation, which is the largest and most enduring community to which they and their fellows belong. The mission of a nationalist is to keep alive the national history and ensure that the symbols of national identity are passed from generation to generation. Gender and social class are important but they are contained within a communal identity that unites people and enables them to work together for the communal good. Race is but one of very many communal boundary markers.

Statists put the interests of the state above the interests of any gender, class, nation or race. Statists demand loyalty to the state, a political organisation with defined geographical boundaries. The state is deemed to have sovereign powers, not its citizens. Statists seek an atomised society in which individual citizens, of whatever race, gender, class, or nationality, are powerless before the might of the state. Liberal statists set about creating a fragmented society and then use it to justify the existence of a liberal governing elite which acts as arbitrator between competing groups; multi-cultural societies serve just that purpose. Liberals use various imaginative social contract theories to justify the power of the state over its citizens but totalitarians are more honest in laying state power bare; citizens obey laws and accept the authority of the state because they are punished if they do not. The most important single part of a person's identity is their citizenship. Statists almost always believe that the institutions and way of life promoted by their own state are superior to those found in other states. Most statists think the world would be a better place if all states were modelled on theirs.

Racists see history in terms of racial groups, racial achievement and racial misfortunes. Race is central to their identity and the way they view others. Racial groups are believed to be the widest groups with which individuals can identify. Race is a boundary marker that is able to unite people in a relationship of empathy and co-operation. Racists not only see race as central to their identity but also central to their politics, which is generally conducted in terms of racial rights and interests. Their aim is to promote the identity and interests of their own race. They use race as a political power base and usually define race in the simplest of terms, namely skin colour. Despite the simplicity of the definition, racists usually attach more than physical characteristics to race. There is almost always a belief in a racial culture (Black-culture/White-culture) and racial behavioural and intellectual characteristics.

147

Some racists are separatists, who do not necessarily believe that one race is superior to another but are concerned to preserve racial identities and characteristics.[96] Others are supremacists. Some White supremacists believe that evolution is a process of natural selection in which Whites have risen to the top by virtue of their natural superiority. Evidence for White superiority is said to be found in scientific, technological, engineering and cultural achievements. White racists usually treat persons of mixed race as outsiders.

According to some Black supremacists, human evolution began and will end with all humans being Black. White people are seen as a freak of nature who have upset the natural order, but in doing so they have ensured their own extinction. All knowledge and civilisations have their roots in Africa and therefore Black people are owed credit and respect for the achievements of mankind. The success of Whites has been built on the achievements of Blacks and the exploitation of Blacks by Whites. By an historical accident (industrialisation) White people gained power over Black people and have continued to exploit and oppress them ever since. The misfortunes of Black people are deemed not to be due to any fault of their own but to the actions of White people. Black racists usually treat people of mixed race as outsiders unless it is politically convenient to include them, which it usually is when Black people are in a minority.

There is a natural and universal reluctance on the part of all communities to admit to their territory large numbers of outsiders. We should resist the propaganda of those who try to confuse this natural and necessary condition of community with hatred founded on race. A general rule applicable in all parts of the world is that the greater the number of outsiders who penetrate communal territorial boundaries and the more different they are from insiders, the greater the hostility and resistance to their intrusion. To put it the other way round, the fewer the number of outsiders, and the more easily and unobtrusively they fit into the host society, the less resentment and hostility they will attract. A few thousand French people living permanently in Germany would not be considered a threat but five million would be considered an invasion. Likewise, if a large number of Germans migrated to France the French would not be pleased. The point at which the size of a foreign population becomes unacceptable is impossible to say but it is certain that race plays a significant part in determining how noticeable the outsiders are and how different they are perceived to be.

---

[96] Many people find any form of separatism extremely offensive but it is difficult to understand the moral argument for believing that wanting to keep races separate is bad but wanting to mix them up is good.

African communities behave no differently to those in Europe. George Orr, a senior official at the South African ministry of home affairs, has been quoted as saying, *Every year more and more come in. One of the troubles is that most of the illegals are unskilled, and they are competition for South Africans. They utilise health, education and housing facilities which are in short supply. And according to the police they often turn to crime.* In the same article, it was reported that 180,713 illegal aliens were repatriated during 1996 and 41,000 were sent home in the first three months of 1997. Despite the attempts of the state to reduce the flow of Black immigrants into a predominantly Black South Africa there are Black citizens who feel strongly enough about the matter to demonstrate their opposition. *Hundreds of street vendors went on the rampage in central Johannesburg last week smashing windows and looting shops to protest against the "invasion" of foreigners.*[97]

In order to absolve Black people from the charge of practising racism and being racist, the terms are sometimes defined by liberals in a way that involves *differential power*. In simple terms it means that racism is a consequence of one race having power over another race. Racism is seen as a vice of the rich and powerful who exploit the poor and powerless. The purpose is clearly the racist one of suggesting that only Caucasians are racist because, it is alleged, they have power over other races and use it to exploit them. The oppressed (i.e. the rest) cannot be racist because they are the weaker party. If a rich middle-class Black or Asian businessman discriminates against and refuses to employ poor working-class Whites, he is not being racist because in the overall scheme of things his race is being discriminated against and exploited by Whites. Poor Whites are not seen as individuals or as members of a class or part of a nation but as members of the White race, and one way or another they are deemed to benefit from that.

Such arguments lack logic or merit but they enable liberals and Black politicians to take the stance that Black people cannot be racist because they are at the bottom of the heap and there is nobody below them to oppress. This approach appeals to the liberal mindset and encourages their one-way view of racism. They are sometimes prepared to concede that in exceptional circumstances Black people can be racist but they give their position away when they call it *reverse racism* or *reverse discrimination*. To use different terms for the same act according to the race of the accused is plain and simple racism. The implication is that only Whites discriminate against outsiders, yet anyone with even a slight knowledge of African and Asian politics will know that claim to be untrue.

Evidence for discrimination and the empathy that exists between members of a community is to be found in the way money for charitable causes is raised and distributed. National communities indigenous to Great Britain tend to give to

---

[97] Quotations in this paragraph are from *The Sunday Telegraph*, 17th August 1997

causes that benefit those defined only by need not nationality.[98] This approach to charity is based on habitual behaviour that lives on from a time when the indigenous communities of the UK saw the benefit of joining together and distributing the proceeds of charity in an equitable manner among themselves according to need. Foreign national communities in Britain have a similar attitude to communal self-help, and it is an indication of their separate communal identity and loyalty that a high proportion of their charitable donations are to charities that benefit members of their own national community, whether they are in Britain or their national homeland. However reasonable and understandable are the arguments given to justify such discrimination, it is nonetheless discrimination and if it were done by the English it would be condemned as racist.[99]

Virtually any expression of communal sentiment by the English is considered racist. The double standard has become so ingrained that it passes largely unnoticed. The following is an example.

> An Englishman laments that an English folk festival is becoming less and less English because Blacks and Asians are increasingly becoming involved in it. He recalls the days when the performers and audience were all English and the atmosphere was relaxed and comfortable. Being surrounded by English people gave a special feeling to the event but with the influx of Blacks into the area that had been lost. He suggests that the festival be moved to an area where there is a strong English community so that the original atmosphere can be recreated.

It is highly likely that liberals would regard a person such as that, and the sentiments expressed as being racist. The views would be thought unsuitable for broadcast, except perhaps as a prelude to an attack on the person and his outlook. But consider the situation with the roles reversed, as happened on the *Today* programme, BBC Radio 4, 23rd August 1997.

> A Black man laments that the Notting Hill carnival is losing its atmosphere and ceasing to be an exclusively Caribbean cultural event. In the early years, being surrounded by Black people gave a special feeling; an ease that could otherwise only be felt in the Caribbean and Africa. That was being lost due to the increasing involvement of Whites and Asians in the carnival and the movement of trendy White liberals into the area. He suggested that the carnival be moved to nearby Brent where there is a strong Black community.

---

[98] There are disaster appeals that raise very large sums of money to help people in foreign countries but the recipients are selected on the basis of need not nationality or race.

[99] A look at a directory of grant-giving trusts will reveal that many charities and trusts have the aim of helping particular foreign national communities in Great Britain and abroad. None, as far as is known, raise money specifically for groups of needy English people.

The issue and the concern felt were presented in a sympathetic way and there was no hint of a suggestion that the person or sentiments were racist. How could they be racist when expressed by a Black person?

Another example of racial discrimination is revealed in fertility treatment and the donation and use of eggs and sperm. A White couple are likely to want a White donor and a Black couple are likely to want a Black donor. Advertisements in Black newspapers ask for female Black donors because there is a shortage of Black eggs. Such advertisements are not considered racist despite the clear discrimination on the basis of race. This is not to suggest that there is anything unnatural or harmful in what is an entirely understandable and justified practice. The point is that it is clearly discriminatory and it suggests that in matters relating to identity and inclusion, race is as important for Blacks as it is for Whites. It reflects the fact that when couples specify the physical characteristics of a sperm or egg donor, they almost always choose those characteristics that are likely to produce a child which looks as if it could be their natural child and part of their community. A White child brought up by Black foster parents in a Black neighbourhood is as likely to feel out of place as a Black child brought up by White foster parents in a White neighbourhood. In a mixed-race society, race is an important factor in an individual's identity and it is foolish to pretend that it is not.

Racism and Immigration

In the first few months of 1983 the Nigerian government carried out a mass expulsion of foreign workers who had entered the state during the oil boom. In an announcement during January 1983 it was made clear that all those who failed to leave the country as ordered would be repatriated, and their names put on a stop list to ensure that they did not return. All companies illegally employing foreigners were threatened with severe penalties under the law. The main relevant law being the 1963 Immigration Act which made illegal the employment of non-Nigerians in the private sector without the written consent of the Director of Immigration. By April 1983 2,200,000 foreigners had been repatriated.

In the Indian state of Assam in January 1983 it was announced by the Chief Minister, Hiteswar Saikia, that the construction of a fence along the Indian border with Bangladesh would be resumed. The Indian Government had decided to construct the fence in order to prevent the migration of Bangladeshis into India. Between 1961 and 1971 about one million Bengalis had crossed the border and the government believed that the latest wave of migration had contributed to the outbreak of serious communal violence in Assam. An Assam Movement gained wide popular support for its demand that the aliens be detected, disenfranchised and deported.

In 1985, a representative of the Chakma tribe, brought to the attention of the UN Human Rights Sub-commission that the Bangladeshi armed forces and police were violating the human rights of the Buddhist tribes-people who faced virtual genocide unless they converted to Islam.

In an article by Fergal Keane in *The Sunday Telegraph* (11th May 1997) a pupil at a Middle School in Hong Kong is reported as saying, "We were invaded by the British and we were forced to share our country with other races. Now I feel good again because we are to live with our fellow Chinese in one country," Later in the same article there is mention of a Chinese film about the Opium War in which the British are portrayed as foreign devils.[100]

During March 1999 it was reported that after ethnic clashes in the Indonesian part of Borneo 90 people were dead and 11,000 terrified refugees had fled after being attacked by gangs with swords, spears and poisoned machetes. The perpetrators of the worst violence were the indigenous Dayaks.

> The main object of their anger – and victims in the current violence – are migrants from the overcrowded Madura island, who were encouraged to move under former President Suharto's trans-migration programmes, designed ostensibly in the interests of racial harmony. Though only a tiny minority, the Madurese are fiercely resented for taking jobs on the plantations, logging concessions and gem mines that have severely encroached on Dayak lands. Two years ago several hundred Madurese were massacred by tribesmen.[101]

The examples given above are just a few of the very many similar events that occur every year throughout the world. Clearly there are many nations that wish to protect their culture and their communal territory. It is also evident from the way events are reported that statists think it perfectly proper for states to control immigration into their territory but usually find it abhorrent when nations try to impose similar restrictions. The following widely accepted, long-standing conventions of a state-dominated global system reflect that view.

1. States have the right to defend their territory against invasion and occupation by other states.

2. States shall not interfere in the internal affairs of others states.

3. States have the right to determine who is a citizen, who shall be allowed to enter the territory of the state and under what conditions.

Nationalists believe that nations naturally have the same rights and obligations commonly accorded to states, indeed, states are political structures for securing the rights and interests of nations; that is the justification for their existence. States should be subordinate to nations, and promote their interests. If they fail to do that,

---

[100] Fergal Keane, BBC's Asia Correspondent
[101] *The Daily Telegraph*, 22nd March 1999

nations owe no loyalty to the state and have the right to defend national interests by any appropriate means. Some nations are vigilant in defending their cultural and territorial boundaries, and mount an active defence at an early stage. Others are very lax and complacent, only being roused to action when it is already too late to successfully resist.

In advancing their model of civic society, and denouncing nationalism, liberals promote the idea that all European states are or should be multi-ethnic and multi-racial. It is deemed to be a moral obligation deriving from colonial guilt to rid Western Europe of single-race states. To oppose that crusade is to be a racist – or so liberals tell us.

We must judge the wisdom of mixing many nations together by the results. At the moment, the prospects for the success of this naive experiment do not look good. Where there was community and order there is now ever increasing alienation, fragmentation and disorder. While it would be a great mistake to blame every problem on the pressures and resentments created by immigration, it can be justifiably argued that large-scale immigration worsened some existing problems and created others. There is certainly a tension and feeling of unease amongst the English population that did not exist before the 1960's. If liberals were to listen to the indigenous population instead of continually berating them, they would discover just how much resentment and anger there is bubbling away beneath the surface waiting to erupt.

There have been earlier periods of immigration but due to the similarity of the people involved and the comparatively small numbers, the immigrants were assimilated into the English population. In modern times the differences are so great and the numbers so large that we have many nations where there was once one. Whatever the supposed advantages that are alleged to accrue to a nation that permits mass-migration into its homeland, there are very few Englanders who believe that they are better off in a multi-cultural, multi-racial England than they were in a one nation England.

The English are not alone in their anguish at what is happening to their country and their community. Feelings of resentment and anger are generated everywhere in the world where a similar situation exists. As a general rule, the greater the differences between insiders and outsiders, the greater the number of outsiders involved and the larger the territory they occupy, the greater the hostility to them from the indigenous population. The resistance to immigration is not born of ignorance, stupidity or fear of the unknown, as liberals would have us believe, but by a wish to preserve a communal identity and way of life. The motive is defensive and not born of a dislike or hatred that arises from racism. It does not matter what the race of an outsider is, all that matters is that they are outsiders and there are a lot of them.

Vigorous nations throughout the world endeavour to protect their geographical and cultural territory. Europeans are no different to anyone else in wanting to live in their own land among their own people. Their problem is that after years of propaganda, many of them feel guilty or even ashamed of their feelings. The good news is that the pendulum has passed the end of its multi-cultural swing and increasing numbers of people are realising that liberal views and assumptions about immigration and racism are not ones that they are bound to accept or even to accord any respect. The utterances of liberals are merely a point of view and not the self-evident universal truths liberals assume them to be. We are not obliged to play by a rulebook written by liberals. The English are a nation and like any other it has the right to determine where it draws its communal boundaries and how it defends them.

Summary

All nations endeavour to maintain their cultural and territorial space. All communities discriminate between members and non-members. To discriminate between insiders and outsiders is not racism, it is human nature. Humans are communal animals; without discrimination, communities cannot exist.

National communities usually consist of people who belong to the same race. When the members of such a community see a stranger of another race, that factor alone is sufficient to determine that the stranger is not an insider. For racists, that is as far as the process need go but for nationalists race is only one element among many that distinguish an outsider from an insider; sometime it is a factor, sometimes not. Other markers, of varying sophistication, include language, dress, accent, mannerisms, beliefs and attitudes. A community is more than a one-dimensional relationship based only on race.

Those people who define race solely in terms of skin colour, namely Black and White, and then relate every person and every issue to that division, are racists of the crudest kind. Liberals are amongst the worst offenders. Their obsession is such that they define race and racism in a way that suits their political purpose and then use it as a weapon. To accept their definitions and the perceptions linked to them is to give them power over us. Liberals are free to define and use words as they wish but nationalists are equally free to reject those definitions and use their own.

Economic-Liberals and Social-Liberals

The influence of the English on the birth and development of liberalism was considerable. Liberalism grew out of rationalism. It was a creature of its time. Much of classic economic-liberal theory presents capitalism and the free market as the servant and tool of human need. Economic-liberalism was inspired by a desire to harness the new technology and the economy it gave rise to and use them to make the world a better place. As with many ideologies, the early sparkle, clarity and brilliance of thought was lost as it was taken up by those who used it to justify the pursuit of selfish interests. A radical approach to economics ossified and became dogma. The world changed but economic-liberals failed to move on. Social-liberals did the opposite, abandoning the hard rationalism and pragmatism of the early liberals. They wanted to help the unfortunate and deserving but nowhere in that early approach was there room for the lazy and dishonest. Charity began at home and was guided by what are now called family values. The aim was to give unfortunates the opportunity to better themselves. Modern social-liberals have taken from classic liberalism the belief that we can control our environment and perfect human nature but in the place of rationalism and open argument they have put good intentions and dogma. Early social and economic-liberals would turn in their graves to see the flabbiness of most of those who now call themselves liberal. Today's liberals would be better called *modernists*.

Liberalism was born into a world very different from the one we live in. It is time to move on and use an approach that addresses the problems that modern liberals have largely been responsible for causing.

Modern liberalism promotes the view that freedom belongs to individuals and that there should be as few restraints as possible on their ability to make choices. Each person should be free to choose how they live and not be constrained by custom or culture or communal obligations. The right to choose lies with individuals not communities, which have no place in modern liberalism. Instead of communal constraints on freedom of choice and action we have ideological constraints. Conformity is not restricted to a given community or culture but to the whole world. Thus, we are allowed the freedom to choose what we say and how we live provided we do not offend liberals.

Concern for individual human rights is to be welcomed but those rights need to be balanced by the needs and rights of communities, which sometimes require that individual rights be subordinate to community interests. Achieving a successful balance between the two is a matter of judgement, and not something that can be determined by the application of hard and fast rules.

The unit of human organisation preferred by liberals is a society rather than a community. Communities, especially national communities, are only deemed worthy if they are small and can be contained comfortably within a liberal political society. Large core-national communities are seen as threatening because they are incompatible with an atomised society where liberals manage and manipulate the parts. Liberals prefer societies where relationships are contractual and valued in money terms. In place of community and empathy we are given *rights* and it is for each person to enforce their rights and seek compensation when they are infringed. If an individual suffers a misfortune or loss it is presumed that it must be due to an infringement of their rights and that fault lies with a person or company or the state or *society*. Fate, accident and personal responsibility are no longer regarded as adequate explanations for misfortune.

Liberals dislike strong traditional communities because they restrain and moderate the behaviour of individuals by means of informal rules and sanctions over which liberals have no control. In other words, they are not open to liberal social engineering. Worse still, they sometimes promote illiberal values and perceptions.

Economic-Liberals

The term economic liberal is used here to mean that group of persons who believe:–

1. human beings are primarily economic animals who act in a way that maximises their economic wellbeing (rational decision-making in pursuit of wealth maximisation);

2. free enterprise, free trade and market forces (i.e. capitalism) are the most efficient ways to distribute scarce resources;

3. the consumption of goods and services can be equated with happiness;

4. the unrestricted right to engage in free trade is a human right;

5. capitalism can be equated with democracy;

6. those who seek to restrain capitalism are enemies of democracy;

7. globalisation is good, inevitable and to be welcomed;

8. states and nations are obsolete and a hindrance to free trade and the greater prosperity of all.

The dominance of economic liberalism is such that if political arguments are to be taken seriously they usually have to be put in economic terms. For example, those opposed to the building of a fifth terminal at London Heathrow airport were primarily concerned about the prospect of an increase in the number of flights and the increase in noise and road traffic that would result. However, in order to be listened to they had to argue that the project was economically flawed because passenger traffic would not increase at the projected rate and that even if it did it would be cheaper to develop one of the other London airports. Those in favour argued that the new terminal would bring more local jobs and that if it was not built the projected extra air traffic would go to an airport outside the UK and income would be lost. The argument, *if we don't do it someone else will*, is nearly as popular as the lemming argument, *they are all doing it and if we don't join them we will be left behind*.

Not only is almost every dispute reduced to economic terms but the more unpopular an economic development is the more certain it is that we will be told, *it will create jobs and be good for the economy.* However, when there is a proposal for something that will create jobs in the Public Sector, the issue of jobs is seen not as a benefit and a boost to the local economy but as a burden and a waste. Proposals for constitutional reform and the creation of a Welsh Assembly and Scottish Parliament were at first criticised primarily in terms of cost, which suggests that democracy has to be cost effective. Different rules seem to apply to the EU, which has what is politely called *a democratic deficit,* because matters of cost, bureaucracy and waste are not dwelt upon.[102]

An ideal world for the economic liberal is one where the earth's population consists of deculturalised individuals who have no sense of community (an atomised society) but share sufficient common values and perception as are necessary to make them susceptible to the same types of advertising, want the same type of goods and services, and have as their prime motivation the desire to maximise their personal wealth. In other words, the dream is of a global consumer society in which luxuries become essentials and human happiness is seen as something to be achieved through consumption. The underlying theme is perpetual economic growth, with much of it brought about by the absorption of new markets into the global economy.

Economic-liberals have as their goal a global market place and a global workforce. They argue that the providers of goods and services are usually able to operate at a higher level of efficiency and profit in a large homogeneous market than in many small markets where for cultural and other reasons the requirements of consumers vary. In the 1950s and 1960s unemployment rates in liberal industrial states were low, and as a result labour costs rose. The solution adopted in the UK and some other Western states was to encourage the migration of cheap labour from the Third World to increase the size of the unskilled workforce and reduce labour costs. In recent years the aim has been to attract highly skilled labour, especially those with programming and other computer related skills. The prime consideration and justification throughout has been economic need, as defined by economic-liberals. At no time has it been thought necessary to either consult the host nations or give them a formal opportunity to express their opinion on the matter.

Social-liberals supported the migration policies of economic-liberals because it fitted with their desire to create multi-cultural, multi-racial societies. Even now,

---

[102] The EU is a device for entrenching liberal economic and social values in Europe. With the growth of wider liberal institutions, such as the World Trade Organisation, the EU has ceased to be as attractive to economic-liberals as it once was. Many economic-liberals are now critical of the EU because they see it as a ponderous bureaucratic machine moving in the direction of Soviet style central planning and economic management.

they use the arguments of economic-liberals when they refer to the positive economic benefits that the immigrants bring to the host states. The alleged benefits are often said to be due to the immigrants' business skills and their willingness to work hard.[103] This attitude persists and is used to argue for a change in attitudes to immigration and economic migrants.

> Home Office ministers are studying a Canadian scheme which would enable more economic migrants with professional and specialist skills to work in Britain as part of a possible shake-up of the immigration laws.
>
> The immigration minister, Barbara Roche, said in a speech in Paris yesterday that the government believed it was time to start a debate on finding ways to meet "legitimate desires to migrate" to Britain and called for an "imaginative rethink" of existing immigration rules so migration could meet economic and social needs.
>
> She wanted to see "innovators with good ideas to take the economy forward" and add to national wealth, as well-skilled specialists come to Britain.[104]

In order to increase the size of homogeneous markets it became fashionable in the 1960's to suggest that to succeed in the global economy it was necessary to benefit from economies of scale. Corporations needed to be bigger and they needed bigger *home* markets to operate in. This lent support to mergers and trading blocs such as the European Common Market. Various theories have been right for their time and served a useful purpose but others have owed their popularity to sounding *neat*. The enthusiasm for *downsizing* (staff reduction) demonstrated how a large number of apparently intelligent individuals could act like lemmings. Another example was the European Monetary System (EMS), which was based on corporate self-interest, political wishful thinking and ideological convenience rather than a realistic assessment of its viability. In other words, the needs of large corporations fitted neatly with the political objectives of social-liberals. From that came the *indisputable truth* that large home markets are an essential ingredient of economic success.

The *economy of scale* argument was used despite Japan's success in becoming a world economic power with a comparatively small home market. Liberals largely ignored Japan's success because it was due, in the main, to a mix of central planning, in the form of co-operation between the state, banks, and business, and a large dose of protectionism. Japan also enjoyed the benefit of being a nation-state

---

[103] Liberals would never suggest that the English work harder, or have better business skills than, for example, Jamaicans, but it was thought acceptable to suggest that Asians work harder and have better business skills than the English. Those immigrants who, in the main, did not do well (e.g. West Indians) were consoled and told that it was not due to their lack of willingness to work hard or to their poor business skills but to the racist nature of White Western societies.

[104] *The Guardian,* 22nd July 2000

and having a strong community with comparatively low social costs, including those associated with crime. All of these factors hold good despite the economic recession that Japan has endured for many years now. There is a limit to what any community can suffer but the Japanese have so far survived conditions that would have already brought turmoil to multi-cultural societies. Liberals find it impossible not to be smug and satisfied when the Japanese face economic or social difficulties. The smugness will vanish if the problems in Japan contribute to a global recession. If that happens, England is more likely than most to suffer serious social unrest.

The resentment felt by Western liberals about Japanese success gave rise to stories about them being unable to match the achievements of the West because the Japanese approach to life and business was not conducive to individual freedom of thought and expression, i.e. not liberal. It is still sometimes claimed that this means that the Japanese are not very good at creative thinking and the production of original ideas and that their success is based on copying and improving the ideas of others. It is interesting to note that if such remarks were made about a Third World nation they would be considered racist.

Liberals are reluctant to look too closely at Japanese society because neither its economic success nor its recent difficulties have been accompanied by the disintegration of its national community. For the most part, Japanese society functions in a peaceful and orderly fashion because of its rejection of social-liberal policies. Although Japanese society is far from perfect (e.g. political corruption and Mafia-like criminal organisations) it does enjoy many of the benefits of a national community, some of them being politeness, the observance of civic and community rules, and lower crime rates than exist in other industrial societies with the same size and density of population. For example, there is far less vandalism and street crime in Japan than in the UK.

It has been suggested by Western liberals that Japan should reform its economy by, among other things, bringing in immigrants to increase the size of the unskilled workforce and reduce labour costs. The Japanese do not regard that as a serious option because they do not want the sort of society that immigration brings. They enjoy the luxury of being able to reject multi-culturalism without the risk of condemnation from within Japan. Many of them have visited England and been shocked by the number of foreigners living here. They cannot understand why so many have been let in to settle and feel no guilt about saying what others dare only think. But that is only possible because they live in a society that is not dominated by social-liberal dogma.

Those who benefit most from the liberal economic system have massive economic and military power with which they can punish those states that shun *free trade* and resist being drawn into the global economy. Free trade is a policy of the strong because it makes possible the transfer of resources from *the edge* to *the centre*.

Until recently *the edge* was the Third World and *the centre* the mainly liberal industrial states. The centre is now less geographical and has more to do with elites, corporations and financial institutions, although it remains true that they tend to be based in the liberal industrial states, particularly the USA. The purists who occupy and control the centre see their interests, i.e. the interests of the global economic and financial system, as being above those of any one state. They view states as a means for controlling populations in a way that is helpful to the interests of the new centre; the Global Elite. States are factors to be manipulated and encouraged to compete for the favours that global corporations can bestow upon them. They also act as tax collectors, keep internal order and, by providing appropriate education and training, produce a workforce suited to the needs of the global economy. No state is more important in this respect than the USA because it finances and controls the military power necessary to protect the vital interests of the Global Elite.

The changing nature of industrial production and low shipping costs has made it possible for trans-state corporations to move production from high cost economies to low cost economies. In other words, to move factories and assembly plants to the workforce instead of moving the workforce to existing places of production. The modern logic of liberal economics is that services are provided and goods are manufactured where labour costs are lowest and sold where prices are highest. For example, transferring the production of sports shoes to low-wage states has not led to a reduction in the prices charged in high-wage states but it has increased the profits of the corporations involved. It is difficult to understand how the labour force in liberal industrial states can gain long-term benefits from the transfer of jobs and technology to places where labour costs are low. In theory, low technology and low-skill jobs are replaced by high technology, high-skill jobs, and the quality of the work force is constantly upgraded to keep it ahead of workers in the emerging industrial powers. In fact, that does not happen because high-technology industries are capital intensive and use comparatively little labour. Many of those who lose their jobs are not capable of re-training for high-tech jobs, even if they are there to fill. It is difficult to see how it can be in the English national interest for manufacturing and service jobs to be moved from England to Asia when those who lose their jobs are generally offered work in a low-tech low-pay service industry or face unemployment.

The transfer of resources and their ownership makes sense in a liberal global economy where the aim is to draw all states into a web of interdependence from which they cannot break free. But there is no sense in it for nations and states because in addition to losing assets they are losing control of their economies and the mix of production and research resources needed for a healthy mixed economy. It was not, and is not in the English national interest or the interest of the UK for capital and technology to be exported from the UK to other states so that they can be industrialised and modernised and made into powerful competitors. It will not be long before the transfer of capital and technology to China and other Asian states will be seen to have been a strategic folly on a massive scale. Many of those involved in the transfers must have at least an inkling of the consequences but their primary interests are short-term profit and access to markets. Their motto is, *the future will look after itself.*

We have been told for very many years that it does not matter who owns or finances the means of production because what is important is where it is placed. It is said that if we provide corporations with financial and fiscal incentives, and a cheap trained labour force, they will create jobs and boost the economy. Likewise, it does not matter if foreign corporations buy UK businesses because they are investing in the economy and employment will be unaffected. Passing control of businesses abroad is a technicality that brings the practical reward of inward investment.

The *it's a mere technicality* argument usually goes with the words, *it helps us compete in the global economy.* How such nonsense can be uttered and believed is beyond belief. The control of corporations and where they are based is of paramount importance for investment, research, and the flow of profits. Despite the pressure on managers to think globally, many retain local loyalties and instinctively do what they can to further the interests of their nation and state. Their influence can be an important factor in deciding where corporations expand and which branches of a business are closed down in a recession. For instance, Japanese corporations invest overseas but they have not lost their Japanese identity. The core of the corporations remain in Japan with Japanese management, which is why they are described as Japanese corporations and we talk of Japanese investment in the UK and USA.

Most of those who control global corporations are compelled to follow the prevailing global ideology because it is difficult, if not impossible to break out of the system it creates. They would prefer not to transfer technology, production, and services abroad but if they do not do so their corporations will become less profitable than competitors who are willing to do anything that reduces costs and increase profits.[105]

When, during the next global recession, the UK branches of foreign-owned companies start to close and jobs are lost it will become clear for all to see that it does matter who owns and controls factories and financial institutions. Even when the economy is doing well, it can be seen that some companies are bought by foreign buyers solely to gain that company's market share or take over lucrative

---

[105] Those with a feeling of guilt about what they feel compelled to do are in a similar position to farmers who are subject to the authority of the EU Common Agricultural Policy and the web of grants and subsidies it has spawned. They might regret the farming techniques they are encouraged to use and are aware of the damage they are doing but they are fixed in the web like flies. The pressures of the system are such that it is not possible to opt out and survive.

161

contracts. In such cases, the acquired company may continue as a legal entity but domestic production is shut down, and goods and services are supplied from the purchasing company's existing foreign plant. As a result, the UK becomes dependent on a foreign supplier and the balance of trade is worsened. In the short-term the manoeuvre is recorded as an inflow of capital, which is seen as a good thing.

Those politicians who accept the myth that the global economy has made nations and sovereign states obsolete are blind to the foolishness of losing control of strategic industries. They are fond of using the term *UK plc* and believe that states can, and should, be run like corporations. They fail to realise that corporations are responsible for only one aspect of life and are able to buy in the factors needed while discarding what is not. They use labour that has been educated by the state and is sometimes housed by the state. The state provides among other things medical care, defence, fire and police services. The directors of a company are only responsible to the shareholders to the extent that they must produce a profit. Welfare, culture and social cohesion are not their concern. When it is not profitable to employ members of a workforce they fire them (let them go) and the state has to deal with the consequences. The managers of companies have only a very narrow and short-term view of interests, costs, and profit. A state cannot be run like that, and the pretence that it can will eventually lead to ruin.

In theory, a free-market global economy will result in similar wage and price levels around the world as a vast labour market competes for jobs and corporations compete for sales. In practice that does not happen. The relocation of production might be beneficial for those with well-paid secure jobs but for many others it means insecurity and unemployment. Relocation also fails to take account of the fact that in an emergency nations and states sometimes need secure access to certain strategic goods. What is a disadvantage for nations and states is an advantage for the Global Elite because dependency is a deterrent to those who wish to opt out of the global economy. States that attempt to take that option are penalised in a way that deters others from trying the same thing. Rebellion is met with direct financial and trade sanctions, and other economic weapons, including the undermining of currencies. The resulting hardship stands as a warning to others that there is no alternative to capitalism. The blame is put on the rebels and their economic mismanagement rather than on those imposing the sanctions.

The enthusiasm for a globalisation of labour, production and capital has not been matched by a globalisation of prices. When the issue is wages and productivity we are told that we have to compete in a global economy but when it comes to pricing goods, the global market is divided into price zones. Corporations are careful to sell their products in each market at the highest price that market will bear. There are plans to institutionalise these price blocs so that retailers can be prevented from buying in a cheap bloc and selling in an expensive bloc. The EU is, for example, doing its best to help the producers of *designer label* products keep their prices high in Europe and sell at lower prices elsewhere. How such action can be squared with the idea of a global market place is difficult to understand. Neither is it clear how price blocs bring the alleged benefits of globalisation and free trade to the people of the EU.

The aim of creating a regional trading bloc operating according to the principles of liberal economics was central to the creation of the European Common Market. Linked to that was the long term objective of creating political structures and institutions that would lock the member states into a liberal political and economic system. Thus we have the European Union and European Monetary Union (EMU). If the currencies and economies of the member states are merged it will be extremely difficult for the inhabitants of what was once a member state to take back the powers ceded to the EU. Being at the heart of Europe will be like being wrapped in the embrace of an octopus whose tentacles make escape very difficult. The threats and warnings of economic doom directed at French-Canadians in the lead up to their referendum on independence for Quebec would be nothing compared with the barrage that would be directed at those voting in a referendum on withdrawal from the EU. Such a referendum would probably be deemed illegal by the European Court, which has the prime purpose of bringing about, and then maintaining, an unbreakable political and economic union.

The EU is structured in a way that is designed to ensure that social and economic liberalism endures in all the member states until they merge into one. With the devolution of member-state powers downwards to EU-approved regions, and the handing up of strategic powers to the EU, the individual member-states will have few functions to perform and will melt away, thus enabling the harmonisation of economic, political and legal systems throughout the EU. Without states to represent their interests nations will find it difficult to resist the onslaught of global culture and the bureaucratic tidiness which demands ever greater standardisation. The governing elite in France sees things differently and believes it can control the EU and use it as a shield to protect French culture from the materialistic values of economic globalism in general and the USA in particular. Unfortunately for the French, a European Union state will have no interest in defending national cultures because its aim is to engineer and promote a concocted European identity that will belong to everyone but no one.

Fortunately, the EU is likely to collapse under the weight of its internal contradictions and absurdities. From the wreckage it might be possible to build an organisation that enables European nation-states to co-operate on matters of common concern and jointly confront global corporations rather than bow to them.

The imposition of global uniformity and the creation of an EU state is opposed by most nationalists but some believe that the EU is helpful to them because it will result in the break-up of multi-nation member states and enable small nations to flourish in a *Europe of the regions*. Scottish Nationalists, for example, appear to

163

think that a worthwhile political independence can be won for Scotland while the economic and financial integration of the EU proceeds at speed. They do not appear to have a long-term view as to how the creation of a European superstate, dedicated to harmonisation (the elimination of differences), will assist them in asserting a Scottish identity and obtaining national self-government. Perhaps they are anticipating the collapse of EU economic and political union and the opportunity it will provide for a fully-fledged Scottish state to emerge. A Scottish identity has survived 300 years of union with England and Wales, so it should survive a shorter period locked into the EU. On the downside, the EU might survive for longer than Scottish Nationalists would like. They should not underestimate the determination of the Eurocrats to atomise national communities in the interest of promoting a European identity

Nationalists prefer to retain those things that are peculiar to their nation and do not feel the necessity to harmonise and be like everyone else, – especially not for the convenience of corporations. Nationalists are united in their opposition to a global economic and political society, particularly one where a junk-culture reigns, the market economy is sacrosanct, and it is thought that everything of value has a price and everything can be bought.

To suggest that economic considerations should not always be treated as paramount is not to suggest that trade and competition are bad or that cost, waste and inefficiency are unimportant. It is merely to point to the fact that there are different ways of managing and measuring those factors. For example, *the market* might determine that it is efficient to grow vegetables in Kenya and air-freight them to UK supermarkets, but if cost, waste and efficiency were assessed not by an accountant but by an environmentalist or someone concerned about the nature of the global economy, it could be shown that transporting vegetables thousands of miles is an absurdly costly, wasteful and inefficient use of resources.

Community, democracy, culture, the environment and quality of life should be given the consideration that they deserve and not made slaves to alleged *best economic interests*. The important things in life should not be ignored just because a price cannot be put on them. Politics should not be treated as a branch of economics and the currency of political debate should not be tax rates, economic growth, and how best to compete in the global economy. A society modelled to meet the needs and interests of global corporations (profit and survival at any cost) is not a pleasant society to live in. Greed, and an obsession with the bottom line are not virtues.

The social and economic strands of liberalism have been intertwined for many years but they are beginning to unravel because they are becoming increasingly incompatible. Capitalism requires open stable markets but social-liberalism creates instability. As liberal societies become more chaotic and crime-ridden, the two strands of liberalism will become increasingly incompatible. Social-liberals will be cast adrift to perish. Economic-liberals will find something that better meets their needs.

The following quotation is an apt comment on liberal democracy.

> All forms of government destroy themselves by carrying their guiding principles to excess. Democracies become too free in politics, in economics, in morals, even in literature and art until even the dogs in our homes rise up on their hind legs and demand their rights. Disorder grows to a point where a society will abandon all its liberty to anyone who can restore order.[106]

Free Trade

Free trade is a term used by economic-liberals to describe trade unhindered by protective duties and import restrictions. Real free trade is trade unhindered by other, often hidden factors such as coercion and subsidies. Free trade cannot be said to exist when one party has little choice but to sell a commodity (usually a primary product, e.g. mineral and agricultural produce) on terms determined by the buyer (usually a global corporation). Any attempt by producers to regulate supply and price is condemned as price fixing. Those concerned are invariably accused of holding the West to ransom and pressure is brought to bear to end the arrangement. They are compelled to return to a market that is biased in favour of the buyer.

The producers of strategic primary products (e.g. oil) are deemed to be morally obliged to sell to those who are willing to buy in a theoretical *free* market, that is one where the price is determined by unrestricted supply and demand.[107] To restrict supply for political/diplomatic reasons is considered to be blackmail. The producers of strategic manufactured goods (e.g. armaments) are deemed to have the right to choose their customers and the price of their products. In other words, they are not bound by the *free* market. Since it is the manufacturers of strategic goods who make the rules, it is hardly surprising that the rules are favourable to them.

The terms and conditions of trade between states reflects the power relationship between the parties concerned. Powerful states are generally able to get a good deal while weak states generally get a poor deal and have to be thankful for it.

In liberal economic theory, states produce those commodities for which they are best suited (comparative advantage) and all states benefit from it. Free trade is seen as not just being efficient but virtuous. The mantra is, *free trade benefits*

---

[106] In the place from which the quotation was taken it was attributed to Plato. Whoever the author, the point is well made.

[107] Oil is clearly under-priced because European governments are able to get more from taxing oil products than the producers get from selling it.

everyone by creating wealth. Some doubters question how free *free trade* really is and who it makes wealthy. Is free trade merely a device used by the rich and strong to exploit the poor and weak? It can be argued that those who gain most are the global corporations which play off one party against the others thus securing for the corporations the following:

1. primary materials at low prices;

2. production with low wage costs:

3. sales in high price markets;

4. government grants and tax concessions.

In reality, *free trade* allocates resources between states according to their ability to pay. The international market is like a domestic market in that it is geared to supplying the needs of those with high disposable income. The market only recognises need if it is backed by the ability to pay.

Those governing elites that benefit from the activities of global corporations do their best to promote and protect the interests of global corporations. The ideology of free trade is a device by which those with wealth and power gain access to markets and resources. It is also used as a cover for *dumping*. Farmers in one state are, for domestic policy reasons, given a subsidy to produce a crop which is then sold (dumped) in another state at a price local farmers cannot compete with. For example, US maize dumped in the Philippines and, in times of surplus, EU agricultural produce of all kinds dumped in any market except the EU. Meanwhile the EU is careful to exclude low-price agricultural produce that competes with its internal producers. Despite that, we are told that those who receive *cheap* produce benefit from it. When it is pointed out that it destroys local economies and communities, and encourages agricultural workers to move to cities and live in poverty, it is said to be good because it enables that state to use labour and land more efficiently. More efficiently for whom or what?

What actually happens is that the former farmworkers help swell the low-paid urban labour force and farmland is turned over to producing crops for export. The state that *benefited* from the *cheap* produce becomes increasingly enmeshed in and dependent upon the global economy. It needs to export cash crops, low-price manufactured goods and primary produce in order to buy the food from abroad that it can no longer produce for itself. Thus, it loses much of the control it had over its economic, political and cultural development. If states that have been integrated into the global economy try to restrict entry to their market or subsidise domestic manufacturers, they find themselves open to sanctions that are difficult to resist. Interdependence is a weakness. The refusal of a World Bank loan or the hint of trade sanctions can cause a currency to plummet and make the governing elite unpopular and vulnerable. The suffering of those who resist sets an example to others. There is little choice but to abide by the rules of the economic order.

An illustration of how free trade and the global economy draws victims into a system that destroys them, is illustrated in *Reservations are for Indians*, by Heather Robertson, pages 16–19.[108] (The Slaveys are a North American Indian tribe.)

> The year followed a regular cycle based on spring trappings, summer fishing, winter trappings. Life was utilitarian and absolutely efficient. Each family unit was stripped bare of everything which did not contribute directly to survival, with no excess baggage allowed. It was ruthlessly self-disciplined way of life, including the murder or suicide of those who became a burden through illness or age. When the population grew too large for the game in the area to support, the people began to die of starvation until the proper balance was restored. When the treaty was signed in 1899, the entire Slavey population was only 175.
>
> The first link with civilisation was established by the Hudson's Bay Company. The Slaveys began to move in diminishing circles around The Bay so they would be close enough to bring in their furs or get supplies when game ran low. Dependency took root. The circumference of the people's world became narrower, with The Bay at the centre. The family lost its self-sufficiency and the people became employees of The Bay. The fur trade bound the people ever more tightly to the company. The Indians were valued in terms of the amount of good fur they could bring in, and were paid not in money but in food. The more daring and successful a hunter was, the more dependent and enslaved he became to The Bay. The more food he brought in the more food he would receive. He and his family soon began to depend on this "store food" as the staple of their diet and in order to get it, the hunter would work even harder. By becoming an employee of The Bay, the Indian entered an economy which was not essentially different from that functioning in the rest of Canada and with the world. The Slavey's produce – fur – found a worldwide market.
>
> The Hudson's Bay Company was the only business in the area. The Indians bought their food from the same company to which they sold their produce. Money was unnecessary for food and fur where bartered. The Bay, completely in control, set the prices and the standards and the Indians were forced to abide by the decisions of The Bay manager. It was simple for The Bay, dealing with an illiterate, non-English-speaking population over which it had complete control, to make sure that the value of groceries always

---

[108] *Reservations are for Indians*, by Heather Robertson, published by Lewis and Samuel, 1970. Reprinted 1990 and still available.

equalled or exceeded the value the fur brought in, so that the people were perpetually in debt or breaking even. Although they were now laborers, they lived on the same subsistence level as before. All they had lost was their independence. Their relationship with The Bay contained no prospect of their becoming richer or more powerful and The Bay did not suggest to them that one day they too, the Indians, could be Bay managers or operate a store of their own.

In order to save time lost in hunting, The Bay would grubstake the Indian trappers before the season opened with enough food to see the family through. The normal economy was thus reversed, since the Indians got the food first, and worked later. They had a big grocery debt at the store before they went trapping and they were expected to bring back at least enough fur to pay it off. A bad season put the Indians deeply in debt to the store. And it was not long before the whole community was under obligation to The Bay. The Bay would grant the most credit to the best trappers; a man's worth was measured by the size of his bill at the store. Debt made the Indians vulnerable to threats and pressure from the Bay manager. It was important to be friends with him or he would cut back credit, and this could mean death.

Pressure became severe in the period when The Bay was also the government. A resident Indian agent did not establish himself in the Hay Lake until 1957. Until that time, the Indians received their government information and assistance, a family allowance, rations, pensions, through The Bay. The people couldn't speak English so the Indian agent consulted with The Bay manager.

A shattering change came in 1952 when the Oblate Fathers built a huge residential school on the reserve. The Slaveys were to be educated. Children had to attend school every day for ten months of the year. Suddenly, the balance swung from emphasis on the old leaders to emphasis on the children and the future. The hunting pattern was broken when the children began to attend school. It was then almost impossible for the parents to continue to follow the trap lines. The necessary labor of the children – wood-gathering, baby-sitting, water-carrying – was missing, and no family wanted to leave its children for six months of the year. The Slaveys gambled on the future. They sent their children to school and settled down in their little log cabins around Habay and Assumption. The men continued to trap and hunt, but they were unwilling to leave their families alone for five or six months at a time. The circle shrank again. They trapped closer to home. Soon the area was trapped-out by too many hunters, and game and fur became scarce. The people came soon to depend almost exclusively on The Bay, for their food and game was a supplement, something to eat when the rations ran out. The population grew rapidly, since the food supply from the government and the store was inexhaustible. By 1963, the Slavey population numbered 767 and 33 children were being born every year. The little log cabins became crowded.

The simple act of establishing a school completely revolutionised the Slavey economy. Not only did trapping become almost impossibly difficult but the population soon destroyed the game. The Slaveys assumed, in all good faith, that the government, which was insisting they attend school and thus abandon their way of life, would provide new jobs for the children when they finished school and alternative employment for the men until their families were grown. But Indian Affairs found it easier to dole out increasing quantities of rations as the game dwindled. No attempt was made to retrain or re-employ the Indian men. By 1963, the entire community was on total welfare. The initial dependency on The Bay was multiplied into total dependency on the government. The government now provided what nature had formerly supplied. The complete switch from subsistence based on the land to subsistence based on government handouts took only ten years.

The traditional way of life of the Slaveys was the result of natural selection. Their self-sufficiency was sustainable in a particular environment. The arrival of The Bay changed that environment. The best response to that change, if they had the power to do so, would, perhaps, have been at an early stage to use any necessary means to drive The Hudson's Bay Company and all interlopers out of the Slavey homeland. Given the impossibility of doing that, they should, perhaps, have not traded with The Bay and lived as before. That was probably not a realistic option either because The Bay would have eventually drawn some Indians into its economic web by offering enticements and an apparently easier and better life.

The outline above sets out how one Indian community was destroyed. It shows how that destruction was accompanied by the fine-sounding words and theories, and the paternalistic attitudes, of those who destroyed them. Many Indians believed that adapting to the new economic order would bring prosperity to them and their community. They did not appreciate the intertwining of cultural, political and economic life. The way we build shelter, how we get food to eat, how we care for the unfortunate, these things are bound up with cultural, political and economic values. Self-government and freedom are impossible for a community that is subject to an economic structure controlled by outsiders. A community that places its economic wellbeing in the hands of outsiders is doomed because outsiders have no interest in preserving the communal way of life except in as far as it serves outside interests. The general rule to follow is, do not become dependent on outsiders and hand them control of your economy, culture or political system because in doing so you will hand them the power to destroy you and your way of

169

life. Do not be tempted to wear the one-size-fits-all global identity that some are so eager to see you wear – it is a straightjacket.

The sad tale of the Slaveys shows that trade is not neutral; it has cultural consequences. Trade freely entered into can benefit all involved but the advantages gained from the *free trade* promoted by those who extol the liberal global economy, are greatly overstated. As a general rule, free trade is desirable if the parties are at equal stages of economic growth and trade is freely entered into. It should be on a selective basis that serves the interests of the community. Trade is not an end in itself; and need not be an all or nothing option. Nationalists judge the worth of a global economy by its ability to meet the needs of individuals and nations, rather than by its ability to serve the needs of the Global Elite and those corporations, individuals and states that have the ability to pay for the resources they *need*.

Many of those who are enthusiastic about real free trade and the benefits it brings are justifiably irritated by those who claim to support free trade but in fact support subsidies, dumping, import controls, central planning and bureaucratic regulation. For that reason, many *free traders* oppose the EU.

> We are different than we used to be. The government has us in a little box, with a lid on it. Every now and then they open the lid and do something to us and close it again. We are a dying race. Not this generation but the next, will die.
>
> Willie Denechoan, medicine man, Hay Lake. [109]

Advertising

Advertising is an essential part of economic liberalism and the creation of a global consumer culture. One of the main aims of corporate advertising is to restrict access to the market place, and thereby decrease choice, by making it too expensive for new competitors to enter the market.

Advertising is a form of pollution that becomes ever more intrusive and polluting. Yet, there is little opposition to it, perhaps because we have been exposed to it from birth and many people cannot imagine a world without it.[110] Advertising is the face of economic liberalism that we are exposed to daily: on radio and television; in newspapers and magazines; in and on public transport; at bus and railway stations; in the street on billboards and buildings; on shoes and clothing; it

---

[109] *Ibid.*

[110] A glimmer of light is provided by *Adbusters*, which publishes an excellent journal that ridicules and attacks corporate advertising. *As citizens look for a foothold in the struggle between democracy and corporate rule, Adbusters presents key strategies for bringing corporations back under civil control.* www.adbusters.org

comes through our letter-boxes and down our telephone line; it appears in post-marks and amongst our email; at sporting events, in hospitals and on hospital appointment cards. Feature films are increasingly being financed through the inclusion of products, brand names and logos. Some feature films and television programmes are made specifically for the purpose of marketing goods. In other words, the film is an advertisement loosely disguised as entertainment. It has been suggested in the UK that police uniforms be sponsored and carry a logo. An idea for the future is to use earth-orbiting satellites and lasers to project advertisements across the night sky. In Sweden, a telephone company is able to provide cheap telephone calls for those who are willing to have their conversation interrupted from time to time by advertisements. Companies have been invited to provide, or finance, local government services in exchange for advertising space in the streets of the town concerned. There would be advertising on lavatory paper if it didn't harm the product image.

The constant barrage of false perceptions and shallow values is the stuff of brainwashing. If you really think that having the right label on your clothes or badge on your car makes you a better person than those who have not, you are either stupid or have been brainwashed into becoming a fully-fledged member of the consumer society.

Why do we accept this massive intrusion of advertising? Imagine how the quality of our lives would be improved without the polluting effect of the unsolicited advertising that is thrust at us at every opportunity. Imagine, if you can, towns and cities free of the clutter that advertising brings.

We need be no less well informed if we have the choice when needed of going to certain journals, websites, radio and TV stations to obtain information about products. Such an arrangement would encourage information advertising rather than the usual life-style advertising which tells us nothing about the product other than that those who consume it will become sexy, sophisticated, popular, intelligent, etc. It would be some consolation if only fools were brainwashed but even the intelligent are taken in by a barrage of advertising that massages status-seeking instincts.

A particularly irksome turn of events for many motor racing fans was the transfer of Formula One coverage from the BBC to ITV, a television station that carries advertising. What benefit did the change bring to viewers? Much the same teams and drivers are competing and the racing is no more interesting or exciting. The big difference is that instead of uninterrupted coverage of the event we have inflicted on us regular breaks for advertising. Any motor racing enthusiast knows that this spoils the enjoyment because it breaks the flow of the race, but we have no choice. Advertising is so much part of the junk-culture to which we are exposed that if Formula One cars, racetracks, and drivers were not covered with advertisements, the event would for many people seem unreal.[111]

Afterword

For thousands of years the members of different communities, cultures, and civilisations have traded and exchanged ideas. What is so different about the modern global economy is that one economic system and ideology has become so powerful and dominant that it has enabled one set of values and perceptions to infiltrate and weaken all others. The liberal global economy is not inevitable or *natural*. It is governed by man-made rules that are imposed and enforced by those who benefit from them. The structure of the global economy and its institutions is difficult to reconcile with the idea that democracy is about the members of a community or the citizens of a state having a large measure of control over those things that affect them as individuals and as a group. Being enmeshed in a web of dependency greatly narrows the choices open to them.

Social-Liberals

In the same camp as economic-liberals, but looking at a different horizon, we have social-liberals. They channel their quest for individualism in a different direction. There are many values and perceptions associated with social-liberalism but the concern here is to deal with those that directly conflict with the values and perceptions of nationalism.

The term social-liberal is used here to mean that group of persons who:–

1. equate social-liberalism with democracy;

2. believe that those opposed to social-liberalism are also opposed to democracy;

3. attach greater importance to the rights of individuals than to those of communities;

4. believe that all disputes can be settled given good will on all sides;

5. extol multi-culturalism and multi-racialism as things that are inherently, and unarguably, good and desirable;

6. believe that their ideology is valid in all circumstances, in all places, at all times;

7. advocate loyalty to political constructs such as the state, the EU and UN rather than to organic groups such as families and nations;

---

[111] The Wimbledon lawn tennis championship gives an idea of how things could be without advertising. The lack of advertisements around the courts is spoilt only by corporation logos on the players' clothes, their equipment and the players themselves.

8. are internationalists as opposed to nationalists;

9. in the name of progress promote every social innovation that furthers the above values and perceptions.

To be more concise, social-liberals generally favour rights over obligations, individuals over groups, societies over communities, states over nations. It can be seen that those who are here called social-liberals are sometimes called *Leftists* or *Left-liberals*.

To criticise social-liberalism is not, as they would have us believe, to attack democracy or human rights. It is to criticise a narrow, liberal view of democracy, rights, obligations and human worth. Liberal representative democracy is not as representative or as democratic as liberals would have us believe. It tends to only represent views that accord with liberal ideology and its political agenda. Contrary views, including public opinion, are generally ignored or suppressed. If the electorate is to enjoy real representative democracy, it will need the ability to elect those who are appointed to positions of power in the institutions of the state. A start could be made by electing those who should be responsive to public opinion, which should include police chiefs, and local representatives of the Lord Chancellor and the Director General of the BBC.

A choice every few years between similar packages of goals and policies is not everyone's idea of democracy because the choice is limited to variant forms of liberalism. Political debate in the UK during general election campaigns amounts to little more than claims and allegations about tax rates and the cost of competing policies. There are many issues about which the electorate is concerned but unable to express an opinion. The reason is that the political factions of the governing elite share a common position on many issues and have a mutual interest in not raising them during election campaigns. Public opinion on the issues of immigration and capital punishment are two of the more obvious instances of ignoring what is inconvenient. Any politician who attempts to represent public opinion on those issues is treated as a leper. Thus, the liberal governing elite is able to set the electoral agenda and keep it in safe territory. This cosy arrangement will at some stage fall apart because the English will feel so frustrated by the failure of the political establishment to address their concerns on important issues, that they will turn to political groups outside the elite. It is only then, when the elite itself is threatened, that something will be done to satisfy public opinion.

Social-liberals show the greatest concern for *middle-class rights*. They have a preference for individual rights over group rights, and for the right to do things rather than the right to be free of things. For example, the rights to freedom of expression and behaviour are given to individuals but not to communities. There is no recognition that individual and communal right conflict. Communities are not deemed to have the right to set standards of behaviour and enforce them. This is not to deny the importance of individual freedom of speech and expression but it is to question the way those rights are framed.

Rights, if they can properly be called that, are best expressed within a community where rights and obligations can be balanced and adjusted according to the needs of the time. Communities have the right to expect members to observe certain standards of behaviour. In return for compliance, members enjoy benefits when through misfortune they suffer hardship. Those who receive help do not do so as of right; no person has the *right* to expect help from others. Instead, those who give it do so because it is good for the community, and what is good for the community is, in the long-term, good for them. When those who give are in need others will come to their aid. This enlightened self-interest is the fuel that powers communities. Once this point is understood, it can be seen that no person has the right to break communal rules and thereby bring misfortune on himself or herself, and then demand that others give help. The liberal emphasis on individual rights undermine communal institutions and abuses communal instincts by compelling the prudent to aid the reckless and feckless.

The outlook of social-liberals on the matter of rights can be seen in their position on the use of swearing in films, drama and literature. Those who object to swearing or even *excessive* swearing, are dismissed as narrow-minded and dictatorial for wanting to tell others what they can and cannot see and hear. The old cliché about the need for art and drama to reflect real life is invariably trotted out, and in many cases it is a valid argument. However there are words that many liberals cannot bring themselves to use, and object to others using, despite them being necessary to reflect real life and the language people use. They become coy about what they call the *C* word because it is offensive to women, and the *N* word is out of bounds because it offends Black people. Such concern is not extended to those offended by the *F* word, even if they are Black women.

Communities overcome the problem of offensive language by reaching an informal consensus about where and when such language is acceptable. I will not use language offensive to you if you do not use language offensive to me. The approach of social-liberals is to say, I can do and say what I like because that is my right, but you cannot do or say as you please because I find it offensive. In a similar vein, social-liberals are dismissive of those who express concern about sex and violence in videos and television programmes that can easily be seen by young children. They argue that it is for parents to supervise their children and use the off-switch. Further, it is said that even if children do see such things it is of little concern because:

1. they are able to distinguish between fiction and reality;
2. they cannot be protected from reality for ever;
3. there is no evidence that it does any harm.

Despite this apparent desire to resist censorship, liberals try to prevent children, or anyone else, being exposed to views that are offensive to liberals. For example, they seek ways of preventing access to Websites that promote political views with which liberals disagree. The supervision of parents and the availability of an off-switch is no longer seen as adequate protection, and neither is the good sense of the children. Nor do we hear about the right of individuals to be free to pick and choose the Websites that they visit.

In a community, the conflict between individual and communal rights is much reduced because there is a consensus as to what is and is not harmful to the community and its members. Those things that are thought harmful are discouraged and punished; those that are beneficial are encouraged and rewarded. Communal culture provides informal guidelines to acceptable behaviour. In liberal societies, it is mainly middle-class liberals who set the guidelines as to what is and is not acceptable to the public taste. Do liberals have a greater right than communities to set standards?

Social-liberals are unable to recognise that in some disputes the interests of the parties are irreconcilable and for one party to be satisfied another must be denied; i.e. a zero sum game. They also fail to acknowledge that communities have interests and that different communities have different and sometime conflicting interests. It is perhaps their unwillingness to accept these facts that leads them to believe that all disputes can be settled in a peaceful way *given goodwill on all sides*. All the goodwill in the world cannot settle some disputes, especially those arising from different values and perceptions.

Liberals find it difficult to accept that some cultures are incompatible with others and that when those cultures are brought together in one society, conflict is certain to occur. To admit that would undermine their case for multi-culturalism. Nationalists accept that such difficulties exist and that each culture is valid in the community in which it has grown. The best way to minimise conflict is through cultural self-government. Where that is impossible because one or more nations have settled in the homeland of another, the guiding rule should be that where there is cultural conflict, the values and interests of the indigenous culture must prevail. If the cultural norms of the settler-nations are of critical importance to them, they should move to their own homeland, or another place, where they can enjoy their national way of life. If they have no homeland of their own that is unfortunate and a problem to which a solution should be sought but it is not a reason for destroying the culture of the indigenous nation or robbing it of its homeland. One nation should not be expected to bear the burden of another nation's negligence or misfortune.

Social-liberals find such an outlook offensive and try to overcome the conflicts inherent in multi-culturalism by promoting a civic society where the special link between a nation and homeland is denied. They advocate a policy of give and take that erodes the cultural rights and interests of the indigenous nation in order that the interests of outsiders can be satisfied. In practice, the indigenous always give and the settlers always take. Where it is not possible to find a compromise between incompatible cultures, liberals simply impose their own values and thereby subvert the cultures and rights of all sides but their own.

Social-liberals take the attitude that only they are concerned about furthering human rights. They have made themselves arbitrators of what are and are not rights, and the order of priority that should be given to them. Further, they insist that the rights they promote are absolute and should be observed everywhere regardless of the communal and societal cost of doing so. Thus, liberal rights are deemed to be universal, i.e. good for all places at all times. This view overlooks the different cultural, economic and political circumstances that exist for different communities in different parts of the world. The approach is like that of economic-liberals who insist that all economies should be subject to the same rules. That leads to policies that compel small industrial states to expose their industries and markets to trade rules that suit the corporate predators that dominate the global economy. In a similar way, social-liberals do their best to compel all states and all communities to open their cultures to liberal values, however destructive they are to the indigenous way of life.

Some are better able to afford rights than others. Rich and poor have a different idea of what should be a right. The poor tend to give higher priority to rights that involve the provision of food, housing, work, healthcare and education. It is only when these basic human needs are equated with rights, and are met, that people become especially concerned about what for many is the luxury of liberal rights. Many of the human rights that are claimed by liberals as their own are in fact common to many cultures and political ideologies, and accord with instinctive notions of natural justice and natural morality. What is peculiarly liberal is that individual rights are given high priority while communal and cultural rights are lowly rated or excluded, unless they belong to fashionable minorities.

At the heart of social-liberalism is the notion, *if I want to do something I should be free to do it.*[112] Sometimes the qualification, *provided I do no harm to others* is added but even then it is often interpreted narrowly. An example of this is to be

---

[112] The qualification, 'provided I do no harm to others', is often forgotten. For example, a few years ago there was much debate about the right of severely mentally handicapped people to have sexual relationships and their right not to have to use contraceptives or be sterilised. Social-liberals argued that it was a human rights issue and that everyone had the right to a sexual relationship and that no one should be compulsorily sterilised. Little regard was given to how such individuals would raise and support their children or whether the *right* of such people to have children was in the interest of the society in which they lived. The rights of individuals were seen as being more important than all others, and the consequences of exercising those rights were divorced from the social consequences and costs incurred by others. The child is not seen to have the right to be born into a viable family unit.

found in the way social-liberals approve, as a matter of principle, of the easy availability and widespread use of various *recreational* drugs. While concerns about the use of soft drugs and their side effects have been widely overstated, it remains true that dependency on any drug, including alcohol, gives rise to problems for the individual addict and the wider community or society.

The topic of *drugs* is very complex and there is no intention of getting bogged down in it here. The point at issue is the way it is debated. Social-liberals take the view that it is a denial of individual liberty to make the supply and consumption of certain drugs a criminal offence. They use the economic argument that legalisation would incur fewer costs for the state than prohibition. The crux of their approach is that legalisation would undermine criminal networks and reduce related crime. Whatever the merits of the arguments, there seems to be little concern for the question of whether it is in the best interests of communities and societies that a large proportion of their population be frequent users of, or addicted to, drugs.[113] A youth culture in which drugs play a prominent part is likely to encourage attitudes, behaviour and a way of life that makes large numbers of people incapable of functioning within a viable community.

Marx called religion the opiate of the people but in our time it would be nearer the truth to say that hashish and television (especially sport and soap operas) are the opiates of the people.[114] They are commonly used as an escape from a reality over which individuals feel they have no control. Those who smoke dope often reject the values of the society they live in but drugs seem to reduce their will to do something to change it. Indeed, prolonged immersion in a youth culture wedded to image, drugs and consumerism is a form of conditioning that promotes liberal values. It is certainly not a culture that encourages effective resistance. Yet, despite the liberal way of life being an easy option, there are, thankfully, many young people who reject it.

The young have a natural tendency to challenge communal conventions and norms. Successful communities make rebellion by the young possible but place limits on it. Questioning values and conventions serves the useful purpose of helping communities adapt to a changing environment. Adaptation is something that all living things need to do in order to survive and prosper but social conservatives often find it difficult to understand this. They resist change as a matter of principle, believing that the old is better than the new merely because it is old. Social-liberals do the opposite and welcome change for the sake of change

---

[113] (a) Some of the arguments are considerably weakened by their failure to account for the psychological effects of drug taking and the sort of youth culture it gives rise to. (b) Pointing to the availability of nicotine and alcohol, and the damage they do, is not a logical argument in favour of the consumption of yet more harmful substances. It does however point to the hypocrisy implicit in many of the arguments used when the matter is discussed.

[114] Hashish is, of course, not literally an opiate.

in the naive belief that what is new and fashionable must be better than what went before. They seek change without having any clear idea of where it will lead. The new is deemed better than the old for no other reason than that it is new and those who resist change are dismissed as being out of touch with the modern world. Social-liberals believe that change is good because it brings *progress*. But what do they mean by progress, and progress towards what? Does anyone know what the liberal destination is or how we are supposed to get there? It seems that aiming for a destination is not fashionable and we are supposed to just hang on and see where we are taken. In the event of a destination and route being offered, they are usually vague and materialistic. This *leap into the dark* approach to politics is responsible for subjecting communities and societies of all kinds to destructive experiments.

Communities have a sense of continuity and permanence that is essential to their good health. To tamper with the long-lived customs and traditions that underpin that health is foolish, especially when it is carried out on an ideological whim and the effects are impossible to reverse.

The flouting of convention can be useful and is to be welcomed, provided it does not go too far and is not taken too seriously. Many teenagers, with little experience of life, think they have a unique insight into the troubles of the world and have all the answers, which appear to them to be obvious and simple. The arrogance of youth is well known. Most of us have been guilty of it but we eventually come to understand that the world is more complex than it first seemed. We develop a sense of history and do our best to understand the purpose of conventions and institutions, and how they have evolved. Unfortunately, social-liberals never lose the selfish and simplistic approach; they remain obsessed with personal freedom and the need to assert it. A simple example of this was to be seen a few years ago with the campaign to change the Sunday shopping laws in England and Wales. It brought together social and economic-liberals in a common cause. Their argument was in essence as follows: If I want to go shopping on a Sunday and it is more convenient for me, why shouldn't I be allowed to do so? If I want to open my shop on a Sunday and by doing so I can make a higher profit why shouldn't I be permitted to do so? Regulations concerning Sunday trading were seen as being a hindrance to personal freedom and a restriction on trade. [115].

The original reason for Sunday closing had outlived its purpose (to satisfy the sensibilities of Christians and the Church) but it had gained new justifications. For example, Sunday had become an important day for sports clubs because members were available on that day. Also, families had a day when they were better able to enjoy, and sometimes endure, being together. Those who lived in and around

---

[115] It can be argued that stores face higher costs and reduced profits as a result of Sunday trading but the point is that the owners and managers of the stores believed that Sunday opening was in the interest of their business, for to have argued otherwise would have been to suggest that they wished to open as a public service, perhaps in the cause of personal liberty? Many of the guarantees given concerning the employment and payment of staff were quickly eroded.

shopping centres were able to benefit from one day at home in comparative peace and quiet. The vast majority of people were able to have a day free from work and the consumer society, while those who had to work were rewarded with extra pay or benefits. The law concerning Sunday trading needed reform but many would argue that instead of concentrating on the economics of the issue, greater attention and weight should have been given to wider social and cultural considerations. Surely it is conceivable that the temples of consumerism can be closed on one day of the week without causing too many people to suffer withdrawal symptoms. The point is not whether allowing more Sunday trading was a good or bad thing but how the argument was conducted. As it happens, the compromise settled on seems to be reasonably satisfactory.

It is curious that so many of the English people who are so enthusiastic about multi-culturalism are reluctant to live their dream. They can generally be found living well away from the multi-cultural districts they profess to find so appealing. Some young English multi-culturalists go to live in cosmopolitan Brixton, Notting Hill or some other fashionable *exciting* and *vibrant* area that is *enriched by the coming together of races and cultures*, but they soon move away for one reason or another. Perhaps they are perturbed to find that the people living in those areas do not respond well to being patronised by trendy liberals. Most English multi-culturalists do not even venture into the areas that are supposed to be so culturally invigorating and attractive, and when one looks at their friends and those they live with it is difficult to understand why there are so few Black and Asian people among them. There are some who abandon their English identity and try to adopt another but they are never fully accepted and are regarded as a joke, sometimes being referred to as *wiggers*. Most of them see the futility of trying to become something they are not but a few become more determined and attempt to gain acceptance by becoming extremely hostile to and contemptuous of everything English. The ploy always fails because instead of being accepted as insiders they gain only the contempt of those they are trying so hard to impress.

It can be observed that very many liberals lead comfortable middle class lives. The louder they shout the more likely it is that they are in secure, well-paid jobs with a well defined career structure and a good pension scheme. Their practical involvement in what they think of as liberal activities usually amounts to little more than recycling their rubbish and showing a concern for the environment. They have no wish to challenge the power structure or call for greater democracy. Instead, their radicalism amounts to a concern for the welfare of pandas and dolphins. They demand an end to whaling and fox hunting but keep eating factory-farmed chickens and battery eggs. It is so much easier and cheaper to demand that others change their ways than to do so oneself. It's always easy to find an excuse for hypocrisy.

Eating in *ethnic* restaurants, cooking *ethnic* food, listening to *ethnic* music is deemed sufficient to demonstrate a commitment to multi-culturalism. For some, it is enough to drink Irish beer and listen to Irish folk music. One can only envy these culture vultures as they soar in the swirling thermals of a multi-cultural sky.

Those settlers who make a career from proclaiming the desirability of a multi-cultural, multi-racial society usually behave in much the same way as their English counterparts, with the exception that they feel no need to adopt another culture as their own. Black people and Asians live in predominantly Black and Asian districts; their friends are predominately Black or Asian, and the political, cultural and social organisations to which they belong are predominantly Black or Asian in membership and outlook.

The political strength of the Black and Asian settlers is now sufficiently great for them to do without the support of their liberal allies. They no longer feel the need to lend support to liberal slogans about different races working together or to view multi-cultural societies as an ideal. Instead, they see multi-cultural societies for what they are, a place where communities compete. They know that communal identity and unity is important and that individual interests are often best served by pursuing communal goals. The primary task of ethnic minority *community leaders* is to represent and promote the interests of their community. That is not a route English liberals take because to do so would be regarded as nationalistic. Instead, the more multi-cultural and fractured a society becomes the more intent liberals become on advancing the interests of other communities and criticising their own.

A Liberal Dilemma

English social-liberals are uncertain as to what their attitude should be to Islamic states and Moslems living in the UK. On the one hand, they feel that they should patronise non-Europeans but on the other, they feel hostility towards the ethos of Islam, which is incompatible with liberalism. Moslems are not prepared to compromise their beliefs and values. Islam does not promote the cult of the individual or consumerism and the free market. Economic-liberals therefore see Islam as a long-term threat but in the short term they want to trade with them and make a profit. Because of the need for secure oil supplies and the wish not to offend Islamic allies, liberals are reluctant to use their human rights weapon. They know there is often little difference between a friendly Islamic governing elite and one that is a foe.

Many European nationalists are also unsure about how to view Islam. Most nationalists see the growing Moslem population as a greater threat than any other to European nations but there is nonetheless some sympathy for Moslems living in their own countries because Islam offers resistance to liberal values. Moslems, like nationalists, are demonised by liberals for not being liberal. Both are invariably portrayed in an unsympathetic and negative way.

Most liberals muddled through the Salmon Rushdie affair in some confusion because it was not clear what the correct line should be. Should they support free speech or should they condemn a miscalculated insult aimed at what is essentially a Third World religion. If Salmon Rushdie had been an Englishman there would have been no problem because his comments would have been construed as a form of racism. In the end most said and did nothing, although some, like Fay Weldon, had the courage, despite the air of intimidation, to publicly support the principle of free speech.

When not confronted with stark ideological choices liberals tend to extend their sympathies to Islamic national groups living in the UK and appear to put their trust in the conviction that liberal ideas are self evidently true and that given time Moslems will come round to seeing that truth and adopt liberal values and perceptions. In this way foreign national and religious groups are allowed to established themselves in England and to thrive and grow with no thought being given to the consequences should they decide to retain their culture and most of what goes with it, including large families. Mixing together in one state several national communities with irreconcilable values and perceptions is bound to lead to resentment and conflict. The only surprising thing about it all is that liberals expect the indigenous population to bear their dispossession and its consequences in silence.

European social-liberals are often burdened with feelings of guilt because they believe their ancestors are unique in having inflicted harm on others. As a result they subject their own societies to critical examination but fail to apply the same rigour to the cultures, societies and histories of those they regard as victims. Indeed, non-European cultures are generally viewed with great sympathy and even reverence. Their ethnocentric perceptions of the world and its history are rarely challenged. For instance, many North American Indians insist that they were in possession of their homelands from the time of the creation until they were dispossessed by Europeans. Yet, 8–9,000 year old skeletal remains found near Kennewick, USA are not Indian, and fit the theory that the Indians, after migrating from Siberia to North America, probably replaced an earlier established population. Whether that process was one of extermination (genocide) or displacement (ethnic cleansing) is open to speculation but the discovery could lead to a view of the past that contradicts the Indian version. Because of that possibility, attempts were made to have the remains destroyed before they could be scientifically examined. This is not meant to suggest that the plight of North American Indians should not be dealt with in a sympathetic manner, it is merely a call for consistency and a move away from the racist idea that if it were not for Europeans, the world would be a place of peace and innocence. The sensitivity with which liberals treat Indian beliefs can be contrasted with their attitude towards Christian fundamentalists and their creation model of the Earth.

This form of ethnic discrimination extends into schools and colleges with the result that the education system, is no longer socialising English children into their national culture and their national community, but is instead making them critical of it and forcing on them a liberal-centric world perspective. Fortunately, there are many on the treadmill of the global economy who are disenchanted with liberal theory and practice, and are rediscovering their communal identity. In many places the task of reviving and repairing national cultures is underway.

The Triumph of Liberalism?

In *The End of History*, Francis Fukuyama expressed a belief shared by many liberals that with the end of the Cold War and the destruction of *the Evil Empire* the last ideological war had been fought and won by liberal democracy. He hoped to convince us that all the ideological enemies of liberalism have been vanquished and that there is widespread recognition throughout the world that liberal societies provide the model to which all societies aspire. That outlook is much the same as Marx's view that the destruction of capitalism and the arrival of communism would mark the end of an inevitable historical process. One of the shortcomings of this approach to history is that it overlooks the fact that evolution does not have a destination. It keeps working away but there is no telling where it will lead.

Not everyone is prepared to accept that ideological warfare is at an end and we now live in the best of all possible worlds. Professor Samuel Huntington, *The Clash of Civilisations*,[116] takes a different view and suggests that global society is moving away from a period of war between states to war between civilisations. He rightly observes that those with a similar history, culture and religion are drawn together. He characterises the great divide as being between the West (Europe and North America) and the non-West, which includes Asian-Confucian, Oriental-Islamic and Tartar-Orthodox spheres of influence. Latin America is seen as a possible addition to the Western sphere, "a third pillar of Western civilisation", but for that to happen "democracy, free markets, the rule of law, civil society, individualism and Protestantism" will need to "take firm root".

Professor Huntington's model has been criticised as being a new means of justifying high levels of military spending. In addition, despite his liberal credentials, he has been condemned by social-liberals as, you guessed it, a racist, a Nazi, an imperialist and a Social Darwinist. What seems to have escaped the attention of his critics is that Professor Huntington links capitalism with Western culture as if the two things were the same. Some see a conflict between the two and believe that although liberalism is a strand of Western civilisation, it is one that the West would be better off without. The kindest thing to be said is that liberalism has served a purpose but its many excesses need to be undone as we

---

[116] In the journal *Foreign Affairs*, 1993.

move on to something better. Liberalism is an evolutionary dead-end, like modernism, and has to be abandoned because it promotes an unsustainable way of life. Professor Huntington's work does not suggest that we move to a post-liberal Western culture but it does mark a retreat from universal liberalism. He suggests that the limits of the West (the liberal empire) be defined and Western *culture* (i.e. liberalism) be preserved (presumably by force) within the Western hemisphere.

Nothing lasts forever. The collapse of empires and political dogmas often follow a victorious but long and expensive war. Liberal states have tough economic and military shells but to varying degrees they are weak at the core because of diminishing communal cohesion. Liberals are so firm in their belief that they and their ideology are inherently superior to all others, that it has made them careless of those things that hold a nation and a state together. Man cannot live by image and style alone.

In their moment of victory liberals are ready for a fall. We have heard much about the post-Marxist, post-socialist ideological landscape but we will soon hear the term *post-liberal society*. When the liberal age has passed a vast number of people will wonder how it could have been widely believed that such a jumble of ideas so destructive of community would end in anything but the disintegration of the societies that lived by them. Liberal societies are unable to attain a self-sustaining internal equilibrium. Instead, they need to continually expand and devour external human and material resources.

The Rise of Multi-Culturalism

Multi-cultural and multi-racial societies have existed throughout recorded history but their promotion as an ideal form of society is new. What is certainly new, is the zeal with which economic and social-liberals have, for different reasons, adopted multi-culturalism and set about weakening their own communities. It is much like the way they set about vandalising English towns and cities during the 1960s and 1970s in order to *redevelop* and improve them. The wholesale destruction of old housing and its replacement with modern housing schemes took no account of the needs of community and its importance in maintaining a pleasing social environment. Both of those waves of ill-thought-out destruction were seen for what they were by just about everyone except those responsible. Fortunately, it has long been recognised that the housing and redevelopment schemes of the 1960's and 1970's were a great mistake, and in some places an attempt is being made to put things right. Recognition of the damage done to communities in the name of multi-culturalism is slower coming, but the truth is dawning on some of those responsible. Others are so committed to the ideology that they press on in the hope that despite evidence to the contrary, everything will work out for the best.

In the decades following World War II, multi-culturalism assumed the status of holy writ. It is extraordinary that an ideological whim with such important consequences for England and the English should have been pushed through by such a small liberal priesthood. Their mission was to create multi-cultural societies where none had existed before. They went about the task with great determination and at no time did they feel the need to produce rational arguments with supporting evidence for their views. Instead, they managed to attain an unchallenged position of moral supremacy on the strength of emotional moral platitudes and the suppression of dissent.

Following the end of World War I, the leading statesmen of the time were in agreement that the best hope of securing peace was to apply the principle of national self-determination. This pragmatic policy sought the creation, as far as was possible, of a state for each nation and an adjustment to existing borders in accordance with that principle. The aim was to remove one of the main causes of conflict and one of the principal justifications used by one state to either attack another or interfere in its internal affairs. The League of Nations was created for the purpose of enforcing both the principle of national self-determination and the peaceful settlement of disputes between states. Unfortunately, in some places it was not possible to draw viable nation-state boundaries because the mix of nations was so great.[117] In other places it was thought necessary to reward the wartime victors and punish the losers and, as a result, parts of pre-war Germany and territory occupied by Germans were included in other states, notably Poland and Czechoslovakia. That failure to apply the principle of national self-determination was an important factor in the rise to power of Adolph Hitler and the events that led to the Second World War. When Hitler set about recovering German territory and bringing German people into the German state it was difficult for others to deny that it was a job that should have been done at the Paris Peace Conference.

This is not to deny the likelihood that Hitler would have eventually invaded Poland and Russia whether all Germans lived in Germany or not, but it gave him a popular cause that could be used to further his other objectives. It can be seen in *Mein Kampf* that it was not the ideal of a world of nation-states that led Hitler to war. He was a statist who used the German nation as a vehicle for very different objectives.[118]

---

[117] The option of giving grants to appropriate groups to encourage then to move to other areas for the purpose of creating viable nation-states was not taken. This is not to suggest that everything and everyone can be bought, but merely that financial inducement might have formed part of an equitable solution to some long-standing problems.

[118] It can be argued that the Nazis were more concerned with the philosophy of Neitzsche than with nationalism. It was ideas concerning the will to prevail and the role of supermen that drove them. According to this view, the majority has no claim to happiness or wellbeing but exists only to make possible a process that produces great men. The suffering of a whole nation is of less importance than the suffering of a great man. This view conflicts with the communal concern of nationalists for the

World War II and its aftermath provided liberals with the opportunity to link the ideas and ideals of their ideological enemies, especially nationalists, with the Nazis. Later, when kindly Uncle Joe Stalin was transformed into a demon, though not as evil as Hitler, twentieth century history increasingly became the preferred period of history for liberals. It offered the opportunity to teach *good and evil history* and show how *the West*, and its liberal values, overcame the twin evils of communism and fascism. One of the non-too-subtle messages is that it is difficult to distinguish nationalists from racists and Nazis. The success of that sustained propaganda campaign has disarmed European nationalists for the past fifty years and prevented any effective resistance to the widespread imposition of multi-culturalism. To challenge it was to invite condemnation as a Nazi seeking racial purity and *a return to the politics that caused two world wars.*

With the end of the Cold War and the demise of the Soviet Union, scorn was rightly heaped on the concept of a command economy.[119] What was not deserved was the view that all government interference in economic affairs is bad or that the collapse of the Soviet Union proved the moral superiority of *free enterprise* and *free market capitalism.*[120] Again, the propaganda was successful. Those who suggested restricting the free market and subordinating economic activity to communal needs were condemned for advocating a Soviet style economy that would bring inefficiency and hardship. Surely it is clear for all to see (so they tell us) that only capitalism and liberal democracy offers a future of peace and plenty for all mankind.

The last ideological battle had been won and liberals could look forward to the collapse of the Chinese and North Korean communist states, which were certain to quickly follow. With the introduction of liberal democracy, those who had suffered under communist rule would never allow it to return. Much to the surprise of many liberals, some former communists won elections and attempted to create stability from the economic chaos and collapse that followed the fall of the communist states and the move to market economies. Some politicians won office on a policy of protecting their societies from the devastating power of the global free market economy that had gained access to the markets of the former Russian Empire. However, those states that had been freed from one empire quickly became part of another. They were so vulnerable to outside economic and political pressure that it was impossible for them to resist being rapidly drawn into the

---

wellbeing of all members of their nation, who are not to be treated as *small folk* who amount to nothing *except in the feelings of mighty men*. Leading Nazis appear to have used the German nation as a vehicle for their belief that they were heroic men whose nobility and great deeds counted for more than all the suffering they caused.

[119] An economy where resources are allocated by government command rather than market forces.

[120] It is sometimes overlooked that the arms race, which was central to US strategy during the Cold War, was made possible by central planning. Also, it was not private enterprise that took Neil Armstrong to the moon.

liberal global economy. Global corporations saw the opportunities offered by a generally well-educated but poorly paid labour force and moved in with ruthless efficiency. The sudden introduction of a free-market economy, along with the privatisation of state-owned industries and the complete collapse of others, led to the transfer of valuable assets to Western companies at knockdown prices. The opening of the Soviet bloc market and a new trading relationship with China gave birth to a massive and sustained boon. However, there is no getting away from the truth of the old saying, the bigger they are the harder they fall.

Despite the great misery and loss of life caused by Stalin and other communist leaders, the criticism levelled against communists since the collapse of the Soviet Empire has not been as fierce as that directed against the Nazis. There is no hunting down of Communists and no demand for the trial and punishment of those who committed crimes against humanity. One explanation for this is that communists, socialists and social-liberals share certain ideals, values and perceptions; their belief clusters tend to overlap. Many social-liberals sympathise with the avowed aims of communism and find it hard to criticise it in the same venomous terms used for Nazis. Bernard Shaw and other *Left-liberals* visited the Soviet Union and found little to criticise. They saw what they wanted to see because they hoped the system would work. Likewise opponents saw what they wanted to see. A similar thing happened with the Third Reich and Mao's China; sympathy promotes leniency. The crimes of communists are overlooked even though they have been responsible for far more deaths and human suffering than the Nazis. Some people have been impudent enough to claim that the liberal global economy has caused more deaths and suffering than the economic policies and social reforms of Stalin.

Communists, such as the likeable Mr Gorbachev, appear on television chat shows and are treated as members of *polite society*. This despite the fact that his part in bringing an end to communist rule and the destruction of the Soviet Union was an unintended effect of his policies. Mr Gorbachev was trying to reform the Soviet Union so that it could successfully compete with capitalism. He wanted to save the system not destroy it. He sent Spetsnaz (Soviet Special Forces) death squads into Lithuania and other republics of the Soviet Union in an attempt to prevent them ceding from the union. Many people where killed in those operations but little mention is made of such actions. Mr Gorbachev is an intelligent and charming man but so was Josef Goebbels.

An example of unequal presentation of Soviet and Nazi activities was to be seen in the television series *Cold War*, written by Jeremy Isaac. Nazi atrocities were prominently featured in the programme but there was little mention of Stalin's terror; the millions who died in the famines caused by agricultural collectivisation; the millions who died in the gulags; the murder of kulaks; the forced deportation (ethnic cleansing) of nations from their homelands.

In addition to there being greater liberal sympathy for the ideals of communists, and a greater understanding of the problems they faced, there is the fact that a physical war was actually fought against the Nazis and when blood is spilt antagonisms and hatred tend to run deeper. A common factor in the rehabilitation of communists and Nazis is that just as some Nazis were useful after the Second World War, so some communists were useful after the Cold War. They were often the only people practised in government and able to keep order while the economies and markets they nominally controlled were exploited. Yeltsin, a former communist, proved useful in the job of preserving the Russian state while Russia was plundered in the name of creating a free-market economy. Russia became enmeshed in the liberal global economy and so dependent upon the goodwill of *the International Community* and its financial institutions that it was unable to resist the policies of the New World Order.

The Liberal Political Spectrum

Liberals like to think of political philosophies as occupying places in a political spectrum from the extreme Left to the extreme Right. They see themselves as occupying the middle ground, which is taken to confirm the validity and truth of their ideology. Being in the middle is regarded as normal, neutral and virtuous. Those outside that middle band are to varying degrees seen as extremists and cranks who need to be clearly and repeatedly labelled as such so that their ideas and opinions are treated with hostility. Thus news bulletins warn us of organizations and person who are left-wing or right-wing but never that they are liberal.

The linear Left-Right political model, which has its origins in the French Revolution, is useful as a shorthand for describing political activity within the liberal political elite, with social-liberals on the middle Left and economic-liberals on the middle Right. However, it is a very simple model which does not adequately explain or represent the complexity of politics and the mix of ideologies and instincts that we all subscribe to in one way or another.

The Political Ring

The young, and those new to the study of politics, are often attracted to the idea that if you go far enough to the Left you appear on the Right, or vice versa. This ring model at first glance seems neat but it is inadequate, simplistic and unhelpful. It is rarely used by liberals, except to imply that all those ideologies of which liberals disapprove are but varieties of the same tyranny. The main problem with this model for liberals is that a ring is a continuous band with no left, right, and middle.

Political Clusters

Politics is more complex than either the spectrum or ring models allow for. A better model is a three-dimensional galaxy where clusters of values and perceptions are drawn together by ideological gravity. Ideologies that seem to be completely different from one another contain similar ingredients but in different proportions and mixed in different ways. For example, it is possible to be a totalitarian centralist communist or a democratic decentralist communist. The two clusters produce very different types of communist but the Left-Right model does not take account of that because one communist is seen as much the same as another. The same superficial treatment is given to nationalists.

The cluster model encourages us to look more closely at ideologies and the basic elements from which they are constructed rather than accept the place that liberals allocate them in their Left-Right spectrum.

Political ideologies evolve and adapt to changing circumstances, knowledge and perceptions. The ingredients and the emphasis put on each of them vary over time. Those models of reality that are rigid become stressed and eventually shatter due their inability to reconcile reality with theory. Even religions that claim adherence to a body of divine law tend to re-interpret that law from time to time to make it accord with the needs of the time. One major problem with reinterpretation is that it undermines the credibility of what are supposed to be absolute truths. One remedy is for a law to remain sacrosanct in theory but ignored in practice, as for example with many Roman Catholics and birth control. Another solution is to gradually change absolute laws into conditional guidelines, as in the Anglican Church where moral relativism reigns supreme.

Many liberals genuinely believe that all rational, well-meaning, intelligent people are liberal by nature. They find it very difficult, if not impossible, to accept that there are clusters of values and perceptions that are at least as coherent as their own. Liberals are often far more closed to ideas and knowledge than those they condemn.

Liberals and Bigotry

It is a curious feature of liberalism that its fundamentalists try to present themselves as open-minded rational beings who are prepared to listen to all points of view and see both sides of an argument. In practice, liberals are no more tolerant than anyone else. They portray their opponents as ignorant narrow-minded bigots, and seem to do so on the grounds that only a bigot or fool could fail to see the truth of liberal assertions.

All ideologues are to some extent intolerant of ideas that conflict with their own. We all believe that our views are *true* and that others are necessarily *false* or misconceived. One of the peculiar things about liberals is that they believe their views are self-evidently true. Their mere assertion that something is true or desirable is thought to be enough. An example is their assertion that multi-cultural societies are *a good thing* and something to be encouraged despite there being a great deal of evidence to show that multi-cultural societies are not *a good thing* and that they are usually unstable due to the resentment, tension and conflict they generate. When the tensions inherent in multi-cultural societies flare into open conflict and violence, liberals do not see multi-culturalism as the cause but lay the blame elsewhere.

A bigot is a person firmly wedded to a particular set of ideas and intolerant of any others. Bigots are generally not content with believing something, they want everyone else to live according to those beliefs.

Liberal bigotry manifested itself in the political correctness that swept North America. Its progress in the UK was hindered by those in the media and elsewhere who challenged it and pointed to its absurdity. Despite scattered resistance it took hold in the institutions controlled by social-liberals and is still firmly entrenched.

The principal aim of political correctness is to alter perceptions. It sets out to make normal those communal arrangements and relationships that instinctively seem abnormal. In attempting to do that, they institutionalise discrimination in the name of undoing it. Those who speak out against the absurd dogma face being called bigots.

In 1997, Lord Tebbit made a speech in which he condemned multi-culturalism on the grounds that it causes divisiveness within a society. As might be expected, he was roundly condemned for daring to suggest such a thing. The hypocrisy of those scolding him was not difficult to see. The Conservative Party opposition leader, William Hague, keen to show that he is *a regular guy* in touch with the young and modern attitudes, was reported as saying, "We are going to be an inclusive party. We are a multi-cultural society. We want to be part of that. We want to celebrate that." "I have my own cricket test now: if you don't want to be part of the team, then get off the field." "I want a Conservative Party that embraces people, that doesn't attack people. I stand for patriotism without bigotry."

Paul Tyler, chief whip of the Liberal Democrats, said, "If Mr Hague has one tenth of the integrity and political courage of his predecessor, he will insist the Conservative whip is withdrawn from Lord Tebbit."

Keith Vass, an Asian MP, supported the demand that the whip be withdrawn and said, "It is not enough for William Hague to distance himself from Norman Tebbit. Lord Tebbit's comments were deeply offensive and insulting and characteristically stupid." It should be pointed out that there are many people who have found remarks made by Keith Vass over the years to be deeply offensive, insulting and characteristically stupid but have not said so because they believe that personal attacks are not helpful to an intelligent discussion.[121]

Many in the media picked up William Hague's use of the word bigotry and took it to be directed at Lord Tebbit. If we accept that a bigot is a person who is unquestionably devoted to a particular set of ideas and intolerant and dismissive of other ideas, what reason is there for thinking that Lord Tebbit is a bigot but not those who are intolerant and dismissive of his views? The critics did not address the issues but sought to deny Lord Tebbit the right to express views that challenged liberal orthodoxy. In addition, there was the usual predictable reaction from the usual sources. *The Independent* carried letters and articles directing personal abuse at Lord Tebbit without addressing the points he made. An article, *British Muslims horrified by Tebbit's dark vision*, typified this less than intelligent responce and ended with a quote from Meena Chaudhury who gave a carefully considered opinion on the appeal of the Conservative Party to ethnic minorities. "They must be bloody stupid to want to join a clapped-out old party anyway. Let's face it, what we have is a bitter old man speaking at a fringe thing of a party that does not matter." Presumably, this comment was regarded as witty?

What did Lord Tebbit say that was so terrible?

"Multi-culturalism is a divisive force."

"One cannot be loyal to two nations any more than a man can have two masters."

"Youngsters of all nations born here should be taught that British history is their history. If they are not they will be forever foreigners holding British passports and this kingdom will become a Yugoslavia."

"Unless we share standards, moral values, language and our own national heritage, we will constitute neither a society nor a nation but just a population living under the same jurisdiction." "Humans cannot really talk to each other beyond fairly restricted groups such as a family, a club or a gang – even a political party – without holding some over-riding beliefs and standards in common.

"Unless there is a shared commitment to the common values on which the law is based, the friends of a transgressor will support him rather than the forces of the law. Without shared values, the law is ineffective against crime."

Many people believe that Lord Tebbit's views make perfect sense and that he is entitled to express them. Yet, liberals portray him as the devil incarnate. What reason can there be for that other than their inability to address and answer the issues raised.

---

[121] All of the quotes given are from *The Daily Telegraph*, 9th October 1997.

It is not difficult to detect a similarity between the sentiments of Lord Tebbit and those expressed here but there are important differences relating to what is a nation, a community and a society. These differences make it necessary to reject the remedy offered by Lord Tebbit. His suggestion that the "youngsters of all nations born here should be taught that British history is their history" would not produce the result he seeks. Settlers can be taught the history of another people or nation but it will never be their history because their ancestors were not on the inside of that history. A person's history is the history of their family and their wider community. It is the history that has shaped their culture and their sense of who they are and where they belong. History is not like a wardrobe of clothes that can be slipped on and tried for comfort. The fit would not be good and those trying them on would always feel uncomfortable and want to go back to the clothes that had been made for them and in which they felt at ease. Those who are forced to share their history with strangers will find that history being re-tailored to fit the needs of others. A history with large sections cut from it and patches added from elsewhere is of little use to anyone.

Lord Tebbit appears to be a British nationalist (i.e. a British statist) who is advocating a British melting-pot society along the lines of the supposed US melting-pot. His aim is to avoid division and conflict by assimilating the settlers into an existing British identity. That was also the aim of liberals in the 1960's. They asserted with confidence that outsiders would, with the next generation, be assimilated into the indigenous way of life but the forecast was predictably wrong. It is clear that settlers cannot and do not want to be assimilated. There is now little realistic chance of such a policy succeeding or even being pursued. Multi-culturalism is even more divisive than Lord Tebbit thinks.

On the same page of The Daily Telegraph, 9th October 1997, that carried the headline, "Hague slams Tebbit over race" there was an article, "I live in England but I never say I am English". Godfrey Jones, a Black clothes salesman explained his position as follows: "When I go on holiday and people ask me where I'm from, I tell them I live in England but I never say that I'm English. When England are playing football, I usually find myself rooting for the opposition – especially if it's Brazil or another team with black players. It's not that I hate this country. I love the place, but not what it stands for. I don't really feel part of it. Maybe one day attitudes will change, but I can't see it."

Dennis Marshall, from Barbados, said, "I have always got along with everybody but at the end of the day your culture is your own and if you dilute it too much, you are left with nothing. I am West Indian and I live here. I respect the views of the English but I have my own views and my own ways and there is nothing that can change that."

Shahar Ali Imran said, "I came here twenty years ago, I was educated here and have friends of all races and religions. When the English go abroad, they hold onto their traditions and cultures so why shouldn't we. You can't take away people's roots and transplant new ones."

Godfrey Jones, Dennis Marshall and Shahar Ali Imran expressed sincerely held views with which nationalist would sympathise. Perhaps liberals should get out more and actually talk to Black and Asian people and ask them for their feelings on these matters.

Education, Socialisation and National Identity

Socialisation is a process that is essential to the continuing life of a nation. Until fairly recently, children were socialised into their community by their family and communal institutions. That arrangement now has to compete with the resources of modern states, which have the power to promote loyalty to the state, its civic society and the ideology that governs it. National identities and loyalties are tolerated provided they do not threaten state identities and loyalties. It is possible to see this strategy being employed in the teaching of history in English schools.

- First, there is no teaching of the history of the English and England, there is only British history. This serves to deny English national identity and promotes a British civic identity. More recently, school children have been subject to *information* produced by the EU that promotes a European identity and the concept of European citizenship.

- Second, the histories and cultures of non-European settlers are deemed to be self-contained exclusive cultures that are part of an inclusive British culture. English culture, in as far as it is acknowledged, is nothing more than a blend of imported cultures. Likewise, the English are merely a mix of assorted immigrants. Englishness is an inclusive identity, no group or way of life within it being any more English than any other.

Thus, English children are subject to a system of official socialisation that does not recognise their nation and its history The English, a nation with a recorded history that is nearly two thousand years old, are made invisible in their own country.

In most Western states the primary formal institution for passing on the history, language, culture, values and perceptions of a nation is that of formal education i.e. schools, colleges and universities. In the UK that function is rarely performed because those who dominate the educational establishment find the existence of an English nation ideologically inconvenient. School children have no inkling that the Anglo-Saxons are the early English; the people who created and populated England. No hint that it was in those so-called Dark Ages that the origins of English language, culture, attitudes, and institutions are to be found. Pupils are given no sense of continuity from that time to this. The special importance of that early period in English history is completely lost.

The reasons for this approach is that a link between a long-lived English nation and the land that they live in would bring home to foreign communities that their forebears lived in another part of the world and played no significant part in English history other than as outsiders. It would also make English children and adults less accepting of the idea that they belong to just one of many groups of migrants living in England. The long association between a nation and its homeland would get in the way of an inclusive identity.

Liberal educationalists are faced with the problem that despite their best efforts, the young members of foreign nations soon realise that England is not their homeland. Most can see that they and their family do not look like the English and that their own cultural icons are alien to England. Even the endeavours of developers and builders have failed to break the link between the history of the English and the villages, towns, cities and countryside of England. A nation that has lived in its homeland for fifteen hundred years makes its mark on the landscape. A village church is part of the English countryside, it belongs and is an agreeable and comforting site even to Englanders who have no religion. A church is seen as a symbol of a local community, in much the same way as a village pub might be. It is also part of the history of the village and of England, having probably been there for many hundreds of years. Even Norman churches have become symbols of continuity. A mosque, however, appears to the English as an intrusion and a threat because it indicates that people of an alien culture have occupied a piece of England. This instinctive reaction does not accord with the unrealistic hopes of liberals that colonisation should be seen as an enriching process. But however much they may dislike such feelings, liberals cannot stop them.

The attempt to destroy the special link between the English and their homeland has created a situation where the English are made to sacrifice their communal identity so that others may enjoy theirs without feeling like outsiders.

These liberal policies can be contrasted with those of their ideological brethren in the USA where it is thought desirable to promote the culture and history of the indigenous North American Indians, and to denigrate the history and culture of European immigrants. Perhaps when the English form a minority of the population of England and they are not seen as a threat, their existence will be recognised in the school curriculum under the heading *The Native English – History & Culture*.

Most states in Europe contain an indigenous nation that forms the core population and gives its identity to the state and its institutions. In such places there is a very strong case for the institutions of that state promoting the history and culture of the core-nation. The situation in the USA is different because the indigenous North American Indian population is not the core-nation of the USA and its values do not underlie the core culture on which the state was founded.[122] Despite that, and the liberal notion that all citizens are equal, Indian histories and cultures are rightly accorded special attention in the educational system and the link between nation and land is recognised in special land rights. Unfortunately, English-Americans (Anglos or plain Americans[123]) are not accorded special treatment or recognition even though their history and culture formed the core of the original United States and the original American dream. Surely, English-Americans are entitled to have their history and culture accorded as much respect by the educational establishment as any other?

In the United Kingdom, the English are both an indigenous nation and the core community. In view of that, English parents have not only the right to have their children taught their national history but also the right to have the educational establishment accord English history and culture at least as much respect as any other. What actually happens is that English history, when it is not ignored or made into British history, is usually presented in a negative way, while the histories and cultures of *ethnic minorities* are taught in an uncritical and positive manner. The shortcomings of those foreign communities and the hardships they have endured are invariably blamed on some oppression or wrong done to them by the English or the British. This oppressor/victim mentality is encouraged by people like Baroness Sarah Ludford, a Liberal Democrat MEP, who was responsible for a resolution, passed in 2000 by the European Parliament, which among other things demanded that schools throughout the EU teach their pupils about Europe's role in slavery and colonialism. Why limit it to Europe's role? Perhaps she naively believes that non-Europeans did not have a role in slavery and colonialism. Is she unaware that even now there is slavery in Africa and Asia? Does she not know that Tibet and other parts of the Chinese Empire are colonies? If the history of slavery and colonisation is to be taught it should be the whole history and not a portion of it that serves a racist agenda.

Liberal educationalists are well aware of the power they have to influence the perceptions of the young but few are prepared to admit it. They think it better to preserve the illusion that education is a value-free process. However, others are more forthcoming. Shortly before Hong Kong merged back into the Chinese state, the head of the Professional Teachers Union said of the Chinese communists, *They want to control our politics, our media and now our education system. They know*

---

[122] There is not, and was not, a single North American Indian culture but instead a variety as wide as that found among the indigenous nations of Europe.

[123] *American* in this context can be taken to refer to that group of people who think of themselves as only Americans and not, for example, as Irish-Americans, Polish-Americans, Italian-Americans, Chinese-Americans, Afro-Americans etc.

that you can change the mind of the child through education.[124] Are we to believe that it is only Chinese communists who use education for ideological purposes?

The following is an extract from an article by Nicholas Tate, chief advisor on the curriculum, which appeared in the *Sunday Times News Review*, 27th August 2000. It shows that even when an individual within the establishment believes that English culture and history have a place in English schools, their good intentions can be frustrated by those with closed minds.

> Over the years a range of incidents has sapped my confidence that the cultural and political intentions of the national curriculum will necessarily be converted into reality: a poetry anthology derided because it focused on the English literary heritage (the inclusion of Wordsworth's *Daffodils* occasioning particular outcry); a teacher telling me it was racist to devote 50% of the history curriculum to British history; a lecturer instructing teachers that their role was to educate a "generation of cosmopolitans"; a college principal explaining that she did not regret her students being unable to observe Remembrance Day given that it was an event that involved "an implied unity which I'm not sure everyone can sign up to".

Despite subjecting two or three generations of English children to liberal propaganda most are aware of their English identity, and as they get older they start to explore it.

Liberals and the Media

All governing elites contain competing factions. In liberal states the factions compete, within ideological and perceptual boundaries set by themselves, to become the elected government. The system of government and the electoral process are structured in a way that favours the governing elite and makes effective opposition within the system, impossible. The issues around which elections are fought relate to how the status quo can be best managed. The core values and perceptions on which the state is founded are not challenged; only fanatics and extremists would do such a thing. At the heart of every liberal democracy is a governing elite that has as much power after an election as before it. Gore Vidal's suggestion that the National Security Council effectively governs the USA, whoever is President, is much nearer the truth than many people realise. Only candidates who have the support of a section of the governing elite have any chance of effectively running for President.

Liberal governing elites behave like any other in uniting to defend their core interests. All governing elites strive to quell opposition but where liberals excel,

---

[124] Article by Fergal Keane in *The Sunday Telegraph*, 11th May 1997. Fergal Keane is the BBC's Asia Correspondent.

and often by a very great margin, is in hypocrisy. Despite their claim to favour democracy and freedom of expression they do their utmost to dominate and control the media and the news agenda. This is not done in the crude way known in some states but in a more subtle way that relies heavily on self-censorship. Even in apparently unimportant programmes, such as *phone-ins*, perceptions are controlled by having the right presenter with the right invited commentators. A typical example follows.

On 28th October 1997, BBC Radio 4 broadcast a *phone-in* which was supposed to bring enlightenment to the debate over whether the UK should join the European Monetary Union (EMU). Both the presenter and the *studio expert* were clearly supporters of the EU and the Euro. Callers who expressed doubts about the aims of the EU and the practicality of the Euro were challenged and corrected while supporters were given free reign and backed up. A man who made the point that the result of EMU would be a federal European state which would suffer the same fate as that of the Soviet Union and Yugoslavia, was treated as if his suggestion was farfetched and plain silly. Another caller who babbled in a utopian way about EMU bringing an end to war in Europe was not challenged and brought down to earth but merely listened to at length and thanked for his contribution.

Despite the inability of the presenter and *expert* to grasp the realities of international politics, bigger states have bigger resources and fight bigger external wars. If, as we are told, the EU will not become a state, why is it acquiring all the attributes of a state? Why is there such concern to build an EU *defence* force?

Why were the programme presenter and the *expert* unwilling to even consider the possibility that multi-cultural states, and especially big ones, are inherently unstable and prone to internal communal violence and conflict that eventually cause them to break up? History suggests that multi-cultural states sometimes have an interest in promoting external conflict because it is the only thing that can hold their divided society together.

Much of the liberal opposition to Rupert Murdoch is not because, as is often suggested, his newspapers or television stations are of inferior quality but because his newspapers often give vent to popular views and frustrations that are not on the political agenda of the liberal governing elite. In other words, Mr Murdoch's newspapers are not always supportive of liberal values and institutions, and therefore not someone that the liberal elite can trust. The late Lord Rothermere and his father were also seen as being unreliable.

The Murdoch newspaper that British liberals detest above all others is *The Sun*. They are very free in their criticism of it but have little to say about *The Mirror*, a pro-liberal version of *The Sun*. The following extract is from a piece by Kevin Maguire, Political Editor of *The Mirror*, on 2nd December 1998:

So who favours the euro replacing the pound? Most top businessmen and union leaders, Tory big guns Ken Clarke and Michael Heseltine, Lib-Dem leader Paddy Ashdown and – at least in private – Tony Blair and Gordon Brown.

And who is against it? Tory leader William Hague and his MPs plus a rag-tag band of entrepreneurs, Little Englanders and right-wing nutters.

The Guardian, a broadsheet newspaper, suggests much the same thing but in a less crude way. The presentation is different but both are hostile to nationalism and support the dismantling of European states to create a European super-state. The pursuit of a European identity is regarded as progressive. Those opposed to the EU are not seen as advocates of greater democracy but as dinosaurs resisting the inevitable march of *progress*. That view, which is so freely disseminated through the broadcasting media, is challenged by *The Sun* and some other newspapers.

Newspapers are generally less conformist than the broadcasting media. The reason is perhaps that many of the people working for newspapers are less likely to be part of the governing elite and are more often critical of it than is commonly supposed. Press criticism of the *establishment* might not go very deep, and is often mixed with the trivia of soap operas and party politics, but at least there is some questioning of some liberal dogma some of the time. This is more than can be said of the broadcasting media, which is tightly controlled and follows the approved line.

Rupert Murdoch's growing influence in television broadcasting is seen as a more important threat to the governing elite than his control of newspapers because television is a far more effective medium for propaganda. The viewer does not select television and radio news in the same way that they select a newspaper. People tend to read those newspapers that reinforce their perceptions and prejudices but broadcast news is much the same in content regardless of the channel. This sameness is possibly one of the reasons why television and radio news is widely considered to be impartial and objective, and is therefore more believable, influential and powerful. However, the optimism of the audience is misplaced because there is no such thing as a neutral selection and presentation of news. What is left out is as important as what is put in and how it is presented. There is so much happening in the world yet it is hard to believe it from UK news broadcasts. Foreign news is almost exclusively about disasters in one form or another, and domestic news is dominated by political trivia and crime. When Parliament closes for holidays and weekends, political news makes way for sports news.

Those who control news and current affairs broadcasting avoid letting the news agenda get out of their control by not employing *extremists* (i.e. non-liberals) as journalists or editors. When did you last hear anything favourable said about any of liberalism's ideological competitors? When did you last hear anyone challenge

197

the interests, values and perceptions of the governing elite? On the rare occasions that it does happen, dissident views are nearly always voiced by someone who can easily be portrayed as an extremist. Giving such people an opportunity to air their views, often in heavily-edited fragmentary form, allows the broadcasters to claim that they give access to all views and are thus *democratic*.

One of the arts of media control is to appoint editors who will manage news in the desired way without close supervision. News editors with the correct ideological outlook are likely to select the correct stories, give them the right order of priority and present them in an appropriate way. Liberal values and perceptions are internalised to an extent that those involved in collecting and editing news are largely unaware of their bias, and in that they are no different from those involved in broadcasting in other political systems. The appointment of Andrew Marr, a pleasant man, as BBC Political Editor in 2000, lends weight to the idea of a self-perpetuating liberal elite. The government appoints the Director General of the BBC and he plays a part in appointing *reliable* people to important positions within the organisation.

> Marr, a former editor of the *Independent*, accepted the job "a few weeks ago" at a breakfast meeting in the Halcyon hotel in Holland Park, west London, with Greg Dyke, the BBC director general, and Tony Hall, head of news and current affairs. [125]

It was also reported that Greg Dyke, who made £12 million from the sale of London Weekend Television, was appointed as director general of the BBC despite having donated £50,000 to the Labour Party and having "bankrolled" several Cabinet ministers while they were in opposition. This is the same Greg Dyke who complained that the BBC is "hideously white".[126] What if he had said that the Great Britain athletics squad is hideously Black, or, better still, that the Commission for Racial Equality is hideously Black?

In most states the governing elite exercises control over the media through its power to licence broadcasters and appoint those who manage broadcasting authorities. The arrival of satellite broadcasting changed the rules because it enables persons outside the governing elite to broadcast direct to the citizens of a state and influence them in a way that might be unwelcome to the elite, which loses control of the news agenda. Such concern is probably behind the hostility shown by liberals to BSkyB and Rupert Murdoch. If a satellite service can attract a large audience through its acquisition of exclusive broadcasting rights for various popular sporting events, it will be able to promote a different political agenda to the one promoted by the governing elite. Perhaps that, rather than a sudden

---

[125] *Daily Telegraph* 15th May 2000, report by Michael Smith and George James.
[126] *BBC Online* - The BBC: Leading Cultural Change For A Rich And Diverse UK
[Greg Dyke's speech, Race in the Media Awards 2000] – Commission for Racial Equality

concern for the workings of the free market or consideration for *the man in the street* and his ability to watch popular sporting events, was behind moves to prevent BSkyB acquiring exclusive broadcasting rights to certain sporting events.

In the UK, all forms of broadcasting are regulated by bodies which issue licenses and impose conditions. In order to obtain a licence it is necessary to provide what is considered to be an adequate amount of news coverage in the programming. Such a provision is expensive for one broadcaster to provide so it is usually bought in from one of the specialists news agencies. The concern that news should be included in programming is rather curious and seems to indicate that the governing elite does not want to allow anyone to be able to escape from the daily promotion of the elite's values and perceptions. The regulatory authorities were concerned when it was suggested that *News at Ten* might be ended and the news slot moved to a later time. Gerald Kaufman, a member of the Labour Party, appeared on Channel 4 news and suggested that if *News at Ten* was scrapped it would count against those responsible when their licences came up for renewal.[127] Another instance of such concern was shown when a bid for a broadcasting licence was rejected, at least in part, because of an insufficient provision of news coverage. Why should an agent of the state be concerned about when and how much television news is shown? Admittedly, other aspects of programming are controlled to provide an approved balance but why control broadcasting in that way and not newspapers and journals? What would be the reaction if it were announced that newspapers had to bid for a limited number of licences and their contents had to meet certain requirements and conditions?

News is as persuasive as advertising and there is a lot of it about so it is hard to avoid. Television news is made easy and, where possible, entertaining to watch. The introductions to news programmes generally convey the impression that something new and dramatic has occurred and that what is about to be shown is *the* news and not a selection of news. The presenter is a familiar, friendly but authoritative figure who is able to impart information in a way the viewer believes to be impartial.

The BBC World Service broadcasts radio programmes around the world and its success is founded on its reputation for reliable and accurate news coverage. It is certainly less overtly biased than most other radio stations of its kind but *reliable* does not mean *neutral*. The World Service would not be funded by the UK government, through the Foreign Office, if it was not fulfilling its task of projecting the values and perceptions of the UK governing elite. Being factually correct and reliable 99·9% of the time builds confidence in the news supplier and makes it easier to plant the all important 0·1% of deception.

---

[127] *Channel 4 News* during the week ending 5th September 1998.

When socialisation, regulation, and self-censorship fail to control the news agenda, laws are introduced to deter or punish those who express opinions that are deemed unacceptable. Such suppression is clearly at odds with the ideals of free speech and free expression, and with the spirit of the European Declaration on Human Rights and the UN Charter. Either there is free speech or there is not. To suggest that free speech is permitted within the law is a rather flimsy attempt to evade the charge of censorship. Governments of all types introduce laws prohibiting the expression of opinions with which they disagree and put a gloss on it by suggesting that such laws are there, for example, to protect democracy or state security.

A *good* reason can always be found for a law that suppresses political opposition. The Algerian government cancelled a general election it was certain to lose and then in 1996 gained approval by means of a referendum for banning the main opposition party. The referendum was widely recognised as being *fixed* but it enabled the governing elite to take action against its political opponents under the guise of upholding the constitution and the law of the land. This is an extreme example but governing elites are generally able to make unlawful those things they regard as a serious threat to their wellbeing. All statute law is man-made; none of it is neutral.

Afterword on Liberals and Liberalism

To criticise liberals and liberalism is not to condemn everything they believe in or to accuse them of evil intent, it is merely to reject many of their ideas and beliefs as unrealistic, ill-conceived, and harmful. In a free society it is not a crime, civil offence or social disgrace to reject an ideology and point to its flaws. Opposition to cultural and financial globalism, multi-culturalism and internationalism are not born of xenophobia but concern that they are harmful to communities and democracy. The resistance of the English to an ideology that undermines and threatens the existence of the English nation is something that should be expected; it is a natural and necessary defensive action.

Liberal globalism is destroying the diversity of nations, cultures, and languages. It destroys previously cohesive and stable communities. Has anyone ever voted for liberal globalism? Has any nation living in its own nation-state ever voted for the introduction of a multi-cultural society? The English certainly haven't but those things have nonetheless been inflicted on them. Where is the democracy in that?

Liberals and Nationalism

The Demonisation of Nationalists and Nationalism

Nationalism and *nationalist* are neutral terms which are often used as a form of abuse. Those who are scornful of nationalist sentiments try to depict nationalism as unthinking or fanatical devotion to a nation, and link it to aggressive and militaristic behaviour. Nationalists are commonly portrayed as people who believe that their nation is superior to others. Liberal propaganda almost always makes a link between nationalism and a highly centralised authoritarian military state. Nationalism is depicted as a reptilian instinct that needs to be overcome and discarded; something that appeals to the stupid and unsophisticated; something to be avoided or, if possible, exterminated.

There are undoubtedly aggressive and militaristic nationalists but there are also aggressive and militaristic liberals, communists, Moslems, and Christians. Nationalists generally accept and welcome the existence of many nations and cultures but not in one state. Because of that, they have no missionary zeal to bring others into the fold. For example, the Japanese feel no need to make others Japanese. They, like the members of other nations, are mostly defensive in that they wish only to secure or retain their nation's self-government, independence, identity and way of life within the borders of their homeland. Their mission to convert others is restricted to promoting;

a)   the acceptance of the nation-state as the building block of global society, and

b)   the principle of non-interference by one nation in the affairs of another. What nations do within the privacy of their own homeland is for them to decide.

A diversity of nations and cultures is as essential to the evolution of communities as biological diversity is essential to plant and animal life. Liberals make much of the benefits to be gained from cultural cross-pollination but if we all live in a global liberal mono-culture, where is the variety to come from? Each culture and community offers a different insight into how to tackle the problems that face all communities. Cultures are survival strategies; all preserve the solutions to problems. One day that information may be useful to other cultures.

Nationalists seek a global society in which, where possible, there is self-determination for all nations. It is not the business of nationalists to say how each nation should organize itself; they do not seek uniformity. The doctrine of nationalism provides a model for how global society should be organised to minimise conflict. Nationalism provides the broad framework, it does not determine the detail. The sovereignty of all nations and their states should be respected.

Liberals take an almost completely opposite position to that of nationalists. They are unwilling to accept that other ideologies are better suited to certain cultures, places and times, and they reserve the right to demand that all states conform to liberal values and perceptions. Despite the guise of a concern to promote free expression and diversity, their aim is the subordination of all cultures and their political and economic systems to a global liberal norm. A liberal multi-cultural society contains only cultural shells; it is like a nest full of bird's eggs that have

201

been pierced and sucked dry. In other words, cultural diversity is a wonderful thing provided non-liberal core values and perceptions have been removed. For that reason, liberals see the Notting Hill carnival as a wonderful advertisement for multi-culturalism. Lots of gloss and glitter but little that is challenging or threatening to liberals. In contrast, Islam is seen as dangerous because it is a complete way of life; a sophisticated culture that directs its followers in every aspect of their lives. Behind the costumes, beards and rituals of Islam there is a substance that it is impossible for liberals to suck out. They cannot even patronise Moslems because they mostly have contempt for liberals.

It has become common practice in some quarters to use nationalism and nationalist as terms of abuse. That, combined with propaganda which suggests that nationalists are necessarily right-wing, gives rise to two problems. The first is that it is difficult to discuss the subject in a sensible unemotive way; the second is that it takes no account of the fact that nationalism goes beyond issues of left and right. Many of the revolutionary and liberation groups of the post World War II period were nationalist groups that turned to the Soviet Union for support because it was the only state willing to help them. For example, Ho Chi-Min and Fidel Castro were nationalists as was Gamal Abdal Nasser, the President of Egypt, who was compelled to seek help from the Soviet Union when Western financial assistance for the construction of the Aswan Dam was withdrawn.

The communists, socialists and liberals who tacitly and overtly supported Third World national liberation movements, tended to ignore the nationalist element of the struggle and concentrated instead on the avowed struggle for social justice and freedom from oppression. In short the wars of national liberation were seen as being against colonialism rather than as a struggle for national self-determination.

Nearly all of the groups that fought for independence from colonial rule were tribe/nation based. In most places, the zeal of leaders for national self-government waned as they took over fledgling states and became the new governing elite. Recognition of national homelands and the principle of national self-determination was rarely given high priority as they set about the task of holding together multi-nation-states within existing colonial boundaries. Many of the attempts to create civic societies (so-called *nation-building*) have been less than successful. Some of the new states are so large and the resources available to their governments so comparatively slender that they are unable to effectively govern or defend the whole territory of the state. In many cases national boundaries are regaining their importance and national governments and administrations are being formed without regard for state boundaries. Africans are no fonder of multi-culturalism than anyone else.

The term *nationalism* is often deliberately confused with loyalty to the state, and portrayed as a tool or device invented by governing elites for the purpose of manipulating those they govern. While it is true that governing elites often appeal to the communal instincts of nations, it does not follow that the concept of nation or national identity were invented by those who sought to use those instincts in the service of the state. That something is sometimes misused does not necessarily make that thing bad.

Those responsible for the demonisation of nations and nationalism run into difficulties when they want to promote the interests of, for example, North American Indian nations that are asserting their claim to a homeland and the right to preserve what remains of their culture and way of life. Likewise when small South American Indian nations (tribes) attempt to resist the advance into their homeland of alien people and an alien culture they are generally sympathised with, and rightly so. In a similar way, Ken Saro-Wiwa was not condemned for his nationalism when he bravely campaigned on behalf of the Ogoni nation against the exploitation and pollution of their land by the Shell Oil Company and the Nigerian state. He was shrewd enough to present the campaign as an environmental issue because he realised that it would be difficult to get the support of Western liberals if it was seen as a campaign for national self-determination.

> "He [Ken Saro-Wiwa] used to tell me, in fairly bitter tones, that whale-loving White liberals don't care about the Third World's 'real' problems. "But environmental complaints will get to them," he would add.[128]

That members of the Commonwealth failed to save Ken Saro-Wiwa from execution was not due to a faith in quiet diplomacy but to the fact that many of its member states, particularly in Africa, have problems similar to those of Nigeria. Most are multi-nation-states with governing elites recruited from the dominant nations within the state. Nelson Mandela, for example, was unable to enthusiastically support a campaign by the Ogoni for self-government when the South African state was, and still is, unwilling to support or recognise the distinct and separate nature of nations such as the Zulus within its own state boundaries.

Liberal Nationalism

Some liberals have come to terms with nationalism and accept that national cultures provide the perceptual and value environment in which real freedom can flourish. They argue that liberalism is above all a concern for personal freedom, and that freedom implies choice. *Personal freedom demands a wide range of choice between meaningful options.*[129] In other words, there is no meaningful choice between two options if one of them is regarded as illegal or immoral or improper. *Freedom involves making choices amongst various options, and our societal culture not only provides these options, but also makes them meaningful*

---

[128] *The Independent* 12th November 1996 – in an article by Donu Kogbara.
[129] Joseph Raz, *Ethics in the Public Domain*, 1994, OUP.

to us.[130] Culture provides *a background against which more individual choices about how to live can be made.*[131] This can be taken to mean that we have more real choices in a community of like-minded individuals than in a society where there are many sets of often-conflicting values and perceptions.

Humans have evolved instincts for communal living. We need to *get along* with those we live with. The way we live and the choices we make are moulded by our communal life. Our instincts are not suited to life in a society where there are many conflicting cultural norms. The social fabric of a civic society cannot match the sophistication, balance, depth and completeness of a communal culture that has evolved in an organic way over a long period. It follows that it is advantageous for the members of a national community to preserve their culture and the space within which it can flourish.

Although some liberals have recognised the importance of communal cultures and their importance to freedom and democracy, most reject that stance because they see it is favourable to the nationalist position. Liberals cannot totally ignore and deny the existence of nations so they set about an intellectual unravelling and examine each strand in isolation. For example, it is sometimes suggested that nationalism takes two forms, *political* and *cultural*. Political Nationalism is motivated by the belief that the interests of each nation are best served by the creation of a state within fixed boundaries that enclose the national homeland. The second, Cultural Nationalism, is motivated by the belief that the purpose and justification for the existence of a state is the preservation and promotion of the national culture and way of life. To dissect nationalism in this way can help the observer gain insights but to view the parts in isolation, as if they can exist alone, serves only to distort and misunderstand the thing being observed. For example, using *nationalism* in the terms *ethnic nationalism, social nationalism*, and *civic-nationalism*, suggest that there are ethnic nations, social nations, and civic nations. The parts belong together; nationalism is a living whole and it is only as a whole that it can be properly understood. Dissection does not reveal the communal soul that binds the part together. They are intertwined and inseparable in the minds of nationalists who, depending on the needs of the time, lay emphasis on one or the other.

The separation of nationalism into its parts can be useful as an analytical tool but creating several types of sub-nationalisms and trying to apply each of them as if they have a separate existence gives a false impression of the whole. It also gives rise to arguments about whether a particular strand of nationalism is good (e.g. civic-nationalism) or bad (e.g. primordial nationalism). A better approach would be to use completely different terms for the parts so that they are not individually mistaken for the whole. All of this should be borne in mind for what follows.

---

[130] Will Kymlicka, *Multi-cultural Citizenship*, 1995, OUP

[131] David Miller, *On Nationality*, 1995, OUP

Ethnic and Primordial Nationalism

Ethnic nationalism is an exclusive nationalism based on a shared history, culture and a common ancestry. It is not possible to join an ethnic group, one has to be born into it. To be a Zulu it is necessary to be born a Zulu. To belong to an ethnic nation is like belonging to an ethnic group, it is *in the blood*.

Primordial nationalism is much the same as ethnic nationalism but the term is usually used when emphasis is placed on the ancient and instinctive roots of nations. Primordialists believe that nations are a natural human grouping; an extended kinship community. Mankind has always lived in communities; which are the origin of language, culture and religion. Our human instincts have evolved within a communal environment. We have a psychological disposition to live in communities and instinctively defend their cultural and geographical space. Kinship is the natural basis for co-operation, which is the key to survival. Communities give us our sense of who we are and where we belong. The kindred community of mother, father and children is the building block for other wider and more complex communal organisms.

Early or traditional human communities contained the elements of modern nations; one has evolved into the other. Nations are not *invented*; they do not exist only because they have been defined.

The term *virulent nationalism*, used in the derogatory sense of meaning *poisonous* or *infectious* nationalism, is sometimes used by liberals to describe ethnic or primordial nationalism. Those who use *virulent* fail to understand that nationalism is found in all normal people, they do not need to be infected with it. Nationalism is not something that is caught like a cold, and neither is there a cure. It is a natural communal sentiment that is part of being human.

Social Nationalism

Social nationalism is an inclusive nationalism based simply on the fact of being a member of a society and sharing the rudiments of a common way of life. The term is used for the feeling of belonging that is shared by *a people*, which is a group that lacks sufficient unity and common identity to be called a nation.

Although social nationalism has its root in a shared culture, it appears to be something that can be acquired and dropped according to circumstance; we can leave it behind when we move on; it is not something we carry around for life.

Civic and Official Nationalism: State Nationalism and Statism

Civic-nationalism and official nationalism are similar to social nationalism but with the addition of *identification with a state* and *loyalty to a state*.

The distinction between *civic* and *official* nationalism, in as far as it is possible to see one, does not seem to be significant. Some use the terms in slightly different ways, others lump them together under one heading.

Official nationalism, which can be called patriotism, is an inclusive nationalism based on identification with, and loyalty to, the state and its political culture. Civic-nationalism suggests something additional; an identification with a public culture. Both *official* and *civic-nationalism* could be lumped together and labelled *statism* or *state nationalism* because both rely on the existence of a state, and both are used in various ways to justify the existence of a state. But, for the sake of convenience, the broad term *civic-nationalism* will be used.

The United States is sometimes given as an example of a state with citizens who share a civic-nationalism. The great *American melting-pot* is said to bring together people of all races and cultures and blend them together into one nation; an American alloy. That metaphor is less appropriate now than ever before but it is such an important part of liberal mythology that they feel the need to protect its sanctity. Some think the US bears greater resemblance to a bucket of pebbles collected from around the world. They are of different composition, shape, and size. Only if they are rubbed together for a very long time will they produce the fine sand of a nation.

Civic-nationalism fits the liberal ideal of a multi-cultural society where the state pursues, protects and arbitrates between the interests of all individuals and groups. Citizens are united in their loyalty to the state, its constitution, institutions and public culture, which together promote the bundle of shared values and perceptions that make citizenship meaningful.

In a multi-nation-state, the more nations there are, the more difficult it is to find a consensus. The greater the cultural differences, the lower the common denominator is likely to be. It might be so low that there is not enough common ground to produce an effective constitution and code of law which all can respect and feel comfortable with. The various groups could probably agree on a few basic definitions such as those for murder and theft but would probably have difficulty agreeing on the penalties. Should the aim be punishment, deterrence, retribution, or compensation? Perhaps penalty is the wrong word. Some may prefer to place the emphasis on reform and help for the offender.

Without a broad range of shared values, it is impossible to construct a political and legal framework with which all communities can identify. In such circumstances, there is no focus for a civic-nationalism. The remedy suggested by liberals is that all groups should accept liberal political institutions and ideology as a universal political currency. That is unacceptable to many groups. Moslems, for example, are no more likely to accept liberalism as neutral common ground than are liberals to accept Islam. What actually happens is that nations continue to value their organic communal identity and only look to their manufactured civil identities when it serves their communal interest.

A civic-nationalism of sorts may develop over time in a multi-nation state but it is not something that can be engineered as a cure for disunity. It is certainly not something that is bound to happen. Civic-nationalism can also decline, as it has in the UK and the USA. The introduction into the UK of many new nations and greatly differing cultures has broken the consensus and weakened loyalty to the UK. At one time, the interests of the UK overlapped those of England but that overlap has dramatically shrunk as the UK governing elite attempts to appease Scots and draw the various settler-nations into a British identity.

In a similar way, civic-nationalism flourished in the USA when it had a core English-American population. As the number and size of nations within the USA has increased, so the sense of oneness has decreased. Most Latinos in the USA are likely to feel a closer affinity with Mexicans than with Anglo-Saxon-Americans. This suggests that a *civic nation* and *civic-nationalism* are not as inclusive as liberals would like them to be. What of those who do not feel loyalty to the state or their fellow citizens? Are they excluded from the nation? If loyalty and identification are removed from the relationship, little is left other than a population sharing a common citizenship.

Liberals are committed to the incompatible ideals of civic-nationalism and multi-culturalism. They think that given sufficient determination and cajoling they can create strong and united multi-cultural states. This despite strong evidence to show that more multi-culturalism means less civic unity.

One of the ploys they use to put flesh on the bare bones of citizenship is to merge civic and national identity. Thus, if you are a citizen of France you are deemed to be French. According to the state, no citizen of France is any more or less French than any other citizen. And none have any more or less right to be in France because no special connection between ethnic French and France is recognised. It follows from this that the cultures and religions of all citizens are deemed to be equally French and of equal importance and worth to the state. Such a view is of course completely unrealistic; the state's decree has clearly exceeded its powers. Just as more multi-culturalism means less civic unity, so the greater the number of cultures crammed into a national identity the weaker that identity becomes. In the end, what does it mean to be French other than to be a citizen of France? What becomes of those who were once called French? Are they to be called ethnic-French or would that get in the way of stripping them of their special link with their land and the state?

Civic-nationalism involves the stretching and distortion of nationalism. Algerians with French citizenship are not French and pretending that they are is wishful thinking. It is as much an insult to Algerians as it is to the French to suggest that one can become the other by means of a legal nicety. Even in the USA, where the indigenous nations have for the most part been ethnically cleansed, it is difficult to get people to give up their national identity when they adopt a US civic identity. They cling on to their ethnic identity however thin it might be. Many Americans think of themselves as being both American and Irish even though they have never been to Ireland and have to go back through many generations of ancestors to reach someone who lived in Ireland.

The situation in France is different because the indigenous French are still a majority and it is they who determine who is and is not French. Being French is more than a civic identity; it is a cultural and ancestral identity. Algerians in France, whether second, third or whatever generation, will never be French until they are absorbed into, and indistinguishable from, that group of people who are commonly acknowledged to be French. When that process is complete, everyone who calls themself French will look to a common French history and feel that it is their history. That is even less likely to happen in France than in the US, unless the ethnic French population shrinks and melts away. This is not to suggest that Algerians want to be French or that they believe it is possible for them to become French. It simply means that national identity is more enduring than a civic identity.

Most states do not grant citizenship to just anyone who applies for it. With the exception of Anglo-Saxon and some West European states, citizenship is usually only granted to those who can show that they have some connection with the core-nation or nations. German citizenship is granted to *ethnic* Germans from Eastern Europe who have never before set foot in Germany because it is felt that the German state exists to represent and protect the interests of ethnic Germans, i.e. members of the German nation as determined by ancestry. Israel has a similar policy for Jews. Palestinians have already made it plain that the fledgling state of Palestine welcomes the *return* of Palestinians, even if they have never before set foot in Palestine. In all cases, nationality is determined by parentage rather than by place of birth or residence. The Republic of Ireland discriminates in favour of those with an Irish line of descent and nearly every other state does likewise when granting citizenship because it is natural to believe that community, identity and belonging pass through families. People with a link of kinship to the indigenous core population of a state are widely thought to have a natural right of entry because it is their homeland and that they will better fit in with the way of life. Nationalists regard the maintenance of a core culture and core national identity as essential to the wellbeing of a civic society. Liberals on the other hand find such selection and discrimination offensive and often term it *racist*. Furthermore, they do not believe that a state has the right to pursue such a discriminatory policy, whether the majority of its citizens want it or not. Surely, if the indigenous population of a state wish to select who they allow to enter their country and live with them that is their business? By what right do outsiders tell a nation how they should manage their affairs?

The nationalism of the Scottish National Party (SNP) is often described as civic-nationalism but just what that means is not clear. If members of the SNP really believe in civic-nationalism why do they not cultivate and promote their British civic identity? Why do they want to abandon one civic identity (British citizen) for another (Scottish citizen)? Why is their Scottish identity more important to them than their British identity? What is it that makes that group of people so different from other citizens of the UK that they want to govern themselves and believe that they have the right to do so? Perhaps more telling is the fact that outsiders recognise the right of some groups to govern themselves. Outsiders may resent or disapprove of Scots wishing to break away from the UK but they recognise their right to do so. The people of Nottinghamshire do not assert a right to self-government in a state of their own and outsiders would not acknowledge a right to self-government because they are not a nation and Nottinghamshire is not a national homeland. But why is one notion of self-government scorned and the other accepted? The explanation is that nations living in their own homeland are seen to naturally have a right to self-government. It is real nations (groups bound together by history, culture, ancestry, language, perceptions and a common identity) that are recognised as having that right.

We must presume that members and supporters of the SNP have an idea of who is Scottish and who is not, but inclusion or exclusion from Scottishness cannot be based on citizenship or loyalty to a state because no Scottish citizenship or state existed when the SNP was formed. There is also the point that a Scotsman who, for example, gains Canadian or New Zealand citizenship is still accepted as being Scottish. In other words, Scottishness is founded on something far more complex that mere citizenship.

It seems that there is a group of people calling itself Scottish which has a loyalty to something more enduring and important than a civic identity. The SNP is clearly appealing to that higher loyalty and identity. Its struggle for independence is based on the belief that there is a Scottish nation, defined in terms of culture and history; that it has a homeland and the right to govern itself if it so chooses. In this, Scottish nationalism is little different from Irish, English, Kurdish or Palestinian nationalism but the SNP has adopted the fig leaf of civic-nationalism in order to overcome two major obstacles to its progress. The first is the opposition of liberals to European ethnic or kindred nationalism, and the resulting need to appease them in order to avoid vilification. The second is that the SNP has to appeal to a population that has a fragile national identity divided along cultural, religious and historical fault-lines. Because there are in effect two loosely connected Scottish nations, each with its own history, culture and origins, it is necessary for the SNP to appeal to a social or civic-nationalism, and to take advantage of a widespread dislike for a common enemy, the English.[132] It was for this reason that many members of the SNP were so pleased about the film *Braveheart* which contained far more fiction than fact and was a vehicle for a very crude anti-English sentiment.[133] For example, the circumstances of the battle won by Wallace were nothing like those shown, and the seduction of King Edward's wife by Wallace was sheer invention since she was not married at that time and could not have been more than ten years old. But there is little to be gained from going through a long list of the very many faults in such a bad film; its propaganda purpose has already been served. The SNP appealed to the *Braveheart spirit* and saw no contradiction in doing so while claiming to be civic nationalists promoting a Scottish identity that includes the many English living in Scotland. English liberals probably also enjoyed Braveheart and found the thinly veiled expressions of dislike for the English uplifting. The political masochism of English liberals could be brushed aside and treated as the ridiculous abnormality it is if it were not for the fact that they have the power to inflict their perceptions on others, and in particular the young.

Another equally bad film that presents fiction as history is *The Patriot*. The anti-English nature of the film and its simple-minded story line will no doubt appeal to some. Some English people believe, perhaps mistakenly, that Mel Gibson was attracted to the film for that reason.[134] *The Patriot*, which is known to some English people as the *The Dwarf*, perhaps a reference to Mel Gibson height, was to be based on the life of Francis Marion, a brilliant strategist, known as the Swamp Fox, who was inspired by ideals of liberty. The rebellion was started and led by men like him who wished to preserve the rights of freeborn Englishmen. Unfortunately, for the makers of the film, Marion did not have the background needed for a hero.

> But as the historian Robert D. Bass has pointed out, Marion also "failed to honour flags of truce and knowingly violated international law". And his worship of liberty had clear limits: he would rape his female slaves and hunt Native Americans for sport. It was when these uncomfortable facts came to light that the film-makers changed the character's name to Benjamin Martin. In the film, needles to say, Martin has no truck with slavery whereas the British – who in reality fought the slave trade long before the Americans did – are presented as thoroughgoing racists.[135]

---

[132] The euphemism used for the English is *London* or *Westminster*.

[133] Some Scottish nationalists found *Braveheart* an embarrassment, in the same way that some Welsh nationalists wince when King Arthur is used as a prop for Welsh nationalism.

[134] It has been suggested that Mel Gibson would do better to make a film about any of the various real atrocities inflicted on Australian Aborigines. It would certainly be a treat to see him decorated with war paint and leading an Aboriginal tribe to victory.

[135] *The Week*, Issue 264, 15th July 2000

Spike Lee has criticised the film for ignoring the existence of the Black population in general and slavery in particular. Other uncomfortable facts are that the British government wanted to limit settlement in North America to the eastern side thus leaving the west for the indigenous Indian nations. The Indians fought on the British side because they wished to preserve the existing boundary. There are other *difficulties* that make the events of the time impossible to portray in terms of good versus evil. There were atrocities committed on both sides but they were rare.

The British officer, Banastre Tarleton, who is the main villain of the film, was indeed guilty of breaking the codes of war but not in the way shown in the film. Like Marion he was a brilliant soldier who had an unpleasant side to his character. The important thing is that his behaviour was the exception not the norm.

What is reasonably certain is that if such films depicted, for instance, the Irish in the same way that they depict the English, there would be allegations of incitement to racial hatred and the threat of prosecution. There is no doubt that the films will cause many people throughout the world to dislike the English but what effect will it have on an English audience? Perhaps it will make some of them ask who is making these films and why? But perhaps that is too much to ask for. More likely, they will leave the cinema with a view of history that no amount of written rebuttals will change. It is for this reason we must welcome the revival of a Russian film industry which presents a different view of the world to the one Hollywood gives. The lead character in *The Brother 2* is Danila Bagrov who, during a four-day visit to Chicago, kills a variety of unpleasant individuals.

> *The Brother 2* is Hollywood turned upside down, with Russia and Russian values taking on and triumphing over the West.

> "Tell me, American. What is power? Money?" he [Danila Bagrov] asks an organised crime boss against the backdrop of the city's skyline after massacring his way into his office. "I think power is truth. Whoever has truth on his side has power."[136]

The filmmakers of other countries should follow the Russian example and turn Hollywood values against the things Hollywood represents.

The crude hatred of the English revealed in films like *Braveheart* reflects the feeling of a large number of Scots for the English. There are many instances of Englanders living in Scotland being discriminated against in employment, suffering abuse, and being subject to violent assault. *The Sunday Times Magazine*, 4th October 1998, carried an article, *Scotch Wrath* by Jean Rafferty, which gave many instances of discrimination by Scots against the English. This included abuse in and out of the workplace.

---

[136] *The Daily Telegraph*, 8th July 2000. Article by Marcus Warren

People who would be shocked at anti-Jewish jokes or the idea of calling black people "niggers" are quite happy to speak out openly against the English. The words "English bastard" are heard everywhere.

The case of Mark and Paul Ayton is referred to. The two brothers were walking home after a night out when they were accosted by two young men singing *Flower of Scotland*. The brothers were called "English bastards" and a fight followed. After that, two more youths became involved and Mark was attacked by three of them, who kicked him as he lay on the ground. *Then they left him. He died alone, choking on his own vomit.* It does not seem unreasonable to suppose that had the brothers been Black and been called Black bastards, the story would have been more widely reported and a public enquiry demanded.

Throughout the article, anti-Englishness is called racism, which it is clearly not. It is hostility to outsiders that focuses on a history of conflict between the English and Scots, and is re-enforced by the sense of frustration that arises from the large-scale migration of English to Scotland. Much the same happened in Wales when the English migrated there in large numbers during the 1960s and 1970s.

Another example of discrimination involved James Cairns who joined the Scottish Black Watch regiment and suffered constant physical and verbal abuse for being English. His story was reported when he sued the Ministry of Defence because of the brutal treatment he received.[137]

To suggest that some members of the Catholic community in Scotland dislike the English is an understatement. Many Protestants share that sentiment but the antipathy that they feel for Catholics is probably at least as great and in many cases more deeply felt. Many Protestants are also inclined to support the Union because of their support for the Protestant *Ulstermen* whose identity is in many ways linked to the UK. Some Catholic Scots also favour the union because they believe their position is more secure in the UK than it would be in an independent Scottish state dominated by Protestants. Religion is not yet an important issue in England but it is likely to become so as the size of the Moslem population increases.

When Scotland attains independence it will presumably have a constitution that defines the Scottish nation in terms of citizenship and loyalty to the state. But that will give rise to difficulties. Will those English people living in Scotland when a Scottish state is created be deemed to be Scottish and become Scottish citizens unless they opt out? Or will the English be labelled as ethnic English and thereby gain the recognition in Scotland that is currently denied them in England? How will a Scottish government regard those citizens of Canada, New Zealand and the USA for whom a Scottish ancestry is an important part of their identity? Will a

---

[137] *News of the World*, 1st November 1998

Bengali or Englishman living in Glasgow really be regarded as a Scot while a Scottish migrant to Canada, with or without Canadian citizenship, be seen as a foreigner?

Scottish nationalism is not civic-nationalism but plain and simple ethnic-nationalism but it has been given the label civic-nationalism to appease liberal opinion. Because of division within Scotland, it has proved necessary to play on an ethnic Scottish identity and old feelings of rivalry with the English. The SNP leadership neither approve of nor condone violence and *racist* behaviour against the English or anyone else but they nonetheless gain some satisfaction in being able to harness the *Braveheart spirit*.

Summary

The conclusion drawn from this is that civic-nationalism is strongest in nation-states, where it exists naturally as a strand of ethnic-nationalism. The desire to create a state, which is sometimes described as civic-nationalism, rarely exists other than as an expression of ethnic-nationalism. The more nations that there are within a state and the greater the difference between them, the weaker a civic identity and the state itself will be. In other words, civic-nationalism is an expression of unity, it does not create it.

Other Nationalisms

Further misuses of *nationalism* are to be found in such phrases as *Islamic nationalism* and *Arab nationalism*. Likewise, the term *African nationalism* is often mistakenly used in place of *Pan-Africanism* despite the fact that there is not one African nation but many. African nations have rich and distinctive cultures; there are many African languages, cultures and histories. Pan-Africanism is a political movement that seeks to bring African states together so that they may better pursue common interests. Pan-Africanism gave rise to the creation in 1963 of the Organization of African Unity, the members of which are states.

Real Nations and Real Nationalism

Nations and nationalism are centred on people. States and civic-nationalism are centred on political structures. Real nationalism is, as we have seen, more complex than the one-strand *civic-nationalism*. The threads that run through a nation's identity and bind its members together are so varied and numerous that the breaking of some, or even many, of those threads is not fatal to their national identity. Englanders might believe in one god, several gods or none. They might be nationalists, internationalists, communists, fascists, liberals, anarchists, monarchists, republicans, centralists or decentralists. They might live in China or be citizens of Spain. They might wish to change the structure of the state or preserve it. They might do any or all of these things, and more, and still be English. Nationalism is not fragile.

Nationalists have to protect different strands of their national identity according to the needs of the time. When they do that they are sometimes labelled as cultural or political or economic or linguistic nationalists. For example, resistance to the highly Americanised global culture is often called cultural nationalism.[138] There is also French resistance to linguistic invasion by English/American words and phrases. Another example of so-called linguistic nationalism is the attempt by Welsh nationalists to establish the dominance of the Welsh language in Wales. Political nationalism is an expression of the desire to form a nation-state or to retain or regain control of it. The Basques are just one of many nations seeking self-determination.

If it could be commonly accepted that there is only one nationalism (the real thing) and that what is called civic-nationalism is something different, it would be easier to avoid the tendency to a polarised 'this or that', 'good and bad' argument. That in turn would make it easier to promote a more helpful and realistic view which recognises that people have many overlapping identities and loyalties. The citizens of a real nation-state have no need to distinguish between their national and civic identity because the two are so closely entwined; the state is the political embodiment of the nation. The citizens of multi-nation-states need to distinguish between two identities if they are to survive. A nation that does not assert its identity and interests will be ignored and become politically invisible. The English have suffered that fate because for many years they have mistakenly believed that the institutions of the state represent English national interests. Fortunately, there is a dawning realisation that the governing elite will only take notice of the English if they organise themselves and push their interests in the same way that other nations do. The English have to quickly learn the art of *ethnic* and *multi-cultural* politics. What better way is there to succeed than to study the best practitioners and adapt their ways to our needs?

Nationalists and Patriots

Because liberals wish to portray loyalty to a state as good and loyalty to a nation as bad, they have attached positive connotations to patriotism (a noble loyalty) and negative connotations to nationalism (a bigoted and xenophobic loyalty).

---

[138] Using the term *Americanised* and Americanisation in a derogatory way is not meant as criticism of the many American communities that promote and protect traditional communal values. It refers to the spread of a hard, shallow, money-orientated culture that afflicts much of the US and is taking hold in the UK and other parts of the world. It is perhaps understandable that the US should try to remake the world in its own image but it is sad and amazing that others should be so keen to help.

Patriotism

Patriotism is often defined as devotion to one's country and concern for its defence. It is not clear whether *country* is taken to mean simply a geographical territory or if it includes the indigenous people of that country and their culture, i.e. a nation.

A wider definition gives a patriot as a person who vigorously supports his country (native land) and the way of life of its people (nation). It is difficult on this definition to distinguish a patriot from a nationalist but nevertheless patriotism is often used in a way that suggests loyalty to the state. Thus we have those who are proud to be British, Spanish or Indian patriots, and others who are proud to be English, Basque or Bengali nationalists.

Prime Minister Tony Blair uses *patriotism* as meaning loyalty to the state, as can be seen from his appointment of a Minister for Patriotism. The task of the minister is to promote a British identity and loyalty to the British state. So desperate is the Labour government to stop the rapid decline in a British identity that Home Secretary Jack Straw suggested that, except for domestic competitions, the *national* football teams for England, Scotland and Wales should be abandoned in favour of a Great Britain team. The aim is to promote an inclusive civic identity and enable the members of ethnic minorities to identify with the team. As usual the concern is with giving priority to ethnic minorities. What does it matter to the likes of Jack Straw that the English, Scottish, and Welsh will find it less easy to identify with a British team and feel that they have been robbed of one of the very few outlets for an expression of their national identity? That of course is the very reason for the suggestion, which shows a complete lack of understanding of national identity and loyalties. It is probable that most English, Scottish and Welsh people would rather have their own teams and fail to win competitions than have a winning team made up of foreigners. The only surprise is that Jack Straw, and the famously out-of-touch Tony Banks (former Minister of Sport), have not suggested a European Union team, but perhaps that is the next step. That would give a real chance of winning nearly every competition. But who would feel good about them winning or even care? Where would a Great Britain team play its home games? The whole thing is just too absurd to be true.

Patriotism is a term often used by those who are defensive about being called a nationalist. They try to draw a greater distinction between the two terms than is justified.

Patriot – from Greek *patris* native land; related to *pater* father.

Chauvinism

Chauvinism is aggressive or fanatical patriotism; jingoism; enthusiastic devotion to a cause; smug irrational belief in the superiority of one's own state, nation, race, party, sex, etc.

Jingoism

Jingoism is the belligerent spirit or foreign policy of jingoes; chauvinism.

A jingo is a loud and bellicose patriot, a chauvinist.

Realpolitik

Realpolitik is practical politics based on an understanding of the realities of how political systems work and what motivates political actors. It is Machiavellian in that it is not good or bad in an ethical sense but is concerned with who has power, how they gained it and how they use it. It is also an understanding of how those with power justify their actions, policies and goals.

The systems approach to *international relations*, which is not currently fashionable, suggests that states have instinctive interests and reflexes which are independent of their internal structure and the interests of those who govern them. This causes states to behave in certain predictable ways whether acting alone or in groups. The approach does not deny that governing elites have their own interests and that they use the state to further them. It suggests that, despite the differences, governing elites behave in similar ways in similar circumstances and that state interests can be separated from elite interests.

Few accept that states react to external stimuli like the hard-shell billiard balls they were once commonly compared with, but the analogy is often a useful one. The internal structure of states, and the ideology and interests of their governing elites are important but they do not explain everything. A state is a *whole* system and as such it has inherent interests and instincts that are separate from those of its parts. However, the interests of nations and governing elites often overlap with those of their state, not least because their wellbeing is often furthered by the survival of the state. It is because nations and governing elites are usually prepared to subordinate their short-term interests to those of the state that states behave in a more or less predictable way. The task of *realists* is to observe the instincts and behavioural characteristics commonly displayed by states, and to use that information to establish general rules that help predict how states will behave in any given situation.

Human institutions tend to reflect the fact that humans are communal animals with communal instincts. For example, states and nations have the territorial instincts of humans and all react in a similar and largely predictable way when their territory is threatened or invaded. Realpolitik suggests that whatever the ideology of those who make decisions on behalf of the state, they will tend to be presented with a choice between a limited number of realistic options (often there is no real choice) and the decisions they make will unavoidably be influenced by communal instincts.

Hypocrisy is to be found everywhere and is not restricted to the leaders of any particular state or the followers of any particular ideology. When US military forces invaded Cambodia the United States was widely condemned but when China invaded Tibet and absorbed it into the Chinese state, few took to the streets to show their opposition. The cases are not exactly parallel but the invasion of Tibet was a greater threat to the existence of a nation than was the invasion of Cambodia. The Chinese government tried to justify its invasion on the grounds that Tibet is part of the Chinese state. Statists, whether liberal, communist or whatever, find it difficult to counter such an argument because they give state boundaries priority over national boundaries. Nationalists have no problem in rejecting the Chinese position because any nation living in its homeland has the right to self-government, and the Tibetans are a nation living in their homeland. They are not ethnic-Chinese and the Chinese state has no proper claim to govern Tibet or Tibetans.

Indigenous populations are best able to care for their own culture and wellbeing, and that is confirmed by the actions of the Chinese in Tibet, who have as a matter of policy set about destroying the symbols of Tibetan national identity. Many traditional Tibetan buildings have been destroyed and some important Tibetan cultural and religious customs have been banned. The Chinese government also supported their own candidate as the successor to the Dalai Lama and have encouraged Han-Chinese (ethnic-Chinese) to migrate to Tibet to create a multi-national, multi-cultural civic society.[139] That policy of colonisation is clearly being used to weaken the Tibetan nation and prevent it enjoying self-government in its own country. The Chinese strategy is made easier by the fact that Tibetan national institutions have evolved in a comparatively isolated country and are vulnerable to the pressures and divisions created by multi-culturalism. In other words, Tibetan culture and social organisation has not evolved the defensive mechanisms that are essential for the survival of national communities in a multi-racial, multi-cultural society.

The strategy of the Chinese government might already be successful in that the process is unstoppable. There are now more ethnic-Chinese in Tibet than Tibetans. The Dalai Lama has accused the Chinese of cultural genocide and social-liberals have sympathised with him but they find it difficult to argue in favour of a mono-cultural national community. They instinctively feel that what is happening is wrong but are ideologically opposed to the measures necessary for the Tibetans to regain control of their homeland.

---

[139] China contains several nations that wish to be free to govern themselves. The Chinese governing elite uses a strategy of encouraging the movement of people from one part of China to another (e.g. Xinjiang Uygur region) in order to dilute and weaken national identity. The leaders of liberal states make no objection to such ethnic engineering because they use or support similar policies elsewhere – e.g. in Indonesia.

When the Dalai Lama was asked in a televised interview how he would deal with the matter if Tibetans were to recover the political power they once had in their own country, he replied that those Chinese who had positive feelings about Tibetan culture would be assimilated but that it would be desirable for those with negative feelings to leave. Such a view is completely at odds with liberalism and multi-culturalism, yet he was treated with great respect, even reverence, by the interviewer, who did not ask him to explain how Tibetans could gain political control of a country in which they are a minority by peaceful or democratic means. Neither was the Dalai Lama asked to explain how the Chinese who did not want to be assimilated would be expelled. There was no hint of an accusation of ethnic cleansing.[140]

The English are in a similar position to the Tibetans in that they have traditionally defended themselves at their geographical borders; much of the English border is coastline while that of the Tibetans is mountains. Because the English were for the most part successful in defending their territory, they were able to develop and enjoy a live-and-let-live attitude to others that permitted greater individualism and deviation from the norm than found in many other communities. In other words, territorial security made possible a confidence and diversity that is not seen in a community that feels threatened. Unfortunately, this free-and-easy attitude is a source of communal weakness in a multi-cultural society where other communities have evolved strong cultural defences to compensate for their lack of secure geographical boundaries. It is evident that as a general rule, nations with secure geographical boundaries often have soft cultural boundaries, while those with insecure or non-existent geographical boundaries evolve hard cultural boundaries.

The UN Charter, Article 1(1), states that one of the purposes of the UN is, "To maintain international peace and security, and to that end to take effective collective measures for the prevention and removal of threats to the peace, and for the suppression of acts of aggression or other breaches of the peace, and to bring about by peaceful means, and in conformity with the principles of justice and international law, adjustment or settlement of international disputes or situations which might lead to a breach of the peace." However, when China invaded Tibet little was done by other states to remedy the situation. Another example is that of the people of Spanish Sahara who were not given the opportunity for self-determination when the territory was decolonised in 1976 and split between Morocco and Mauritania. Morocco was more concerned with gaining control of the valuable phosphate deposits than with seeing the creation of an independent state. The mainly nomadic people living there were unable to resist the military power of Morocco and a former Spanish colony is now a Moroccan colony. Much the same happened when East Timor gained independence from Portugal in 1975. Indonesia invaded and occupied the territory and brutally suppressed resistance. It

---

[140] BBC Television, *Breakfast with Frost*, 21st July 1996.

then sold oil exploration rights in East Timor's offshore waters. The people of East Timor, like the people of the Western Sahara, were unable to benefit from the exploitation of *their* mineral resources. The ideal of free trade and the necessity of making more resources available to the insatiable appetite of the global economy is apparently more important than ideals concerning self-determination, freedom and justice.

Realpolitik suggests that in certain situations <u>all</u> states tend to act in a similar way regardless of the ideological stance of their governing elite. It is often only the ideology (moralising) used to justify policies and actions that differentiates one government from another. Most governments and their leaders are aware that the reasons given for actions and policies are usually a cover for the pursuit of state interests. The most dangerous people are the statesmen who adopt a crusading approach and really believe the sanctimonious moralising that they indulge in. When governments make human rights an issue, as is frequently done by the USA in its dealings with China, it usually has more to do with using human rights as a weapon in a battle about access to markets than with a genuine concern for the welfare of people. There is plenty of evidence to show that in a contest between a trade deal and human rights, trade comes first. Even Foreign Secretary Robin Cook was silent about an ethical foreign policy when he visited China for the purpose of furthering trade deals. In fact the longer Robin Cook is Foreign Secretary, and the more he learns about the realities of world politics, the less we hear from him about an ethical foreign policy.

The Global Jungle

The *International Community* was not outraged by events in East Timor but when Iraq invaded Kuwait and the interests of the *International Community* were threatened there was much talk of the need to resist aggression and preserve the independence of states. The usual references to *freedom* and *democracy* were not much used in this instance because there was little that was free and democratic about the system of government in Kuwait. Had the interests of the *International Community* been served, or at least not threatened by the invasion, there is little doubt that nothing would have been done to resist it. It is widely known that the conflict was about oil, its price, and who controls it. Why pretend it was a struggle between good and evil?

The reaction to the invasion was not surprising and it would be naive to expect states and their governments to act differently. It does, however, demonstrate that states are more ready to act to protect their own interests than they are to protect human rights or the interests of others. Such a view better explains the actions of states and the development of global society than the simplistic good against evil model. It is also apparent that those who advocate free trade do so not out of idealism but a belief that it serves their interests.

Liberals appear to believe that we live in a global village, but nationalists know that we live in a global jungle where it is for each nation, and each state, to look after its own interests and defend itself. Sometimes it is necessary for states to co-operate with others to defend common interests but such interests have traditionally been related to some kind of external economic or military threat. In modern times, alliances such as the EU, NATO and the defunct Warsaw Pact came into being to defend an ideological status quo.

Whatever the reason for the creation of an alliance, its justification ends when its purpose has been served. Some alliances endure out of habit long after the reason for their creation has passed. Others are given a new lease of life by the manufacture of a new threat. Alliances can be prolonged but eventually they all end. In view of that, each party to an alliance should ensure that when it ends, they are in a position to regain their former independence and not be needlessly dependent upon others. If an economic, political or military alliance endures for more than a generation there is a danger that some or all of the allies will come to believe that the alliance will last for ever and fail to make any provision for the time when the alliance ends. For example, the British governing elite appears to assume that the European Union will endure indefinitely. As a consequence it does not see the folly of allowing much of British industry to become foreign-owned and controlled; of integrating British defence companies with foreign ones; of allowing fish stocks to be lost to foreign control; and much more. By the time governing elites recognise that the ideal of a European state is impractical and damaging, the UK will be even more at the mercy of other states than it was before it joined, and even more dependent on the goodwill of others for food and the planning, financing and evolution of its industries and services. Complete self-sufficiency (autarchy) is not a realistic aim but states, and nations, should keep their dependency to the minimum possible because it limits their options and is a source of weakness during times of conflict.

It is sometimes necessary for a weak state to rely on other states for its defence against a strong neighbour but it is not something to be recommended. For example, Japan might one day find itself in conflict with China and discover that the US government does not believe it to be in the best interest of the US to stand by its commitment to the defence of Japan. For all its technological and economic power Japan might find it is unable to successfully confront Chinese military power. An alliance formalised by a treaty is of little worth if the interests of one of the parties, particularly the more powerful party, are no longer served by that treaty.

States and nations have to stay alert and not grow fat and lazy. Long periods of success usually lead to complacency. The survival skills and social cohesion that enabled nations to become rich and powerful are often lost or undone in a fit of reckless disregard for long-term survival interests. There is a tendency to project the present into the future. In Western states this takes the form of believing that the future will be much like the present but with more technology and consumption.[141] There is little awareness that civilisations have a life cycle and that they die of complacency or exhaustion or a loss of the will to perpetuate themselves. Nations can survive the collapse of states and the wider civilisation of which they are a part but if they do not work hard to preserve their identity and boundaries, they too disappear. The greater the proportion of a nation that cares little about its history or its future, the more certain is that nation's demise. Those who "don't care" about keeping alive their communal history and identity will come to care but by then it will usually be too late.

National Self-Determination

Self-determination means self-government. A nation has self-determination when it is able to determine its own interests, actions, way of life, laws and form of government. A self-governing nation is able to set its own goals and pursue its own policies.

United Nations Charter, Article 1. The purposes of the United Nations are:

> (2) To develop friendly relations among nations based on respect for the principle of equal rights and self-determination of peoples, and to take other appropriate measures to strengthen universal peace.

It is not clear what is meant by *peoples*, as used in Article 1, but the term was probably meant to refer to the indigenous peoples of the post-World War II European colonies. The right to self-determination was seen by the American drafters of the Charter as a device for bringing about the break-up of the European empires and the opening of those markets to US business interests. The US did what states commonly do, it used its pre-eminent position to pursue its interests in the guise of a moral agenda.

The use of *peoples* suggests that an American civic society view of self-determination was intended. There was little attempt, during the process of decolonisation, to recognise real nations and re-draw political boundaries to form nation-states and bring about national self-determination. Two notable exceptions were the creation of the states of Pakistan and Israel. The first came about as the result of the political situation within India, and pressures the British colonial power was unable to resist. The second was the result of intense external pressure on the UK from the US.

There was no general intention to create nation-states. If there had been, the US would have put pressure on the European colonial powers to achieve that end. The world would now be very different because many of the ancient African countries

---

[141] There is also a tendency to project the present into the past and re-interpret history in the light of current values and perceptions.

would have been recognised. For example, the colony of Nigeria would have been broken up into several states corresponding with the boundaries of national homelands. One of those states would have been Biafra. Instead, colonies became states and a struggle began in which those who took control offered the thin manufactured identity of citizenship in place of the rich ancient communal cultures to which the people had a natural loyalty and affection.

It is possible that the drafters of the UN Charter believed that nations have the right of self-determination but having already misused *nation* in the American fashion to mean *state*, they needed a synonym for *nation*, and thought *people* suitable.

In addition to lacking any guidance on the vague term *people*, the UN Charter is also unhelpful in that it does not provide any mechanism or guidelines for *peoples* to achieve self-determination. For example, there is no obligation on state-governing elites to recognise the right of self-determination of *peoples* within the territory of the state, or to assist them achieve it. There are two principle reasons for the lack of guidance. The first is that most state-governing elites have an interest in preserving the state system as it is. The break-up or division of one state could set a precedent for others. Many multi-nation-states have potential breakaway groups within their own territory and it might prove embarrassing to champion independence for a nation elsewhere and then deny it to another nearer home. Both India and China are multi-nation-states which have a history of championing independence movements abroad yet both are reluctant to recognise the right of national self-determination within their own borders, e.g. Sikhs in Punjab and Tibetans in Tibet.

Another reason for the UN Charter remaining vague on the matter of self-determination is that it would be very difficult, if not impossible, to establish rules for governing the process by which a nation can properly seek and attain self-determination. In most cases nations have to fight to attain a state because what a new state gains an old state loses, and states do not give up territory willingly. Because the matter is complex and the outcome unpredictable (much depending upon the relative power of the parties involved) it is a convention (ignored by NATO states in respect of Yugoslavia) that the society of states treat a bid for independence – Irredentism – as an internal matter and wait to see what happens. If those attempting to break away are able to establish effective control of the territory and population they are claiming for the new state, and the state from which the territory has been seized appears to acquiesce, perhaps after a long and expensive war, other states give recognition to the new state and its government. In the terminology of international law, a *de facto* situation is made *de jure*.

As far as nationalists are concerned, the UN Charter can neither give nor deny the rights of self-determination and self-defence to nations because they are inalienable rights. Every nation has the inherent right to govern itself in its homeland, subject only to it having the means to gain or retain that objective.

The *right* to national self-determination is not something that most states, and especially liberal states recognise, unless it weakens the position of an enemy state. States do not usually press their friends and allies to recognise the right to national self-determination or to assist those seeking it. The struggle by Chechens to create their own state is a war in which the *people* of a former Russian colony are seeking self-determination and they might reasonably expect the support of those members of *the International Community* who so often speak of the need to uphold freedom and democracy.[142] The action taken by the Russian government against the Chechens was as brutal and costly in lives as anything undertaken by Bosnian Serbs, yet only weak formal objections were made to the Russian government. The reason for *the International Community* being so restrained was that President Yeltsin was introducing a free market economic system and integrating Russia into the liberal global economic system. It was necessary to avoid doing anything to undermine his position. If a communist president had authorised the invasion of either Chechnya or of the Russian parliament building, he would have been condemned for being a Stalinist.

The admission of Russia to the Council of Europe, an organisation concerned with upholding liberal ideals, was a further sign that opening Russian markets to global corporations had a higher priority than human rights or self-determination. Yeltsin's respect for democratic bodies and procedures was not high but nothing could stand in the way of presenting him as a Russian champion of freedom and democracy.

National self-determination in its purist form is impossible to attain; it is an aspiration, as are other ideals such as democracy and freedom, but nationalists think it is something worth striving for. That means resisting and undoing the work of those who are attempting to submerge national identities under civic identities. It also means supporting those, wherever they might be, who resist the imposition of a global culture and identity.

---

[142] There is little doubt that the Chechens are not part of the Russian nation; their language, culture, history and religion are very different from that of the Russians. Although the states of The *International Community* have objected (half-heartedly) to the way the Russian government has fought the war in Chechnya, they have not challenged the right of either side to fight. In other words, in the case of Chechnya, there is recognition of an absolute right to national self-determination but the Chechens have to fight and win it.

Other examples of attempts to create states are Biafra attempting to break away from Nigeria in the late 1960s, and the current war conducted by the Tamil Tigers in Sri Lanka. Also, Pakistan attempted to prevent East Pakistan breaking away to form Bangladesh.

National Interest

Mention is often made of the national interest but what is usually meant is the interest of the state or the group that controls the state. It is very difficult to arrive at an objective assessment of what is the best interest of a nation but nationalists would argue that in the long-term the core interests of a nation are best served by leaders who see it as their primary duty to safeguard the existence of the whole nation (people and culture), defend its homeland, and promote its interests and wellbeing. That means ensuring that all sections of the nation have adequate food, housing, healthcare, education and access to a fair judicial system. It is for the nation to judge if its leaders are doing the best they can in the circumstances to fulfil their duty. Such a relationship can only work in the long term if there is a free and open democratic system that makes the governors accountable to the wishes of the governed.

The nationalist position is that nation-states and their governors exist for the purpose of pursuing the interests of the nation. Unfortunately, it is generally the case that governing elites use their control of the state to promote their own interests over the interests of the nation or nations they govern. Disregard for real national interests are most likely to occur when there is no recognition of the fact that nations, states, and governing elites sometimes have conflicting interests. What usually happens is that governing elites suggest that there is only one interest, the national interest, and they are pursuing it. For example, in a one-party state the interests of party, state and nation are deemed to coincide. If the governing elite is recruited primarily from the business elite, it will promote an ideology that favours business interests.

Elite, state and national interests do not always conflict and even when they do there are certain situations where the geopolitical strategic interests of the state are accepted by all parties as being paramount. Despite the inevitable conflicts that arise, it is usually in a nation's interest that it has its own state, a nation-state, to represent its interests in global society. In all but exceptional circumstances, it is in a nation's best interest to defend and preserve its state.

An example of an exceptional circumstance is a situation where a nation-state is unable to effectively deter or defend itself against total destruction by another state. In such circumstances, it would be in the best interest of the nation for the state to surrender and die so that the nation might have the chance to survive. A nation can survive without a state but not without its people and culture. Similarly, if a governing elite acts in a way that unnecessarily threatens the survival of the nation or its state, it would be proper and necessary for the nation to rid itself of that elite. Indeed, it has a duty to do so.

Liberals often suggest that the only ascertainable common interests of a nation or any other group of people are the survival and economic wellbeing of its individual members. They also argue that if there is a national interest, there is no way of knowing what it is or what policy should be pursued in its furtherance. This is a dangerous argument for liberals to follow because it can be used against them when they assert that it is the task of government to pursue the greater happiness of the greater number. Nevertheless, they use the survival and economic wellbeing argument to justify the merging of two or more states into a super state. For example, they argue that the EU offers the prospect of greater wealth and prolonged peace for the people within its borders. It is therefore in the best interests of the citizens of the existing member states that their states merge into a new civic-state.

The liberal view overlooks the fact that there are ascertainable communal interests, such as the preservation of communal culture and identity. It is in the interests of a community that those who govern it are accountable to the community, and are obliged to pursue communal interests. In other words, self-government is an interest, and that means that those who govern should be drawn from the community. Two things follow from this: communal interests translate into individual interests; the EU is unable to further those interests.

Part of the argument in favour of the EU is that merging the states of Europe into one super-state will enable the people of Europe to gain greater influence in the world and thereby better pursue their interests in the global economy. One of the difficulties with this is that in order to *gain more influence in the world* the people of Europe will have to accept less influence (control) over those who govern them. The *influence* argument is one that globalists often us, never mind the loss of democratic accountability, look at the influence that will be gained. Influence over what and for whom?

Another part of their argument is that the EU will prevent conflict and war by creating a web of economic interdependence that makes war impossible. Conflict will be channelled into competition in sporting events and song contests. Englishness will, so they hope, mean little more that identifying with the England football team. With the fading away of national identities, and the adoption of a European civic identity, we will enjoy peace, goodwill and prosperity. This overlooks the fact that big states try to establish and preserve a sphere of influence. The creation of one sphere means challenging the boundaries of another sphere. That, and the compulsion to meddle in the affairs of other states, gets them involved in foreign wars. Like other imperial powers they will describe their wars as peace-keeping missions. A better, but not conclusive, indication of who is the aggressor and who the defender in a war is to look at which side is fighting on their home territory, and which is in foreign territory. A nation or a state or an alliance that fights its wars abroad is nearly always an imperial or aggressive power.

Another shortcoming in the peace and prosperity plan is that large multi-nation states are prone to internal liberation wars. All in all, the chances of a fully-fledged EU bringing greater peace and stability to the world are remote.

The EU provides an example of how governing elites create states in their own image and subordinate national interests to state interests. All the while they are doing this they deny it. For example, there is the supply of pro-EU *educational* material to schools and the promotion of EU symbols, such as the EU flag on car number plates and public buildings. They want us to become familiar with and identify with the flag and think of ourselves as Europeans who owe an allegiance to the flag and what it stands for, which is a European civic-state. While they promote an inclusive identity, they also undermine exclusive identities. In England there is the promotion of manufactured regional identities and interests that involves stirring up resentment and conflict between the EU administrative regions to promote regional loyalties that detract from national identity. It is the classic policy of divide and rule.

Regional government is being introduced through the creation of Regional Development Agencies and administrative reorganisation before the people of England have had an opportunity to express an opinion on it or opt for an English Parliament. The prize for regional politicians is the greater glory of being a member of a Regional Assembly, or its Executive or even First Minister. EU regional identification on car number plates is just one of the many ways in which they encourage us to build a regional identity. It is only a matter of time before we have regional flags and Latin mottoes. Perhaps Jack Straw and Tony Banks will suggest regional football teams and the merging of county cricket teams.

The EU does not promote national identity unless it fits with its regional policy. Thus Scottish and Welsh national identity is acceptable, at least for the time being, but English national identity is a problem because England is too big and potentially too powerful to fit into the EU regional plan. The opportunities for the expressions of English national identity are therefore minimised. The Europhiles purr with satisfaction every time England football supporters are involved in trouble because it provides an opportunity for liberals to ridicule and denigrate the English flag and those who espouse a pride in England and Englishness.

The EU governing elite is promoting its own interests and not those of the member states or the nations within them. The flaw in their plan is that nations will find that their interests are being denied and ignored because there is no institutional arrangement for pursuing those interests. Dissatisfaction and social stress will rise above the froth of multi-national civic society dogma. Nations will find that they have no way of pursuing their interests other than by asserting their right to govern themselves. It is merely a question of how long it will take to reach that stage.

The prize on offer in this cost-benefit deal is a future where a new improved superstate cares for all its citizens in a way that nasty old-fashioned nation-states are unable to match. An EU superstate will usher us into the gleaming global economy of the twenty-first century. Please jettison your history, culture and national identity before the flight starts.

Such a bargain could only be put forward by people with an impoverished idea of what is important in life; who but a liberal could believe that a nation should accept the offer:

> What shall it profit a nation if it shall gain the whole world, and lose its own soul.

The theory that economic wellbeing and individual survival are the prime interests of all nations is a liberal view based on the false assumption that a nation is merely a group of individuals who share membership of a political unit that exists to pursue economic goals. The liberal argument that citizens have many conflicting interests and that it is not possible to pursue all of those interests, is a statement of the obvious. They could add that there are also communal interests that sometimes conflict. However, the art of political leadership is to make a judgement as to how conflicts of interests can best be minimised and common interests maximised. The way in which the problem is tackled depends upon one's perception of it.

Liberal social-contract theory deems that individuals live together in a civil-society because that is the best way for them to pursue the greater happiness of the greater number. As we have seen, happiness and standard of living are measured primarily in economic terms, with culture, identity and place being treated as having little value. A nationalist view is that individuals live together in communities because natural selection has made humans communal animals. Community has proved to be a successful way of managing conflict and improving the odds for survival. Other benefits include a communal culture, identity and a sense of belonging. So the nationalist answer is yes, individuals do have conflicting interests but they also have shared communal interests, the first of which is the preservation and welfare of their community. The most effective way of pursuing those interests is to create a state which has as its primary goal the preservation of the nation. Greater individual consumption might play a part in improving individual and communal welfare but it is not the first or only goal.

The economic wellbeing theory (or consumer theory) is therefore not one that nationalists can support because they are aware that nations are more than a collection of individuals seeking material gratification. The people and their institutions are bearers of a history, language and way of life, they are members of a relay team that carries from one generation to the next memories, values and perceptions that are unique to that nation and essential to its regeneration. The survival of a nation therefore has a cultural as well as a physical aspect. If the population survives, perhaps enjoying great wealth, but the national culture dies, then the nation has not survived.

That individuals are willing to forfeit wealth or even their lives, in defence of their nation is something liberals find difficult to adequately explain. Chechnya provides an example of individuals joining together in a common cause and fighting against great odds in an attempt to preserve their nation and the state apparatus that co-ordinates and organises the nation's resistance. Chechens do not want to be part of a centralized superstate, they prefer to be free to govern themselves and are prepared to fight for it despite the material and human cost. That does not support the idea that individual survival and wealth maximisation is the prime concern of human beings.

It can be concluded that governing elites of all kinds use whatever means necessary to enlist support for policies and goals that advance their interests. Even those who are critical of nationalism appeal to it in one form or another when they need to rouse a population to the defence of its homeland. The willingness to fight is not born of aggression but is an instinct for individual and communal self-preservation. Nations are generally only roused to fight when they are attacked or threatened with attack. Nationalism is not usually an effective call to arms when the aim is to gain support for an attack on another nation's homeland; the reason being that it is instinctively thought to be wrong. For that reason, wars that entail fighting in other lands are usually justified by an appeal to a universal political or religious creed. Such wars take the form of a crusade of good against evil. An example of this was when war broke out after the secession of Slovenia, Croatia and Bosnia-Herzegovina from the multi-nation-state of Yugoslavia. It was members of the British Labour Party, which has a history of condemning the use of military force, who favoured bombing Serbia into submission and were the most strident in demanding that British troops be sent to *enforce a peace*.[143]. The fervour was due to it being seen by them as a war to defend multi-culturalism.[144] It was a Conservative government, which is usually seen as more warlike, which was reluctant to get involved. The former saw the conflict in terms of the need to

---

[143] *Enforcing a peace* means using force to compel a person or group of persons to abide by the wishes of the enforcing body. If the underlying conflicts are not addressed and resolved it is highly likely that when the compulsion is removed the peace will break down.

[144] There must be a suspicion that many but not all members of the Labour Party supported Bosnian-Moslem aspirations for self-government, and opposed similar Serbian and Croatian aspirations, because they mistakenly saw Bosnia as a multi-racial, multi-cultural society where Bosnian-Moslems, Orthodox Christian Serbs and Roman Catholic Croats had lived happily side-by-side until disturbed in their idyll by Serb nationalists. The reason for casting Serbs as the villains was not that they were the only ones to move populations so as to create secure areas with firm national boundaries, it was because in most places they had a military advantage and were best able to carry out such a policy. The Croats forced 250,000 Serbs out of Croatia but throughout the conflict the *International Community* supported the Croats and their policy of ethnic cleansing did not become a human rights/war crimes issue. The US government, which was arming and training the Croatian army, urged them to do their ethnic cleansing quickly and instigated media diversions while it was taking place. The Serbian refugees were expelled from Croatia with the knowledge and approval of the US government, and there has been no demand from the *International Community* that Serbs be allowed to return to their homes. One has to conclude that President Milosevic was seen as someone who had to be removed from power because he did not accept the ideology and objectives of the *International Community* and was beyond its control. Economic-liberals oppose him because he is a socialist, and social-liberals oppose him because he is a nationalist. Better, therefore, to support Croatian nationalists while they are useful but after the war to back their liberal opponents.

impose their values on others while the latter saw it in terms of state interests. For the Conservative government, the interest being threatened was that of the UK's permanent seat on the UN Security Council and it was probably for that reason that they agreed to get involved.[145]

The first interest of nations and nation-states is survival of the nation, which means survival of the people and the culture. The first interest of liberal states is survival of the state and its ideology. Nations have national interests; states have state interests. Nations usually want to protect what they have; liberals feel the need to impose their values on others.

Nationalists and Realists

Machiavelli devised a set of rules or strategies for the guidance of princes.[146] The rules relate mainly to the internal affairs of a kingdom or state, and explain the means by which political power can be gained and retained. Machiavelli described the reality of politics as he saw it practised. The advice he gave dealt with the practical means of dealing with political problems. Similar rules to those set down by Machiavelli are applicable to the affairs of nations and states in the modern global system where each nation and state has ultimately to depend upon itself for its survival and wellbeing. Liberal principles (professed but not acted on) have little bearing on those rules and their application. The rules of global politics are concerned not with how nations and states ought to behave but with how nations and states actually behave. That information (the rules of the game) is necessary for those who wish to survive within the global system. It is for politicians to justify their actions and dress them in the appropriate ideological clothes. Even the most blatant pursuit of narrow self-interest can be presented as the selfless pursuit of a noble ideal.

It is extremely difficult, if not impossible, to take an active part in global politics and always operate within a set of narrow moral principles. Success in matching actions with ideals is more likely to occur if the ideals are founded on a realistic view of the world and human behaviour. A morality that is divorced from reality is

---

[145] In order to preserve the UK seat on the UN Security Council it is seen to be necessary to always be willing to respond to UN needs. If the UK's permanent seat was taken by Japan or Germany or the EU, it is unlikely that the UN could rely on them for the same degree of co-operation and expertise.

[146] *The Prince.* It is often mistakenly believed that Machiavelli necessarily approved of what he described. He set down general principles for gaining and retaining power. His rules were based on observation and study of how the world is, not how it ought to be. The Realist School in International Relations adopts a similar outlook, describing world politics in terms of such traditional concepts as balance of power, spheres of influence, power vacuums, etc. Like Machiavelli, they are not offering a guide on morality and virtue. It was for the Prince to decide the purpose to which the knowledge was put.

less likely to be observed and less likely to serve as a useful guide in the setting of realistic goals. The greater the mismatch the greater the hypocrisy that arises from it.

Nationalists tend to have fewer problems in matching their words to their deeds for the simple reason that their perception of how nations and states behave tends to be a closer match with reality than that of social-liberals. For example, nationalists understand the limitations of the United Nations and are not surprised when shortcomings are revealed. The UN provided the dominant liberal states of the time with an institution that would better enable them to pursue their interests and project their shared liberal values as global values. The creation of the Security Council, which institutionalised the dominant position of powerful states, was an act of Realpolitik. It is therefore futile and naive to argue that the UN would work as intended and bring peace to the world if it were not for states and other global actors pursuing their interests. Similarly, it needs to be recognised that nationalism is an enduring fact of life that should be catered for. It is less than sensible to denigrate nationalists, ignore the widely felt sentiments that they express, and claim that the world would be a better place if nationalism did not exist. It does exist and is a natural expression of a communal identity that will not go away. The pursuit of peace, or any other goal, needs to take account of nationalism and the other realities of global society, and not try to wish them away. The problem for liberals is that their pursuit of internationalism and multi-culturalism takes little account of the realities of the world. It is their denial of those realities that gives rise to many conflicts and prevents long-lasting solutions being found for them.

The Governing Elite

Marxist theory holds that in all but the most primitive of societies there are two groups of people: a ruling class, and one or more subject classes. The dominant position of the ruling class rests on its ownership and control of the major economic resources. Economic power is the root of political power, which enables the ruling class to shape the state in a way that best furthers its own interests. Members of the ruling class do not owe their dominant position to any intellectual or moral superiority, but to their economic power. The subject classes, the proletariat, are wage-earners who own no economic asset other than their labour.

Vilfredo Pareto and Gaetano Mosca put forward a different theory.[147] Pareto observed that in all societies there are two classes: the governing elite, and a non-elite, i.e. the rest. Elites exist in all spheres of human activity. In mathematics, music, morals, etc., there are those who excel and those who fail. Those who excel form the elite within their given speciality and from them the governing elite is

---

[147] Vilfredo Pareto: *Les systemes socialistes*, Paris, Marcel Giard, 1902; *Trattato di Sociologia Generale*, 1915–19. (English language translation in *The Mind and Society*, 4 vols. London, Jonathan Cape, 1935.)
Gaetano Mosca, *The Ruling Class*, New York, McGraw-Hill, 1939.

formed. The governing elite consists of sub-elites that directly or indirectly play an important part in government and the shaping of society. The governing elite described by Pareto is unlike that of Marx's ruling class in that it is composed of people who have excelled in one area of activity or another, rather than with people who own or control economic resources.

Pareto was concerned primarily with emphasising the division between the governing elite and the non-elite, while Mosca gave greater attention to the composition of the governing elite. He started in the same way as Pareto by pointing out that:

> Among the enduring facts and tendencies that are to be found in all political organisms, one is so obvious that it is apparent to the most casual eye. In all societies – from those that are very simple and have barely attained the dawning of civilisation, down to the most advanced and powerful – two classes of people appear: a class that rules and a class that is ruled. The first class, always smaller in number, performs all political functions, monopolises power and enjoys the advantages that power brings, whereas the second class, the more numerous, is directed and controlled by the first, in a manner that is now more or less legal, now more or less arbitrary and violent.

Mosca also argued that:

> an organized minority obeying a single impulse will inevitably rule over an unorganised majority for the reason that each member of the majority stands alone before the totality of the organized minority. Members of the organized minority have some attribute, real or apparent, which is highly valued and very influential in the society in which they live.

The dominant minority owes its position to good organization and the will to govern. Mosca did not exempt from his theory parliamentary democracies, which he believed to be controlled by a political elite divided into factions which compete with each other for office. Representatives are not elected by the voters but, as a rule, have themselves elected. Or, to put it another way, the governing elite arranges the electoral system in a way that suits it and, with the help of those of its members who are able to manipulate public opinion, has itself elected. The rules of the political game are fixed in a way that prevents strong counter-elites emerging and gaining power.

Governing elites are recruited from among the economic, military, political, religious, cultural and other elites within a society. Elites justify their power by claiming to be superior to others in some way, perhaps by having valued attributes or by being the guardians of certain values. A governing elite might be challenged by an internal counter-elite or an external foreign elite. Whatever the reasons for

231

the formation of elites and the means by which they obtain power, once a governing elite is in place it does its utmost to stay there.

Elite theory has developed and become more sophisticated since Pareto and Mosca but the fundamentals remain unchanged. Elite theory is as applicable to liberal societies as it is to any other.

Governing elites are able to restrict access to the political system by various means. They make the rules and impose their values and perceptions upon it. Such an arrangement favours the governing elite and makes it difficult for a group which has an ideology that fundamentally conflicts with it from competing for political power. The hurdles and hoops placed in the path of non-elite politicians are many and varied. For example, in the UK from time to time there is discussion of the merits of using a system of proportional representation to elect the government, the latest giving rise to the *Jenkins Report*. Proportional representation is a useful ploy for a governing elite because under the guise of greater democracy it is able to distance policy-making even further from the electorate and ensures that all sections of the elite are able to enjoy positions of power. The problem for the governing elite is to devise a system of proportional representation that prevents non-elite politicians and their ideas from gaining publicity. After all, it would not be desirable for extremists (i.e. non-elite politicians) to gain a platform from which they could air their subversive views. Hence, when there is discussion about which system of proportional representation would be best for the UK, it is openly stated that the system should be such as to keep out extremists. The barrier usually takes the form of a cut-off point that excludes those who receive less than a certain proportion of the votes cast, or a requirement that candidates put up a very large deposit or need their nomination papers signed by an unreasonably large number of electors. The methods are many but they are always made to appear reasonable and merely technical.

Electioneering in the UK is becoming more and more expensive despite rules which seek to limit expenditure. The main parties spend more than they can afford during election campaigns and find themselves dependent on large donations from individuals, many of who are rewarded in one way or another. It is sometimes suggested that a solution to this difficulty would be for the state to fund political parties. If such a proposal was ever put into effect, it is certain that the rules would be framed in a way that ensured that only the parties of the governing elite received substantial funds, thus preserving the status quo. The method used might be to simply give financial support on the basis of the number of votes won in the previous general election. A different approach would be to greatly reduce the amount spent on elections. A cut in election advertising would not be welcome because, as with commercial advertising, the aim is in part to exclude non-elite groups from the contest by making entry costly. Political advertising and campaigning rarely has the positive purpose of informing the electorate about policies but instead aims to create an unfavourable image of opponents.

In the USA the political system is such that although in theory every citizen is able to run for president, only the very rich or those who have the support of the governing elite and its wealth have any chance of taking part in, let alone winning, what is a hugely expensive competition between advertising campaigns.

The Internet offers cheap access to the political market but it does not have anything like the power of television advertising. Websites can at least make information available for those who are looking for it but if the Web proves to be an effective way of challenging the status quo it is certain that a means will be found to control it. Iran and China are examples of states that have introduced measures to restrict and control use of the Web.

Elites and the Political System

The governing elite (aristocracy – ruling class – the establishment) exercises its power through its control of the institutions of the state. Those institutions are sometimes collectively called *the state*. The primary institutions of the United Kingdom are Parliament and the Monarchy. The branch of the governing elite that exercises formal control of the state is the political elite, from which members of the government are drawn.

The sub-elites that make up the governing elite share many common values and perceptions, and generally occupy strategically important positions in both the formal institutions of the state, such as the judiciary, education and armed forces, and the informal but important areas of activity such as industry, banking and the media. It is impossible for a state to function efficiently or at all, in the long term, unless all the institutions of the state are controlled by the governing elite, and all its parts share core values and perceptions.[148] Stability requires that all formal and informal institutions reflect and promote the values of the governing elite.

Within the governing elite there is a political elite which is either contained within one party (a one-party state) or split into competing political parties or factions. In political systems like those in the United Kingdom and the United States, many of the members and supporters of the main political parties believe that their political philosophies and ideals are far removed from those of their main political opponents but in reality, their ideologies spring from eighteenth and nineteenth century liberal political philosophy. Each faction has tended to emphasise a

---

[148] In some states where there are two or more large nationalities, the political, economic and military elites reach agreement on the sharing of power and structure the state accordingly. For example, in Rwanda the political elite consisted of Hutus and the military elite of Tutsis. Such arrangements are usually fragile and sooner or later one of the elites will attempt to oust the other. A similar situation exists in neighbouring Burundi.

different aspect of that philosophy, and this has given rise to social-liberals and economic-liberals. In theory, their shared priority is for individual rights and freedom of choice. For social-liberals these rights and freedoms relate mainly to social relationships and political institutions. Economic-liberals express rights and freedoms in terms of freedom to trade and consumer choice. It is usual to think of social-liberals as being on the Left and economic-liberals as on the Right. The degree of hostility between them varies but recently in the UK these factions have moved closer together, the Left having probably moved furthest.

The Labour Party has its origins in the non-elite members of the industrial working class and was, at one time, a socialist party which promoted and campaigned for values and perceptions which conflicted with those of the liberal governing elite. It represented a socialist counter-elite opposed to a free-market economic system and threatened to overthrow *the system*. Since those days, the leadership of the Labour Party has increasingly been recruited from the governing elite and with Tony Blair as Prime Minister in a Labour government, the process of absorbing the Labour Party into *the system*, and taming it, has been completed. Far from overthrowing capitalism, the leadership of the Labour Party suggests that it can run the capitalist system more efficiently than the Conservative Party. The Labour Party is still committed to policies dear to the hearts of Left-liberals but only when economic circumstances permit. The heavy reliance on *the market* and economic growth indicates that this is capitalism with some of the rough edges smoothed off and re-labelled as The Third Way.[149]

The Global Elite and the New World Order

Members of the governing elites in industrial states increasingly see themselves as divorced from, and above, any emotional attachment to nations or states. Instead they identity with, and form part of, a global-elite consisting of professionals who manage information, images, money and other similar resources across state boundaries. The members of this global professional elite, who have been called *symbolic analysts*,[150] believe they have more in common with fellow professionals across the world than with their fellow citizens or members of their own nation.[151] They substitute civic-globalism for civic-nationalism, and have a greater loyalty to the organization that employs them than to any state or nation. Their values can be expressed in monetary terms and the global culture of which they are part gives priority to style and image over substance. They judge their worth and that of others by job title, income and *life-style*. They have been seduced by economic liberalism and are unable to understand the motivation of those who act in an

---

[149] Not to be confused with the political party, The Third Way.

[150] Robert Reich, *The Work of Nations*, New York, 1992

[151] The Global Elite is explored in, *The Revolt of the Elites* by Christopher Sara, published by W. W. Norton, 1995.

apparently irrational way by subordinating their immediate personal interests to those of a nation. Personal sacrifice for the common good is not something that they subscribe to, unless perhaps it is sacrifice for the good of a corporation.

The global professional elite is more like a global middle class than a ruling class. Its members think in terms of a global economy and global society, and identify with the global governing elite but are mostly on its fringe. It is those with effective strategic control of global economic, military and political resources who form the core global-elite. That elite does not concern itself with directly manipulating public opinion but instead uses its power to influence governments, businesses and bankers from above. The name increasingly used for the Global Elite, along with their interests and policies, is the New World Order. President George Bush (1989-93) used the term to describe post-Cold War global society and the values that would dominate it but it is increasingly seen as an expression of a global governing elite and its liberal ideology. All states and nations are being compelled, one way or another, to abide by values and perceptions imposed from above. Key groups of statesmen, bankers and industrialists are able to manipulate events in a way that compels states to open their markets and dismantle their economic and cultural boundaries. The states and cultures that resist the pressure to conform face powerful political, financial, economic, and even military, consequences. Once states are enmeshed in the global economy and its global culture, there is little chance of them gaining freedom of action because those who step out of line face the prospect of economic ruin. Even the people of the United States are being manipulated in a way that suits the needs of the New World Order. The North American Free Trade Area was created as a device to merge the Canadian, Mexican, and US economies. The continuous step-after-step-after-step approach is similar to that used in Europe to form the EU. A single market and common levels of taxation are the last major economic steps in the binding together of states. When those things are in place, some form of political union and common system of law becomes inevitable. The long-term aim is to merge the European and North American blocs.

The Bilderberg Group

The Bilderberg Group was formed in 1954.[152] Its purpose is to promote liberal political and economic culture with the aim of bringing about the conditions favourable to the creation of a liberal world government. As a means of furthering that objective, people with political and economic power from around the world are brought together in an informal way. A wide range of issues is discussed *off the record* and a political and ideological consensus is reached. The founders agreed that historical trends were leading inevitably towards world government, whether by consent or force, and it was for them to ensure that when it came it

---

[152] The Bilderberg Group is named after the Bilderberg Hotel where its first meeting took place.

furthered their interests. Their long-term aim was to create an *International Order* founded on economic-liberal values and perceptions.

The idea of a global-elite promoting a common agenda and having the power to manipulate states might at first be disregarded as a figment of the imagination of conspiracy theorists. That view is understandable because some of the sources of information about the Bilderberg Group can be seen as cranky. Some of them claim that the Bilderberg Group is a communist conspiracy, while others see it as a Nazi plot. However, there are many reputable who see it as simply a body for furthering a liberal global agenda. If the list of people attending these meetings, and what they do and say, is scrutinised, it is not unreasonable to conclude that Bilderberg is a thoroughly liberal organisation.

Many find it difficult to accept that there is a Bilderberg group because they believe that if it existed they would surely have seen something about it in their newspaper or on television. Their disbelief becomes even greater when they are told that information about Bilderberg is suppressed and its existence and activities kept from public view. It is not surprising that such an allegation should seem fanciful to the vast majority of the population in Western states who are convinced that their news media is impartial and free. Fortunately, there are some politicians and members of the press who are willing to defy those who try to prevent any mention of Bilderberg, but they face an uphill struggle.

Following the first conference held in The Netherlands, the influence of the Bilderberg Group spread. It has promoted its ideas through various institutes that provide a forum for liberal intellectual debate on international or foreign affairs. A name that is often mentioned in this context is the Royal Institute for International Affairs (Chatham House).

Bilderberg is not a hidden world government that gives orders or directs events in far-off places. It is an organisation that enables people with power within various elites to come together, exchange ideas and build a consensus for the general direction of policy. Bilderberg has the role of formulating and promoting elite opinion, which filters down and moulds public opinion and domestic political agendas. It was in meetings of the Bilderberg Group that the outline of the European Union was shaped.

The World Economic Forum (WEF), which has existed for over 30 years, performs a similar task to the Bilderberg Group. The Davos meeting of WEF early in 2000 was attended by thirty presidents and prime ministers; over one hundred ministers and nearly two thousand business people.[153] At that meeting (27th January 2000) President Clinton emphasised the need to continue to push for "open markets and rule-based trade".

---

[153] *The Daily Telegraph*, 31st January 2000

The information that follows has been taken from an article in *The Social Crediter*.[154]

THE 1998 BILDERBERG MEETING [from *The Social Crediter*]

"The world's most powerful secret society" –

Punch magazine, 23rd May – 5th June 1998

by Alan Armstrong, with Alistair McConnachie at Turnberry.

Punch magazine's report continued, "Few have heard of the Bilderberg Council. But its 120 members are some of the most powerful people on the global stage. It meets amid unparalleled secrecy to discuss the future of the world." *Punch* was referring to the meeting held at Turnberry Hotel, near Girvan on the West coast of Scotland on Thursday 14th–Sunday 17th May 1998. Until very recently, any reference to even the existence of the highly secretive Bilderberg Group was greeted with great scepticism by the world's media. *Punch,* along with the *Mail on Sunday,* the *Scotsman,* the *Scottish Daily Mail,* the *Scotland on Sunday* and *The Social Crediter,* met outside the gates of Turnberry to find out what was going on.

The 123 participants at the meeting, conducted as always in secrecy and accompanied by a powerful police presence, included Lord Carrington, Chairman since 1990, UK Defence Secretary George Robertson, William Hague Leader of the Opposition, Kenneth Clarke ex-Chancellor of the Exchequer, Henry Kissinger and a great clutch of other heavyweight movers and shakers from the world of international banking, industry, multi-national corporations, and senior politicians, of whom some are still in power and some others showing real potential!

Investigatory journalist Robert Eringer, in his book *The Global Manipulators* (Bristol, England: Pentacle Books, 1980) notes that "The steering committee certainly has an amazing eye for choosing guests who are on the way up. Most of the current leaders of the West have emerged from the depths of Bilderberg ... Every British Prime Minister of the past thirty years has attended Bilderberg ... (and) Denis Healey was an early member of Bilderberg and was on the steering committee long before he became Chancellor of the Exchequer." Tony Blair attended the meeting on 23–25 April 1993 at Vouliagmeni in Greece when he was Shadow Home Secretary.

[154] My sincere thanks to Alan Armstrong for giving permission to print the article in full. Congratulations to Punch for first publishing the article, *The world's most powerful secret society* and congratulations to those who publish *The Social Crediter* for a journal which provides much useful information and opinion about the global economy, banking and much else. It is recommended despite its apparent hostility to nationalism. *The Social Crediter* is published by KRP Ltd, 16 Forth Street, Edinburgh, EH1 3LH. Tel. 0131 550 3769

WHY THE SECRECY?

Punch noted, and Bilderbergers would not deny, that the Council meets "amid unparalleled secrecy to discuss the future of the world." But why? In this context, Robert Eringer wrote to David Rockefeller, Chairman of Chase Manhattan Bank to enquire about Bilderberg. An assistant directed him to a Mr. Charles Muller, a Vice President at Murden and Company, "the organisation which assists with the administration of American Friends of Bilderberg Incorporated." (p.11) Muller sent him a printed message which included the suggestion that it was: "In order to assure perfect freedom of speech and opinion, the gatherings are closed and off the record. No resolutions are proposed, no votes taken, and no policy statements are issued during or after the meetings."

Eringer subsequently established that in fact this is not so. He managed to obtain a copy of a "Strictly Confidential" record of the meeting held in Barbizon, France in March 1955 and one of the September meeting in Garmisch, West Germany the same year, which records that "Participants in this conference may, in light of the consensus of opinion expressed during the discussions, be able to pass these views on to public opinion in their own spheres of influence, without disclosing their source." (p.30)

Finally, in a letter to Eringer, one-time member Sir Paul Chambers wrote, "I am under obligation not to disclose anything about the Bilderberg Group to anybody who is not a member of that group. I am very sorry that I cannot help, but I am clearly powerless to do so and it would be wrong in the circumstances to say anything to you about Bilderberg."

There is enough here to allow us to insist that if there are grand strategies to be developed, presumably in the "best interests" of the world's peoples, they should be made in forums that are subject to full democratic scrutiny and accountability. Not behind locked doors at private meetings of a largely self-appointed elite establishment.

Why should democratically elected representatives attending these meetings feel it necessary to maintain complete secrecy over what is discussed? It is also open to question whether the British Police Force should have provided armed security for such a "private meeting" or whether an Army helicopter should have been used to ferry Defence Secretary George Robertson. According to his spokesman, "He was fulfilling an official engagement as Secretary of State for Defence and, as such, transport was met by public expense." *(Mail on Sunday, Night and Day* supplement, June 14, 1998, p. 15.)

THE TURNBERRY AGENDA

According to the official *PRESS RELEASE Bilderberg Meetings,* dated May 14, 1998: "Among others the Conference will discuss NATO, Asian Crisis,

EMU, Growing Military Disparity, Japan, Multilateral Organizations, Europe's social model, Turkey, EU/US Market Place."

Hopefully, journalists are beginning to wake up, at long last, to the idea that Bilderberg is real and that it is a very important influence in the world. Perhaps, the veil of secrecy can be lifted if only a little and with that hope, Alistair McConnachie set out to find participants who might be willing to say something about what was going on inside the hotel.

Hotel staff coming and going would just look at their feet without uttering a word. A reporter for the *Scottish Daily Mail* who knocked on the doors of the staff accommodation block was arrested, handcuffed and detained for eight hours in Ayr Police Station under Section 14 of the Criminal Justice Act (Scotland), which is invoked when police have reason to suspect an offence has been committed! This episode is reported in *The Press Gazette* of 22 May.

However, for a few hours on Saturday, between 12 noon and 3pm, the delegates spent time in the grounds, either playing tennis, playing golf on the course by the sea, or visiting Culzean Castle a little up the coast. Alistair McConnachie and a colleague had time to speak to delegates as they passed.

Otto Wolff von Amerongen, Chairman and CEO of Otto Wolff GmbH in Germany was the first to stop and explained that the meeting was structured with short introductions to a chosen topic and then a general discussion. Two British delegates explained that there is a panel which consists of a moderator and two or three people. They have about 10 minutes each on the chosen topic and then there are "discussion questions", which last for 5, 3 or 2 minutes. There are no introductory documents, and there are no records. At the most there is a page on a 3 hour debate. It doesn't circulate documents between its members. One of the British delegates believed it was not possible to mount a conspiracy in a group like the Bilderbergers because it has no existence between its meetings.

George Papandreou, Greek Alternate Minister for Foreign Affairs was out jogging and came over to speak. He said that they had been discussing, "Everything. Everything from the Asian crisis to Portugal to whatever else." He was happy to have his photo taken, "You want to put me in the paper like this? They'll love it in Greece." He jogged off, urging, "Be strongly critical, whatever you write!"

A little light is beginning to shine on this group. For example, Will Hutton, Editor of *The Observer,* who was an attendee at the 13–15 June 1997 Bilderberg Conference at Lake Lanier Islands outside Atlanta, Georgia wrote on 1st February 1998 ("Kinder capitalists in Armani specs") that "the Bilderberg Conference ... is one of the key meetings of the year ... the consensus established here is the back-drop against which policy is made worldwide".

A recent former delegate who "holds a senior position in the media" *(almost certainly Hutton – TSC)* was quoted anonymously at length by Malcolm Macalister Hall in the *Mail on Sunday* article of June 14, 1998. Macalister Hall writes: "But he says that Bilderberg is part of a global conversation that takes place each year at a string of conferences, and it does form the backdrop to policies that emerge later. 'There's the World Economic Forum at Davos in February, the Bilderberg and G8 meetings in April/May, and the IMF/World Bank annual conference in September. A kind of international consensus emerges and is carried over from one meeting to the next. But no one's really leading it. This consensus becomes the background for G8 economic communiqués; it becomes what informs the IMF when it imposes an adjustment programme on Indonesia; and it becomes what the president proposes to Congress.'"

The Bilderberg Group is one of a constellation of "private groups" with related global agendas. They include the Trilateral Commission, the Council on Foreign Relations and the Royal Institute for International Affairs (Chatham House). Arnold Toynbee, the central figure at Chatham House for thirty years from 1925 to his retirement in 1955 might have been speaking about the ethos of any one of these groups when he commented that they were "denying with our lips what we are doing with our hands" *(International Affairs,* Vol. 10).

The Social Credit Secretariat is keen to contribute what it can to ensuring that the agendas of such organisations are made fully open to democratic scrutiny and that especially our elected politicians cease attending such group meetings for so long as they are subject to any instruction to secrecy.

Finally, we put the following comment on record, passed to us, from one of the many people we spoke to and who shall remain nameless, "Book your holidays in Portugal next year".

The Social Crediter Vol.77 No. 4. 1998

Bilderberg members are drawn from the Western liberal governing elites. This geographical and political bias is reflected in the fact that meetings are held in Europe and North America, and that security at meetings is undertaken by the secret services of the United States and several European nations who co-ordinate their activities with local police.

Although many people with power in the media are invited to Bilderberg meetings, most journalists are excluded and measures are taken to prevent them revealing information about the group and its activities to the public. Invited guests are bound by the same convention of silence as are its members, thus they are obliged not to speak or write to outsiders about the meetings. This has not prevented a few journalists and politicians from gathering information about the group but the problem until recently has been making that information widely known. Thankfully the World Wide Web now makes that possible.

Some of the Bilderberg's past "guests" from the corporate media include:

News Corporation director Andrew Knight;

Reuters CEO Peter Job;

Henry Anatole Grunwald, former editor-in-chief of *Time* and Council on Foreign Relations member;

Mortimer B. Zuckerman, chairman and editor-in-chief of *US News and World Report*, *New York Daily News*, and *Atlantic Monthly*, also a Council on Foreign Relations member;

Robert L. Bartley, vice president of *The Wall Street Journal* and member of both the Council on Foreign Relations and the Trilateral Commission;

Peter Robert Kann, Chairman and CEO of Dow Jones and Company, and member of the Council on Foreign Relations;

Katharine Graham, owner and chairwoman of the executive committee of *The Washington Post*, also a member of both the Council on Foreign Relations and the Trilateral Commission;

Jim Hoagland, associate editor, of *The Washington Post*;

New York Times editor and Council on Foreign Relations member Arthur Sulzberger;

Former *Newsweek* editor Osborn Eliot;

London *Observer* editor Will Hutton;

Canadian press baron Conrad Black;

Peter Jennings, anchor and senior editor of ABC's World News Tonight;

Lesley R. Stahl, CBS national affairs correspondent;

WETA-TV president and CEO Sharon Percy Rockefeller;

William F. Buckley, Jr., editor-in-chief of the *National Review*, host of PBS's Firing Line and Council on Foreign Relations member;

Prominent political columnists Joseph Kraft, James Reston, Joseph Harsch, George Will, and Flora Lewis;

Donald C. Cook, former European diplomatic correspondent for *The Los Angeles Times* and Council on Foreign Relations member;

Albert J. Wohlstetter, *Wall Street Journal* correspondent and Council on Foreign Relations member;

Thomas L. Friedman, *New York Times* columnist and member of both the Council on Foreign Relations and the Trilateral Commission;

New York Times book critic Richard Bernstein;

Hedley Donovan, Henry Grunwald, and Ralph Davidson of *Time*;

Joseph C. Harsch, former NBC commentator and Council on Foreign Relations member;

Bill Moyers, executive director of Public Affairs TV and former Director of the Council on Foreign Relations;

Gerald Piel, former chairman of Scientific American and Council on Foreign Relations member;

William Kristol, editor and publisher of the *British Weekly Standard* magazine;

Toger Seidenfaden, editor in chief of Denmark's Politiken A/S.

Source: *The Bilderberg Group: Planning the World's Future Behind Closed Doors*, by Charles Overbeck, www.parascope.com/mx/articles/bilderberg.htm

BILDERBERG CONFERENCE – Turnberry, Ayrshire, Scotland

14–17 May 1998
Participants/Attendees
Current list of participants
Status 13 May 1998
  Chairman
  Honorary Secretary General
  Participants
  Rapporteurs

CHAIRMAN:
Carrington, Peter – Former Chairman of the Board, Christies International PLC; Former Secretary General, NATO (GB)

HONORARY SECRETARY GENERAL:
Halberdstadt, Victor – Professor of Public Economics, Leiden University (NL)

PARTICIPANTS:
Agnelli, Giovanni – Honorary Chairman, Fiat S.p.A. (I)

Allaire, Paul A – Chairman, Xerox Corporation (USA)

Almunia Amann, Joaquin – Secretary General, Socialist Party (E)

Balsemao, Francisco Pinto – Professor of Communication Science, New University, Lisbon; Chairman, IMPRESA, S.G.P.S.; Former Prime Minister (P)

Barnevik, Percy – Chairman, ABB Asea Brown Boveri Ltd (S)

Bayar, Ugur – Chairman, Privitization Administration (TR)

Bernabe, Franco – Managing Director, ENI S.p.A. (I)

Bertram, Christoph – Director, Foundation Science and Policy; Former Diplomatic Correspondent, *Die Zeit* (D)

Beugel, Ernst H van der – Emeritus Professor of International Relations, Leiden University; Former Honorary Secretary General of Bilderberg Meetings for Europe and Canada (NL)

Black, Conrad – Chairman, The Telegraph plc (CDN)

Bonino, Emma – Member of the European Commission (INT)

Brittan, Leon – Vice President of the European Commission (INT)

Browne, John – Group Chief Executive, British Petroleum Company plc (GB)

Bruton, John – Leader of Fine Gael (IRL)

Buchanon, Robin – Senior Partner, Bain and Company Inc. UK (GB)

Burda, Hubert – Chairman, Burda Media (D)

Carvajal Urquijo, Jaime – Chairman, Dresdner Kleinwort Benson S.A. (Spain) (E)

Cavalchini, Luigi G – Permanent Representative to the European Union (I)

Cem, Ismail – Minister of Foreign Affairs (TR)

Chretien, Raymond A.J. – Ambassador to the U.S. (CDN)

Chubais, Anatoli B. – Former First Vice Prime Minister; Chairman RAO EES (RUS)

Clarke, Kenneth – Member of Parliament (GB)

Collomb, Bertrand – Chairman and CEO, Lafarge (F)

Courtis, Kenneth S. – First Vice President, Research Dept., Deutsche Bank Asia Pacific (INT)

Coutinho, Vasco Pereira – Chairman, IPC Holding (P)

Crockett, Andrew – General Manager, Bank for International Settlements (INT)

David, George A. – Chairman of the Board, Hellenic Bottling Company S.A. (GR)

Davignon, Etienne – Executive Chairman, Societe Generale de Belgique; Former Vice Chairman of the Commission of the European Communities (B)

Deutch, John M. – Institute Professor, Massachusetts Institute of Technology, Dept. of Chemistry; Former Director General, Central Intelligence Agency; Former Deputy Secretary of Defence (USA)

Dion, Stephane – Queens Privy Council for Canada and Minister of Intergovernmental Affairs (CDN)

Donilon, Thomas – Partner, O'Melveny & Myers; Former Assistant Secretary of State, and Chief of Staff, US Department of State (USA)

Ellemann-Jensen, Uffe – Chairman, Liberal Party (DK)

Engelen-Kefer, Ursula – Deputy Chairman of the Board of Management, Deutscher Gewerkschaftsbund, DGB (D)

Feldstein, Martin S. – President and CEO, National Bureau of Economic Research Inc. (USA)

Fischer, Stanley – First Deputy Managing Director, International Monetary Fund (INT)

Forester, Lynn – President and CEO, FirstMark Holdings Inc (USA)

Gadiesh, Orit – Chairman of the Board, Bain and Company Inc (USA)

Gregorin, Jean-Louis – Member of the Board of Directors, Matra Hachette (F)

Gezgin Eris, Meral – President IKV (Economic Development Foundation) (TR)

Goossens, John – President and CEO, Belgacom (B)

Grierson, Ronald – Former Vice Chairman, GEC (GB)

Grossman, Marc – Assistant Secretary, US Department of State (USA)

Guetta, Bernard – Editor in Chief, *Le Nouvel Observateur* (F)

Hague, William – Leader of the Opposition (GB)

Hannay, David – Prime Ministers Personal Envoy for Turkey; Former Permanent Representative to the United Nations (GB)

Hoagland, Jim – Associate Editor, *The Washington Post* (USA)

Hoegh, Westye – Chairman of the Board, Leif Hoegh and Co A.S.A.; Former President, Norwegian Shipowners Association (N)

Hoeven, Cees H. van der – President, Royal Ahold (NL)

Hoge Jr, James F. – Editor, Foreign Affairs (USA)

Hogg, Christopher – Chairman, Reuters Group plc (GB)

Holbrooke, Richard C. – Former Assistant Secretary for European Affairs; Vice Chairman, CS First Boston (USA)

Horta e Costa, Miguel – Vice-President, Portugal Telecom (P)

Ishinger, Wolfgang – Political Director, Foreign Office (D)

Issing, Otmar – Member of the Board, Deutsche Bundesbank (D)

Jenkins, Michael – Vice Chairman, Dresdner Kleinwort Benson (GB)

Johnson, James A. – Chairman and CEO, FannieMae (USA)

Jordan, Jr., Vernon E. – Senior Partner, Akin, Gump, Strauss, Hauer & Feld, LLP (Attorneys-at-Law) (USA)

Kaletsky, Anatole – Associate Editor, *The Times* (GB)

Karamanlis, Kostas A. – Leader of the Opposition (GR)

Kirac, Suna – Vice Chairman of the Board, Koc Holding A.S. (TR)

Kissinger, Henry A. – Former Secretary of State; Chairman, Kissinger Associates Inc (USA)

Kohnstamm, Max – Senior Consultant, The European Policy Center (INT)

Kopper, Hilmar – Chairman of the Supervisory Board, Deutsche Bank A.G. (D)

Korteweg, Pieter – President and CEO, Robeco Group (NL)

Kovanda, Karel – Head of Mission to the Czech Republic to NATO and the WEU (CZ)

Kravis, Henry R. – Founding Partner, Kohlberg Kravis Roberts & Co (USA)

Kravis, Marie-Josee – Senior Fellow, Hudson Institute Inc (USA)

Leschly, Jan – CEO SmithKline Beecham plc (USA)

Levy-Lang, Andre – Chairman of the Board of Management, Paribas (F)

Lipponen, Paavo Prime Minister (FIN)

Lykketoft, Mogens – Minister of Finance (DK)

MacMillan, Margaret – Editor, International Journal, Canadian Institute of International Affairs, University of Toronto (CDN)

Manning, Preston – Leader of the Reform Party (CDN)

Masera, Rainer S. – Director General, I.M.I.S.p.A. (I)

Matthews, Jessica Tuchman – President, Carnegie Endowment for International Peace (USA)

McDonough, William J. – President, Federal Reserve Bank of New York (USA)

Nass, Matthias – Deputy Editor, *Die Zeit* (D)

Netherlands, Her Majesty Queen of the (NL)

Olechowski, Andrzej – Chairman, Central Europe Trust, Poland (PL)

Ollila, Jorma – President and CEO, Nokia Corporation (FIN)

Padoa-Schioppa, Tommaso – Chairman, CONSOB (I)

Papandreou, George A. – Alternate Minister for Foreign Affairs (GR)

Prendergast, Kieran – Under-Secretary General for Political Affairs, United Nations (INT)

Prestowitz, Clyde V. – President, Economic Strategy Institute (USA)

Puhringer, Othmar – Chairman of Managing Board, VA-Technologie AG (A)

Purves, William – Group Chairman, HSBC Holdings plc (GB)

Pury, David de – Chairman, de Pury Pictet Turrettini and Co Ltd (CH)

Randa, Gerhard – Chairman of the Managing Board, Bank of Austria (A)

Rhodes, William R. – Vice-Chairman, CitiBank, N.A. (USA)

Robertson, George – Secretary of State for Defence (GB)

Rockefeller, David – Chairman, Chase Manhattan Bank International Advisory Committee (USA)

Rodriguez Inciarte, Matias – Vice-Chairman, Banco de Santander (E)

Roll, Eric – Senior Advisor, SBC Warburg Dillon Read (GB)

Rothschild, Evelyn de – Chairman, N. M. Rothschild and Sons (GB)

Schremp, Jurgen E. – Chairman of the Board of Management, Daimler Benz A.G. (D)

Seidenfaden, Toger – Editor in Chief, Politiken A/S (DK)

Siniscalco, Domenico – Professor of Economics; Director of Fondazione ENI Enrico Mattei (I)

Solana Madariaga, Javier – Secretary General, NATO (INT)

Sousa, Marcelo Rebelo de – Leader of the PSD Party (P)

Storvik, Kjell – Governor, Bank of Norway (N)

Suchoka, Hanna – Minister of Justice (PL)

Summers, Lawrence H. – Deputy Secretary for International Affairs, US Department of the Treasury (USA)

Sutherland, Peter D. – Chairman, Goldman Sachs International; Chairman, British Petroleum Company plc (IRL)

Taylor, J. Martin – Group Chief Executive, Barclays plc (GB)

Thoman, G. Richard – President and CEO, Xerox Corporation (USA)

Udgaard, Nils M. – Foreign Editor, Aftenposten (N)

Vasella, Daniel – CEO Novartis (CH)

Vink, Lodewijk J.R. de – President and CEO, Warner Lambert Company (USA)

Virkkunen, Janne – Senior Editor in Chief, Helsingin Sanomat (FIN)

Vits, Mia de – General Secretary, ABVV-FGTB (B)

Vranitzky, Franz – Former Federal Chancellor (A)

Vries, Gijs M. de – Leader of the Liberal Group, European Parliament (INT)

Wallengerg, Jacob – Chairman of the Board, Skandinaviska Enskilda Banken (S)Whitman, Christine Todd – Governor of New Jersey (USA)

Wissmann, Matthias – Federal Minister for Transport (D)

Wolfensohn, James D. – President, the World Bank (INT)

Wolff von Amerongen, Otto – Chairman and CEO of Otto Wolff GmbH (D)

Wolfowitz, Paul – Dean, Nitze School of Advanced International Studies; Former Under Secretary of Defence for Policy (USA)

Yost, Casimir A. – Director, Institute for the Study of Diplomacy, School of Foreign Service, Georgetown University, Washington (USA)

RAPPORTEURS

Micklethwait, John – Business Editor, *The Economist* (GB)

Wooldridge, Adrian – Foreign Correspondent, *The Economist* (GB)

Source: www.bilberberg.org/1998.htm#Turnberry

Those who control the Bilderberg Group see nothing sinister or improper in the aims of the organisation or the way they go about achieving them. The end justifies the means. Not everyone is as enthusiastic about economic and social-liberalism as they are but it is difficult to see how the Global Elite can be defeated. At the moment, there is no mass opposition from within the liberal system. The small groups that demonstrate against the policies of the Global Elite cannot agree on an alternative model for a global system. Many of the objectors are Leftists-liberals who want to tinker with the present system to reduce pollution or help wildlife. They offer no real alternative. The *rogue states* appear to be contained and liable to succumb one by one to the power deployed against them. Perhaps it will take a very deep and long world economic recession to shake up public perceptions and start a groundswell of opinion that will eventually bring the system tumbling down. Whatever it is that breaks the camel's back, it is likely to be associated with structural weakness or internal stress. Until then the Global Elite will continue to use the *peace-keeping forces* of the *International Community* to extend its power and reach.

The Bilderberg Group's aims may seem unrealistic to some but there is little doubt of its intent. The existence of the elite and its strategy are manifest in the institutions through which global political, economic and financial power are focused, such as the World Bank and IMF. Those organisations are able to impose economic and political policies on states that are straight from the economic-liberal textbook but which take no account of local conditions. The purgative, which is thought by the fundamentalists who prescribe it to be a universal cure-all, is accompanied by a tonic consisting of loans that tie borrowers into a web of debt. To compliment that, there is a continuous and seemingly never-ending movement of sovereign powers away from individuals and communities to remote organisations over which there is no democratic control. Indeed, it is difficult to see how they could be subject to democratic control because they exist to serve the needs of a particular ideological elite. The IMF would have to change beyond recognition if it was part of a democratically controlled global political and economic system.

The world government that the Bilderberg Group seeks will not be democratic because the governing elite will not be able to create the worldwide ideological and cultural uniformity that is necessary for democracy to work. Without common agreement on the values by which a world government operates, it will have to be imposed.

In its efforts to produce the commonality necessary for world government, agents of the New World Order continue to undermine national cultures and promote a global junk-culture and a *citizen-of-the-world* identity. Moslems are among those resisting the spread of the liberal wasteland. Many Moslems do so because their Islamic identity is part of their national identity and they wish to protect both. Unfortunately, Islam is as aggressive and universalistic as liberalism. Moslems are not content with defence but have the same desire as liberals to see their own creed win universal domination. Islam is therefore at least as much of a threat as liberalism to the cultural diversity that nationalists wish to preserve.

Elites and Models of Reality

Communal cultures socialise children into a way of life and provide them with a model of the community and the outside world. Ideologies are sometimes used as a supplement to communal instincts and culture, at other times they compete and seek to overlay the communal view with something better suited to the interests of the ideologues. Sometimes the ideology takes the form of a theology.

Ideologies provide either a partial or complete model of the world. They offer a framework for filtering and storing information. Every governing elite seeks to promote, and if necessary impose, its ideology and world-view on the population it governs. Having done that it is able to manage a flow of information to its population and influence the way unmanaged information is handled. In other words, governing elites always strive to provide their population with information and a mental processing system that generates a certain view of the world.

The shaping process starts with an education system that exposes children to the *correct* values and perceptions during their formative years. Following that there is a constant drip of public propaganda, which ensures that a large majority of citizens accept the elites world-view even when it is contrary to their personal experience and commonsense. Some people resist indoctrination and question propaganda more successfully than others. The governing elite keeps the number of *freethinkers* to a minimum and renders them harmless by making them appear as cranks or the friends of outsiders.

Successful socialisation produces a brain programmed to filter and store information in a way that overrides personal experience and instinct. Information that reinforces desired perceptions is stored but other information is rejected. The filtering process is a subconscious one that leaves us unable to recall the specific information or combination of information that has made us think as we do on any given subject. Sometimes it is not easy to explain or justify all or part of our model because much of it consists of what we have come to accept as being true and obvious.

Well-managed information passes through the system and is stored in a way that strengthens the model of reality. Unmanaged information is filtered. Some is rejected, and some is interpreted and stored in a way that reinforces perceptions.

It is impossible to manage all information and no system is perfect so there are many occasions when unmanaged information gets through the filter and causes discomfort because it cannot be made to fit into the perceptual framework. When that happens it suggests that the framework needs adjusting but because that could lead to a complete rebuilding job, the information is rejected.

In order to avoid the inconvenience of awkward information, it is usual for individuals to seek information from sources, such as newspapers, that can be relied upon to weed out hard to process information and views that might cause the filtering process difficulties. Readers are thus able to prevent the discomfort of cognitive dissonance, which is mental stress arising from trying to accept two or more conflicting ideas or pieces of information as true.

One way of managing information is to *tag* it or its source so that the filtering process knows how to handle it. In crude terms, a tag makes an association with good or evil, friend or foe. It is for that reason that we are warned in news bulletins about the source of information, e.g. right-wing, left-wing, nationalist, communist. The tag acts as a warning to those suitably conditioned that they need not bother giving the troublesome information serious consideration because it is from a dubious source. An example of a source from which all information should be rejected is *an Islamic fundamentalist*.

The liberal mental framework is unable to cope with many types of information. Rejection is not due to any assessment of its intrinsic merit but on the basis of whether it fits their ideas of how things ought to be. Such is the hostility to some categories of information that it suggests fear of a threat to the structure of an ideological model. For example, liberals recoil from and condemn information which suggests that intelligence is determined by genetic inheritance, or that there is any merit in Social Darwinism.

Despite the wishes of the makers, some people tinker with the approved model so as to accommodate awkward information. Soon they have a ramshackle structure in danger of collapse but they stay with it to avoid the inconvenience of starting afresh and building something much better. The longer one stays in one place the harder it can be to move on. Sometimes, in the face of imminent collapse or the weariness of constant maintenance, the old structure is abandoned and a new more sophisticated model built. What joy and peace of mind this can bring; low maintenance and space for all those interesting things that keep coming along.

The guiding rule for construction of a model of reality is to ensure that it accommodates communal instincts, which we all have direct access to. The parroted ideological orthodoxy of the day is best ignored because it is unlikely to contain any deep truths or insights. If our model of reality cannot cope with behaviour and ideas that accord with the principles of natural justice (i.e. what we instinctively feel to be fair and reasonable) there is something wrong with it. Some people spend all of their lives adhering to an ideology that conflicts with their communal survival instincts because they mistakenly believe that to do so indicates moral and intellectual superiority. Others are aware of a conflict between what they say and instinctively feel but they endure the mental discomfort because much intellectual and emotional investment has been made in their model of reality. The bold make a fresh start and are rewarded with the very real and refreshing intellectual freedom that comes when a person can say and do what they instinctively and intellectually believe to be true and proper. There is no need to endure the constraints of an ideological straightjacket.

New Realities for Old

A model of reality that is accurate and able to explain, and to some extent predict, events in the real world will not need to reject information and it will be able to process it quickly and efficiently. It will make sense of the world and make possible the setting of realistic goals and policies. If the model of reality is inaccurate, it will give rise to unrealistic goals and policies which in the long term will fail. Despite clear evidence that ideology does not explain reality, a governing elite is sometimes so firmly committed to it that it would rather follow a course to inevitable destruction than admit the shortcomings and face an unravelling of the whole ideological fabric. Censoring and attacking dissidents is a far easier option. This happened in the Soviet Union where the governing elite was committed to a form of state communism that was never going to work. At the last moment, when collapse was inevitable, they tried to adapt to reality but it was too late. The Chinese governing elite, with better anticipation and more skill, has been reformulating its ideological stance and economic practices in the hope of preventing a catastrophic collapse of the system it controls.

Liberal governing elites face a similar problem but are as yet unwilling to change course. In the meantime, we recklessly hurtle into the future, going where technology and market forces take us in the forlorn hope of a soft landing in a pleasant place. If we run into problems on the way, we must hope that a fix will be found for them. In a sane world, the passengers would mutiny and throw overboard those who are leading them on such a high risk and unnecessary journey. They would halt a globalisation that seeks standardisation, centralisation and conformity and in its place pursue diversity and an outlook that recognises the precarious and tenuous nature of human existence. It is for each community to decide upon the destination it wishes to reach and the route it wishes to take.

Governing Elites and Social Control

It is essential to the existence of a stable and long-lasting state that its institutions and those who control all-important areas of activity within the state, share common values and perceptions. This does not mean that governing elites are free from differences, factions and competition; uniformity is a near impossibility in any group. What unites a governing elite is a will to govern combined with agreed ideological reference points, within which debate and competition are permitted. The Communist Party of the Soviet Union contained factions advocating different points of view and at the highest level there was competition between factions for control of the government.

Before the Russian revolution of the early 1990's, the governing elite of the Soviet Union consisted of members of the Communist Party. Any Soviet citizen prepared to declare an acceptance of Communist Party ideology was able to join and, in doing so, gained the opportunity, if suitably qualified, to occupy a position of power in the institutions of the state, e.g. the judiciary, media, armed forces, industry. Because the Communist Party determined what was taught in schools it was not surprising that many pupils developed the necessary ideological outlook. Some joined the Party not out of conviction but because they knew it was helpful to their careers. That approach was tolerated by the governing elite because it was more concerned with eliminating active opposition than with promoting enthusiastic support. In all states it is necessary for those who wish to obtain positions of power to agree with, or at least not to openly disagree with, certain fundamental values and perceptions. The extent to which the values and perceptions are made explicit, the extent to which disagreement and free expression is tolerated, and the severity of the penalties for dissenting, varies widely.

Following the disintegration of the Soviet Union, the new Russian free-market governing elite gained control of the institutions of the new Russian Federation. Members of that elite filled top positions but many of the existing managers in the bureaucracy and industry were not, and still have not, been converted to the new dogma.[155] It is difficult to know how large the new governing elite is and how deep its ideology has penetrated. The struggle for dominance between the old and the new continues and it is by no means certain who will win in the long term, although in the contest for control of the media the *liberals* had an early victory. The physical battle for the Moscow TV broadcasting station was crucial to the outcome of the power struggle between Yeltsin and the Russian parliament. By the time of the 1996 presidential election the new governing elite had control of radio and television broadcasting and much of the press. As a result, Mr Yeltsin received widespread positive coverage during the election campaign while his opponents

---

[155] The new Russian governing elite sprang from the old Soviet governing elite. In totalitarian states counter-elites are more likely to exist as factions within the governing elite.

received very little. It was hardly surprising that Mr Yeltsin moved steadily from a lowly position in the opinion polls to take a lead and win the election. The bias and unfairness of the broadcasting media was such that even liberals in the West thought it deserved some comment, although it was not reported as something that invalidated the election result. The army was less easy to manipulate than the media so Yeltsin set about weakening and rendering ineffective that which he could not control.

Some governing elites tolerate greater dissent than others but all keep it under control although techniques of control differ, some being more subtle than others. Some elites resort to overt forms of censorship, as all do in time of war. Most of the censorship we are faced with is not of the overt kind but a subtle self-censorship. For example, not all journalists are supporters of the political system within which they work and live. Opposition cannot be openly declared if they are to retain their jobs. If a dissident were to get through the formal and informal vetting system at the BBC and become, say, an economic correspondent, he or she would not remain in the job for long if their opposition to economic liberalism became apparent in reports. For instance, a world economic recession would have to be presented as a threat to the global economic and financial system – *upon which our prosperity depends* – and not as something that might herald the welcome collapse of global capitalism.

In many areas of news production journalists are obliged to produce news reports and articles that accord with, or are supportive of, the governing elite's interests, perceptions, values and goals. Criticism and debate is centred on efficient management of the existing political and economic system and the performance of individuals and institutions. There is no serious criticism of the ideological status quo and no advocacy of alternative ideologies or perceptions.

Those who own or control the news media naturally only appoint as editors and programme controllers, individuals who will work within unstated political boundaries. With power delegated to a safe pair of hands there is no need for day-to-day control. Who would expect otherwise?

Most groups, in whatever sphere of activity, create a system of self-selection by which only those who identify with the group and its values attempt to join it. This situation exists in all media corporations and institutions whatever the ideology of those at the top. Nonetheless, there are some *subversive* journalists, although they have to be careful and subtle about the way they air their views. Journalists, like businessmen and everyone else, often have to work within the system as it is. They have to go with the flow because it is difficult to fight it alone. Once a system is in place it tends to stand until inherent weaknesses emerge and bring it to an end. It is when systems collapse or are in a period of transition that opponents within can emerge and influence the formation of a new system.

Elites, Principles and Pragmatism

No governing elite can be relied upon to uphold its declared principles when its existence is threatened. In such circumstances it will be even more ruthless in using its control of the state and the opinion-forming news media to discredit and attack the opposition. If that fails it will rarely wait to be deposed by constitutional means but will instead manufacture a crisis of some kind to justify its suspension of constitutional government. All governing elites can find a pretext for using any means necessary to hang-on to power. They will also help other friendly and preferred governing elites retain power. An example of this occurred in Algeria where it was certain that an Islamic counter-elite would win the general election. The governing elite knew that once it lost power it would have great difficulty regaining it. It therefore cancelled the elections and set about attacking the Islamic opposition both physically and in the controlled media. The aim was to win internal and external support by projecting an image of a *progressive* government valiantly fighting against Muslim terrorists. The situation was presented as one justifying the cancellation of the general election. It also prepared the way for the EU to intervene on the side of the elected government and support it in its *fight against terrorism*. The governing elite was placing itself in a position from which it could attack and weaken the counter-elite before calling and winning a rescheduled election. The government action was clearly unconstitutional and undemocratic but there was no great condemnation from liberal governing elites in the West. No sanctions of any kind were used or even threatened.

Compare with that the case of Serbia, where in 1996 the governing elite rigged local elections. The central government, headed by President Slobodan Milosevic, was dependent for its survival on benefits gained through local government corruption. If the opposition won the local election and took office it would have revealed the extent of the corruption and that would have undermined Slobodan Milosevic's position. Milosevic refused to recognise opposition victories and the evidence that electoral malpractice had taken place. Supporters of the opposition held a large demonstration in Belgrade against Milosevic but his control of the news media enabled him to prevent knowledge of that and other demonstrations spreading. The considerable television coverage in the UK of the demonstration in Belgrade was somewhat different to the coverage given of anti-government demonstrations in Peru or the horrific violence taking place in Algeria, which was deemed to be the work of Islamic extremists.[156] The reason for the difference in approach was that Milosevic and the governing elite was seen as communist and nationalist. Unlike their opponents, they were not sympathetic to economic or social-liberalism. The Algerian governing elite is generally pro-Western but the Moslem counter-elite is not.

---

[156] *Channel 4 News* challenged this view and suggested, rightly, that the Algerian government and army were responsible for much of the violence.

Algeria is only a news story when the Islamic opposition can be shown in a bad light or there appears to be a threat to the flow of oil and gas. Algeria then becomes a humanitarian problem, which in the future might need some form of outside intervention to restore order and save lives. If that happens, any suggestion that the sudden concern is due to a perceived threat to the supply of oil and gas to the EU, principally Italy, will be dismissed as pure cynicism.

The reaction of liberal governing elites to events in Serbia and Algeria had more to do with self-interest than a concern to uphold democratic principles. Likewise, the principle of national self-determination was abandoned with the Russian invasion of Chechnya and the destruction of Chechen towns. The contrast with Bosnia is stark. If the Serbs had wreaked the same destruction on Sarajevo as the Russians did on Grozny, the outcry and call for intervention and punishment of the Serbs would have been very loud and long. The difference in reaction was due in part to the overt nationalism of the Chechens and the need to protect President Yeltsin and his economic liberalism from domestic opposition. While many Serbs behaved in a barbarous manner deserving of condemnation and punishment, the war in Bosnia was not a conflict between good and evil. Such a simplistic view does not accord with reality.

It was the desire for self-government that caused the Moslems to break away from Yugoslavia but the territory they occupied was insufficient to form a viable Bosnian state. The Moslems therefore wanted to include territory occupied by Serbs and Croats, who in turn wanted to exercise the same right to self-determination that the Moslems were seeking.

The principle of national self-determination suggests that the Serbs and Croats in those territories adjacent to Serbia and Croatia should not have been forced to become part of a Bosnian state. The difficulty was that their territory was needed to create a viable Bosnian state for the Moslems. There is no easy solution but a long-term remedy will probably need to include an agreed movement of population and exchange of territory backed-up with external financial support. Money cannot buy everything but given the choice between enduring conflict, and moving to an area inhabited by fellow nationals and being generously compensated, it is probable that many would choose the latter. The difficulty is that such a solution is not even open for consideration because it does not accord with liberal ideology. Instead of encouraging people to move, liberals prefer to force people to live together. Thus when open conflict next breaks out, liberals will blame nationalists rather than their own short-sighted policy which does not take account of the sentiments of the people involved.

Elite Ideals, Interests, and Actions

The declared ideals of elites and states are not a reliable guide to how they will behave in a given situation. A more reliable way of anticipating behaviour is to look at interests and how they are perceived.

If proclaimed ideals served as a good guide to what elites and states actually do, the *International Community* would have been expected to take action when Russia invaded Chechnya. That it did nothing suggests that on balance it was not in its interest to do so. When Iraq invaded Kuwait, it was a real threat to the strategic status quo and the vital interests of the Global Elite. The *International Community* quickly declared the need to uphold the principles of international law, which it conveniently forgot when it attacked Serbia in 1999. The real concern, of course, was with the threat posed to the control, price and supply of oil. Suitable action was taken to expel Iraqi forces from Kuwait.[157]

The traditional *realist* approach suggests that in all but exceptional circumstances, governing elites pursue goals and policies that they believe to be in their own best interests. An ethical foreign policy will be pursued only in as far as it helps to further interests or does not hinder them. A vital interest ranks higher than an ideal, which can always be *put into context*.

Governing elites promote certain *official ideals*, which they claim to posses and uphold. Guardianship of those ideals is taken to be a necessary condition of controlling the state and its internal and foreign policies. Ideals do not always fit with the needs of Realpolitik. They are therefore appealed to selectively, as the following examples show.

When communist governing elites were preventing their citizens from leaving communist states, liberals condemned them for infringing the right of free movement. When the *Iron Curtain* fell, freedom of movement ceased to be an issue, and governments in Western Europe kept out, or restricted, the entry of migrants from the former communist states.

When the government of Taiwan held elections and moved towards formal independence from China it was warned against such action and threatened by the government of the Peoples Republic of China. In response the US government lent diplomatic support to Taiwan and showed a readiness to back it with military support. But, as we have seen, when the Chechens sought independence from the Russian Federation, they did not get strong backing. All they received were feeble declarations to the effect that the amount of force used to end the bid for independence was regrettable.

---

[157] This is not to suggest that expelling Iraqis from Kuwait was improper. Indeed it was a necessary and right thing to do, as was the introduction of exclusion zones to protect various groups in Iraq, including Kurds.

The slaughter and destruction that followed the break-up of Yugoslavia was seen to warrant the setting-up of a war-crimes tribunal but similar action in Chechnya did not. It is clear that war-crimes tribunals are a political weapon directed against enemies but not allies.

The same lack of impartiality was shown during and after the Nato-Serb War of 1999. When Nato attacked Yugoslavia it broke the rules of the Nato Charter and what its members at other times call International Law. As is customary in today's world of so-called ethical foreign policies, there was no declaration of war, only a demand for surrender followed by an attack.

A new level of hypocrisy was reached when following the Nato attack on Yugoslavia, the aggressors set about prosecuting and punishing as war criminals the political and military leaders of the state they were attacking. The matter was made worse by the US governing elite demanding the prosecution of Serb war criminals secure in the knowledge that US citizens were immune from such prosecutions because the US refused to recognise the authority of War Crimes Tribunals to seek out, try, and punish US citizens.

This is not to suggest that those responsible for war crimes should not be punished, only that the initiation of such attempts should be based on objective rules and applied equally to all. Thus, if individuals are kidnapped or extradited from some states in order to stand trial for crimes against humanity, it should be accepted that individuals can be kidnapped or extradited from all states, including the UK and USA.

Elites and the Media

Within every governing-elite there is a political elite. In some states, factions within the political elite form parties that compete with each other to form the government. Competition takes place within agreed ideological boundaries. In order to take part in political debate it is necessary to tacitly subscribe to the ground rules. The broadcasting media acts as the gatekeeper and generally only gives access to those who conform to the rules. When the UK governing elite does not directly control broadcasting bodies, a system of licensing is used to ensure that only *responsible* organisations obtain licenses and that they broadcast *responsible* news, i.e. news provided by *responsible* news agencies.

Parties promoting values and perceptions that conflict with those of the governing elite are occasionally mentioned for the purpose of ridiculing, demonising or otherwise attacking them but they are not presented as *serious politicians* and their ideas are not presented as worthy of serious consideration. Professor Noam Chomsky has argued that many of those working in the media are unaware of the censoring function they perform.[158] They have internalised the fundamental values and perceptions of the governing elite and believe that those who deviate from them are extremists, and because of that there is no obligation on broadcasters to report their actions and views in an objective way. Other political philosophies are seen as undeserving of serious consideration and need not be given intellectual credibility. Indeed news managers find it very difficult to discuss opposing ideologies because many of the concepts involved are alien to them. Because liberal broadcasters rarely have their own values and perceptions challenged, they are not practised in justifying and debating them. This can be seen when usually calm and polite interviewers, who are supposedly obliged to be objective and fair, become short-tempered or patronising when faced with someone who challenges or dismisses the prevailing ideological norms.

The hostility, irritation and underlying bias of the broadcasting news media is revealed in the way dissidents and their ideas are discredited before they are heard. When dissidents are given the opportunity to speak they have to overcome associations of stupidity or fanaticism. For example, if a quotation is preceded with, *an Iranian government spokesman said*, the vast majority of the audience in a liberal state has been conditioned to dismiss what follows without giving it serious consideration.[159] Likewise, the Iranian broadcasting media do not quote the words of Western liberal politicians unless they reinforce a cultivated stereotype.

No such tags are attached to information from liberal sources. In fact, much of the information that passes as news comes from unattributable liberal sources such as spokesmen giving background information for the Royal Institute for International Affairs (Chatham House).

The attitude to dissidents in *enemy* states is quite different. They are given publicity and a credibility that gives the impression that they have widespread popular support. It is suggested that if it were not for ruthless suppression of dissent by the state, the dissidents (a counter-elite) would be swept to power on a wave of popular support. At the same time, home-grown dissidents are ignored or treated as criminals. This dual approach can be seen in the relationship between liberal states and China.

This is not to say that dissidents are never given exposure in their *home* media, it is just that they are rarely, if ever, given the opportunity and necessary time to explain the values and perceptions that underpin their world-view. Without that background it is impossible to effectively challenge elite values and perceptions in short interviews dominated by sound bites. Another difficulty is that questions are

---

[158] Noam Chomsky, *The Manufacture of Consent*. An excellent study of how *news* is managed.
[159] The hostility lessened early in 2000 because a reformist Iranian government was pursuing some policies that the BBC could describe as 'liberal'.

not ideologically neutral. What is viewed as good and helpful from one ideological perspective can be seen as bad and problematic from another. Questions or issues are presented in ways that reveal the ideological framework of the person asking the question or presenting the issue. For example, liberals see the expulsion or detention in prisons of those refused political asylum as a problem. Others are reassured by it and would see it as a problem if those making false claims were not expelled or detained. The approach taken reveals the underlying views and assumptions of the editor.

A further difficulty created by a style of political debate dominated by sound bites is that it is very difficult to challenge the ideological status quo when an answer that takes more than twenty seconds is considered longwinded.[160]

Propaganda

Propaganda is the organised spreading of opinion, ideology, perception or information, which might be true or false. Propaganda can be positive, promoting ideas and perceptions by associating them with *good* images or values. It can be negative, discrediting ideas and perceptions by associating them with *bad* images or values. All governing elites use propaganda to promote their values and perceptions and to discredit their ideological opponents. The difference between the propaganda of various ideological warriors is style rather than technique.

The primary channels through which propaganda is spread within states are the education system and the broadcasting media. Both channels provide excellent opportunities for the mostly unnoticed use of constant drip-feed propaganda which, among other things, suggests that some sources of information are more trustworthy than others. Values and perceptions are implanted which help build a model of reality that determines how new information is handled. In some political systems the process of indoctrination is so thorough that many young people regurgitate with great zeal the values and perceptions that they have been fed by the governing elite during their formal education, and think themselves radicals. In reality, they are guardians of the ideological status quo.

For several years there has been a fashion in the UK for Media Studies, where much is made of the need to look for bias in the media, especially newspapers which are an easy target because it is not difficult to discover their political preferences. The broadcasting media is portrayed as being generally neutral, which it is not. One explanation for the different treatment is that newspapers are more likely to challenge liberal views than are the almost wholly pro-liberal broadcasting media. How often has a student of Media Studies had liberal bias in the broadcasting media pointed out to them? Is the unwritten assumption that multi-culturalism is a good thing ever questioned? Is attention drawn to the fact

---

[160] op. cit. Noam Chomsky deals with all these points and much more.

that arts programmes on radio and television are dominated by social-liberals and their agenda? Why do soap operas deal with social issues of particular interest to liberals and provide liberal solutions to the problems that arise? Why is there no examination of the bias in the education system that affects the way Media Studies is taught and the perceptions it promotes? Why are media study students not asked to look for bias in their course material and in the views of their lecturers? Are the political views of those teaching media studies representative of the population as a whole? Education is no more neutral than broadcasting and a look at the standard course material makes it clear that the bias is in favour of social-liberal values and perceptions.

We need to be able to organise the limited information we have about others to see if our outlook is similar to theirs and to improve our chances of predicting their behaviour. We build a complete picture by linking small amounts of information in a way that enables a model to be built and gaps filled. Once a person has been categorised, additional information is interpreted in a way that fits the preconceived model. When that person expresses an opinion that does not fit the model, it is often *misheard* or misinterpreted in a way that enables it to fit. Things are assumed even though they are not said.

This method of placing and storing information in a way that makes sense of it is similar to that used by intelligence services (secret police) when they keep watch on dissidents. *Friendship tree software* such as WatCall by Harlequin is able to detect friendship networks. Similar pattern-recognition programs are used for email and to check on website and newsgroup visits. The principle behind it is much the same as the one that notes which library books a person borrows and which newspaper they read. For example, if a person reads *The Guardian* and is a member of Greenpeace, or some other environmental organisation, it can be assumed that they support CND, vote for the Labour Party, are anti police, anti monarchy, anti capital punishment, anti hunting, anti private education, anti private medical care, anti censorship, for 'artistic' freedom of expression and freedom of movement, for the welfare state, for redistribution of wealth, concerned with the problems of the Third World, anti American (USA), anti immigration controls, pro immigrants. In other words they are likely to be a social-liberal. On the other hand, a reader of the *Daily Telegraph* and a member of a Chamber of Commerce is likely to vote for the Conservative Party and hold the opposite views on most or all of the policy areas given above. They are also more likely to be Freemasons and regularly attend church services.

These are generalisations but ones that are commonly made because that is how we store and use information. Better information in any individual case enables the stereotype to be modified. Political propagandists make use of our information storage and retrieval systems by linking together certain words, concepts and pieces of information. They create associations that encourage us to perceive people and events in the way the propagandist desires. *Nationalist* is one of the many words to which liberals constantly attach negative connotations. If we hear or read the words *nationalist* and *England* the links we are encouraged to make are with *Little Englander, xenophobic, bigot, racist, Nazi, uneducated, aggressive, skinhead.* The words *nationalist* and *Scotland* make positive links and a more attractive image. Evidence of this was seen in Channel 4's Powerhouse programme in April 2000. In a discussion that touched on a proposal that only MPs representing English constituencies should be able to vote on matters that affected only England, the words *English nationalism* were mentioned. Upon hearing this, Glenda Jackson, Labour MP, exclaimed, "Oh no! We can't discuss that here, that's Nazism!"

Free Speech

Free speech is near to being an absolute; either you have it or you do not. It might be necessary and reasonable to have laws to protect state secrets or make it an offence to slander or libel a person, but even if such restrictions on free speech are discounted it is evident that in one way or another states restrict what can be freely said and published within their jurisdiction.

Free speech is generally taken to mean the free expression of ideas and beliefs. States that deny citizens the right to express an opinion on any political matter cannot be said to uphold the right of free speech. Persons imprisoned for expressing political views are political prisoners whether their imprisonment is secured through the criminal or civil law. Punishments sanctioned by the state which fall short of imprisonment, however they might be disguised, are deterrents to free speech. For example, the prospect of financial ruin due to defending a prosecution or paying damages is a constant threat held over those who challenge liberal values and perceptions for which there is little public support.

Some states make very little effort to justify the restrictions they place on the free expression of political views but others raise hypocrisy to rarefied heights when they claim that it is necessary to deny the right of their citizens to express certain political views in order to uphold freedom and democracy.

Free speech is essential to the working of democracy, which is in effect a free market where the electorate has a choice between competing political ideologies. As with an economic free market it is essential that the electoral consumer has free access to information about all the options available so that they are able to make a considered rational choice. In reality, consumers of goods and services do not have the perfect knowledge or make the rational choices that theory suggests is essential to the proper working of a free market. The large corporations that dominate manufacturing and retailing spend vast sums of money on advertising for the purpose of: a) persuading consumers to behave irrationally, and b) to exclude potential competitors from the market. Political elites play a similar game with the electorate and rely heavily on the tendency of people to stay with the brand they know rather than risk a change. For that reason, brand names such as Labour, Conservative, Democrat, and Republican, are valuable. As with the commercial marketplace, new brands are kept out by the high cost of entering the market. Politics is an expensive business in a market controlled by monopolies.

When liberals campaign for free speech, it tends to mean free speech for liberals. It does not mean free speech for those who express anti-liberal views. Liberals first attempt to suppress *disagreeable* ideas by "not giving them the oxygen of publicity" but if that fails they use ridicule or intimidation to silence dissidents. Financial punishment forms the next line of defence because it avoids the embarrassment of openly political trials and political prisoners. Violence and intimidation are not ruled out but they are a sanction that is usually applied through a non-state organisation that is tolerated and unofficially encouraged by the state. Thus, organisations that exist to intimidate opponents of the governing elite and prevent them from exercising the supposed right to free speech are portrayed as noble defenders of democracy. Those that they try to silence are of course extremists who deserve what they get. One of the great unsolved political mysteries is why liberals think it their right and duty to silence their ideological opponents but squeal with indignation when there is any attempt to silence them.

Is there free speech when it is known that what is said and written privately can be listened to and read by agents of the state? Does such knowledge inhibit free expression, and is freedom of speech diminished by self-censorship – *the censor in the head*? What justification can there be for a state to hinder or prevent their citizens encrypting email in an unbreakable code? Why is it thought acceptable for liberal states to monitor all forms of electronic communication but for other states to be condemned as police states because they open their citizen's letters?

Nicky Hager, in his book, *Secret Power*, sets out how a computer system named ECHELON scans all email, faxes and telexes for target keywords and numbers.[161] This system complements another called Oratory that can listen to telephone calls and recognise target keywords. It has been suggested in an informal way for many years that such systems exist but Nicky Hager explains in great detail how the system works. It might be suggested that such arrangements are necessary to protect democracy, the Free World, the *International Community*, etc., but the foreword to the book by the former New Zealand Prime Minister, David Lange (1984–89), makes it clear that he, as Prime Minister, was not provided with information about the matter.

> Life at the time was full of unpleasant surprises. State-sponsored terrorism was a crime against humanity as long as it wasn't being practised by the allies, when it was studiously ignored. In the national

---

[161] *Secret Power*, Nicky Hager, ISBN 0908802358, Craig Potton Publishing, Box 555, Nelson, New Zealand.

interest it became necessary to say 'ouch' and frown and bear certain reprisals of our intelligence partners. We even went to the length of building a satellite station at Waihopai. But it was not until I read this book that I had any idea that we had been committed to an international integrated electronic network.

... this raises the question of to whom those concerned saw themselves ultimately responsible.

Should citizens of the USA, UK, Canada, Australia and New Zealand be concerned that a computerised system of information gathering has been introduced in those states without public discussion or consent? Why, when the existence of such a system was revealed several years ago, did it not reach the top of the news agenda and spark public debate? Is liberal democracy as free and democratic as liberals claim?

The various human rights declarations and conventions give no absolute right to freedom of speech because governing elites, through state legislatures, are able to make exemptions. We have a right to free speech unless the state says otherwise.

The Universal Declaration of Human Rights

Article 19,

Everyone has the right of opinion and expression; this right includes freedom to hold opinions without interference and seek, receive and impart information and ideas through any media and regardless of frontiers.

Article 29 (2)

In the exercise of his rights and freedoms, everyone shall be subject only to such limitations as are determined by law solely for the purpose of securing due recognition and respect for the rights and freedoms of others and meeting the just requirements of morality, public order and the general welfare in a democratic society.

The European Convention on Human Rights

Article 10.

1. Everyone has the right to freedom of expression. This right shall include freedom to hold opinions and to receive and impart information and ideas without interference by public authority and regardless of frontiers. This article shall not prevent states from requiring the licensing of broadcasting, television or cinema enterprises.

2. No restrictions shall be placed on the exercise of these rights other than such as are prescribed by law and are necessary in a democratic society in the interests of national security or public safety, for the prevention of disorder or crime, for the protection of health or morals or for the protection of the rights and freedoms of others. This article shall not prevent the imposition of lawful restrictions on the exercise of these rights by members of the armed forces, of the police or the administration of the state.

In other words, everyone has the rights listed unless there is a law that removes them. The scope for justifying the denial of free expression is certainly wide. The *get out clause* explains why so many of the states that are signatories to the various Declarations and Conventions are widely regarded as repressive. The inclusion of the *Universal Declaration of Human Rights* and the *European Convention on Human Rights* in a state's domestic law offers little protection to those citizens who are ideological enemies of the governing elite.

Is there any absolute right of free speech? The answer is 'no' but some states tolerate greater freedom of speech than others. There is undoubtedly greater freedom of speech in the USA than in the UK or the Peoples Republic of China. Being free to express an opinion is only half of a right. The other half involves making freely expressed ideas and information known to a wide audience. Money and an outlet in the media obviously help. Freedom of speech without the ability to communicate ideas to a wide audience is like having goods to sell but no way of selling them. Freedom of speech and the freedom to address an audience are essential to the proper working of democracy; a denial of one diminishes the other. Freedom of speech is of little value unless it is accompanied by a free and varied media, and in modern times that means a free and varied broadcasting media.

In liberal democracies, the suppression of unwelcome ideas is accompanied by slogans extolling the need to uphold freedom, democracy and the rights of those who might be offended by the expression of those ideas. The right of a small group not to be offended is often deemed greater than the right of a large group to enjoy freedom of speech on matters relating to their wellbeing and survival. The majority must be silenced so as not to offend the minority but it is deemed acceptable for the minority to offend the majority.

To ban something because it gives offence is an odd argument for liberals to use because they are not concerned about the offence they give to others and do not believe it to be a good guide as to what should be permitted. Liberals usually argue that those offended by what liberals deem to be radical and daring in the arts and entertainment are small-minded and undeserving of sympathy. When liberals boldly push back the bounds of what is publicly acceptable, it is thought unfortunate but unavoidable that some will be shocked. What a difference though, when liberals are offended or they believe some other group worthy of their concern is offended. Such inconsiderate behaviour is deemed to be a contemptible outrage. Just how small-minded can these liberals get.

Sovereignty

To be sovereign means to be answerable to no higher authority in law.

The state is an abstract legal entity in much the same way as is a business corporation but whereas a corporation is restrained in many of its internal and external actions by laws imposed upon it, a sovereign state is not so constrained. A sovereign state enacts its own laws and enforces them. An independent sovereign state is able to enter into agreements with other global actors if it chooses to do so.

A question frequently posed is "Where does sovereignty formally lie?" For instance, does sovereignty lie with the monarch, the president, or parliament? Less rarely asked, but perhaps of greater importance, are the related questions, where does sovereignty come from, and to whom does it belong?

The terms *state sovereignty* and *sovereign state* are commonly thought of as something to do with the ability of states to act alone, to be independent. Independence is the freedom to act without external restraint. Although there is a link between sovereignty and independence, the former term has a more particular meaning. Sovereignty is a legal concept that originated with the power of a sovereign to create, enforce and repeal laws. The sovereign is answerable to no higher worldly authority and the sovereign's subjects have no right of appeal to any higher legal authority. Absolute monarchies have given way to republics, and the powers of the sovereign have generally passed to the state and its legislature.

A sovereign state is able to regulate the affairs of its citizens within its borders by means of laws that are enacted and enforced by designated institutions. The legislature might be a monarch or a dictator or a political party or a parliament or some other body that either assumes the right to exercise sovereign powers or is given the right by the state's constitution. In the case of an absolute monarch (absolute sovereign) or other dictator, the constitution is whatever they say it is.

In its external relations with other states and other international actors, a sovereign state recognises no higher legal authority. However, because of the nature of the global state system, governing elites have to take account of conventions governing the relationship between states, and the power and interests of other states. Powerful states are less constrained by conventions and other external considerations than are weaker ones. Some states are less independent than others but all are sovereign if they make and enforce their own law.

A sovereign state is able to make and repeal laws, and to police and enforce those laws within its boundaries. A state's sovereignty is diminished if its citizens are subject to laws made and enforced (directly or indirectly) by an outside body. A sign of diminished sovereignty is the right of citizens to formally appeal to a legal authority outside the state. States sometimes grant outside bodies the right to exercise certain sovereign powers on the state's behalf. A test of independence and sovereignty is whether the state is able to recover those powers.

An example of a state attempting to directly assert an extension of its sovereignty is to be found in the case of the USA threatening to implement the Helms-Burton Act. That legislation gave the US government the right under US law to punish companies trading with states on a US government list. For example, a British company trading with Cuba could be prosecuted and penalised in the US. The states of the EU refused to accept that attempted extension of US sovereignty, and threatened retaliation against US companies operating in the EU.

Sovereignty, Interdependence and Power

It is often suggested that the economies of modern states are so interlinked and interdependent that the governments of those states have little ability to control economic activity, and consequently states are viewed as outdated relics of a past era. Leaving aside for the moment the contention that states are outdated, we will briefly look at what is meant by interdependent.

Interdependence is generally used in a way that implies a system where all parties benefit and none have control. It would be more realistic to see the global political system in terms of power and dependency. It is a system where powerful states are able to enmesh less powerful states in a web of interdependence that serves the interests of the most powerful states. Each party is dependent on the other but some are more dependent than others.

Being a large importer of goods and services is a factor in the calculation of power. Refusing to buy goods can be a more powerful weapon than refusing to sell them.[162] This is especially so where the economy of an exporting state is dependent upon the market in one, or a few, other states. Examples of such imbalances in commodity dependency are very common between Third World states (less developed states, LDSs) and the European Union or USA. If the USA bans the import of a certain commodity from a certain state it is likely to have serious consequences for the exporter but little, if any, for the USA. Further, the exporter is unlikely to have sufficient power, either alone or as part of an alliance with other producing states, to be able to do anything about the situation other than to appease the US government and comply with whatever demands it makes. If, on the other hand, a weak state were to ban the import of a commodity from the USA, or otherwise act in a way harmful to the interest of the USA, there is little doubt that the USA would employ whatever diplomatic, economic or military power it felt necessary to persuade the offending state to change its policy. If that failed, the

---

[162] An idea promoted by Kenneth Waltz.

US could, by various means, undermine internal support for the government of the weaker state or help internal opponents of the government to overthrow it. The weaker state is therefore in many ways dependent and unable to act in its own best interests but it is still sovereign if it is able to enact and enforce laws internally. It can be seen that the difference between independence and sovereignty is sometimes a matter of judgement. If a state enacts or repeals laws as a result of external pressure, both its sovereignty and independence are diminished.

The USA is used in the example above because it is the dominant world economic and military power. If, or more likely when, China succeeds to that position it too will use its power to its own advantage with consequences other states may not regard as an improvement on what we now have. The Chinese government is currently using the power derived from controlling access to a large market to drive hard bargains with global corporations, especially in relation to the transfer of technology and manufacturing capacity. Economic-liberals rationalise their desire to gain access to the large Chinese market by suggesting that the absorption of China into the global market will inevitably bring a market economy, the overthrow of the Chinese governing elite, and the birth of Chinese liberal democracy. Trade is being used as a Trojan horse for liberal values. On the other side, the Chinese governing elite is using the bait of trade and profit to acquire technology and other resources from the West and thereby rapidly increase its economic and military strength. When it is the dominant global power it hopes to be in a position to dictate terms to global corporations. The outcome of this game of poker is hard to predict.

Where Does Sovereignty Lie?

We will for the moment ignore the issue of where sovereignty comes from and look only at who or what exercises sovereign powers. In many situations it is difficult to know where sovereignty actually lies until a dispute arises between two or more bodies claiming sovereign powers in the same territory. The test of where sovereignty lies is in its enforcement. For example, if the European Court of Justice (ECJ) gives a judgement and the UK government, with the backing of parliament, refuses to abide by that judgement and cannot be compelled by the EU to do so, it is evident that the UK parliament is, in that policy area, sovereign.[163]

If the UK parliament were to make a law that conflicted with EC law, the English and Scottish judicial systems would have to decide which law to uphold? If an Act of Parliament stated quite clearly that English and Scottish law had primacy over EU law but the English and Scottish judicial systems refused to recognise the validity of that Act and continued to give primacy to EU law, and could not be dissuaded from doing so, it would be clear that sovereign powers lay with the ECJ and the EU. However, if those judges who refused to accept the sovereignty of

---

[163] The European Court of Justice is an institution of the European Union.

parliament were simply dismissed and others, willing to give effect to the will of parliament, were effectively appointed in their place, it would be clear that sovereign powers lay with parliament. If UK judges were appointed and paid by the EU, it would indicate that sovereign powers had passed to the EU.

If the European Court of Justice were to decide that the British government had broken European law and as a consequence instructed it to take a certain course of action and the government refused, what would be the consequence? If a punishment was imposed on the British government how would it be enforced? If it were a fine and the fine was not paid, could the European Court order the arrest of members of parliament or government ministers, detain them and bring them to trial? Who would carry out the arrests and where would those arrested be detained? Under what law would offenders be charged and who would try them? What if there was a popular anti-EU uprising? How would it be suppressed? Part of the answer is to be found in a speech (9th May 2000) by the Prime Minister of France, M. Jospin, in which he spoke of the pooled armies of member states being used "to maintain internal security".

The determining factor in deciding where sovereignty lies seems to be in enforcement. If the UK parliament has effective control of the police forces and the armed forces it possess sovereign powers because where two judicial systems claim jurisdiction in the same territory it is the system that can be enforced that prevails. If the day comes when the European Union controls the police and military forces in the United Kingdom, determines its laws, and the European Court is the highest court of appeal, then the parliament of the United Kingdom will not be sovereign. An indication of loss of sovereignty would be members of the armed forces swearing an oath of allegiance to the European Union or its president instead of to the British monarch. There is also the matter of who pays the police and armed forces. That issue might not be far away because in 1992 Germany's Chancellor Kohl said, "A European army and a European police force lie at the end of the road to European Union." However that objective is pursued, we will be assured with all possible sincerity by those favouring an EU state that no such thing is planned. So, the creation of an EU Rapid Reaction Force (RRF) has nothing whatsoever to do with the creation of an EU army. No, it is merely a *peacekeeping force* to be used in humanitarian missions. Just why the member states of the EU need to combine forces for that purpose is hard to tell. The UK plans to contribute 12,000 people, 72 combat aircraft and half the Royal Navy's surface fleet to the force.[164] Other member states will between them contribute equipment and people as and when they express a willingness to do so.[165] The

---

[164] Information available mid-November 2000

[165] Other than the obvious problem of having people with different first languages fighting in one force, there is the difficulty of combining the professional forces of the UK and France with the mostly conscripted forces of Germany and other EU states.

makeup of the peacekeeping force makes it look very much like an invasion force. What is not clear at the time of writing is whether there will be a bar on the Force being used within the EU. Suppose the electorate of a member state elects a non-liberal government or one that wants to withdraw from the EU. Will it be possible to deploy the Rapid Reaction Force in that *rogue state* to restore truth, justice and the liberal way? If there is no specific prohibition on internal deployment it must be assumed that it is a possibility that has been deliberately left open. Big questions to be answered are who will have ultimate control of the Rapid Reaction Force, and to whom or what will members of the force owe their loyalty?[166]

A more immediate question is, are UK armed forces being over-stretched? They have training and personal skills that are equal to that of any other forces but do they have the equipment and numbers? Is this bid by the UK government for European political glory backed with the necessary resources? The short answer is no. British forces are being asked to do more and more with less and less. Eventually they will be asked to undertake a task that will result in defeat and embarrassment. Humiliation will shatter the prestige and morale of the UK's armed forces and create long-term problems, such as making recruitment more difficult. And all because of the political posturing of a government that has no real grasp of military matters or grand strategy.

There are also questions relating to sovereignty. The core of the RRF command structure is to be British but will the UK government have control over its own forces? Will it have control of those of other member states? Or will a body within the EU have control and be able to order the RRF to invade, for instance, an African state (perhaps a former French colony) for the purpose of keeping its government in place against internal opposition?

It can be argued that these questions are no different from those that could be asked about the commitment of UK forces to NATO but there is a difference. The members of NATO are recognised as separate states even though the organisation is completely dominated and controlled by the USA, which supplies the bulk of

---

[166] The French want to create an EU military capacity that is able to meet EU political aims. They are quite clear about the need to have a military force that is able to play a part in achieving foreign policy goals – whether of the French state or the EU. They see the RRF, however humble its beginnings, as the kernel of a force that will be able to operate independently of NATO and US control. The French have a long-term strategy, which is more than can be said of the UK government. The US strategy is to retain control of military resources in Europe while: (a) getting European states to meet more of the cost – preferably by buying more US equipment; (b) creating a military force that can act independently of NATO – thus avoiding the need for the agreement of all NATO members and getting around the deployment restrictions inherent in the NATO Charter. There is therefore some overlap in US and French objectives; the difference relates to control. The prime concern of Prime Minister Blair is to make a political gesture and show that *Britain is at the heart of Europe*. The proposal, as advanced by the UK government, points to muddle and wasted resources. The RRF will add nothing to the overall military capability but will duplicate existing political and military command structures.

just about everything, including combat forces and transport capability. In the EU the distinction between member states is fading and majority voting is, little by little, becoming the norm. Unlike NATO, the EU is not principally a military alliance of states but a state in the making. The political control of NATO is such that involvement in *out of area* missions is by consent and a force can be withdrawn by its government.

In addition to the above, there are matters of principle to be considered. What of the notion that you should do to others as you would have them do to you? Would member states of the EU think it acceptable for African or Asian states to send a peacemaking force to intervene in the affairs of a European state?

The creation of an EU fighting force is relevant to sovereignty because the line of command indicates where sovereignty lies.

The EU and the British Monarchy

One of the problems to be overcome by those who favour the European Union is what to do with the British monarchy. Although the direct power of the monarch is very limited, he or she is Head of State and thus holds an important position in the constitutional structure of the UK. That position symbolises among other things the sovereignty of the UK and as such is not compatible with a European Union state. Perhaps for that reason, the governing elite became less supportive of the monarchy during the 1990's. A steady drip of propaganda from *opinion formers* was set on persuading public opinion that we should *become more European* and do away with the monarchy or strip it of any constitutional power. That offensive suddenly stopped when the more immediate threat of the break-up of the UK loomed with devolution and the creation of a Scottish Parliament. The British monarchy again became the focus for a British identity and the British state. Members of the political elite no longer called for the royal family to move out of its palaces, get proper jobs, cycle to work, and in general to be more like other Northern European royal families. Instead, snippets of *news* about the royal family began to reappear in the broadcast media and the reverential approach to coverage of the monarchy returned. Lots of respectful coverage of the Queen Mother and her latest birthday, cold, or fall.

That rehabilitation of the monarchy for the purpose of underpinning Britishness will eventually conflict with the need to remove the monarch's status as Head of State. As the process of EU state building goes on it will become necessary to transfer some of the constitutional powers held by the monarch to an EU president. One of those powers could be the right to authorise the opening of Parliament. The ceremony by then will be an inconsequential formality because Parliament will have lost many of its powers. Perhaps Parliament will still be opened by the monarch but only with the approval of the EU president. It will become an occasion that serves merely to keep the natives happy and preserve the illusion that Parliament and the monarchy are meaningful institutions.

What constitutional function will the monarchy serve if the UK is totally absorbed into a European Union state? There is widespread respect for Queen Elizabeth among Englanders but the long-term future of the monarchy in England has been weakened by the Queen being seen less as Queen of the English and more as head of the British state and Commonwealth. A monarch who is the symbolic head of a nation is in a more enduring position than one who is only head of state. States come and go but nations live on.[167]

HRH Princes Charles sees himself as a future king of a multi-cultural, multi-racial, multi-religious society and not as king of the English and symbolic head of that nation. If a monarch owes no loyalty to the English nation then the English nation owes no loyalty to the monarch. A king without a nation or a state becomes a short-lived curiosity.

Where Does Sovereignty Come From?

It is difficult to argue successfully that sovereignty *in the beginning* or *in the natural order* lies with individuals because mankind is a communal animal. We are subject to the higher authority of our parents from birth. The family is the smallest community to posses sovereign powers. Families as individuals and as groups, are part of a network of larger communities to which sovereign powers are lent for specific purposes. Something lent is something retained – ownership remains with the lender.

Communities exist within and alongside other communities; they are grouped together in clusters with boundaries that exist in the imagination of insiders and outsiders. The outer communal boundary is that of the nation and the innermost boundary, the family. As the layers of community have been built up from the inside outwards, so sovereignty has become more remote from its source. The democratic nation-state is generally the largest and most remote unit to which individuals are willing to lend their sovereign powers. The reason for that is simply that to lend sovereign powers to a body outside the nation-state is to place them in the hands of outsiders (non-kin, foreigners) who have interests, values, and perceptions that are to varying degrees different from, and sometimes in conflict with, those of insiders. We instinctively want those who exercise our sovereign powers on our behalf to be fellow insiders who share our communal interests.

---

[167] The determined effort to make the monarchy more acceptable in Scotland and Wales has meant it becoming less English. Various English symbols have been removed from royal insignia while Scottish and Welsh symbols have been added.

Sovereignty originates with communities, and is lent to individuals and institutions for the purpose of managing the community in a way that members of the community think beneficial and acceptable. If the community believes that its sovereignty is not being used as it wishes it has the right to reclaim it. To deny such a right is to deny the basic principles of democracy. If, for example, the Scottish people wish to re-allocate their sovereignty from the UK parliament and lend it to a Scottish parliament, they are entitled to do so and it is not for any other nation or state to deny that right. The English likewise enjoy the same right to cede from the UK, and the EU, and create their own state.

Those who are lent sovereign powers generally want more and come to believe that they hold them by right. Governing elites have encouraged both the movement of sovereign powers to the state, and the perception that the state possesses those powers as of right. That movement, combined with the deliberate confusion between *nation* and *state*, has enabled governing elites to get away with treating sovereignty as the property of the state, and theirs to do with as they wish. They deem it to be their right, if they so choose, to give it away or *pool* it with the sovereign powers exercised by other governing elites.

Sovereignty belongs to communities. Those to whom sovereignty is lent have no right or irrevocable authority to pass it on to any other body. Sovereignty is to be used by insiders for the benefit of insiders. To place sovereignty in the hands of outsiders is to invite tyranny. If a national community has its sovereign powers seized from it, and is compelled to observe laws and a system of government imposed from outside, then that nation has the absolute right to rebel and reclaim its sovereignty. Without sovereignty there is no freedom.

When the state of South Carolina attempted to repatriate its sovereign powers from the Union in 1860, the Union government claimed an absolute right to exercise sovereignty on behalf of the people of South Carolina and used military force to assert its claim. There are an increasing number of citizens in the US today who feel that the governing elite has, through its control of the Federal Government, seized the sovereignty of the people as of right and is using it to further elite interests rather than those of the people. Hence, the interests of corporations and bodies outside the US are given priority over the interests of US citizens. One expression of the theft of communal sovereignty was the formation of the North American Free Trade Area (NAFTA).

The alienation of citizens from the state (people from government) is found in many places but in the US there are people who are prepared to make it an issue. As might be expected, those who seek decentralisation and repatriation of sovereign powers are patronisingly dismissed as fools. Some are, but the vast majority want greater control of their lives and see no reason why they should abide by the laws of a government that does not pursue or even acknowledge the values and interests of the communities it governs.

If modern American rebel groups such as The Freemen were Marxist, it is certain that those who deride them would instead be treating them as revolutionary heroes. However, Marxists do not seek the repatriation of sovereign powers because they are centralists rather than decentralists. Marxists, like liberals, tend to favour strong governments that are able to coerce and direct the people. They favour centralisation, bureaucracy, social engineering, and regulation. They need the power of the state to suppress the communal instincts of the people. They see it as their mission to *enlighten* and *educate* those who resist, and use a vast body of law and regulation to enforce that enlightenment and wean the people away from the instincts that have served them and their ancestors well. They do not ask the people what they want but tell them what is best for them. Most of the Americans currently rebelling against the power of the Federal Government are seeking greater democracy through decentralisation and the ability to exercise their communal sovereignty.

In a democratic nation-state it is the duty of those who govern to use communal sovereign powers to preserve the community and further its interests. It is their duty to listen to the people and do as the people want. There will always be conflicting interests in a community, whether it be large or small, and as a result there will from time to time be winners and losers. It is the task of wise governors to ensure that it is not always the same people who win and lose.

At no level in the web of linked communal institutions are the collected sovereign powers *owned* by those exercising them. No government body has the right to lend sovereign powers to any other body without the consent of those to whom sovereignty belongs. No body can give away what it does not own; sovereignty belongs to the people and they have the right to reclaim it as and when they see fit.

Sovereignty and International Law

Most of what is commonly called international law is elite law, which is a body of rules created by an authority in order to punish those who offend against the interests and values of that authority. Laws usually prohibit certain acts and behaviour, and encourage others. To be effective laws need to be enforced.

Law is an enforceable *rule* or *body of rules* established by custom or an authority for the purpose of regulating certain human relationships. Law can be *natural* (customary), having grown and evolved within communities and between communities, or statute law, the law of a state. Natural law evolves within a community and is enforced by it, often by informal means. State law (statute law) is made (codified) and enforced by a state. Natural or customary law usually reflects the common interests of all parties that observe it. Statute law tends to reflect and further the interests of those who make it.

The rules that regulate the conduct of the citizens of states in their dealings with the citizens of other states is called *private international law*. It is usually enforced internally by the contracting states according to rules that apply equally to all citizens of those states.

Agreements between sovereign states (e.g. treaties) that regulate the relationships between states is *public international law*, which is usually enforced by powerful states against less powerful states.

Human communities and societies have evolved and become more complex at a rate that has, in the past few thousand years, outstripped the ability of natural law to keep pace. Various authorities, religious and secular, have filled the gap by creating law which meets practical needs and furthers ideological ends. Formal law codes have taken on a life and logic of their own, while natural law has increasingly taken second place to ideology and interests. Relying on the letter of codified law without testing it against the principles of natural law, can produce results that offend our instinctive sense of natural justice and morality. Public opinion is usually a better expression of natural justice than is *the letter* of statute law. The jury system could be used to ensure that statute law does not conflict with natural law. A defendant who is clearly guilty of offending against statute law but has acted in accordance with natural justice is likely to be found innocent by a free jury. For that reason it would serve natural justice if juries had the power, presently exercised by judges, to recommend or pass sentence. It is important that public opinion has a place in the judicial process because that system and those employed there, including judges, are the servants of the people, which is something they often forget. More democracy and accountability to public opinion is needed in the judicial system not less.

Natural law, and the principles that underlie it, has evolved in a way that best meets the needs of individuals and their communities. Natural law is an expression of the behaviour and attitudes that enable individuals to live together in a community to their mutual advantage. It is the body of general rules (common law) that enable a community to survive and prosper. Behaviour that does not serve the common good is discouraged. What is good for the community (whole and parts) is thought of as just, moral and lawful. What is bad for the community is seen as unjust, immoral and unlawful. These communal instincts for what is right and proper cannot be destroyed by ideological conditioning but they can be suppressed. Some are made to feel ashamed of their communal instincts and are instead guided by dogma, i.e. political correctness.

Murder and theft are natural law crimes. In those and similar instances statute law overlaps with natural law. However, statute law often parts company with natural justice when it comes to punishing offenders and compensating victims; in fact, natural justice remedies and those who advocate them are often regarded, in a sneering way, as barbaric.

273

The principles of natural justice are evident in the international law that has its origins in longstanding conventions (a form of common law) but little if any is to be seen in manufactured international law. For example, *laws* relating to war crimes and crimes against humanity are couched in terms that enable them to be used by the winners of a conflict to prosecute, judge, and punish the losers; none of which accords with natural justice. The judicial system is not independent and the crimes are not framed in a clear and impartial way that makes it possible to indict and prosecute the citizens of any state. In other words, the winning side is often as guilty of war crimes as the loser but escapes prosecution and punishment. For example, Chechens were unable to have Boris Yeltsin tried as a war criminal, and Tibetans are unable to have Chinese leaders prosecuted, yet the *International Community* is able to deal as they choose with those they regard as war criminals. The general rule is that war crimes and crimes against humanity are only committed by the citizens of defeated or small states and those prosecuted are always associated with an ideology to which the prosecutors are opposed. It should also be noted that unlike their position on crime within the state, liberals are keen to see their ideological enemies severely punished. It seems that vengeance, deterrence and retribution are valid justifications for punishing offenders when it suits liberals. No mention is made of the need to help offenders reform their ways so that they can once again take their place in society.

It is much easier to be righteous about crimes against humanity if you are able to define the crimes, initiate prosecution and punish offenders. It is an added bonus when, as with the USA, a state is able to exempt its citizens from the jurisdiction of the International Criminal Court.[168] War crimes were committed on a vast scale in Vietnam and many believe that Henry Kissinger should be put on trial but we all know that will never happen because the US would not extradite him. However, that did not prevent President Clinton's government from urging the Italian government to extradite a Kurdish leader to Turkey so that he could be put on trial for terrorist offences.

Clearly, much international law has little regard for natural justice, which demands that a common body of law be applied equally to all within the jurisdiction of the sovereign authority, and be enforced equally against all who offend. Those who act as judges and impose penalties should not be parties to the case. A system of law that is arbitrary in its enactment and enforcement cannot be said to accord with the principles of natural justice or with democracy. International law and its institutions have more to do with power, interests and ideology than justice.

The global society of states is an anarchic society in which groups with different interests, values and perceptions, abide by conventions which make their dealings with one another less strained and prone to misunderstanding than they might

---

[168] The International Criminal Court is to be set up and start work when the membership treaty has been signed by sixty states. The US is not a signatory (year 2000).

otherwise be. Those conventions, which are a form of natural law, are much the same as they were thousands of years ago. For example, there are conventions concerning the treatment of diplomats and envoys that do not need to be enforced because it is in the interests of all states that they are observed. If a party abuses a trust they forgo the benefits that trust can bring. Offenders are shunned and placed at a disadvantage in dealing with others. It is for this reason that honourable conduct and a good name are so important within and between traditional communities.

The structure of the UN, and in particular the existence of the Security Council, shows that despite the fine words of the UN Charter, the UN is founded on realpolitik. It cannot be otherwise, as was shown by the shortcomings of the League of Nations, which was structured to suit the outlook of US President Woodrow Wilson and American constitutional sentiment. The structural weakness in the League of Nations was corrected when the UN and its Security Council were created. The UN, like other institutions of its kind, is undemocratic; does not have an independent judiciary; does not apply its law impartially; does not have an independent means of enforcement; and does not punish offenders with equal severity.

The existence of the UN Security Council is a formal recognition of the fact that:

1. only the most powerful states are able to both make and enforce international law;

2. it is not possible to enforce international law against the most powerful states.

3. powerful states only observe laws for as long as it furthers their interests to do so. Weak states abide by formal laws because they are punished if they do not.

Global society is a primitive society which, despite the pretence that it is global village, is, as mentioned earlier, best equated with a jungle. If there is such a thing as a body of international law that applies to the whole of global society it is the law of the jungle, which can be defined as, the rules for surviving in a competitive and hostile environment. Most international law and the means for enforcing it have only a flimsy connection with democracy and natural justice.

Kosovo

Events in Kosovo provide an example of powerful states ignoring treaty law and the principles of international law with complete immunity.

According to its Charter, Nato is a defensive alliance. Yet, it issued, through US envoy Richard Holbrooke, a demand to the Serbs that they comply with the terms of the Rambouillet Agreement, which included the right of Nato forces to enter and move freely in Serbia. Neither Serbia nor any other part of Yugoslavia is a member of NATO, and neither of those entities had invaded the territory of a

NATO member. Yet it was made clear by Richard Holbrooke that if the Serbs did not agree to sign what amounted to a document of surrender they would face a bombardment from Nato forces until they changed their mind. The agreement, which made demands of the Serbs that it was known they could not accept, was intended to be the *justification* (excuse) for launching a war. The aim throughout was to weaken President Milosevic and, in the short term, turn Kosovo into a self-governing part of Yugoslavia. This despite the fact that at the end of World War I, the Treaty of Versailles recognised Kosovo as an integral part of Serbia. That recognition was reaffirmed in 1995 by the Daytona Peace Accord, which the USA played an important part in formulating.

The Albanians claim to have lived in Kosovo for two thousand years or more, thus preceding the arrival of the Serbs in the sixth century. However, they lived mainly in the south while the Orthodox Christian Serbs lived mainly in the north where they have sites of religious and national importance.

At the end of World War II the Serb and Albanian population in Kosovo were of roughly the same size. Since then the Albanians, who are a Moslem nation with a very high birth rate, have migrated into northern Kosovo and beyond into Serbia. Many Serbs felt intimidated by the growing population of people with a different religion, culture and language. That led to a steady migration of Serbs into towns and districts where they felt more secure. They were, in effect, being ethnically cleansed from parts of Kosovo where Serbs had lived for many centuries.

In 1999, the Albanian population in Kosovo was 90% of the total. The Albanians, as might be expected, did not want to be governed by people of another nation and set themselves the objective of gaining independence for the whole of Kosovo. Milosevic saw that the Albanians had gained effective control of Kosovo and that the only way to win it back was to expel them when circumstances were right. In 1989 he dissolved the regional government and established direct rule. Use of the Albanian language was banned in schools and places of work. Predictably, the Albanians took exception to that and set about creating their own state in Kosovo. Under the leadership of Ibrahim Rugova, the Albanians sought self-government by peaceful means but when in 1995 the Daytona Accord recognised Kosovo as part of Serbia, the position of Ibrahim Rugova was undermined and the Kosovo Liberation Army (KLA) gained support.

Over the next few years the KLA received funds, arms and training from Albania. At a politically appropriate time they launched a series of raids on Serb targets in Kosovo, which included the killing of policemen and the occupation of areas that enabled them to block the main road leading north to Belgrade. When Serbs moved to open the road and retake occupied buildings, the fighting was portrayed in the media as a vicious Serbian attack on Albanian civilians. The television pictures of those events provided the opportunity for NATO states to issue a series of demands to the Serbian government. Yugoslavia was at the time recognised as a sovereign state and a member of the UN.

United Nations Charter

Article 2

The Organization and its Members, in pursuit of the Purposes stated in Article 1, shall act in accordance with the following Principles.

1. The Organization is based on the principle of the <u>sovereign equality of all its Members</u>.

2. All Members, in order to ensure to all of them the rights and benefits resulting from membership, shall fulfil in good faith the obligations assumed by them in accordance with the present Charter.

3. <u>All Members shall settle their international disputes by peaceful means</u> in such a manner that international peace and security, and justice, are not endangered.

4. <u>All Members shall refrain in their international relations from the threat or use of force against the territorial integrity or political independence of any state,</u> or in any other manner inconsistent with the Purposes of the United Nations.

5. All Members shall give the United Nations every assistance in any action it takes in accordance with the present Charter, and shall refrain from giving assistance to any state against which the United Nations is taking preventive or enforcement action.

6. The Organization shall ensure that states which are not Members of the United Nations act in accordance with these Principles so far as may be necessary for the maintenance of international peace and security.

7. <u>Nothing contained in the present Charter shall authorise the United Nations to intervene in matters which are essentially within the domestic jurisdiction of any state or shall require the Members to submit such matters to settlement under the present Charter; but this principle shall not prejudice the application of enforcement measures under Chapter VII.</u>

Chapter VII enables the Security Council to determine the existence of a threat to the peace, breach of the peace, or act of aggression and to recommend or take measures to maintain or restore international peace and security.

Chapter VII

Articles

39. <u>The Security Council shall determine the existence of any threat to the peace, breach of the peace, or act of aggression</u> and shall make recommendations, or

decide what measures shall be taken in accordance with Articles 41 and 42, to maintain or restore international peace and security.

40. In order to prevent an aggravation of the situation, the Security Council may, before making the recommendations or deciding upon the measures provided for in Article 39, call upon the parties concerned to comply with such provisional measures as it deems necessary or desirable. Such provisional measures shall be without prejudice to the rights, claims, or position of the parties concerned. The Security Council shall duly take account of failure to comply with such provisional measures.

41. The Security Council may decide what measures not involving the use of armed force are to be employed to give effect to its decisions, and it may call upon the Members of the United Nations to apply such measures. These may include complete or partial interruption of economic relations and of rail, sea, air, postal, telegraphic, radio, and other means of communication, and the severance of diplomatic relations.

42. Should the Security Council consider that measures provided for in Article 41 would be inadequate or have proved to be inadequate, it may take such action by air, sea, or land forces as may be necessary to maintain or restore international peace and security. Such action may include demonstrations, blockade, and other operations by air, sea, or land forces of Members of the United Nations.

In short, the UN Charter recognises the right of self-defence but it denies the right of states or the UN to use force against any state or intervene in the internal affairs of any state unless authorised to do so by the Security Council. Obviously, the Permanent Members of the Security Council will veto authority being given for intervention in their internal affairs or those of an ally. The Nato powers did not seek the approval of the Security Council because they knew that Russia would veto it. Even the threat of force by Nato against Yugoslavia was unlawful.

Nato attacked Yugoslavia without the authority of the Security Council and try as they might they cannot escape that fact. They also contravened the terms of their own treaty which makes it clear that Nato is a defensive alliance which acts only when a party to the Charter is threatened or subject to armed attack.

The North Atlantic Treaty

The Parties to this Treaty reaffirm their faith in the purposes and principles of the Charter of the United Nations and their desire to live in peace with all peoples and all governments. They are determined to safeguard the freedom, common heritage and civilisation of their peoples, founded on the principles of democracy, individual liberty and the rule of law. They seek to promote stability and wellbeing in the North Atlantic area. They are resolved to unite their efforts for collective defence and for the preservation of peace and security. They therefore agree to this North Atlantic Treaty:

Article 1

The Parties undertake, as set forth in the Charter of the United Nations, to settle any international dispute in which they may be involved by peaceful means in such a manner that international peace and security and justice are not endangered, and to refrain in their international relations from the threat or use of force in any manner inconsistent with the purposes of the United Nations.

Article 4

The Parties will consult together whenever, in the opinion of any of them, the territorial integrity, political independence or security of any of the Parties is threatened.

Article 5

The Parties agree that an armed attack against one or more of them in Europe or North America shall be considered an attack against them all and consequently they agree that, if such an armed attack occurs, each of them, in exercise of the right of individual or collective self-defence recognised by Article 51 of the Charter of the United Nations, will assist the Party or Parties so attacked by taking forthwith, individually and in concert with the other Parties, such action as it deems necessary, including the use of armed force, to restore and maintain the security of the North Atlantic area.

Any such armed attack and all measures taken as a result thereof shall immediately be reported to the Security Council. Such measures shall be terminated when the Security Council has taken the measures necessary to restore and maintain international peace and security.

Nato action can also be deemed illegal on the grounds that some of the attacks were deliberately made against civilian targets, which is contrary to the requirements of the Charter of the International War Crimes Tribunal. That Charter declares it an offence to attack or bombard, by whatever means, undefended towns, villages, dwellings or buildings. Nato labelled power stations, bridges and television broadcasting stations as strategic military targets. But what would be the reaction from the leaders of the Nato powers if a group opposed to them were to attack similar targets within their states? At a guess, it would be called terrorism.

What direct penalty has been suffered by the Nato powers as a result of their illegal attack on a member state of the UN and the occupation of part of its territory? None of course but who is going to punish them? Perhaps though they have suffered damage in that Nato can no longer successfully claim to be a solely defensive alliance and China and Russia have been alerted to the fact that the Nato powers, which amount to the US and its allies, are so powerful economically, politically and militarily that they feel able to intervene when and where they like. In future, their appeals to international law and the need for the peaceful settlement of disputes are going to look hollow. The Nato-Serbia war has already had repercussions in that it made the Russian invasion of Chechnya diplomatically possible.

We saw earlier how governing elites appeal to morality in a flexible and selective manner. International law is used in a similar way. After manufacturing the necessary *just cause* (explosions in Moscow) President Putin ordered the invasion of Chechnya in 1999. Russian forces laid waste to the capital, killed about 100,000 people, drove many more thousands out of their homeland, and claimed to be restoring order. If the Nato states had wanted to condemn Russia, what principles of international law or charters or treaties could they appeal to when they had so recently broken every rule in the book?

The ploy of vilifying those you wish to destroy was so overplayed, especially by George Robinson the then Defence Secretary, that it will probably be difficult to use such an outpouring of vitriol for quite some time. But perhaps not; Robin Cook did much the same thing in order to prepare public opinion and justify intervention in the internal affairs of Sierra Leone, a former British colony. The RUF rebels were condemned as torturers who were responsible for the mutilation of innocent civilians. In fact, the fault for such atrocities lay with some but not all of the assorted of groups that made up the often disunited opposition to the Western-backed government. The clear-cut distinction made between the nasty rebels on the one hand and the gallant, upright defenders of democracy on the other bears little relationship to the complex reality of Sierra Leone where groups changed sides. Nevertheless, the propaganda machine ensured that intervention was *justified* and British forces entered the conflict on the side of the angels. The level of abuse directed at the enemy fell short of the crude insults heaped on Milosevic by George Robinson. Milosevic and his supporters were depicted as vermin who were so evil and their case so devoid of worth that any action taken against them and the Serbian people was justified. George Robinson became Lord Robinson and was promoted to Secretary General of Nato. What chance is there that he is indicted as a war criminal, along with Prime Minister Blair, Foreign Secretary Cook? It may well be that a free and fair court would find them completely innocent of the charges. However, there is a reasonable case to answer and many formal applications were made to indict them. These three Scots were bound to go scot-free because no winning side prosecutes and punishes its leaders. Just who or what has the power to detain them and compel them to stand trial? The more the process is thought through the more clear it becomes that the International War Crimes Tribunal is a political tool. It is inconceivable that those appointed to administer the tribunal and consider applications for indictment would offend their political masters by even suggesting that they had a case to answer.

The victors not only write the history of a war but they define and condemn the war criminals – at least in the short term.

Sovereignty and Global Society

The natural limit of a nation-state's territory and sovereignty is the nation and its homeland. Although nation-state boundaries are open to change and interpretation, they are usually widely recognised and accepted as legitimate. Even where there is a dispute, there is a limit to the territory and population that can be claimed by the nation. Civic states are not restrained in that way because they have no natural limits to their size, sovereignty or ambition. Civic societies are not constrained by considerations of nationality or homeland. Those things are seen as divisions to be overcome rather than natural boundaries to be observed. Even oceans are no barriers. It is this outlook that underlies the liberal dream of a liberal world government, which means an empire in which liberal laws and notions of rights and justice are imposed worldwide. Nationalists are opposed to all empires because they remove control over the exercise of sovereign powers from those to whom sovereignty belongs. Empires also bring cultural, economic and political oppression in the name of uniformity. Empires are by nature centralised and undemocratic.

Nationalists recognise the right of states to defend their territorial and political unity unless that right is exercised against a nation seeking self-government in its homeland. Nations always have the right to exercise their sovereignty in their homeland because that is the essence of democracy. Liberals and other statists do not recognise that right because they believe that civic identity always comes before national identity, and the rights of the state come before those of the nation. Thus Russian action in Chechnya is not seen as an invasion (a state cannot invade its own territory) but the crushing of those who refuse to recognise the sovereignty of the Russian state – a civil war. Liberal opposition to the military action of the Russian Federation, in as far as there was any opposition, was not based on the right of Chechens to govern themselves but on the way the invasion was conducted. It was seen as an infringement of civil rights and the rules concerning the conduct of war rather than an infringement of a nation's right to self-determination.

When the governing elite of one state plays an active part in dismembering another state, as was done to Yugoslavia, it will still uphold the principle that the preservation of a state comes before the independence of a nation. National liberation movements are sometimes tolerated and even encouraged (Albanians in Kosovo) because of their usefulness in a wider struggle, but they are expected to respect state boundaries and seek a political entity short of a fully-fledged state;

perhaps as a region within a federal state. Another example is Iraq, where there does not appear to be any liberal support for the break-up of the existing state into several parts, including a Kurdish nation-state.

A state that is able to apply and enforce its laws against citizens and organizations living or based in other states, has effectively extended its sovereignty. The traditional way of doing that is by military conquest. A subtler ploy is for a dominant state, perhaps with its allies, to create and control an organisation that is able to make and enforce a body of rules against other states and their citizens. Those other parties are, more or less, compelled to abide by the rules even though they play little if any part in the appointment of officials or the framing of the rules. Examples of such organisations are the World Bank and International Monetary Fund. The rules and directives of these organisations are law for those compelled by circumstance to obey them. In other words, the states that control the institutions have effectively extended their sovereignty.

If there is such a thing as codified international law it should be possible to identify the body that stands above and apart from all states and exercises sovereign powers, i.e. makes laws and enforces them. The UN is the obvious candidate but its Charter is not a body of law, and the organisation is clearly not sovereign because it is unable to police its Articles and Resolutions or punish offenders without the approval and assistance of those states that have the resources to undertake such action. The UN can therefore only take action when it is not against the *vital* interest of the permanent members of the Security Council to do so. This is not to suggest that the UN is not sometimes a useful organisation. From time to time it helps states avoid or manage conflicts, and it provides a meeting place where informal discussion can take place, which is useful and more productive than formal speeches and resolutions.

As we have seen, *international law* is only law if it can be enforced. The experience of the League of Nations, UN and World Court has shown that only those *laws* that serve the interests of the states capable of enforcing them will be enforced. There is little to be gained from winning a case against the USA in the World Court if the USA refuses to accept the verdict. There is little point in the UN attempting to punish the USA for an infringement of the UN charter because it does not have the power to do so. The UN General Assembly can pass as many resolutions as it wishes but they are unlikely to achieve anything unless powerful states support them.

In a similar vein, if the United States announced an extension of its territorial waters (i.e. an extension of its sovereignty) to four hundred miles and banned Spanish fishing boats from those waters, it is probable that Spanish fishermen would comply. If they did not it is improbable that Spain would send a gunboat to protect them. Yet, that is just what happened when Canada extended its fishing limits.

The constraints on a US extension of its sovereignty would not be the power (economic, military, diplomatic) of Spain (or perhaps the EU) but an assessment of how such an extension might harm other US interests. For example, if other states followed the US lead and extended their territorial limits it could deny the US navy access to important areas and strategic straits. It was such a concern that delayed US acceptance of an extension of territorial waters from 4 to 12 miles in the 1970s.

The lesson here is that if a powerful state like the US unilaterally extends its territorial waters to four hundred miles that extension is likely to become *international law*. Who is going to resist it? Other states usually follow such leads without fear of condemnation because even in the global jungle states do not like to be seen blatantly infringing the principles of natural justice. It is therefore unlikely that any state would extend its territorial waters and deny the right of other states to do likewise.

Political systems are structured in a way that enables the governing elite to control law making and enforcement. The elite is able to ensure that a legal framework exists which protects its interests and promotes elite values. Public acceptance of the status quo is gained through elite control of institutions and the principal means of spreading propaganda. Should persuasion fail, the governing elite has, through its control of police and military forces, the ability to compel compliance with its laws. In this way the governing elite and the state become one. To challenge or attempt to overthrow the state (and the governing elite) is the worst of crimes and the one for which the most severe penalty is reserved.[169] The Global Elite/*International Community*/New World Order, works in the same way as other governing elites. It creates and enforces rules that promote its world-view and furthers its interests. Those who challenge the status quo are treated as outlaws who must be punished and made to comply by any means necessary.

Power and States

Power is, in essence, the ability to manipulate events, impose perceptions, and achieve goals. A goal might be to preserve the status quo or destroy it. Absolute power gives unrestricted freedom of action and the ability to compel others to do what is necessary to help achieve goals. No state has unrestricted absolute power because all need to consider the power of internal interest groups and the external power of other actors in the global system. States project their power within and

---

[169] Treason, which is disloyalty to the state, has its roots in natural law and disloyalty to the community. To be trusted as an insider is to be given access to resources, influence and information denied to outsiders. For an insider to be disloyal to his community, particularly by putting the interests of another community first, is to be disloyal to every other insider and put their wellbeing at risk.

without until it is effectively resisted. A state with absolute power would be able to act without fear of any internal or external resistance.

Power comes from the possession or control of resources, such as: military capability; economic factors, e.g. land, people, agriculture, manufacturing capacity; scientific and technological know-how. A geographical position that gives control of a mountain pass or shipping strait is a source of power (e.g. Turkey and the Bosporus). Some states gain power from being the leading proponents of an ideology or the guardians of a holy site (e.g. Saudi Arabia and Mecca).

Other important aspects of state power are the degree of internal unity and cohesion, and the will and determination of its citizens to act together in pursuit of a common goal or ideal. The strength of a state in a given situation is affected by its will and determination to prevail, which depends to a large extent on the importance attached to the interest being protected or pursued. The will to win can sometimes overcome a lack of material resources. For example, during the so-called Cod War, a dispute between the UK and Iceland over territorial waters and access to fish stocks, the Icelandic government won because the outcome was of much greater importance to it than to the UK government, and its will and determination were consequently greater. The fact that Icelandic economic and military resources were far fewer than those of the UK was not a deterrent.

Each state pursues its own external interests, as far as it is able to do so, restrained only by the power (individual or joint) of other global actors, some of which are non-governmental organizations. Non-state actors are not ideologically neutral and it would be unrealistic to expect them to be so. They reflect and promote the values and interests of those who control them, one could not reasonably expect it to be otherwise.

Organisations created by Western liberal states reflect liberal values and play a part in imposing them on members of global society. For example, organizations like the World Bank promote economic-liberalism and are able to serve the interests of the Global Elite by imposing conditions favourable to liberal globalism. States receiving assistance from the World Bank have to abide by terms that favour free trade/open market policies, and are thereby drawn further into the global economy. In this way the independence and power of some is decreased while the power of others is increased.

Power is in large part a matter of perception, and once formed perceptions tend to endure until events force a re-assessment. An example of this process was the steady decline during the twentieth century of the UK as a world power. In the 1930's the governing elite acted as if it was as powerful as it had been at the beginning of the century. It was in the habit of acting in a certain way and others were in the habit of responding in a certain way. As a result, the British Empire held together and the governing elite of a small state was able to exercise sovereignty over the people of other lands. The surrender of Singapore to the Japanese during World War II shattered that perception of British power, and a psychological advantage held for so long was permanently lost. The British governing elite's perceptions also changed, and there was a subsequent loss of confidence that made the process of British post war decolonisation quicker and less bloody than it might have been otherwise. With the exception of a few small colonial territories, the *reach* of UK sovereignty shrank to match its reduced power. It can be seen from this that the perception of power can be more important than the reality. To be seen to be strong is to be strong, until an event occurs which brings a perceptual reassessment.

Treaties between states reflect the status quo at the time of their creation. As the fortunes of states wax and wane so conventions, treaties and institutional structures become obsolete. Thus the fifty-year Peace and Friendship Treaty between the UK and the USSR, signed shortly after World War II, when those states were allies, quickly became redundant when they became enemies with the start of the Cold War.

No state has ever had absolute power and independence but it is essential to the survival of states that they strive to obtain or retain sufficient power to avoid over-dependence on others. In other words, the fact that no state has complete freedom to act as it wishes is no good reason for a state to give up the limited power, independence and freedom of action it does have.

We live in a world where there is ever-greater control of resources in one state by people and institutions based in another state. This is often called *interdependence* and is said to be desirable, inevitable and for the benefit of one and all. Not everyone believes that proposition to be true, and some reject the suggestion that the global economic order will be with us forever. The global economy is not *the end of history* and it will decay and give way to another system as other systems have before it. It should be the task of national leaders to protect their nations and states as best they can from dependency and the powerlessness it brings. Strong nations and national cultures are the best defence we have against those who are trying to strip us of our communal identity and reduce all cultures to a common global banality. Nations and nation-states are not obsolete and now is not the time to abandon them. Instead, they should be strengthened so that they can serve the interests of national communities. We, as individuals and as communities do not exist to serve the needs of a global economy. The purpose of states should not be that of maintaining conditions favourable to global corporations. States should not exist merely to raise taxes and maintain a minimum level of law and order, basic health care and education. Those who are forever telling us that we have to adapt our whole way of life to fit in with the needs of the global economy have everything back to front. The global economy should serve us. If it does not we should change it so that it does.

285

Terrorism

States assert the right to use or threaten to use armed force (violence) to secure their vital interests, but they do not accord the same rights and justifications to individuals and non-state organisations unless it is in their interest to do so. States generally deploy whatever technologies and weapons they have at their disposal and use them in any way they think fit, including attacks on civilian populations, in pursuit of what they judge to be their vital interests. If a delivery system or weapon is available to a state but not deployed, it is because it is in the best interest of the state not to do so. Morality is rarely a consideration in restraining a state because it is always possible to use one moral principle to over-ride another. The main restraining factor is a cost/benefit analysis of the external diplomatic and the internal political consequences.

States assert the right to determine the rules of armed conflict, which are always framed in a way that accommodates the needs of their weapons and delivery systems. Even when both sides in a war are states, and they fight in much the same way with similar weapons, each will try to show that the weapons, tactics and motives of the enemy reveal its evil intent and complete lack of moral scruple. Despite propaganda that would have us believe otherwise, it is no more moral to kill someone with a cruise missile, bomb, bullet or radiation than it is to kill him or her with gas or anthrax. The former are not right and proper, and the latter sneaky and despicable. It is difficult to see how delivering an explosive device by hand at great personal risk, or even as a suicide bomber, is cowardly but dropping a bomb from an aircraft flying at several thousand feet is heroic and deserving of a campaign medal. All individuals in a war, regardless of the side they are on, are capable of acts of heroism and cowardice. We may condemn the cause they are fighting but recognise their valour.

The only valid rules of war are those that are agreed to by all the participants. Agreed rules are born of practical necessity and common interest rather than moral rectitude. It is disingenuous in the extreme for one party to a conflict to believe that it can set the physical and moral rules of warfare and then accuse the other party of cheating if it breaks them. In other words, there should not be one set of rules for states and another set for the rest.

When non-state actors use violence against a state for political reasons, those actors are deemed to be terrorists by the state concerned and its allies. Yet the main difference between the violence used by states and non-state actors is in the cost and sophistication of the weapons used. States have sophisticated explosive devices which they are able to deliver to a wide range of targets in high-price, high-tech vehicles. Those without the resources of a state are only able to deliver low-cost, low-tech weapons to fewer types of target. Non-state actors usually hit soft-targets, and usually kill a high proportion of civilians, not because they are necessarily cowards or hard-hearted but because they do not have the resources to hit hard targets. [170]

States target civilians when it suits them and the results for those on the receiving end are much the same whether the explosive is delivered in a truck or a missile. The main difference is that states can do far more damage; some have the ability to destroy whole cities and their populations using a nuclear warhead, the ultimate terror weapon.

Nuclear non-proliferation treaties are not created and enforced by nuclear powers because they believe that nuclear weapons are immoral but because nuclear states wish to preserve the nuclear status quo. What principle of natural justice or morality supports the view that it is right and proper for the UK to be a nuclear power but wrong and improper for Pakistan, for example, to join *the nuclear club*? The answer is none. The justification is to be found in realpolitik and self-interest, not justice and morality. Likewise, the main reason for the major powers banning chemical and biological weapons is that the weapons are thought to be unreliable on the battlefield.[171] The other big drawback for the top military powers is that chemical and biological weapons, when compared with nuclear weapons, are relatively cheap and easy to produce and deliver. Powerful states wish to preserve their dominant positions, and do not want to be faced with a world in which every state has the means to destroy any other state. Such a levelling of capabilities would make it very risky for one state to attack another, and that would undermine the position of states that enjoy and want to preserve the military, economic and ideological status quo. The use or threat of military power can be helpful in attaining foreign policy goals but states generally only attack other states when they believe that the benefits outweigh the costs. It is difficult to be a bully and survive in a society where everyone is able to defend themselves. As the saying goes, an armed society is a polite society.

States with nuclear weapons seek to justify and preserve their privileged position over non-nuclear states. In a similar way, states claim the right to use armed force in a way denied to non-state actors. In addition, powerful states assert the right to determine which weapons are acceptable, how they should be used, and which states should hold them. In other words, they assert the right to determine which

---

[170] A *hard target* is one that is either heavily defended or physically difficult to destroy, e.g. a missile silo. *Soft targets* are easy to hit and destroy, e.g. towns and the people in them. The nuclear deterrent strategy of *Mutual Assured Destruction* requires that each side is able to destroy the other after absorbing a first strike. This is sometimes called having a second-strike capability. An essential part of MAD is the targeting of cities, which are soft targets.

[171] The various Cold War treaties on biological and chemical weapons were probably broken by both sides. After the fall of Gorbachev it became apparent that the USSR had been making and storing chemical and biological weapons. Each side probably knew the other was cheating but both had an interest in keeping it quiet so as not to legitimise the possession of such low-price, low-tech weapons. It wouldn't do if non-nuclear states decided to adopt such weapons.

ends justify which means. Those who do not abide by the rules are deemed to be outside the bounds of civilised society, i.e. terrorists.

There is no universal set of rules for defining terrorism. What is needed is both an objective test for identifying an act of terrorism, and the impartial application of that test to both state and non-state actors. The British government announced proposals for anti-terrorism laws (17th December 1998) which included a definition of terrorism borrowed from the FBI.[172] The earlier definition of terrorism referred to the "use of violence for political ends, including any use of violence for the purpose of putting the public or any section of the public in fear". The new definition covers "the use of serious violence against persons or property, or the threat to use such violence to intimidate or coerce a government, the public, or any section of the public for political, religious or ideological ends".[173] How will this affect the support of the UK and US governments for groups supporting, or involved in, the violent overthrow of Saddam Hussein? We have the old and well-known problem of deciding who is a terrorist and who a freedom fighter. In this, the matter of defining terrorism is much like that of defining war crimes: fault always lies with the enemy. Were the destruction of Dresden and the dropping of atomic bombs on Nagasaki and Hiroshima calculated acts of terror? The FBI definition of terrorism suggests that they were. For that reason, it is usual for states to assert that only non-state actors can be guilty of terrorism.

A definition of terrorism that includes the actions of states and those who govern them is unlikely to be acceptable to most states. It is improbable that a nuclear power would agree to it.

Colonisation

A colony is a body of persons belonging to one country or state who settle in another country or state. A colony is also the territory their settlement occupies. Colonists usually retain links with their homeland.

At one time, there were many European colonies around the world. In those places where the indigenous population was sparse, such as North America, Australia and New Zealand, the colonists were able to use their superior military technology and growing population to take control of more and more land, despite attempts by the indigenous population to defend their communities and homelands. In heavily populated places, such as India or China, colonists could not hope to displace the indigenous population and were for the most part restricted to small secure areas. From those strongholds they were able to use their military and economic strength to dominate the indigenous nations and resist a natural and justifiable hostility to their presence.

---

[172] *The Daily Telegraph*, 18th December 1998
[173] ibid.

Colonists take territory from indigenous nations by force and/or by a rapid increase in population and the settlement of land. The latter form of conquest can best be achieved by a high settler birth-rate and a steady inflow of reinforcements from the homeland. A sudden influx of settlers can cause shock and confusion among the indigenous nation in much the same way that an unexpected attack by a powerful military force can throw defenders off-balance and into a disorganised retreat. It is the psychological impact that is so devastating and hard to recover from. Things are made worse if the colonisers keep steadily rolling forward never giving the indigenous nation the time to regroup and make a stand. It is in the interest of the colonisers to undermine the resolve of the indigenous nation to resist by convincing most of them, and especially the political leadership, that what is happening is inevitable and impossible to stop. It is like an act of god, perhaps a punishment for past sins.

In the very early stages of settlement, colonists are usually in a weak position and need to buy time by appearing to be friendly, reasonable and considerate. When they have increased in number and established a strong position, colonist usually become more demanding, showing little concern for the interests and welfare of the indigenous population, who are often treated with contempt. The feebler and more grovelling the resistance the greater the contempt.

A colony with a small population remains vulnerable. A change in the circumstances (military, economic, ideological) that made colonisation possible, can lead to expulsion. Sometimes the expulsion is violent but often the threat of violence is enough to make the colonists see the wisdom of leaving. Many British and other European colonies were granted independence because the use of violence was anticipated rather than actual. The psychology of that time lies behind the "One settler one bullet" slogan that is still used in South Africa as a tool for intimidating and driving out Europeans, who will always be seen as outsiders and settlers regardless of how many generations they have lived there.

No nation willingly gives up its territory to another, and all nations have long memories. When conditions change in favour of those who have been the victims of colonisation, it is likely that the colonists will, if at all possible, be driven out regardless of how long their colony has existed. The Irish have not forgotten nor accepted the colonisation of their country by Scottish Protestants; Sri Lankans have not forgotten nor accepted the colonisation of their country by Tamils. The same resentments are felt by Maoris, Latvians, Fijians and many others. It is clear that the European citizens of Kenya and Malawi are seen as outsiders who do not belong regardless of whether they or their ancestors were born there. In most places in Asia and Africa, European colonists have by one means or another been driven out despite it appearing at one time that they were in an impregnable position and there to stay. In other places, the indigenous nations have not been so fortunate, although the dream lives on of being rid of invaders, colonists and settlers.

Not all colonisation is rapid. Sometimes the process is a gradual one fuelled by a comparatively high settler birth-rate. The expansion of colonies can be so gradual and insidious that the indigenous nation becomes accustomed to it. Each new generation accepts as normal the situation it finds itself in. The position is soon reached where none have had the experience of living without a colonial presence. Some may be aware of and concerned about what is happening but there is not the dramatic change necessary to trigger widespread active resistance. A steady increase in the settler population year by year does not produce the same defensive response as the sudden arrival of the same number within a short period.

European colonisation of North America started in a small way but once the bridgeheads were established, the trickle of new settlers grew until it overwhelmed the indigenous nations. Many within the Indian nations of North America fought with determination from the start to resist colonisation but most only did so when it was too late to succeed. Some migrations once started cannot be effectively resisted however clever and brave the indigenous people because the settlers have a technological, economic, or other advantage that makes them unstoppable.

Even at the end when it was clear that defeat was certain some thought it better to fight against great odds than to meekly submit. Sitting Bull and Crazy Horse, and those who fought with them, are heroic figures from that time.

The culture and way of life of the dispossessed soon crumbled and they found they had no identity other than the one given them by the colonists. The remnants of the Indian nations are reminded everyday that colonists have no interest in preserving the way of life of those from whom they have taken land.

Perhaps some indigenous people see the arrival of settlers in their homeland as an enriching experience to be welcomed; the more that come, the more enriching it will be. Such a response is, however, a historical rarity. Most resist by any means possible because they have a communal instinct that enables them to see that colonisation is a threat to their way of life and their identity. The problem is not one of seeing the danger but knowing how to deal with it. The indigenous community may have no experience of such a threat or have lost its communal memory of how to defend itself. Those who cannot relearn, face being overwhelmed and destroyed. They are either absorbed into the settler identity or live in some form of reservation or ghetto as a group of outcasts, a band of people who generation after generation rue the loss of their homeland and dream of the day it will be recovered. Such dreams are almost always completely unrealistic; the time to change the course of events having long passed.

Colonists are sometimes able to gain a strong economic position that enables them to acquire informal (behind the scenes) political power. The political power of others springs from their large number. A minority that becomes a majority is quick to assert the right of majority rule. By whatever means the settlers gain power and the indigenous nation eventually finds its very existence under threat with no part of its homeland free from occupation. In such circumstances, the fault sometimes lies not with the colonists but with a complacent indigenous nation that puts a misplaced trust in its political leaders. For whatever reason, be it complacency, greed or stupidity, indigenous nations are sometimes at first unwilling and then unable to defend their homeland and way of life. Thus, a country won and defended by many vigorous generations can be lost in a single lifetime.

Colonists are sometimes absorbed into the existing population and become indistinguishable from them. After several generations, the colonists lose their identity and become part of the indigenous nation. When that happens they are indistinguishable from other members of the group into which they have been absorbed. Absorption is only likely when the colonists are small in number and there is little difference in appearance and culture between the indigenous and settler populations.

Colonisation, migration, and settlement have occurred throughout recorded history. They are not something invented by Europeans, a blight on mankind that other peoples and nations have been free of. Colonisation is a continuing fact of life that takes different forms at different times. All have colonised and all are subject to colonisation. Some resist and survive while others disappear from history.

Western Europeans once colonised and settled many other parts of the world but now Western Europe is being colonised, albeit in a different way. In England, for instance, there are colonies of nations which not long ago expelled colonists from their homelands. Many, if not most, of the colonies in England are of nations that where never part of the British Empire and therefore not covered by the assertion: *We are over here because you were over there.* Such *justification*, even if it were valid, is short-sighted because it is a two-edged sword which invites the retort, *We are driving you out by any means necessary because you drove us out by any means necessary.* Such exchanges are unlikely to be productive of good will.

Some of the largest colonies are in Greater London. To the west Southall is occupied by Sikhs and in the east Tower Hamlets is occupied by Bengalis and Bangladeshis. From Notting Hill to Wembley there are a series of West Indian colonies. Irish colonies are dotted about from Kilburn to Harrow. A few of the many others include a Chinese colony in Central London and a Somali colony in Hackney. Very many more are to be found in London and other towns and cities in England. As the number of colonists increases, so the English population declines. There are very few English people to be found in Central London (except those who commute there to work), and the number of English in the outer suburbs is constantly declining. The displacement of the indigenous population has become so great that London has ceased, in terms of population, to be an English city.

Colonisation can take place within a state, as is currently happening in China, or happened in the USSR where Russians formed colonies in the Republics of the Soviet Union. As we have seen earlier, Latvia gained its independence but is faced with the problem of how to deal with its Russian colony, which makes up nearly fifty percent of the total population. Latvians have set about formally establishing who is Latvian and who Russian, and who is entitled to vote in state elections and who is not. They have to tread carefully because they face the condemnation of liberals who see decolonisation as a form of anti-multi-culturalism. This places Latvians in an odd position because their country was invaded and forcibly made part of the Soviet Union and then colonised by Russians. Now they are seeking national self-determination they face opposition from Western liberals who are prepared to sacrifice Latvian freedom on the altar of liberal dogma. Liberals condemn a small nation that is trying to regain its freedom, while upholding the rights of the colonists. Liberals are in effect aiding the aggressors and oppressors, and hindering the oppressed and exploited. They oppose the creation of a Latvian nation-state because they believe that the linking of ethnicity and citizenship could set an example for other European nations. For Latvians the issue is a matter of their national survival in their homeland. They know that their future will be gloomy if they become a minority in their own country and are compelled to abide by the will of a Russian majority.

Multi-Nation States

Some of what follows has already been dealt with in this section but it is reintroduced here to illustrate a particular aspect of state power.

Power and Nation-States – Unity is Strength

The power of one state in relation to others has many strands. Other than geopolitical factors, industrial output and the like, there is the matter of social cohesion, which is founded in a sense of common purpose and interests. Other things being equal, a nation-state is far more likely to be united than a multi-nation-state. The reason is that within a nation there is both greater horizontal and vertical unity between social classes than in a civic society which lacks the communal bonding of national identity. Put another way, the members of a given social class share a sense of unity and empathy that comes from shared experiences. The members of each social class have some sense of unity and empathy with the members of other social classes because they share a national identity and communal history. If the link between classes is broken, as when the Normans established a foreign ruling class, the unity and empathy is broken. If the ruling class does not share a sense of unity and empathy with the other classes, it is likely to exploit them. This is not to suggest that there is no division or class conflict within a national community. The point is that there is likely to be less conflict and greater unity where people share a communal identity and history. There is a two-way bond of loyalty between governors and the governed, which is in part due to their common interest in preserving the state; the political embodiment of their nation.

A state with sympathisers and supporters in other states, gains power in relation to those other states. That power might be exerted through the electoral or lobbying systems or directly through supporters who hold positions within the power structure of the other state's governing elite. Those supporters are citizens of one state but feel loyalty and sympathy for another state, perhaps for reasons of nationality or religion or political ideology.

The advantages to be gained by a state with supporters in another state include the inward transfer of:

- private funds, e.g. for projects and charities;
- state funds by way of grants, loans and the supply of equipment on favourable terms;
- direct commercial investment;
- economic, scientific, technological and military information.

Other advantages include:

- the ability of the supported state to promote its image, ideology and interests in the host state;
- influence over government policy formation in the host state.

All of these transfers are made easier if supporters of the beneficiary state are able to gain positions of influence within the media of the host state. The ability to influence the setting of the news and political agenda is an obvious goal. Ownership or control of the media is beneficial to the beneficiary state but harmful to the host state. By these means, a small state can manipulate public opinion and policy-making in a larger more powerful state.

The power that a state or other organisation exercises on another state through supporters can sometimes be a source of weakness. A beneficiary state that comes to rely heavily on outside support and loyalties may find that in some situations power shifts to those supporters, who are able to demand a political price from the beneficiary government for their continuing favours. Loyalty to the beneficiary state is unlikely to be dimmed, but supporters who disapprove of the policies being pursued by a particular government are able to threaten to switch support to another faction of the political elite. A *beneficiary* government may find that certain of its policies are being controlled from abroad

Links of loyalty may also increase the power of a large state and diminish the power of a small state. An example of that is to be found in the link between Latvia and Russia. The relationship between the two states is strained because the large number of Russians within the borders of Latvia is a source of weakness for Latvia and a source of strength for Russia. The Russian government has in the past made plain its concern to look after the interests of Russians in the *near abroad*. This means that it asserts the right to intervene in the internal affairs of independent states in order to protect the interests of Russians who live there. Such a declared aim of the Russian government conflicts with the assertion of many Russians living in Latvia that because they were born there they are Latvians and should have the same civil and legal rights as other Latvians. We have already seen that whether or not they where born there, and regardless of the number of generations their families have lived there, they are not Latvians and it would be foolish for the Latvian government to rely on their loyalty and support in the event of a military conflict with Russia. There are several things that indicate that Russian-Latvians are not Latvians:

1. a Latvian does not have a hyphenated national identity, i.e. they are not Russian-Latvians;

2. most Russian-Latvians are unable to speak Latvian fluently;

3. the Russian government feels that it has the right to represent the interests of Russian-Latvians;

4. Russian-Latvians feel the need to assert their right to be accepted as Latvians, whereas Latvians are naturally accepted as being Latvians.

The presence of Russians in Latvia is a source of weakness for the Latvian state and for the interests of the Latvian nation.

It is difficult to assess the degree to which the *unity factor* contributes to the power of a state because there are many unquantifiable factors to consider. The extent to which citizens are willing to fight in a war or to support their government in times of economic hardship is not easy to judge because much depends upon perception of the threat faced. The citizens of a nation-state are usually willing to fight or endure hardship in defence of *their* state because a threat to the state is seen as a threat to them as individuals and as a community.

The citizens of a nation-state are usually able to more easily and quickly agree on interests, goals and policies than the members of multi-nation states, where a process of bargaining between the various national groups takes place. If one of the national groups involved in the bargaining process is also part of a nation that is posing the external threat (i.e. the enemy), it makes agreement more difficult and weakens the state. This raises the problem of divided loyalties, which is difficult to solve. Will a person give their first loyalty to their nation or to their state? The pull of nation over state was demonstrated when Jewish citizens of the USA, UK and other states volunteered to join the Israeli army when that state was at war. Those volunteers showed not just a loyalty to their nation but to the state which has as its prime interest the protection of that nation. That they went to fight <u>and</u> that the Israeli army took them and presumed their loyalty shows that nationality is founded on more than place of residence or birth. Greater trust was placed in Jews who were citizens of other states than in Arabs/Palestinians who were Israeli citizens. When it is a matter of life and death, greater reliance is placed on ties of nationality than on ties of citizenship.

In the event of a large-scale war between India and Pakistan, it is unlikely that Englishmen would feel the need to serve in the armed forces of either of those states. But it would be perfectly natural and understandable for British citizens with kin in the Indian sub-continent to want to defend their community.

If the UK were to become involved in a war with, for example, Iran or Pakistan or Somalia or any of a long list of other states, would the government of the UK be able to rely on the loyalty of Iranians and others living in the UK? Or would it be prudent for the UK government to assume that at least some of them would act in the interests of, or actively fight for, their nation and its state?

Conflicts between nations in one part of the world can spread to other places. For example:–

> Weekend arson attacks on synagogues brought the number of violent incidents to 90 in the past 10 days.
>
> Henri Hajdenberg, president of the umbrella body for French Jewish groups, said: "We believe this wave of attacks comes from North Africans or some elements in the North African community in France who want to pit Muslims against Jews".[174]

As it is impossible to know who a future enemy might be, is it sensible to have outsiders in the armed services or in positions where they have access to secret information? Social-liberals argue that it is unfair to discriminate, and that loyalty to state comes before loyalty to nation. They are compelled by their ideology to argue that all British citizens are equally British and equally loyal to the UK. There cannot be many people who really believe that but it has to be acted upon whatever the harm it might do to the effectiveness of the UK's defences, and English national interests. Multi-culturalists are prevented by their ideology from addressing the problem of loyalties and the extent to which someone can be relied upon to put the interests of their state above that of their nation.

---

[174] *The Daily Telegraph*, 17th October 2000.

Would it be appropriate or practicable in the event of the UK being involved in open war to adopt the practice used during World War II of imprisoning/detaining those who are thought likely to sympathise with the enemy? It would obviously be difficult to pursue such a policy if the potential sympathisers number hundreds of thousands or even millions. We must therefore accept that in the event of a war we might have a large number of people living in the UK who it would be impracticable to detain but who would be likely to support the aims of the enemy and be willing to help them. If social-liberals are right in what they say, there will be no problem because all UK citizens will see their first loyalty as being to the UK, and all will fight with equal enthusiasm and determination against the enemy, whoever it might be. However, if nationalists are right, there will be a large fifth column, which will cause considerable problems and be a source of weakness.

Multi-nation-states by their very nature have persons within their borders (citizens and non-citizens) who live there not out of any sense of belonging or concern for the land they live in, but because of political or economic convenience. London is a centre for foreign political groups, many of which are working to influence or overthrow the governments of other states. The difficulties these dissidents pose for the British government have grown in recent years in line with the growth in electronic communication, which makes it possible for a small group in one state to spread political propaganda in another. It is understandable that dissidents should act as they do but often it harms the interests of the UK and sometimes also the interests of the indigenous nations within it. During a review of anti-terrorist legislation, Lord Lloyd, a senior law lord said, "The UK, together with some other western countries, is particularly liable to be caught up in these struggles because of the numbers of ... foreign nationals who live, or seek sanctuary here."[175] Although he specifically mentioned foreign nationals (meaning foreign citizens) the same problem exists in relation to the many British citizens who are involved in political activity directed towards their overseas homeland. For example, the Sikh community in England is known to have within it a significant number of people who are active in promoting the campaign for a Sikh nation-state. The vast majority of nationalists in England and elsewhere probably sympathise with the Sikhs and wish them well but it is possible that at some stage the national interests of Sikhs and English will conflict.

Events in 1998 brought the issue of loyalty and conflict of interest to the fore:

> Calls for leading supporters of Muslim fundamentalist terror groups to be deported were growing yesterday as politicians asked why "fanatics" were being harboured in Britain.

---

[175] *The Independent* 7th October 1996

Donald Anderson, the Labour chairman of the Foreign Affairs Select Committee, said he supported demands for the deportation of the "fanatic" leaders of fundamentalist groups.

"I wonder what his immigration status is and whether we should harbour such fanatics." [176]

It seems that Donald Anderson was referring to Omar Bakri Mohamed, *leader of the London-based Al Muhajiroun, an organisation dedicated to establishing a world Islamic state.*

Support came from the Conservative home affairs spokesman, James Clappison, who wrote to Jack Straw, Home Secretary, asking him to do all he could, *including the use of the power to deport, to counter support for international terrorism.*

Presumably, Mr Anderson and Mr Clappison are supporters of multi-culturalism. If so, they should not be surprised to find a wide variety of views being expressed because that is just one of the *benefits* to be had from the *rich and vibrant* political culture that multi-culturalism brings. It is to be expected that in a multi-cultural society there will be very different ideas about who are the aggressors and who the victims in global politics. Surely the MPs do not expect people of all cultures and political views to share liberal perceptions concerning who is and is not a terrorist? It is hardly in keeping with tolerance, free speech and democracy to seek the deportation of someone who expresses an opinion with which one disagrees.

It is not necessary to be a Moslem fundamentalist to see the hypocrisy of Tony Blair's unqualified support for US attacks on what it regards as legitimate targets (e.g. a pharmaceutical plant in Sudan), while seeking to silence British citizens who have a different perspective on events and see US embassies, military bases, and banks as legitimate targets. NATO thought it legitimate to engage in the strategic bombing of non-military targets in Serbia, so why should those fighting in a war against the New World Order not adopt a similar strategy? One of the most important rules of warfare is that you do not let your enemy set the rules. None of this is meant to condone violence; all that is being sought is consistency.

Multi-nation-states can be compared to ships with multi-nation crews. It has been found that the greater the mix of nationalities, cultures and languages in a ship's crew, the greater the social friction and inefficiency generated. The main concern of owners and insurers is about the ability of such crews to cope with emergencies. English has long been the language of merchant shipping but today most seamen have no English and this obviously hinders co-operation. There are many instances of ships getting into trouble or sinking because of misunderstandings or the total inability of crewmembers to communicate with each other or with outside rescuers.

---

[176] This and the following quotes are from *The Daily Telegraph*, 25th August 1998.

When a state has citizens (a crew) that belongs to one nation (a nation-state), that state is generally more united and its citizens more able and willing to co-operate and make sacrifices to defend and further their collective interests and protect their state. Unity is strength.

Untangling Multi-Nation-States

The division of multi-nation states into their ethnic parts is usually only possible following the collapse of the political authority that held the state together. Examples of multi-nation-states are the Soviet Union, Czechoslovakia, United Kingdom, Canada, Belgium, Democratic Republic of Congo, Nigeria and Yugoslavia. The Soviet Union, Czechoslovakia, and Yugoslavia have broken up and the others might not be far behind.

Some multi-nation-states are easier to untangle than others. Much depends on how the state has been formed, the size of the nations, and the extent to which they have separate homelands within the state. With the demise of the Communist governing elite in Czechoslovakia, that multi-nation state broke into two nation-states, the Czech Republic and Slovakia. The separation of Canada into two states should not pose many problems because of the high concentration of French Canadians in Quebec.[177] Belgium is likely to split into Flemish and French-speaking parts. The policy of the Flemish nationalist group, Vlaams Blok, is to seek the peaceful dissolution of the Belgium state. The response (early 2000) of the Belgium liberal governing elite was to threaten to ban Vlaams Blok. Liberal democracy works in mysterious ways.

The UK is being unravelled and Scottish independence is likely to be the result. If or when it happens it will probably be triggered by a relatively minor issue which results in a constitutional crisis about which parliament has the democratic right to act on behalf of the people of Scotland.

England and Scotland still have large enough core-nations to make viable nation-states but it would be difficult, in present circumstances, to create an independent state of Ulster. Wales could be a viable state but the large English population living there might hinder its stability and unity.

Breaking the USA into nation-states looks an impossible task because the population is more ethnically mixed than in Europe. However, identity in the US is increasingly based on race, and it may be along those lines that the break-up of a Balkanised USA occurs. Until then, the US could be condemned to increasing communal insecurity and conflict.

---

[177] The creation of a Quebec sovereign state would cause difficulties for the Maritime provinces of Canada (e.g. Nova Scotia) but inconvenience to others is not a valid reason for denying a nation its own state.

The break-up of Yugoslavia involved the creation of nation-states and, where that was not possible, a multi-nation state in Bosnia, which is like a mini-Yugoslavia and has the same poor prospects for long-term survival. A state based on the territory occupied by Bosnians (i.e. Moslems) was not viable so it was decided by an external power to compel Serbs and Croats to be part of a multi-nation Bosnia. That state is unlikely to survive because it is probable that when the outside military forces that hold the state together are withdrawn, the Serbs and Croats of Bosnia will declare, perhaps after a referendum, that they are joining Serbia and Croatia. It is difficult to see how such an outcome could be resisted in the name of democracy. The Muslims of Bosnia were not compelled to remain as a minority in Yugoslavia and their withdrawal was rightly accepted and defended by liberals.

Albanians moved into Serbian Kosovo over the centuries, became the majority population and demanded independence. The *International Community* did not officially support that demand because it knew that Serbs and Croats in Bosnia would claim the same right [178] However, the backing of the *International Community* for some form of autonomy for Kosovo has given unintended recognition to the fact that a civic identity is no match for national identity. Albanians living in Serbia, Macedonia and Montenegro did not abandon their national identity and will not do so despite the proclaimed liberal objective of creating a multi-cultural Kosovo. The high Albanian birth-rate and their migration into territory surrounding Albania has not resulted in the cultural enrichment of civic societies in the area but has given rise to colonisation and conflict.

Civic Society in a Multi-Nation State

A growing settler population within a multi-nation-state will eventually become large enough, and have sufficient political and economic strength, to make demands of the majority core-nation. Such demands are usually for cultural or political privileges, and may involve the need for constitutional reform. Possible outcomes include:–

a) the introduction of ethnic monitoring and ethnic quotas, usually in combination with some form of discrimination against the indigenous population;

b) pacifying the minority by formally restructuring the constitution in a way that recognises the different national groups and shares power between them (see below under Power-Sharing in Multi-nation States – Consociationalism);

---

[178] Just about the only concession gained by the Serbs in the surrender document was that Kosovo would remain part of Yugoslavia. That point was not inserted for the benefit of Serbs and has not been observed in practice. It was inserted by the *International Community* because, having played an active part in the dismemberment of the Yugoslavian state, it needed to place limits on the ideal of national self-determination and reassert the sanctity of states. It wanted to avoid giving encouragement to separatist movements of which it disapproves.

c)   dividing the one state into two or more nation-states;

d)   a civil war in which:

   i)   the majority indigenous nation either drives the minority nation out of the state or forces it to recognise that it is in another nation's homeland and should behave accordingly;

   ii) the minority prove too powerful to remove or subdue and win some degree of self-government.

In Fiji, the minority indigenous nation seized control of the state from a majority, mainly Indian, immigrant population. The Fijians acted in the belief that democratic self-government in their own homeland was a higher ideal than democratic multi-culturalism. Sometimes it is necessary to choose between different types of democracy. No model is good for all places and all times.

It is difficult to apply the usual civic-society requirement of one person one vote and majority decision-making in a multi-nation state for the simple reason that minority national groups believe, and usually with justification, that the values, perceptions and interests of the majority prevail over those of the minority. It is in order to overcome this difficulty that power-sharing arrangements are sometimes introduced. The big problem with this approach is that arrangements introduced to meet the interests of settlers and win their loyalty to the political system have just the opposite effect on the indigenous core-nation. Its support for the state declines as it becomes increasingly evident that the first priority of the governing elite is to preserve itself and its hold on power. In its desire to please disaffected settlers, the state and its institutions cease to represent or even acknowledge the interests or even the existence of the core-nation. Principles of democracy and fairness are cast aside in the interest of making outsiders feel like insiders, which they never do. What is supposed to be a solution in fact gives rise to deeper divisions by causing resentment among the majority nation. Its support for the state declines because it no longer sees the state as a means of furthering and protecting indigenous interests. Many Scots recognised long ago that the British governing elite has no interest in protecting Scottish identity and wellbeing except in as far as it is necessary to prevent them leaving the Union. When it eventually dawns on the English that the British governing elite has no concern whatsoever in furthering English national interests, they will hopefully stop apologising for being English and set about recovering control of their sovereign powers. Every self-respecting nation wants to govern itself, and the English should demand nothing less. The problem is that too many English lack self-respect and self-confidence. They have spent so long on their knees being insulted that many of them believe it to be their natural place in the world. Politeness, generosity, and tolerance will be our downfall. We can no longer afford to show concern for every nation but our own. We have to assert our national identity and defend our communal interests. If that means being strident and difficult, so be it. If the United Kingdom and its governing elite will not meet the reasonable demands of the English there is no choice but for England to leave the Union. What a blessed release it would be – no more Scottish-dominated governments diverting massive amounts of English taxpayers' money to Scotland.

Power-Sharing in Multi-Nation States: Consociationalism

When a state contains two or more national, religious or racial groups that are politically powerful but culturally incompatible, there is almost always tension and conflict between the groups. Given sufficient stress, there is likely to be civil war or the disintegration of the state. In order to manage conflict and preserve the state, it is usual to establish a formal arrangement for sharing power between the groups. The name sometimes given to such arrangements is *consociationalism*, which in essence is a combination of consensus politics and power-sharing. It is a model of government favoured by liberals when they are compelled to accept that communal loyalties are stronger than civic loyalties. The idea is to develop and build on co-operation and consensus between communities in the expectation that co-operation will become a habit and help build a civic identity. To help the process along a programme of communal harmonisation is put in place that includes an invented inclusive history of the state. The real communal history and culture of the core-nation is gradually stripped of everything that conflicts with or challenges the official civic history. A recent example of this was a Commission containing a collection of professional Black campaigners and liberals who declared a need for a label to replace *British* and *English*, because they carry the implications of a White identity, and are therefore not inclusive. The Commission also called for a rewriting of history because minorities are left out of the present island story. [179] Stalin would have been proud of them.

What starts out as the recommendation of a committee or commission can soon become law, which means it becomes a criminal offence to oppose what is nothing more than dogma. Totalitarianism often has small beginnings.

Informal recommendations and agreements give rise to informal and formal means of power-sharing, such as ethnic quotas, which require ethnic monitoring and a bureaucracy dedicated to ensuring that the various *ethnic groups* are *fairly* represented in government and in the institutions of the state. Arrangements are also made to ensure that resources are allocated *fairly* among the *ethnic groups*. Thus, competition and conflict become institutionalised.

The problem facing those who seek to engineer new identities and loyalties is that national identities are difficult to destroy. Instead of quietly accepting its demise, a

---

[179] *Report from the Commission on the Future of Multi-ethnic Britain*, published 11th October 2000, Chairman Lord Parekh.

nation usually resists and, if necessary, forms any alliance that is necessary to defend itself. The effect of liberal meddling is to unintentionally strengthen ethnic loyalties and undermine the prospect of generating the type of civic society that liberals have traditionally favoured. The simple reason for this is that multi-culturalism and civic society are incompatible. Try to mix the two and the result is communal, cultural, ethnic, racial blocs competing for resources and power. The competition becomes institutionalised in formal power-sharing arrangements that strengthen communal identities and weaken any sense of a common civic identity.

The rapid decline in a British civic identity, the growth in national and racial identities, and the passing of power from Westminster to the EU, is making the UK and its parliament redundant. If the UK is to survive it will be necessary to introduce constitutional reform that recognises the changing relationship between England, Scotland, Ulster and Wales. Within England there is a politicisation of *race* and religion that could make the problems of Ulster look easy to solve. If existing demographic trends continue, we will eventually have demands for some form of power-sharing arrangement, which will probably start as pressure for ethnic quotas in the institutions of the state, and then move on to constitutional arrangements that secure ethnic blocks in a reformed parliament.

One of the practical problems with power-sharing arrangements is that they need to be revised from time to time to keep them in step with changes in relative population size, which is usually the factor that determines how big a slice of power each group gets. Whatever the adjustment mechanism used, there is likely to be resentment among the group losing power, especially if it is due to other groups having very high fertility rates. The communities that gain power use it to obtain benefits for themselves. The potential for conflict is great, as was seen in Lebanon.

There is a fundamental conflict between the ideal of liberal civic society and power-sharing – *consociationalism*. Each represents a different model of democracy, and each requires different institutions and procedures. In a civic society, political and state boundaries coincide and politicians can, more or less, appeal to the whole electorate. Things are different in a power-sharing system because the electorate is more divided in its outlook, its expectations, and in its demands. In multi-nation-states, cultures generate their own political boundaries, which do no necessarily coincide with those of the state. For example, that part of the Bangladeshi community/nation/ethnic group that lives in England does not see a sharp division between the territory they occupy in England and the territory they occupy in Asia. Their culture and politics flow across state and country boundaries. The views and attitudes of Bangladeshis in England are likely, in many instances, to be more influenced by events and people in Bangladesh than in England. The inclusion of many such national groups in a power-sharing arrangement would not be conducive to the creation of a common civic identity. Society would become more markedly divided along vertical racial/ethnic fault lines. Political parties are likely to reflect this in their composition and the section of society to which they appeal. Effective government would become impossible.

The democracy advocated by Thomas Jefferson was communal democracy and was meant to operate within one community, not between two or more fundamentally different communities. Neither communal democracy nor civic society can work where there are two or more large communities with fundamentally different values, perceptions and interests, sharing one state. Only one set of cultural values can provide the foundations for a coherent system of law, and only one perception of the world can guide state foreign policy. This gives rise to the problem for liberals that if Muslims become a numerical and political majority in a liberal state and want to reject liberal laws and adopt their own, will liberals be true to their proclaimed ideals and adopt Islamic law and an Islamic form of government? Will they observe the will of the majority? Events in Nigeria and elsewhere suggest that non-Muslims are likely to resist the imposition of a Muslim way of life whether or not it is the will of the majority.

Switzerland is an often-quoted example of different nations living together peacefully in a stable and wealthy state. Power-sharing has worked well in Switzerland but only because the different national groups accept a common political culture, and see it in their interest to do so. Each group preserves its own language and lives in its own territory, which adjoins the nation-state with which it feels an affinity. So, although it is a multi-nation-state, each nation has its own clearly defined territory and cultural hinterland.

The Swiss system of democracy permits each of the national groups a large measure of self-government, and the state government adopts a neutral stance in world politics in order to preserve its internal cohesion. If in a dispute between France and Germany the Swiss government were to take sides, the probable result would be conflict between the German-Swiss and French-Swiss. The Swiss state is able to exist because of particular historical and geographical circumstances, and the fact that despite the different identities its citizens, their way of life and interests are sufficiently similar to enable them to live together. The Swiss state is decentralised and adopts a policy of neutrality in world politics. If the territory occupied by Switzerland were flat, it is probable that the Swiss state would not exist.

The decentralised nature of Swiss democracy and its use of referenda is a model that is widely admired. Swiss citizens can, by petition, compel politicians to address issues they might prefer to ignore. A proposal that has sufficient initial support is put to the electorate in a referendum. Politicians who favour centralised states with little popular participation in decision-making (so-called representative democracy) find the idea of petition and referenda unacceptable. Objections are often expressed in the following terms: "it is not part of our political tradition"; "the government is elected to govern" (we the political elite know best and will decide for you); "it leads to populism" (politicians doing what the electorate wants); "it involves the people taking control of decision making on complex matters about which they know little or nothing" (patronising twaddle). That last excuse is surely an argument for doing away with General Elections because if one issue is too complex for the electorate to decide on, how are they to be trusted to make a decision when there are many complex issues. The technicalities of an issue might be complex but the principles are usually not. It is the job of politicians to explain the issues as they see them in as clear a way as possible and for the electorate to make a judgement.

Belgium has a power-sharing structure but it has not helped to engender friendly co-operation between the Flemish and Walloon populations. Power-sharing in Ulster has proved impractical on several occasions and may do so again.

Power-sharing arrangements usually deny the principle that all votes are of equal value, and sometimes the distribution of power within the government is fixed by a constitutional formula. As a result, a large national or religious group which makes up over fifty percent of the electorate might be compelled to accept an arrangement where its opponents are given more power than their electoral support warrants. Such systems tend to perpetuate blocs and institutionalise competition between them. Elections rarely change much because the political system is designed to guarantee representation for different groups by formula rather than according to the number of votes won.

Where the distribution of population is such as to make it possible, the best long-term solution to conflict within a multi-nation-state is the creation of two or more states. That two-state option led to the creation of the province of Northern Ireland; the idea being that Protestants and Catholics (Ulstermen and Irish) would each have a land of their own in which their culture and identity were secure. Unfortunately, for Ulstermen, the size of the Catholic minority population has increased due to a higher birth-rate and in the near future Ulstermen will be a minority. Two options for survival are raising their birth-rate now or fighting a war later. Another option is to become a minority in an Irish state that provides constitutional safeguards for their cultural and religious identity. Unfortunately, constitutional safeguards often melt away once their purpose has been served. The survival of nations sometimes depends on their will to survive and ultimately their willingness to fight.

Two States from One

In 1965 the federation of Malaya, Sabah, Sarawak and Singapore was dissolved and the states of Singapore and Malaysia were created. The situation before separation was similar to Ireland before partition in that there was a large minority Chinese population, mainly in Singapore, which felt insecure as part of a large state in which it was heavily outnumbered. The creation of two states from one was a wise move and both have done well. Some Chinese remained in Malaysia but that gave rise to problems during the economic and political turmoil of 1998 because many Malays resented the presence of a powerful Chinese business community. However, despite the difficulties, the situation is far more stable than it was during the period of the federation, and the solution offers many lessons for the open-minded.

Neither of the governing elites in Singapore or Malaysia adheres to liberal principals and both are generally contemptuous of them. Each state gives preferential treatment to its core-nation and gives them certain constitutional advantages. It is for that reason that many liberals are hostile to the states and their leaders. It also explains why liberals were so obviously smug when the Asian economic recession took hold in the 1990s.

Liberal chagrin is directed at Asian politicians who adopt a holistic approach to government, and try to strike a balance between the interests and rights of communities and their individual members. They do not always get things right but at least they hold some traditional communal values as ideals to be strived for. One objective of government should be to look after the interests of all citizens as best it can in an imperfect world. This has been described as the pursuit of Asian values but it is an approach once practised in Europe.

Singapore has many small national groups but the Chinese population is by far the largest. In order to preserve the dominance of the core Chinese population and enable it to feel secure, laws prevent the immigration of non-Chinese. Those who go to Singapore to work do so for a limited period and do not acquire residential or citizenship rights. These policies have not met with the approval of social-liberals but the citizens are pleased with the results.[180] The Chinese community has worked hard to achieve economic prosperity without bearing the social costs that we see in liberal societies. This is not to suggest that the Singapore system of government is an ideal to be followed slavishly elsewhere, or that it will avoid difficulties during recession. What is being suggested is that (other things being equal) mono-cultural societies which have preserved communal traits and values, are more likely to survive difficult periods than multi-cultural societies with conflicting communal values and little sense of a common identity. *Asian values* enabled some Asian states to enjoy prosperity during the boom years without suffering the social costs seen in the West. *Asian values* do not necessarily bring honest politicians to power or give freedom from economic recession but they offer a good strategy for surviving difficult times.

The test of a community and a society is how it holds together in times of trouble. In those Asian states where there was a corrupt governing elite and financial

---

[180] Marxists explain approval in terms of false consciousness. Liberals see a need for re-education, i.e. unrelenting liberal propaganda. Both try to overcome communal instincts, which are regarded as repressive, rather than working with them.

mismanagement, recession brought social and political upheaval. But one needs to look below the surface froth at the underlying unity of a society to make a judgement as to how well it will pass through difficult times. Not all Asian governing elites and political systems are corrupt, and even where they are, there is often a strong underlying communal fabric which shares burdens, and limits individual hardship, thus preserving unity and stability. Considering the difficulties they have faced, most Asian states have done well to avoid the sort of internal conflict and lawlessness that can be expected in liberal states when times are hard. The main exception is multi-nation, multi-cultural Indonesia.

The Break-up of Multi-Nation African States

Most African states are multi-nation-states. Their boundaries were drawn by European imperial powers without regard for the nations living there, and as a consequence the states are inherently unstable. During the struggle for independence many liberation movements were based on tribal or national groups and when independence was gained, and elections held, voting tended to follow national loyalties.

Nigeria is an example of a multi-nation-state weakened by internal divisions. In addition to being a mix of many nations, it is also divided along religious lines with Moslems mainly in the north and Christians in the south.[181] The power-sharing arrangement introduced to protect the interests of minorities has not been successful and the future for Nigeria looks like one of continuing instability.

> Ethnic clashes erupted in the centre of Lagos for a third day yesterday, leaving more than 80 Nigerians dead and bodies littering the streets.
>
> The fighting between Nigeria's two largest ethnic groups, Yoruba and Hausa, began on Saturday in the central Nigerian town of Ilorin in a dispute over the naming of a Yoruba traditional ruler for the town.[182]

---

[181] Islam was introduced into West Africa by Arab traders who became involved in buying slaves from members of the local Black population and transporting them to Arab countries for sale. At a much later date Europeans arrived in West Africa and became involved in the slave trade. Many of the slaves had been taken prisoner in wars between Black tribes and then sold to Black slave traders. Many slaves travelled from the interior to the coast with ownership passing on the way from one Black person to another until they were sold to White traders.

It is somewhat curious, given the early involvement of Arab Moslems, that many modern-day Blacks in the USA and elsewhere should claim to be adopting Islam because the slave owners were Christians. They ignore the fact that Moslems and Negroes were involved in the trade and profited from it. Indeed, there were Negro slave owners in the US. They also seem to be unaware that the Moslem governing elite in northern Sudan does little to stop the present day trade in Christian Negro slaves from the south of Sudan to the north.

[182] *The Daily Telegraph*, 18th October 2000

In some other parts of Africa, e.g. Congo, state governments have little authority in areas away from the capital city because informal communal boundaries are proving stronger than artificial political boundaries. Communal loyalties are important in everyday life and the networks of communication they create cut cross state boundaries as if they were not there. The governing elites of states tend to live in cities where they act as surrogates of the Global Elite. Multi-national corporations generally agree contracts with the central government of states for the extraction of minerals and other primary products but often they have also to make separate arrangements with, and separate payments to, the tribal and national leaders in the district where extraction takes place. If corporations find it cheaper and easier to negotiate directly with a local ruler they will do so. However, it is usually better for them to deal with a central government that is supplied with military equipment by the *International Community* for the purpose of both maintaining access to primary resources and enforcing trade agreements.

It is probable that within fifty years many African states will have given way to new nation-states. When that happens the people living in those states will be better able to protect, and profit from, their natural assets because multi-national corporations will find it more difficult (but not impossible) to manipulate and bribe local elites. The leaders of a powerful nation might be happy to profit from the pillaging and ruin of the land of a weaker neighbour (as in Nigeria) but they will be reluctant to accept the same treatment for their own homeland. This is one reason why the protection of local environments is better served by nationalism than globalism. A self-governing nation living in its homeland is more likely to care for its land and look to long-term costs and benefits than are global corporations which are concerned only with their own survival and increasing their market share.

Unity and the USA

The English were the core community of the original United States of America and it was American-Englishmen like George Washington and Thomas Jefferson who played such an important part in establishing an independent state and drafting the Declaration of Independence. The American War of Independence was in effect a civil war. One of the curious things about it was that the leaders of the English living in America probably had a stronger sense of Englishness than the governing elite in England. The American-English were very much aware of their English identity and it caused many of them great anguish to rebel and fight their kinsmen. They carried the flag of English radicalism, which had a much greater influence than is commonly believed on the American-English and the writing of their constitution.

Other Northern Europeans, including the Dutch, were involved in the founding and expansion of the United States but they were absorbed into that core Anglo-Saxon

307

community, which still exists. Many of the institutions of the USA have their roots in English institutions and were, because of the influence of radical English democrats, free from Norman attitudes to class, politics and the state.

The numerical and political dominance of the English settlers and their descendants, and the similar cultural background of the other early migrants, helped mould them into a distinct branch of the Anglo-Saxon diaspora. They became a new nation that was able to absorb the relatively small flow of early immigrants from other parts of Europe. They called themselves Americans and the American Constitution was designed to regulate their community. It was a constitution for insiders and the sentiments it expressed should be seen in that light. The declaration that all men are born equal meant that all male insiders are born equal. Negroes and Indians were not considered to be insiders or equals. Even today, long after the drafting of the Constitution and the Gettysburg Address, the descendants of slaves are not part of the core American nation and probably never will be because the two communities have different histories and different identities despite living side by side for many generations. North American Indians, Latinos, Anglo-Saxons (Anglos) and Black-Americans are some of the many separate communities that exist within a US civic identity. Strangely, it is the community that founded the USA that now has the least sense of communal identity. It is also the community that is least willing or able to defend its interests. Perhaps because of that, it is the one community that is subject to unchallenged denigration.

During the 19th and 20th centuries very large numbers of migrants of many different nationalities arrived in the USA. Some of them integrated into the core population and thought of themselves as Americans. Others were unable to give up their attachment to their national identity, history and homeland; they thought of themselves as, for example, Italian-Americans or Irish-Americans (hyphenated Americans).

The descendants of slaves, having lost their national identity and culture, have adopted a racial identity, the only one open to them. They call themselves *Black-American* or the misleading *African-American*. More recently a wave of immigrants, Latinos, have arrived from the south. So large is their number that some of them are able to live in the US without the need or desire to speak English. They can receive television and radio programmes in Spanish, and exist as part of a wider nation that has its own language, culture, history, interests and sense of identity and community. They form a colony, which, as their number and power grows, is likely to seek political concessions, which may eventually include some form of self-government or perhaps a merging of the southern lands with Mexico. Will a US government faced with, say, a majority Mexican population in Texas or California, treat demands for constitutional change or complete succession, in the same way that it demands Serbs treat similar claims by Albanians living in Kosovo? What would be the reaction of the US government if they were instructed by an outside power to reach a constitutional settlement with the separatists and that if they did not do so within a certain time the US would be bombed? It would be treated as an insult and dismissed as interference in the internal affairs of the USA. How would Foreign Secretary Robin Cook have reacted if the Chinese government instructed the UK government to attend talks and reach an agreement with the IRA for the autonomy of Northern Ireland? How much worse it would be if the ultimatum was issued through a puppet state and delivered by an insufferably pompous Foreign Secretary?

The core-American community that was once so bold now lacks self-confidence in asserting its identity. Those among them who dare to suggest that their community has as much right to formulate, express and pursue its interests as other communities, are treated as extremists. Liberals disarm members of the core-American community by encouraging them to feel guilty about who they are. One of the tactics is to portray them as oppressors. The teaching of English-American history is disapproved of unless it is presented as shameful. Even the term Anglo-Saxon is regarded as offensive. American cultural revolutionaries have attacked the teaching of English literature and are very free with their condemnation of just about everything associated with the English-American population. Such behaviour would be condemned if it were directed at any other similar group.

Core-Americans have the same right as other Americans to be taught their own history, culture and achievements in a positive way. They need a sense of identity and solidarity as much as any other community. To treat them less favourably than other groups is institutionalised discrimination.

Melting-Pot or Meltdown?

It is easier for different nations and peoples to live together in one state when citizenship brings them material wealth. Being a citizen of a powerful state can give a feeling of superiority over the citizens of other *lesser* states. This psychological advantage is lost when changes in the global power structure compels citizens to adjust their perception of where they are in the global pecking order. Decline can lead to a loss of confidence in the political and economic system and bring underlying social tensions to the fore. If the vast majority of citizens never travel abroad to see what life is like elsewhere they can be more easily lulled into the belief that *their* state is *the best in the world*.

A powerful state, and especially an economic and military superpower, is able to gain privileged access to, and control of, economic resources around the world. However, all good things come to end and sometimes the end comes quickly and unexpectedly. It can also be a slow and uncomfortable adjustment to reduced circumstances. The longer reality takes to dawn, the greater the shock and damage done when it arrives.

The UK adjusted quite quickly to the changed global power structure that became apparent during World War II. Acceptance of changed circumstances was not due to great wisdom or virtue but to the plain fact that the UK was bankrupt and could no longer afford the symbols of a global power. Assets that had been built up over centuries were lost in two world wars, 1914–1918 and 1939–1945. Ten years of war during a thirty-one year period is a massive cost to bear. The UK was unfortunate in that it had to pay its way through those wars and gained no benefit from them. In contrast, its US ally became the world's most powerful and prosperous state. The defeated enemy, despite suffering great damage and loss of life, emerged from the Second World War with no debts and a massive inflow of capital for the creation of a modern industrial economy.

The armaments and other equipment the UK received from abroad were not free gifts and one way or another they had to be paid for. For a state to start the twentieth century rich (but already in decline) and forty-five years later be broke and desperate for loans, is to compel a rapid change in perception of its place in the world. The UK governing elite made that adjustment. It realised that it did not have the resources to fight many colonial wars, so it set about decolonization in a mostly orderly fashion. Then, mainly as a result of economic difficulties, it reduced the size of its armed forces until it was a regional instead of a world power. The obvious ebbing away of power resulted in not only a loss of status for the UK but also for British citizens. Being British was not what it used to be and the idea that "British is best" was quickly dispelled. A pride in being British faded most quickly in Scotland where the fiction of a British nation had only been accepted half-heartedly. English Conservatives found it particularly difficult to adjust to the post-war world and still desperately hang on to the idea that they have some special right to interfere in the affairs of other states. For them, the last trace of Britishness and what used to be are found in the United Kingdom, which they wish to preserve at all costs. Contrary to popular belief, die-hard British Conservatives are hostile to English nationalism because they see it as a threat to the Union. They are unwilling to accept the final stage of decolonisation, which involves the dissolution of the existing UK and freedom for its parts. Such is their commitment to preserving the Union that they are willing to see the English pay for it, both in terms of money and democratic representation.[183]

The adjustment to reduced circumstances affected perceptions of what it meant to be British. Mass immigration into the UK from former colonies in the Third World hastened the decline in a pride to be British. The English found it difficult to accept that they shared a meaningful British identity with the people who were arriving from all over the world. The Scots and Welsh have tended to see the British state as an extension of the English state and therefore have never been as

---

[183] The dissolution of the UK is likely to be followed by a new form of co-operation between its parts. The new relationship is likely to be based on mutual advantage but it is difficult to see its shape yet because much depends upon the fate of the EU.

attached to the idea of being British as have the English, who tended to give the two identities equal status. As the global standing of the UK decreased, so support for Scottish and Welsh nationalist groups grew. Old nations felt the need, and saw the opportunity, to re-assert their national identity and seek self-government. Those movements are now coming to fruition and they have in turn sparked the re-emergence of a popular English national identity, albeit in what is so far a muddled and embarrassed way. The English had never felt the need to question or even think of their Englishness; it was something they felt and took for granted. Most adopted a British identity because Englishness was at the heart of it; the two became mingled. That British identity had by the mid-1990s become threadbare and the issue of what it means to be English was thrust upon them. The devolving of power to a Scottish Parliament, a Welsh Assembly, and Northern Ireland Assembly, prompted a growing number of English to realise that they had different interests to the Scots and Welsh. It became evident that they too needed a parliament and executive to protect and pursue English interests.

The USA is likely to face problems similar to those of the UK when its relative decline (it happens to all states and empires) becomes plain to its citizens. One of the great areas of study for future generations will be how in the twenty-first century US citizens and politicians adjusted to a world where their state did not have economic or military supremacy. Will they be able to handle it or will the shock speed the disintegration of the USA? How rapid will the decline be and how far will it go? Along the way, many US citizens will do what the British have done; they will look for an identity to replace a citizenship of declining status. The search for roots will probably make hyphenated identities more popular, be they national or racial. With the exception of the indigenous Indian nations, none will have national homelands in the US to which they can withdraw and seek national self-government. Will there be an attempt to create homelands or will the struggle be for power within a reformed federal state? Again, the idea of power-sharing raises its head. Politics will become even more oriented towards groups competing for state resources. It will become more difficult for political leaders to appeal to the common good and a common civic identity when seeking support for their policies. Each group will want to know what is in it for them.

In the scramble for a communal identity, a large number of Americans will come to see themselves as part of the Anglo-Saxon diaspora and realise that they have more in common with many Australians, Canadians, Englanders, Lowland Scots, and New Zealanders than they do with the various hyphenated groups with whom they share a citizenship. When they look to their roots they will find that they share an identity, and a rich and interesting history, with other Anglo-Saxons worldwide.

Summary of Part Two

The observations in this section about what states and governing elites do, is not meant to convey surprise or amazement. The aim is to point to the realities of the world we have to survive in and show that all states and elites behave in much the same way given the same circumstances. Interests and power are the primary factors governing the behaviour of states and their governing elites. Interests are to a large extent determined by geopolitical factors. For example, geography has had an important influence on the interests and foreign policy of the United Kingdom, Germany and Turkey. Their different geographical circumstances and political boundaries have given them different problems to overcome and opportunities to exploit. The outlook of their people (national character) has in part been shaped by geography. Another but often less important influence on real and perceived interests is the ideology of the governing elite, which is itself influenced by geopolitical factors. This is not to suggest that the official ideology or the political system of a state is unimportant. It is often very important, sometimes causing a government to act against the best real interests of the state and lead it to destruction, e.g. Nazism. What is being suggested is that some ideologies (and theologies) are more likely to lead a state into foreign wars than others. Such ideologies are nearly always universalist, i.e. their followers want all the people of the world to believe in and live by the dogma of the one true way. Examples of universal ideologies are communism, liberalism and Islam.

If a state attacks other states and fights its wars abroad in the name of a universalist ideology it is difficult to see how the governing elite of that state can be anything other than aggressive and meddling, whatever the ideological justification it gives for its actions.

Liberals would have us believe that they and the states and institutions they control are above considerations of power and interests, and are instead guided only by the wish to drive the forces of darkness from the face of the earth so that all can bathe

in the light of freedom and democracy. What freedom? What democracy? It is important that we see sanctimonious liberal rhetoric for what it is.

It is difficult to escape the unkind thought that only a village idiot would believe we live in a global village bound together by the brotherhood of man. The world is a hard competitive place where the weak and gullible have their land, culture and very existence taken from them. When the realities outlined in this section are programmed into our world-view it is easier to grasp what is happening and why.

Nationalists are not necessarily opposed to all things that liberals favour. Many ideals and values are shared and are not specifically liberal or nationalist. Neither is it being suggested that liberals are devils and that nationalists are saints; there are, as the well-worn saying goes, good and bad everywhere. What is being suggested is that liberals and nationalists have different ideas about human behaviour and happiness. Nationalists tend to see communities as evolving organisms bound together by links of kinship, culture and shared experiences. National communities provide a sense of place, identity and continuity that are essential to human happiness, health and contentment. Communities and their members consist of layers of instincts and experience that accumulate over many generations. They are the sum of a process that continuously merges the present with the past. Language, art, music, literature and all the other strands of human activity and achievement are mingled together in a way that makes each culture unique and worth preserving. Communal histories are a record of the weaving of cultural threads. National communities have a mass, speed and direction that enables them to overcome hard times and carries them into an unknowable future.

Where nationalists see long-lived evolving communities, liberals see engineered societies. They believe that instincts and customs can be broken and remade so that people behave as liberals deem they should. Liberals are not concerned with how people are but with how they ought to be. Culture is viewed as something that can be manufactured and disposed of. There is no sense of history only of now and self; shallowness permeates everything.

The ideal world for liberals is one where everyone is liberal in thought and deed. At the heart of liberal dogma, behind the apparent concern for individual rights and freedom of choice, is an obsession with materialism and uniformity.

Two of the territories social-liberals claim as their own are human rights and freedom of expression. Their claim is spurious but it enables them to think of themselves and their views as radical and challenging. In reality, they support the ideological status quo, which is not surprising because they are the product of a system designed to churn out ideological clones. Social-liberals have no wish to overthrow or challenge *the establishment* because they either belong to it or are supportive of it. You can have any political system you want provided it is liberal. Despite being intensely conservative and unoriginal, they like to think of themselves as radicals.

Liberals deem that individuals have certain human and civic rights which it is the duty of society to promote and observe. Among those rights is the right to choose an identity and the right to be accepted. Inclusiveness is a virtue, exclusiveness a sin. Liberals are hostile to the concept of nations as exclusive communities founded on common ancestry, history, and culture. They see nations, nationalism and nationalists as incompatible with liberalism and therefore incompatible with democracy. They sometimes concede that nationalism and the sense of separateness that it fosters may have been necessary and desirable in the past, but they argue that in the contemporary world of multi-cultural societies it is harmful and should be suppressed or eradicated for the greater happiness of the greater number. Nationalism and nations are relics of the past that conflict with multi-culturalism, liberal globalism, and a citizen-of-the-world identity.

Liberals proclaim a belief in freedom of speech and tolerance while crushing those who openly question their dogma. Dissidents are demonised, usually being labelled as racists or fascists.[184] One only has to observe the lack of impartiality and tolerance shown to dissidents in the broadcasting media to know that liberal niceties are only extended to those who stay within the bounds of liberal orthodoxy. Liberals undermine communities, cultures and identities. They erode the link between nations and their homelands and insult those who resist their destructive meddling. Liberals push on with their naive policies despite historical and contemporary evidence which shows that such policies do not produce societies brimming with peace and happiness, but instead generate resentment, tension, resistance and conflict. The blame for the problems that arise lie not with those who resist the ideological daydreaming but with those who indulge in it. Liberals are responsible for burdening future generations with the task of unscrambling the mess they are so busy creating.

Social-liberals and economic-liberals usually think of themselves as far apart on a linear Left-Right political scale but they are, in political terms, close relations stemming from the same root. They often engage in bitter disputes and are rivals for power within the governing elite but both are comforted by the knowledge that whatever the result of elections, the nature of the state will stay as it is. The only change will be one of emphasis, according to which faction forms the government. Both wings seek an atomised society in which individuals are free from the constraints of community and culture, and able to seek happiness and personal gratification in the consumption of goods and services. The cult of the individual and the cult of the market are bound together like opposite sides of a coin. They coexist within a liberal political system because each needs the other. Economic-liberals use democracy, human rights and freedom of speech as weapons against those who resist the spread of the free market and the global economy. Social-liberals behave like those Christian missionaries who, during the period of European colonial expansion, advanced into shattered societies and communities on the backs of adventurers and traders.

Economic-liberals see themselves as realists in a world of fierce but free competition where success is measured in wealth. They show little concern for those who do not have the skills and aptitudes necessary to succeed in a cut-throat economic society. Instead they believe that individuals and groups with wealth and

---

[184] It can be observed that there is usually a direct link between the frequency with which someone uses the word fascist as a term of abuse, and the sophistication of their political ideas: the more, the less. *Fascist* has mostly been replaced by *racist* but the same rule applies: the more, the less. Liberal academics redefine *fascist* from time to time to fit the needs of the time (i.e. to include their current ideological enemy), thus it is very difficult to get any agreement on what fascist means. It would probably be better to leave the term in its proper historical context and relate it to the policies and actions of members of the Italian Fascist movement.

power are not only more deserving of it than those who have neither, but also more virtuous in that they are wealth creators; the more they consume the more wealth they create and the more economically virtuous they become. How kind and considerate it is of them to undertake such a noble task.

Both social and economic-liberals are internationalists in that they are opposed to the notion of nationalism and nationality, which they take every opportunity to condemn. The liberal ideal is one where national cultures blur, one in to another, and liberal values and perceptions form a common cultural currency that enables us all to live in peace and harmony. Freedom of individual thought and movement come together with open markets and the free movement of capital and labour. Social and economic-liberals march together ever onward bringing down the petty barriers that separate one nation from another. They see it as their mission to end diversity and bestow on us liberal global values, a liberal global market and a liberal global identity.

Despite liberal missionary work and their constant propaganda, instinctive communal values and perceptions survive. Few members of the Labour Party are so imbued with the brotherhood of man that they are willing to be governed by foreigners. Similarly, many members of the Conservative Party are not so blindly attached to the ideal of free trade that they are willing to sacrifice their national identity to the interests of a European and global economy.

Not all members of the liberal governing elite are zealots but there are enough of them to act as guardians of the faith and prevent the flock straying far from the path of righteousness. They ensure that political, economic and cultural debate at the local, state and global level takes place within a liberal ideological framework. They are so determined to achieve universal freedom of expression that they are prepared to use whatever force and intimidation is necessary to silence dissidents who herald the liberal utopia as a living hell.

Nationalists seek a world of diverse self-governing national communities because they see it as the best model for peace, democracy and human survival. No model is perfect and there will always be conflict but the best models are those that are able to recognise world society for what it is.

315

Part Three   Community and Survival

Darwinian Evolution and the Process of Natural Selection

Organisms

An organism is any living animal or plant, or anything resembling a living creature in organisation, structure, behaviour, etc. The characteristics of life are chiefly the ability to grow, react to stimuli, and reproduce or renew. Physical life is a chemical process; communal life is a behavioural or organisational process.

Darwinian Evolution

Darwinian evolution by the process of natural selection is a gradual, steady, orderly and continuous change in the physical and behavioural characteristics of a group of organisms. Those characteristics that increase the rate of reproduction and survival within a breeding group become more widespread in that group than do characteristics that reduce the rate of reproduction and survival.

For a breeding line to survive, offspring need to have the physical ability to reproduce; the instinct to mate; the communal instinct to raise offspring. Those who live in a communal and cultural environment that re-enforces the desire to have children are more likely to do so than those than those who live in a cultural environment that discourages family life. Non-reproductive human lines become extinct.

Natural Variation

Natural variation occurs when a reproductive process involves the mixing of genes. Each offspring is genetically different from each parent. In other words, every child has a mix of genes and characteristics that is different from, but similar to, those of each parent.

Natural Selection

Natural selection is the process that selects characteristics from among those made available by natural variation and causes them to become dominant within a breeding population. Natural selection is the means by which those characteristics that improve the ability of individuals and groups to reproduce and successfully rear offspring are spread from generation to generation.

Natural selection selects characteristics that are favourable to the group as well as to the individual.

Natural selection is a blind process that is not moral or fair. It is not taking evolution towards some preordained goal. It is a continuous unguided process that operates on individuals, communities, species, and ecosystems.

Darwinian evolution makes it possible for <u>groups</u> of organisms to adapt to a slowly changing environment. The individual parts live, reproduce and die, but in doing so they enable the whole, be it community or species, to adapt and evolve indefinitely. The parts come and go but the whole lives on.

Darwinian evolution selects characteristics that favour reproduction and survival in a given environment and gradually makes those characteristics dominant in the whole species or that part of the species subject to a particular environment. For example, Eskimos and Maoris are members of the same species but in adapting to their different environments they have evolved different physical and behavioural characteristics. Some of these physical characteristics make it possible to classify each of them as members of a different race.

Darwinian evolution gives rise to specialisation, diversity and sophistication but it also tends to produce stability between and within species. For example, species are constantly refining characteristics that favour survival but despite that their overall number remains fairly constant because the number of individual offspring within species that survive and breed, more or less match the number that die. Those species that are unable over several generations to reproduce at a rate high enough to replace those breeding pairs that die, become extinct. A species that reproduces far more quickly than is necessary to maintain a stable population will eventually have its population growth halted or reversed by a limit on the availability of food.[185] In addition to competing with each other for food, territory and other resources, the members of a species will also be competing with other species.

A change in the population size of one species affects other species because all are part of the environment to which others must adapt. If, for example, a prey improves its ability to avoid detection, the characteristic responsible will spread throughout the population because more individuals with the favourable characteristic will survive and have offspring than those who do not. Species feeding on the *improved* prey may decline in number, possibly to extinction, because the prey are harder to catch. Or, the hunter species may adapt to the change by switching to another food source and/or improving their hunting skills. Those offspring that have improved hunting skills will survive and breed more

---

[185] This accords with the proposition made by the Rev. Thomas Malthus (1766–1834) in *An Essay on Population*, that population adjusts to the food resources available for it. Hence, food is often scarce in relation to population.

successfully than those that do not and the improvement will spread through the species, restoring a *balance* between hunter and prey. The adaptation is likely to be by means of natural variation, which gives rise to a wide range of options for change in the physical and behavioural characteristics of the species.

The stability of an ecosystem is usually maintained in a less dramatic and more gradual way than suggested by this account because evolution by natural selection is usually a continuous process involving very small changes. Because hunters usually have more than one prey, and prey usually has more than one hunter, the balancing act is likely to be taking place on many levels. The result is a web of direct and indirect links between the many species of animal and plant life that coexist in an ecosystem. The relationships are so complex that it is impossible to determine the long-term consequences of any given evolutionary step. Several apparently insignificant and unrelated changes can combine in a way that produces a catastrophic environmental change for a given species, making it extinct. That extinction might also be catastrophic for other species or even for the whole ecosystem. On the other hand, a group of interdependent species might disappear with little effect on the ecosystem as a whole.

Darwinian theory suggests that when two populations of the same species become separated for a long period, and each is subject to a different environment, one of the groups is likely to evolve into a new race or species. This tendency to specialisation and diversity is seen, for example, when plants and animals become newly established on an island that has a different environment from where they came. The process of adaptation to different environments causes each separated group to evolve in different ways. The greater the difference in the environments the greater the difference in selected characteristics and the more likely it is that a new species will evolve.

The main shortcoming of Darwinian evolution is that while it can explain gradual change, it has difficulty explaining sudden or dramatic evolutionary changes. Evolution is not always a continuous process of small steps, sometimes there are great leaps. Creationists have rightly pointed to the inability of Darwinists to adequately explain these leaps. An answer may be found in the ability of organisms to store a collection of mistakes and pass them on as a group to the next generation.

Where is this leading you might ask. Well, for the moment it is enough to point out that it has been suggested that communities and cultures are organisms – they live. Like any other living thing they reproduce and are subject to natural selection.

Chromosomes and Genes

A human chromosome is a rod-shaped structure composed of a sequence of genes.

A cell is the basic unit of life. It is the smallest living system that is capable of functioning independently.

Every normal cell, with the exception of reproductive cells, contains at least one pair of chromosomes. Whether a species carries one pair of chromosomes in each cell or several hundred, every member of the same species has the same number of chromosomes. Humans have forty-six chromosomes and about 30–40,000 genes in each cell.

In human reproduction twenty-three chromosomes in the female egg associate with twenty-three chromosomes in the male sperm, thus reforming the total of forty-six. Each chromosome comes together with another carrying the same type of information and splits into two parts. The parts pair off to form a double helix. The result is twenty-three pairs of chromosomes carrying two complete sets of genetic instructions for the construction of a new generation of organism.

Children of the same parents have a mix of genes that are similar to, but not the same as, other children of the same parents. The obvious exceptions are identical twins, identical triplets etc. because the genetic blueprints of each child are identical.[186] Other than those exceptions, each offspring has a unique combination of genes that makes it different from all others. Each mix of genes is one that has never occurred before; each is a blueprint that has never been tested before. It is partly for this reason that most embryos are flawed in some way and are unable to produce a viable fetus. Miscarriage, usually at a very early stage, is part of the process of natural selection.[187] Those fetuses that survive to birth, and then mate, are able to combine their successful blueprint with another, and the process of trial and error goes on.

Mutation

In addition to being part of a process that enables genes to mix, chromosomes also self-replicate as part of the process of cell division which enables organisms to grow and replace cells that die, e.g. skin cells.[188] The replication of DNA, shortly before cells divide, is not always perfect and there are sometimes mutations. For example, human skin cells are constantly being replaced and from time to time the process is imperfect and mutations occur. Such mutations or mistakes are generally due to external factors such as ionising radiation or chemicals. The process is cumulative and more and more blemishes occur because each time the cell divides it copies earlier faults. The damage caused by an accumulation of

---

[186] This is due to each child originating from the same cell and therefore carrying an identical mix of genetic information.

[187] About 80% of embryos are miscarried at an early stage. (Embryo for about the first ten weeks then fetus until birth.)

[188] Each cell of an organism contains a complete set of chromosomes. In other words, each cell contains the same genetic information. For this reason, a DNA profile of a skin cell can be matched with, for example, a blood cell.

faults could lead to disaster but the damage is limited by the ability of genes to repair themselves. The repairs are not always perfect.

The mixing of genes from each parent gives rise to *natural variation*. Mistakes made during the self-replication of genes gives rise to *mutations*. Most mutations are less well suited to their task than the original but some produce characteristics that offer an improvement or advantage. Both forms of variation are tested by natural selection to see if they help or hinder the ability of individuals and species to survive.

Genes – Message or Messenger?

In recent years, natural selection and evolution have been seen as being driven by genes. The term, *the selfish gene*, implies that genes are central to the process of natural selection, and that the whole evolutionary process is driven by their *interests* and *needs*.[189] This approach sees organisms as things created by and for the convenience of genes. It encourages a certain way of seeing and interpreting information. For example, it has been observed that humans, as individuals and as a group, sometimes willingly risk death, injury or economic loss in order to help/protect/save an individual. Instead of viewing such behaviour from the top down as part of a communal survival strategy, it is seen from the bottom up as a survival strategy for genes.[190] A weakness of the gene-centric view seems to be that life existed before genes. Therefore, genes are a product of evolution and natural selection.

Whether the emphasis is put on communities or genes, it can be observed that animals have altruistic instincts towards those with whom they have a close genetic relationship. Thus, altruism is high within groups where the members are closely related (a kindred community) but low in groups where members are distantly related.

A study of human behaviour can lead to all sorts of stratagems and game play for calculating the genetic cost-benefit in any particular situation where a person is faced with the opportunity of doing something that will benefit another person but is potentially harmful to himself. The general rule is that the more distantly related the person under threat is, the less likely it is that another will risk their life to help or save them. The underlying belief is that our behaviour is determined by the need to ensure the survival of our own genes. Therefore, a mother is more likely to risk her life to protect her own child than an unrelated child. Taken further, it can be argued, or predicted, that a mother is more likely to risk her life to protect five of her children than she is to protect one of five. If she is young and able to have

---

[189] Richard Dawkins *The Selfish Gene* (1976) and *The Blind Clockmaker* (1986).

[190] Professor William Hamilton interpreted altruism as a selfish gene strategy – kin selection or inclusive fitness theory.

more children, she is less likely to risk her own life to save her only child tl
she is old and unable to have more children. It can be argued that there is a 1
off between an existing genetic investment and future possible opportunitie
genetic investments.

Such is the nature of the selfish-gene argument that everything, incl
community, can be seen as part of a strategy that has evolved for furtherin
interests of genes. Perhaps it is possible to turn the tables by pointing ou
genes do not act alone but in communities.

The Selfish-Community

Altruism is an instinctive cost-benefit calculation. But is it made for the bene
genes or the individual organism, or the community of which the organism is
Or is it for the benefit of all three interdependent parts? Altruism, and every
else to do with natural selection, can probably be just as well *explained* b
selfish-community, which is guided by communal instincts for survival, as
by the selfish-gene. In short, our behavioural instincts have been honed by n
selection to ensure the survival of our community – the family.

Selfish-community theory suggests that man is a communal animal
communal instincts. Community is a survival strategy and therefore it is in th
interest of individuals to preserve their community. The more immediat
community is, the greater the instinct to preserve it. The smallest and
immediate community is the nuclear family of mother, father and children
nuclear family is part of a wider network of linked kinship communities that
economic and reproductive needs. Each member of each network has an inter
preserving the various layers of an extended community. The size of
community will depend on the physical and social environment in which it e
As a general rule, each individual has a greater interest, from a survival po
view, in preserving immediate layers of community than distant layers.

If altruism is guided by the selfish-community, the parts will behave in the
way as if guided by the selfish-gene. Each approach explains why paren
willing to put themselves at great risk to protect their own children but wil
put themselves at a lesser risk to protect a more distantly related child. The se
community also explains why humans will put themselves at some risk to p
any child. The key to it is that we have within us communal instincts that
been evolving from pre-human times. During most of that time, the only y
children anyone came into contact with were members of their comm
Children are a communal asset and we have an instinct to protect all childrer
instincts have not caught up with our changed environment.

Some reject the cold calculation of game-play because they find it dista
rather than inadequate. Much depends upon how an issue is presented an

question asked. For example, why do humans live longer than is necessary to bring up their offspring? It seems reasonable to argue that for most of human existence, children with grandparents who helped care for them, were more likely to survive and reproduce than children without that advantage. There was therefore an advantage to be had from a longer life span and the evolution of instincts that made grandparents want to care for their grandchildren. This is not to suggest that a rational calculation is made, only that natural selection has made the calculation and provided us with the appropriate instinctive behaviour. It seems as reasonable to argue that the arrangement is to the advantage of the community, as it is to argue that it is to the advantage of the grandparents' genes. What helps genes also helps community.

It might at first seem difficult for either the gene-centric or communal approach to explain why a person should risk their life by jumping into a river to rescue a dog. An unkind interpretation might be that those who die as a result of attempting to save the life of a dog are acting in an irrational way and natural selection is removing their genes from the gene pool. In other words, risking life and limb for a dog is not a behavioural characteristic that forms part of a successful survival strategy. Another view is that such action is a by-product of communal instincts. We all have an instinct to put ourselves at some risk or inconvenience to help other members of our community because we have a reasonable expectation that they will help us. We would take some risk to save our own dog for which we feel affection, a communal sentiment. We might therefore be willing to take a perhaps lesser risk to save another person's dog because we have a reasonable expectation that others would do the same for our dog or other pet or property. The dog might be regarded as an honorary member of the community or as communal property. In some sense the dog is seen as part of the community; an insider; a communal asset. Because communal life provides us with many benefits and has always been part of human life, we have an instinct to protect our community and its assets. For this reason, individuals will incur some risk to themselves to help a communal neighbour put out a house fire.

For nearly all of the long period of human evolution, most human contact was with other members of the kindred community and as a result there was little need in most circumstances to differentiate between an insider and an outsider. Helping others in everyday life was likely to be helping one's kin. Thus we instinctively feel well disposed to helping and co-operating with those with whom we are familiar.

Instincts are not as sharply honed as the gene-centric view suggests, and there are times when the wrong instinct is triggered and inappropriate action is taken. There is no way of avoiding this because natural variation ensures a mix of behavioural and physical characteristics within a breeding population. If everyone was exactly the same, natural selection would have nothing to work with. Perhaps this accounts for what seems to be an instinctive hostility to cloning and the uniformity it suggests.

A gene-centric view of natural selection puts genes at the centre of the process in much the same way as the Earth was once thought to be at the centre of the universe. An alternative view is to see genes as an essential part of an organism but not its reason for existing. They are simply messengers; the carriers of information. One gene or a billion genes, whether selfish or not, cannot survive or give directions except as part of an organism which in turn may be part of a larger organism. Ecosystems are organisms containing many interdependent organisms. Natural selection works on all the many parts of an ecosystem. Each part has an evolutionary path compatible with its individual and communal survival.

Our physical and behavioural characteristics have evolved over millions of generations, going back beyond the start of human life. Each of our instincts is the product of natural selection. We are made up of layers of evolutionary experience, some of which were gained from the earliest life forms on Earth. Humans co-operate with some humans more than with others because it has been found to be in their individual and communal interest to do so. Natural selection has made kindred relationships instinctively stronger and more enduring than other relationships because it has been found to assist survival and successful reproduction. Kin not only share many physical and behavioural characteristics, but also a communal culture and way of life that they have an interest in preserving because in the long term it has proved to be part of a successful survival strategy. One consequence of this is that humans instinctively discriminate in favour of kin with whom they are familiar, and have a history of co-operation in the struggle for survival. Such familiarity originates in the family; indeed *familiar* derives from *family*.

The survival *strategy* for each living system sometimes involves co-operation at one level and competition at another. For example, the individual members of a community compete with each other in seeking a mate, but co-operate in defending the communal territory. In a similar way, communities compete and co-operate with other communities as the needs of survival dictate.

Systems

A system is a collection of elements that form a whole. The relationship between the elements is ordered in some way. A system has a boundary; an inside and an outside.

Systems can be:

1. without life – inorganic	a group of interacting parts, e.g. a solar system;

2. living – organic

a) e.g. plants and animals; true organisms; they grow, produce off-spring and die; their life cycle is powered by chemical processes; they respond to stimuli; they have a limited life span.

b) e.g. communities, species; they have many of the characteristics of true organisms and can be said to live because they have internal organization and communication; they renew themselves; they evolve; they do not have a predetermined life span.

3. abstract

e.g. ideas and concepts; they have many of the characteristics of true organisms; they are born and evolve; they exist in the individual and collective minds of conscious beings; they do not have a predetermined life span.

4. a mix of the above,   e.g. Earth's ecosystem.

Evolutionary progression from a lifeless singularity to a complex universe containing organic life, communities and ideas suggests that evolving systems have a tendency to become more complex and sophisticated. They also combine with other systems to form new more complex structures, and sometimes a new level of existence. For example, inanimate elements combined to form life, which gave rise to consciousness, which led to ideas and the ability to recognise natural laws. It seems probable that this evolutionary process will continue and produce living systems of a kind beyond anything we can imagine.

The universe might be a subsystem of something larger but there is no recognisable evidence of that. What we do know is that it is a system and within it there are layers of subsystems such as galaxies, stars, and our Solar System, which contains the Earth and its ecosystem, which is made up of many subsystems, including humans and their communities. Each of us is a collection of subsystems found in other animals, albeit in a different form, e.g. the respiratory system; nervous system; circulatory system. The breakdown of systems into subsystems can be seen in cells and beyond.

- Lifeless systems behave in way determined by natural physical laws which are formulated and reformulated from time to time.

325

- Living physical systems are subject to natural physical laws but because of their ability to reproduce they are also subject to the laws of natural selection.[191]

- Abstract systems are subject to natural selection.

- A communal system has both a physical and abstract existence.

Systems are a collection of parts (subsystems) that have an ordered interdependent relationship (symbiosis). When that relationship is disrupted the parts may re-establish the old relationship or form a new one. Another possibility is that the parts fail to find a new stable relationship and the system and its subsystems suffer a catastrophic collapse.

Individual animals and plants normally have the ability to live (maintain their system structure and boundaries) for a limited period during which they reproduce. Their subsystems work together in a way that preserves the whole, which is greater than the sum of the parts. Human communal systems are likewise able to maintain their structure and boundaries but unlike the individuals that form the parts, they are able to renew themselves indefinitely.

Biological and communal systems normally have the ability to reproduce but some female bees, wasps, termites and ants are unable to reproduce and instead work to help those who can. Natural selection has evolved a reproductive system, from queen to queen, that produces many sterile individuals who work for the good of the hive or colony (the community) and make possible the creation of a new generation and a new community.

Comparisons between the communities of different animals (especially insects and humans) are fraught with danger but all successful communities are organised in a way that serves the purpose of reproduction. The smallest complete human communal system is the nuclear family.

Living systems normally have not only the ability to reproduce but also the instinct to do so. Such is their imperative to reproduce that it can be seen to be the primary purpose of living systems. When humans reproduce, they pass on in their genes the instructions for both the construction of their offspring and the behavioural ground-rules for the renewal of their community. Communal culture provides a guide to the behaviour necessary for the continuation of the community in the current environment. Culture has a part in determining partners and the opportunity to produce offspring. It therefore plays a part in selecting the genes to be passed on.

Kinship and kindred sentiments help bind a community together: culture is the intellectual glue that reinforces and promotes common behavioural survival

---

[191] Can natural selection be framed as a law or collection of laws?

strategies. Successful cultures employ successful survival strategies; they promote behaviour that has in practice been found to promote communal survival. Part of that success is due to their ability to recognise and make a place for the deeply embedded instincts that look after long-term needs and interests. Cultures constantly renew themselves and evolve in a way that helps individuals and communities adapt in a sophisticated way to a rapidly changing environment.

Abstract organisms evolve in an abstract environment which has roots in a physical world. New ideas grow in the compost of earlier ideas. Given the same intellectual environment, similar ideas and insights spring into life in different places. If many conscious beings are given the same input, some will produce the same output. The implication of this is that ideas and perceptions can emerge spontaneously in different places and times, and become part of equally valid bodies of knowledge.

Chaos and Order

Chaos Theory

Chaos theory suggests that phenomena behaving in an apparently random manner have underlying order based on principles the observer does not understand. It also suggests that if an observer looks close enough at phenomena behaving in an apparently orderly manner, an underlying chaos will be found.

Order is the systematic, logical, predictable and comprehensible arrangement of elements. Order has a perceivable shape or pattern but chaos does not.

Chaos is the absence of a perceived order, structure and understanding. Chaos is order at a level of complexity that is beyond the understanding of the observer. Chaos precludes prediction.

What is chaotic in one age might be order in another because with the passing of time and an increase in knowledge, patterns become apparent where in earlier times none could be seen. With sufficient knowledge, time, and a wide enough view (time and space) order emerges from chaos. This at first suggests that eventually everything will be known and understood, but chaos theory suggests that the more we know the more there is to know and that in every ordered system there is underlying chaos waiting to be found.

Chaos, in the form of chance, is both within natural selection and an outside influence on it. Natural selection relentlessly selects and adapts, bringing order and stability as it does so. It also brings ever-increasing complexity and sophistication that has within it new levels of chaos. Natural selection devours chaos at one level by bringing order to it but it also opens new levels of chaos.

From time to time, chaos disrupts the smooth steady flow of Darwinian natural selection but in doing so it creates opportunities for natural selection to start new evolutionary threads. An example of this is the extinction of the dinosaurs.[192] They were successful animals, well adapted to their environment but they did not have the ability to survive the rapid changes that took place 65 million years ago. The cause of that mass extinction (there have been others) may have been a comet, meteor or asteroid striking the Earth, or perhaps massive volcanic activity. Whatever the cause, it was, in terms of the period during which dinosaurs existed, a chance or random event. It occurred so suddenly, and with such dramatic and widespread effect, that there was not enough time for many species to evolve and adapt by means of Darwinian natural selection. Those life forms, including mammals, that survived, did so because by chance they happened to have characteristics that enabled them to live and breed in the changed environment. If a heavenly body caused the extinction, it could have been bigger or smaller, or impacted on land instead of the sea, or struck at a different angle. Different circumstances would have created different environments, many of which would have caused the extinction of mammals. If mammals had not survived, we would not be here.[193]

The post-dinosaur system of which we are part is not inherently better or superior to the old system it is merely different. It would be wrong to suppose that change necessarily leads to something better. We are living through, and are an important part of, another mass extinction. Perhaps the process is a shift from a period of stability to one of chaos and it has gathered an unstoppable momentum that will see the end of human life and a shift to a new and very different stability in the Earth's ecosystem.

The mass extinction of animal and plant species reduces diversity in the short term but can lead to greater diversity in the long term. Species which have survived virtually unchanged for millions of years are forced to adapt to a new environment or die. Others might have no need to change but nonetheless put on an evolutionary spurt due to the extinction of competing species and access to more resources. The short-term chaos of a chance mass extinction can be like the pruning of a tree in order to stimulate new growth. It can also be like the felling of a tree and the grubbing up of its roots. Some heavenly bodies (e.g. Mars?) may have had their ecosystems totally destroyed by apparently random events.

---

[192] Birds are probably dinosaurs or descended from them. Scientific opinion on this matter varies from time to time, and from place to place.

[193] Although humans would not exist, it is likely that an animal similar to humans would have evolved sooner or later. *Convergent evolution* is a process by which the same evolutionary product is reached by different routes. For example, fossil discoveries made in 1998 indicate that feathers evolved twice. In other words, natural selection produced feathers from two separate and independent lines of evolution. This fits with the idea of convergent cultural evolution in which the same cultural invention can take place spontaneously in cultures separated by time or place.

The nature of the world that followed the destruction and the survival of species in the great extinction 65 million years ago was sparked off by a random, chaotic event. A stable ecosystem was destroyed by a catastrophic event but a new stability emerged through the process of natural selection. The starting point for that new stability was created by chance.

Catastrophe Theory

Catastrophe theory is at least as applicable as chaos theory to the workings of natural selection, and the evolution of communities and societies.[194] It suggests that living systems try to adapt to changes in their environment but in doing so they often create internal structural stresses that gradually accumulate and eventually cause a catastrophic system failure. Catastrophe theory offers an explanation of how chaos can emerge from order.

Catastrophe theory can be expressed in formal terms as follows: the input to a system from its environment is continuously changing and the output of the system is continuously changing. If the system cannot cope with the input, its output is interrupted while the system reorganises itself or disintegrates.

Individuals, communities and species are living systems that adapt to the demands of their internal subsystems and their environment. Systems sometimes have sudden or extreme demands made of them that they are unable to cope with and as a result they suffer a catastrophic failure. In other cases, the environmental demands are small and spread over a long period, causing a gradual build-up of stress within an organism. Eventually the stress is such that one more apparently small demand causes a catastrophic failure. This is much like the straw that breaks the camel's back. The failure of a whole system, like a camel, starts with the failure of one or more subsystems, which cause a chain reaction of subsystem failures and the camel dies.

Some subsystems, like the brain, are able to reorganise themselves after a catastrophic failure and start functioning again. For example, if one part of the brain is physically damaged it is sometimes possible for its function to be taken over by another part. Mind and brain are not the same thing but a nervous breakdown is a form of catastrophic collapse caused by an inability to cope with input. A build up of internal conflict and stress eventually becomes unbearable with the addition of a small input of information with which the system is unable to cope. The breakdown of the system provides the opportunity for an internal reorganisation of information, and the creation of a modified system that is able to process inputs and produce outputs. While that is happening inputs and outputs are interrupted.

---

[194] The French mathematician René Thom discovered catastrophe theory. His work was published in 1972. An English translation, *Catastrophe Theory,* followed in 1975.

A chain reaction of catastrophic subsystem failures can spread up or down through many levels of subsystems, or sideways through one level, or in all directions. Each subsystem affected by the failure of others attempts to adapt to its changed environment. Those that manage to adapt and survive, help absorb the destabilising effects of the chain reaction. This process acts as a shock absorber or sponge that limits the destructive effect of a subsystem failure and helps preserve the boundaries and functioning of the whole system. Those subsystems that are unable to adapt to the demands put on them by failure elsewhere also suffer catastrophic failure and, like a falling domino, help spread the shock-wave. Some chain reactions are suppressed, while others accelerate through the whole system and destroy it.

The Earth's ecosystem can be seen to be attempting to absorb the consequences of subsystem failures and maintain the structure of the whole system. Eventually a point will be reached where stress within the system is such that the effects of more subsystem failures cannot be absorbed. The structure becomes so fragile that the failure of one more subsystem leads to a catastrophic failure of the whole. The last straw might appear inconsequential at the time, if it is noticed at all, being perhaps the extinction of an apparently insignificant plant or animal species, or the evolution of a new virus.

Successful communities and cultures are adept at absorbing stresses and strains but there is a limit to the damage that can be absorbed before the destruction of subsystems starts a chain reaction that ends in the catastrophic failure of the whole. Abstract organisms in the form of ideologies and political systems face similar problems. An example of a catastrophic collapse of a state is the demise of the Soviet Union.

Wyrd

The passing of time, and the continual unfolding of the present, is a seamless process that is given expression in the Web of Wyrd, which is everywhere and continually being woven. Wyrd means *what will be* and is a mix of order and chaos. It is the predictable and the random; the inevitable and the possible. Wyrd is part of the early English concept of time in which the *future* is an extension of the *present* and not something separate and apart from it.[195] The future is not another world but merely the present with additional layers of present added to it. Individual and communal deeds done today shape the next layer of present and help determine tomorrow's opportunities and restraints.

There are an infinite number of possible tomorrows and an infinite number of histories. The unfolding of events is determined by a mix of factors including:

---

[195] In Old English there is no future tense. It comes as a surprise to many that Modern or New English has no future tense.

chance; will; natural laws (physical and evolutionary); the inherent characteristics of systems. Some humans, as individuals and groups, try to consciously influence the unfolding of events at a level beyond their everyday life. Most cannot even attempt it because they have no feel for the forces that are carrying them along and shaping their lives; their view is narrow and they are aware of little beyond the experience of their daily lives. Their view of the wider world and the significance of events taking place there is shaped by others.

Those who prefer not to drift aimlessly but have a goal and attempt to steer towards it, have only limited scope for manoeuvre within larger systems that have their own evolutionary currents. Each system is shaped by its internal characteristics and the characteristics of its environment. There are many histories; one within another; currents within currents; systems within systems. For much of the time, it is only possible for individuals and groups to have a small influence on events within the flow of a strong current that carries all with it. But sometimes there are junctions in the Web of Wyrd where the current slackens and it is possible for individuals and communities, to nudge the course of history in one direction or another. Such places are usually ones where there is a fine balance between conflicting interests. Perhaps it is wise to be like a martial artist patiently observing and waiting until the flow is finely balanced. When the time is right a little pressure can have a great effect. In this way it is sometimes possible for a few people or even one person to do something that is of great historical significance, perhaps by setting in motion a chain of events. The problem with this approach is that the wait might be a long one – more than a lifetime – and the critical period be fleeting or difficult to recognise, except in retrospect. For that reason, the struggle has to be a continuous one with constant pressure applied.

The old question arises as to whether it is possible for individuals, either alone or jointly, to guide and steer the unfolding of events? Are human actions the result of free will and choice or are they determined by the circumstances of the time and the dynamics of the system of which they are part? Did Napoleon or Lenin change the course of history or were they merely products of their time; actors playing a part that might have been played by any number of understudies? Our answer will depend on how wide a view we take of the matter. The influence of humans on the history of the universe is likely to be immeasurably small. Human influence on the history of the Earth is likely to be greater. The influence of parents on the lives of their children can be considerable.

A small well-organised group can manipulate a disorganised and unknowing larger group. The minority shapes the system in such a way that despite the many uncoordinated daily acts and decisions of the majority, the system behaves in a more or less orderly and predictable way. This suggests that a group of people acting together with a common purpose can influence the unfolding of the present and the making of history. But to what extent and for how long? Are there deep historical trends that humans are unable to alter? Yes there are, but not all are so deep as to be unbendable, and some *trends*, when they are tested, are found to be insubstantial dead-ends.

The heroic ideal promotes the view that individuals can challenge the course that seems set for them and their community. A hero tries to bend and direct the unfolding of their life and the history of their community. That may involve a long struggle against a powerful enemy or a short fight to the death against impossible odds, perhaps to inflict a heavier cost on the enemy than they are willing to bear.[196] Or the purpose might be to inspire others to take up arms and confront the enemy. The heroic ideal does not accord with the view that what passes each day is fixed and inescapable. Neither is it about drift or 'what will be will be' or hoping things will turn out for the best. It urges us to direct our lives as best we can along the path we want to take. It is about ideals, the traditional virtues and making a mark, which in early English culture was seen as winning fame. None can pass through life without mistake or shame but all can redeem themselves in this world by acts of heroism. The hero tests the line between what is inevitable and what is possible and in doing so discovers if the dragon is all-powerful or can be slain.

To a large extent, we are bound in life by the lot we have been given. Our life thread has been spun, measured and cut but we can influence the way it is woven into the Web of Wyrd. This way of looking at things has much in common with modern ideas concerning chaos, genetics, natural selection and evolution. For example, our genes fix our mental and physical potential and our maximum life span, but the use to which we put what we have is determined, in part, by our outlook on life and the cultural and physical environment in which we are immersed. We all have our limitations but within them we all have the opportunity from time to time *to make a difference*. What is required is a frame of mind that enables us to recognise those opportunities and to seize them.

Our behaviour is moulded by our external social and physical environment and the internal workings of our brain, which is hardwired in a way that make us think and act in certain instinctive ways over which we have little if any control. But we also have soft-wiring that enables us to innovate and adapt to new developments and, to some extent, redirect and mould them. Similarly, our individual and communal destiny is in many ways fixed but there are opportunities, if we look for them and seize them, to nudge the course of history in one direction or another.

We do not know in any detail what *Wyrd* meant to the early English but we can build on the information we have. Yes, our interpretation will be influenced by modern ideas and needs. Our imperfect knowledge of that time is a handicap but

---

[196] For example, Algerians did not win independence from France by defeating the French in battle but by inflicting casualties and an economic cost that the French government was unwilling to bear. In that way it is possible to lose every battle but win the war.

nonetheless our ancestors and their view of the world can be an inspiration to us. A national history is a storehouse of cultural perceptions and artefacts that can be delved into from time to time in order to find something that can be adapted to current needs. It would be nice if we had a thorough understanding of how our ancestors saw the world and their place in it but that is impossible. We can, however, share their means of giving expression to the joys, hardships and the uncertainties of life. In doing so we give new life to them and their memory.

The Web of Wyrd is a way of showing how the present unfolds and is woven into the unbroken passing of time. Many apparently meaningless days are woven into the Web and together become meaningful. We look back into a past that was chaotic in its making but now reveals regular patterns and currents that help us to anticipate how the future will unfold.

Many people see no patterns, they do not see the Web. Instead, they exist from day to day on the crest of the ever-breaking wave that is the present. They have no sense of history and are unable to see daily events as part of a wider setting. They are aware at a superficial level that change is taking place but it is called progress and deemed to be change for the better. The majority of the population is kept occupied with a familiar, predictable, comforting and trivial *reality*. They accept what is regularly put before them in easily digestible form, and do not look beyond it at who is placing it there and why. A popular culture obsessed with soap operas, sport, fashion and the activities of *personalities*, provides a diet for lazy brains; the higher the consumption the lazier the brain becomes; brain death beckons. Convenience brain-food keeps lazy minds full. Those who look beyond the fodder offered them and gain a knowledge and understanding of the past are potential subversives because they are able to see patterns beyond the daily chaos. They are able to resist and challenge the elite's assertions about the unfolding of the present, and what is inevitable and desirable.

Progress

Time passes; we grow older; some become wiser as they pass through life but others remain as naive as the day they were born. The passing of time is not inherently good or bad. Tomorrow will not necessarily be *better* than today. The unfolding of the present is not a mechanical process moving in a predetermined way to fulfil a grand design. Beyond the certainty of death we have no way of knowing for certain what the future will bring. The best we can hope for is to anticipate problems and either prepare to confront them or try to steer around them.

The European notion of *progress* comes in large part from Christianity and the belief that everything is moving in a predetermined way towards the Second Coming of Christ and the Salvation. This linear view of the passing of time became embedded in Western cultures and took on a secular form in the eighteenth century. Liberals saw the industrial and scientific revolutions as a new kind of First Coming when mankind started to take control of the Earth and harness natural powers to create a better future. The material wellbeing of mankind would be improved and bring with it an improvement in human nature, perhaps to the point of perfection. Both the natural material world and human behaviour would be controlled and directed in the search for perfection. Knowledge and education would bring the light of salvation to the darkness within us all and drive it out. Alleluia!

Thus, history came to be seen as a flow with a direction and a purpose. The future will be a better place than the past. The means of reaching utopia is through social and technological change. Change is progress; progress brings greater happiness.

Many technological developments have indeed brought great benefits to mankind, particularly in the field of healthcare. Also, it cannot be denied that the link between capitalism and technology is one that spews out goods and services in a way that no other known system can match. However, unrestrained technological development has environmental and other costs. Natural resources are not infinite and the Earth is not able to act as a sink for infinite quantities of waste. Technological progressives deny that there are limits to *progress* and claim that given time, science and technology will find a solution to any problem. Such faith in a technological fix around the corner has led to a build-up of problems that have not been fixed despite several corners having been turned; dealing with nuclear waste being just one of them.

If we accept, for the sake of argument, that an increase in technological sophistication brings greater happiness to the greater number, and that happiness is the highest goal, it looks very much as if it takes more and more technology to achieve a smaller and smaller increase in happiness. In other words, the marginal utility of technology, expressed in terms of happiness, is very small. Each additional unit of technological development produces a smaller unit of happiness at an increasingly higher cost, where cost is measured in terms of unhappiness resulting from damage to culture, community, health and environment. For many people the stage has long been reached where more technology produces short-term happiness at the cost of far greater long-term unhappiness. All of these factors should be taken into account when evaluating *progress*.

The nineteenth-century liberal view of progress (meaning improvement) has evolved into modernism and is still with us.[197] Progressives (liberals and modernists) see the chaos of their twentieth-century cultural revolution as a blessing that has given mankind the opportunity to escape from the ideas,

---

[197] *Tony Blair declared yesterday that his ambition was to transform Labour from a class-based party into a force modelled on the Liberals of the last century. "My vision for New Labour is to become, as the Liberal Party was in the 19th century, a broad coalition of those who believe in progress and justice," he said. The Daily Telegraph, 16th December 1998*

outlooks, culture and other restraints of the past and make a fresh start. Just as technology is thought to need constant updating, so cultures and identities are thought to need constant reinvention and redefinition. It is difficult to see how this reinvention can mean anything less than constant cultural revolution, the cutting of links with the past, and the destruction of community.

Cultural evolution provides a better model than cultural revolution for what takes place in long-lived communities and societies. Cultures and communities constantly regenerate themselves and in doing so they evolve but the process is too slow for those with short attention spans who are always seeking something new and dynamic to entertain them. They would prefer to ignore the past which is seen as being full of aliens who were less clever, moral and free than their modern day descendants. This view is a product of the notion that progress makes people *better*. The people of the past and their cultures are regarded as burdens to shake off so that society can be rebuilt from the roots upwards according to the dictates of liberal modernist ideology.

We can look to the past for guidance in many things but some lessons are learnt over and over again. Human nature follows much the same course with each life that unfolds. We all make the many silly and sometimes costly mistakes that earlier generations have made. In some things it seems we can only learn from personal experience. We can only truly know love and loss from personal experience. Nothing else can adequately convey the joy and the emptiness.

Those who crave change see the caution, responsibility and sense of continuity that community promotes as a brake on progress. Community is thought oppressive. In its place, they seek society and constant change. Tomorrow will be different from and better than today. The passing of time is inherently good because it brings the future closer to us. The faster the old is replaced with the new, the faster we will progress to a better future. Those who resist change are out-of-touch reactionaries who must be pushed aside and overcome. Opposition to unrestrained change is seen as an attack on individual freedom and an unrealistic attempt to stop humans striving for something better. "You cannot stand in the way of progress" and if you do you deserve to be trampled underfoot.

Humans are indeed curious and competitive animals but those instincts have evolved alongside others. We are a complex blend of instincts moulded by natural selection in a way that enables us to successfully live in communities. Striving to improve one's lot has generally been seen as natural and acceptable provided it does no serious harm to the community that makes such striving possible. Individualism is welcomed when pursued within the setting of community.

Another consequence of seeing rapid and uncontrolled change as desirable is that it has encouraged children to see themselves as separate and different from their parents. Children accept the liberal message, promoted in advertising, that the new is necessarily better than the old; that youth is better than age. Unsurprisingly, children want to show that they are new and different from the previous generation. This has created gaps in what was a continuity between one generation and the next. There is also much greater division within youth culture, a sub-culture tribalism that is probably an instinctive attempt to create community where none is seen to exist. Many children think it is important that they should show that they are different from those who are a year or two older than they are. Such division and atomisation is welcomed by liberals who find it exciting. Nationalists reject atomisation as a curse that undermines the feeling of empathy, continuity and co-operation that is the cement of community and democracy.

Despite the manipulation of youth culture by corporations (a marketing device), and the propaganda that they are subject to in school, many young people are aware that they are members of a wider national culture and as they grow older they merge into it. Even the most inward-looking are eventually forced to recognise that their youth sub-culture is short-lived, reactionary and shallow. When they realise that they cannot escape the processes of ageing, they are able to join the wider adult community, which they had previously thought to be inhabited by people quite unlike themselves. However, the stronger youth culture becomes the later the transition into adulthood occurs and the more *old young people* we have who cannot accept any responsibility that interferes with their desire to be young and irresponsible indefinitely. The longer people live in that unreal world the more damage they do to the wider community that makes such fantasies possible. Individuals eventually realise that *progress* will not bring them the fame, fortune and happiness they had hoped for or even expected as of right. On taking a close look at the real world, they see that while they are chasing shadows, other people are playing a part in the traditional cycle of life. It is then that the importance of community becomes apparent and it is understood that there is more to life than a career, easy pleasure and possessions. There is no virtue in poverty but neither is it to be found up the empty cul-de-sac of *progress* and self-indulgence.

Society

A society can be defined as a group of people sharing a physical or political territory. Nothing can be implied about the nature of the relationship between them, which might be based on friendship and co-operation or dislike, distrust and hostility. To be a member of a society might require nothing more than living in a territory over which a political organization exercises control; thus the citizens of a state are members of a society. In other words, society is the sum of relationships that exist within a defined group.

Society is to *community* what *citizenship* is to *nationality*. Society and citizenship infer nothing about common values and perceptions whereas community and nationality do. Thus, the states of the world do not constitute an international community, although there are groups of states within world society that can be said to form communities.

A society might include all or part of a community, or several communities.

Community

A traditional human community is a group of persons who have:

1. cultural or religious, racial, linguistic or other **characteristics** in common;

2. an interwoven **ancestry**;

3. common **interests**, whether imagined or real, which are sufficient to bind them together;

4. a greater quantity and quality of **communication** among themselves than with outsiders;

5. greater **co-operation** among themselves than with outsiders;

6. greater **trust, empathy** and a sense of being at ease among themselves than with outsiders.

Communities are usually linked to a given geographical area, or areas, although in modern times, and particularly in cities, communal boundaries are often not fixed or clear. Some communities are so dispersed that they cannot be said to have geographical boundaries. In such instances, the lack of territoriality is usually compensated for by strong cultural boundaries. Other communities have clearly defined geographical boundaries on which they have long relied, e.g. the English, Nepalese and Tibetans. One consequence of reliance on physical communal boundaries is that nations living within them usually lack practice in defending cultural boundaries, and are thus poorly equipped to defend their way of life when their physical boundaries are breached.

Benedict Anderson argues that small *face-to-face* communities are the only real or *true* communities and that once personal contact is lost communities become *imagined*.[198] He suggests that members of a nation cannot know more than a few of their fellow nationals, 'yet in the minds of each lives the image of their communion'.

Using *true* and *imagined* in that way, suggests that small face-to-face communities are not imagined, and that large communities are not real or *true*. Yet it is evident that a few hundred people living in close proximity and having frequent face-to-face contact need not constitute a community while several million people widely dispersed and having little if any face-to-face contact can have a strong communal identity. Many English people living in cities and large towns have almost daily

---

[198] *Imagined Communities. Reflections on the Origin and Spread of Nationalism*, 1983

face-to-face contact with neighbours or shopkeepers but do not share a sense of community with them. On the other hand they may have infrequent face-to-face contact with people living in Australia, New Zealand and North America but nevertheless share with them a strong sense of community. A telephone call, a letter and an email are modern forms of face-to-face relationships and constitute personal contact. Although technology has played a part in changing the shape of communities by making them numerically and geographically larger, they are still real and meaningful because the quality of the contacts counts for more than their frequency. A *real* community is therefore more than a group of people who live in close proximity and have frequent personal contact.

Another factor to be considered is the extent to which the members of a community share a sense of loyalty and identity. Traditional communities promote strong ties because they consist of many intertwined threads of interest and activity. The main threads are kindred, cultural, economic and political. Modern industrial and political societies have pulled and twisted the threads of community. Communities have had to evolve within these societies and adapt to the changing environment. Societies favour the growth of single-issue interest groups, which are sometimes mistakenly called communities. As we have seen, communities have many threads. Thus, the sharing of a workplace does not of itself give rise to a community. Work is but a thread in the fabric of life and community.

Despite the destructive pressures of modern societies, communities evolve and survive. The communities with the greatest sense of loyalty and identity are still kinship based. The strength of that loyalty is in part dependent upon the closeness of the blood relationship (genetic favouritism and kinship inclusion), the frequency of contact, and the benefit gained. Thus the bonding between the members of a vertical two or three generation family of parents, children, grandchildren is likely to be greater than that between members of the wider horizontal family, which includes aunts, uncles, nieces and nephews.

Loyalty, altruism, and a sense of common identity usually diminish with the distance of the kin relationship and the accompanying decline in face-to-face contact and shared interests. However, even slender kinship ties can be remarkably strong, reaching out to encompass those who are not known kin but likely to be so because of shared physical and cultural characteristics. Insiders use instinct and assorted boundary markers to determine the boundary of their kindred community

A traditional or *real* (physically close) community is one where every member of a group of people either knows, or knows of, all other members of the group and lives within reasonable walking distance of any other member.[199] Certain types of

---

[199] Research indicates that the maximum number of faces that can be recognised by individual humans is about 500. It has been suggested that this reflects the maximum size of a traditional face-to-face community.

behaviour are formally and informally encouraged and others discouraged. Customary behaviour evolves in a way that enables members of a community to get along together with the minimum of disputes, misunderstandings and unintentional insults. A member of a community generally behaves in a way that is predictable, acceptable and non-threatening to other members.

All community is imagined in that it is in the mind. A dispersed (*imagined*) community is not a community in the same way as is a face-to-face (*real*) community but both are able to bring together individuals within a common identity and for a common purpose. Indeed, a dispersed community can perhaps better contain individuals and social classes that on a face-to-face basis might have difficulty getting along.

Nations, like other communities, exist in the minds of insiders and outsiders. From each viewpoint there will be different perceptions about the nature and character of a given nation and its boundaries.

Communities, whether real or imagined, consist of a web of personal ties and channels of communication. Communal living is the product of millions of years of trial and error. The rules that govern traditional communities have been crafted by natural selection.

Community and Evolution

Mankind has been moulded by natural selection. Those of our ancestors who had a greater than average disposition to co-operate with others usually had a better-than-average chance of surviving and having offspring than those who did not. That process produced humans with behavioural and psychological traits that made them better suited to living in increasingly sophisticated communities. Indeed it was their ability to adapt and co-operate that made complex communities and cultures possible. Those communities and cultures are also subject to the process of natural selection, and as a result they organize themselves in a way that has proved successful for reproduction and survival in certain environments. The evolution of communal instincts is an essential part of that progression.

The term *survival of the fittest* is often taken to mean survival of the physically strong but it means the survival of those organisms that can best adapt to and are best suited to their environment, which has a communal as well as a physical dimension. A community that fails to adapt and reproduce dies.

The instincts necessary for communal living are broadened and deepened by natural selection because communities provide an environment where co-operation with other insiders wins rewards in the struggle to survive and reproduce. When inborn communal instincts are not rewarded and re-enforced, more basic instincts for self-preservation emerge and communities degenerate into societies where competition rather than co-operation is the favoured survival strategy. The descent is quickened when communal instincts are actively discouraged and the pursuit of unenlightened narrow self-interest is promoted. Successful communities find an appropriate balance between the needs of individuals and the needs of the community of which they are part. The survival and reproduction of both are primary goals.

The members of a community co-operate because it is in their interest as individuals and as a group to do so. What is commonly called altruism is an expression of that co-operation. Real altruism is an unselfish concern for the welfare of others, i.e. no reward is expected. Communal altruism is not an unselfish concern for the welfare of others but an enlightened self-interest. It is a sophisticated form of game-play which serves the interests of all involved. I help you today because I believe that when I need help you or another member of the community will help me. Altruism can take the form of common politeness, which is showing consideration for others in the expectation that they in turn will be considerate. Politeness is a mark of community and it makes the business of everyday life more agreeable and less prone to misunderstanding and conflict. An example of communal altruism is to be found in the generally good road manners that are still to be found in England. For example, when there is heavy slow-moving traffic, most drivers stop to allow other drivers in and out of side turnings. If such behaviour was an unselfish concern for the welfare of others we wouldn't get annoyed when the person we have stopped for does not acknowledge our consideration. Consideration for others and acknowledgement of favours given is an important part of good manners. The truth of this is indicated in a report by Thomas Harding.[200]

> Actions that spark off road rage include middle-lane drivers on the motorway, people who cut in at the last moment at road works, those who do not use indicators or jump red lights and discourteous drivers who fail to acknowledge being allowed to pass in narrow streets.

Although individuals and communities benefit from co-operation, it is in the interest of both that there is competition within the community. The gain is much the same as for a football club when there is competition for a place in the first team. Competition makes the team stronger and better able to compete with other teams.

Competition between individuals within a community is mostly governed by formal and informal rules that represent to a greater or lesser extent a balance between the interests of the individual and those of the community. Similar rules and competitive strategies exist within and between communities but competition between communities is usually less restrained and more aggressive because there are fewer rules and less pressure to observe them. This is not to ignore the fact that

---

[200] *Daily Telegraph* 15th May 2000

communities usually benefit from co-operation with other communities, and in turn that promotes politeness (e.g. rules of diplomacy) and acts as a deterrent to open conflict.

In a healthy community, individuals tend to perceive a threat to their community as a threat to themselves and react accordingly. Survival instincts are pooled and directed outwards in self-defence, an entirely natural and essential response. These bundles of instincts work well together as a unit, some restraining others until the need for them arises. They are triggered in a sequence determined by the needs of a given situation. If the carefully crafted relationship between the various instincts is disturbed, a situation can arise where, for example, the instinct to gather and store becomes unrestrained and turns into greed and acquisitiveness. Dire results can also flow from the separation of aggressive instincts from the instinct to protect and further communal interests.

Community and Kinship

The primary community is the nuclear family of mother, father and children. Beyond that, there are varying degrees of extended family, the largest being the nation. There are also various other groups to which each member of a family might belong depending on their personal interests and friendships. These other groups are many and varied, and include those centred on work and leisure activities.

In earlier ages, during times of peace, individuals tended to identify most strongly with their nearby kindred and small *real* community. In modern times, with greater movement of population, those identities have to compete with others. Communities are less dependent than they once were on insiders living in close geographical proximity to one another. Advances in communication and information technology have made individuals increasingly aware that they share interests, perceptions and values with persons they have never met. It has also brought them into contact with cultures that were once remote and unknown, and with which they have many differences. Much can be learned from such cultures but they are usually best appreciated when they are not perceived as a threat.

During the English industrial revolution, many people migrated from the countryside to towns and cities. In many places, new *real* communities grew up around interlocking kindred communities. There was a tendency for workers to live close to their workplace and their kin, and to stay in the same area for life. This made for strong stable communities built on overlapping ties, interests and shared experiences.

After World War I, and particularly in the 1930s, there was a new wave of migration, this time out of town and city centres into the rapidly expanding suburbs. Much of that migration was of the lower middle classes. Many of the

341

working-class communities that depended on traditional industries were left intact until they were destroyed during the large-scale redevelopment that took place in the 1960s. There was much interest at the time in the fate of the many communities in East London which were broken up by policies that took no account of community. Many of the younger members of those communities moved to New Towns where they were isolated from their extended families. The break-up of multi-generation communities during that period played a part in weakening families and unleashing a separate youth culture which has, as one might expect, become increasingly wilful, shallow and immature.

Most of the more recent kinship communities created in English towns and cities are of foreign immigrants who have transplanted their cultures and institutions from their homelands to the districts in which they have settled. In doing that they have been able to preserve their communal memory and communal boundaries. Their practice of seeking marriage partners in their homeland and bringing them to England helped them maintain a link with their homeland and a strong national identity. The existence of modern transport and electronic communications has enabled these small communities to create, and live within, a cultural cocoon in a foreign land.

Kinship is still at the heart of the most enduring communities. We sometimes prefer the frequent company of friends and acquaintances but they come and go while family is always there, feuds permitting. Despite the wonders of modern technology and the cult of the individual, factors such as kinship, personal contact, predictable behaviour, and shared values are still important to us.

Membership of a family, however extended, is for life. Nations are the most extended of extended families, and their intertwined web of kindred relationships promotes a very strong sense of loyalty and identity. A national community is like a chain-mail garment in that its strength is derived from many small interlocking links.

Community and Land

Communities offer their members a sense of identity, stability and continuity, although that is less so now than in earlier times when most people lived their whole life in one small town or village and shared not only a culture and way of life with their grandparents and grandchildren but also a territory and a landscape. The nature of the land helps mould the perceptions and attitudes of successive generations. It affects the way individuals view themselves and their place in the world. Land is at the core of a community's identity and security. If the communal homeland is lost, the community is cast adrift and placed at the mercy of others. Self-government and the freedom to live a particular way of life are likely to be lost with the land; the very existence of the community is threatened. For that reason, communities instinctively defend their homeland. Territoriality is an essential human instinct.

The land makes its mark on the individuals and communities who live on it but they also leave their mark on the land they inhabit. People adapt their way of life to suit the landscape and the climate but, where possible, they also change the landscape to suit their needs. They become attuned to the environment in which they live and become part of the natural order of things. The members of old settled communities are linked to their distant ancestors through communal memories embedded in the culture in which they are immersed. They can see the works of their ancestors around them and feel their presence, not least because the physical remains of many generations are mingled with the earth of the homeland.

Wherever one travels in England the landscape is like a tapestry that records the history of local communities and the English nation; it is a tapestry that tells a story. Very little of the English landscape is natural in the sense that it is unaffected by the lives of those who have lived on it. Because of that, the land that is England is part of English culture. The English countryside, albeit an idealized vision of it, is at the core of English identity, and that is why those who are opposed to an assertion of English national identity are so keen to mock the association between Englishness and the English countryside.

From time to time there have been changes in agricultural and building techniques but until recently these did not mark a sharp break from the past. People could do, see, smell, touch and hear the same things as their forebears. One generation flowed into another and people of different ages spent more of their working and playing time together; they were part of one community and one culture, subject of course to class differences that are a natural and inevitable part of any long-lived large community. The flow from generation to generation gave a sense of permanence, predictability and security that is essential to a healthy community and a healthy land. No community knowingly harms the land on which it depends for its existence and with which it identifies and has emotional and cultural links. The same cannot be said of states. Governing elites tend to see land as merely an economic resource to be used in any way that meets the needs of the time.

The link between a national community and its homeland grows stronger with the passing of time. Generally, the longer the link, the greater the mark that is made on the landscape. This, in part, explains why foreigners in any country usually live in cities, which are increasingly alike in appearance and reflect the needs of global capitalism rather than projecting the achievements and identity of nations. Capitalism treats national cultures and their symbols as little more than things to be used for marketing and advertising purposes. In such an environment, outsiders are able to regard cities as neutral territory. Those foreigners who step out of the cities to visit or live in the countryside are constantly reminded that they do not belong there and that they live in a foreign country. Yet some people come to

England for the first time and do not feel like strangers and are not treated as such because they have an English ancestry and a psychological disposition that enables them to fit in. They are distant kin.

Cultures and Evolution

Humans inherit a mix of physical, psychological and behavioural characteristics that have helped their ancestors adapt, survive, and reproduce. The lessons learned from trial-and-error testing over many thousands of generations are passed on as instincts which are *hardwired* into each human at birth. Succeeding generations are thus spared the need to learn expensive lessons over and over again.

Humans and other animals are also *softwired* with a problem-solving ability (intelligence) that enables them to adapt to situations of which they have no evolutionary experience.[201] It has been suggested that an important difference between Homo sapiens and Homo neanderthalensis was that the former developed a form of softwiring that enabled them to speed up their ability to improvise, which improved their survival skills. Neanderthals may have been content to make do with what they had, only changing the way they lived when it was felt necessary to do so. Neanderthals seem to have had larger brains than Homo sapiens, and may have been happier and more content. Perhaps they innovated in areas other than technology and had a richer spiritual or artistic culture that Homo sapiens. It has been suggested that Neanderthals became extinct because they were less adaptable, less technically inventive, and, perhaps, less aggressive than those they were competing with for resources.[202]

The human brain has a mix of hard and soft wiring that enables it to combine a store of millions of years of experience with the first-hand experience of one lifetime. Culture performs a similar role in that it combines a store of experience and knowledge with the ability to adapt and apply that information in the current social and physical environment. Thus, individually and collectively we face the world equipped with the experience of our ancestors. In addition, we have intelligence, a problem-solving ability that enables us, when appropriate, to override individual and communal instincts in order to meet short-term needs and take evolutionary shortcuts. That ability to adapt needs to be used wisely because there is the danger of being too clever. The suppression of instincts in the quest for immediate gratification or the fulfilment of an ideological goal can be harmful to long-term interests.

---

[201] Defining *consciousness* and *intelligence* is beset with difficulties and will not be attempted here. An interesting related problem is that of defining *life*. Is a computer virus a living thing and if not why not?

[202] Homo sapiens and Homo neanderthalensis are different species of the same human genus.

Culture is a store of successful survival strategies; it passes on life skills from generation to generation. Culture, like intelligence, gives us the ability to weigh short-term and long-term interests, reach a considered opinion and act on it. Culture gives shape to a community. It provides a structure that helps the parts co-operate and attain more together than they can apart. The institutions that perform that task need to be adaptable.

All cultures have rules but some have so few that they are suited only to short-term day-to-day living; they have no skeleton and are blown like sheets in the wind. There are also rigid cultures, bound by excessive formality and sacrosanct rules. They eventually suffer a catastrophic failure and shatter because they are unable to bend and evolve with the needs of the time. Innovation is stifled and the rules are seen as being good in themselves, their purpose having been forgotten.

Successful cultures, provide a means for regularly testing, adjusting, and sometimes abandoning rules to meet the needs of a changing social and physical environment. Finding a workable balance between excessive rigidity and flexibility is usually a matter of trial and error guided by calculation and intelligent guesswork. Difficulties and even disaster can occur when the making and breaking of communal rules falls into the hands of those who are reckless and lacking in historical perspective. A more humble approach is needed, with every effort being made to anticipate the consequences of deliberate change. This is not easy because the relationship between instinct and culture is complex.

None of this is meant to suggest that a flexible culture can be directed and controlled from the top. Cultures, like language, are subject to many influences, internal and external, that are beyond the power of communal leaders to control. Nevertheless, it is their duty to preserve the shape and structure of the communal culture, which if it is too lose will unravel and lose the wealth of knowledge and experience it contains. They must try to anticipate the long-term consequences of deliberate change, and avoid a headlong rush into change for its own sake. Such recklessness invites a catastrophic systems failure and communal extinction. A cautious holistic approach to these things is better than the short-term piecemeal approach of those given to ideological whims. Cultural boundaries are hard to define but they exist and need to be preserved.

There are certain questions that need answering when the cultural, political and economic institutions of a community are modified. What kind of community do we want? Do the proposed changes help attain that goal? Will the changes help or hinder communal regeneration and the habit of co-operation? Are we able to achieve an acceptable balance between the minimum number of restrictions on individual freedom and the maximum benefit to the community? Are short-term goals compatible with long-term communal and cultural survival strategies? Will change bring us greater control over our culture, economy and political system? Are we giving unelected technocrats and bureaucrats the power to shape our lives?

Anglo-Saxon communities have little conscious sense of cultural purity, and have shown a willingness to borrow and adapt from others. This free-and-easy pragmatism was until comparatively recent times made possible because borrowings were mostly from similar European cultures and fitted comfortably into the host community. Foreign things were adopted, modified to local needs and Anglicised; thus cultural boundaries were preserved. In modern times it has been deemed unacceptable for those communities to maintain and defend their boundaries. Instead, they are berated by ideological tsars and directed to welcome and embrace foreign ways and foreign people as if it is a duty to do so. No concern is shown for the culture and community of the hosts, who do not volunteer for the experiment but are conscripted. There is total disregard for the fact that ideas, perceptions and people torn from one culture can cause stress and conflict when transplanted to another. Multi-culturalism, a variant of the liberal ideological virus, weakens and sometimes destroys the immune systems of infected host communities, making them defenceless. The aim of multi-culturalists is not to promote diversity, which is essential to the working of natural selection and the health and vigour of cultures, but instead to suck out those distinct values and perceptions that conflict with liberal dogma. The intent is to leave the shells in place but to *culturally cleanse* the insides, thus giving the illusion of cultural diversity. We are granted the freedom to be different provided it does not lead us to do or say anything that liberals deem to be offensive. For example, British Moslems are free to visit their mosques, wear their traditional dress, eat their traditional food, and hold their traditional festivals, provided they do not live by their beliefs.

In a real multi-cultural society, people of different cultures would have their own system of law, which reflected their beliefs and values. However, besides the impracticability (chaos and conflict) of having several systems of law operating with equal validity in one state, there is the difficulty that Islamic law is unacceptable to liberals. However much they may promote multi-culturalism as an ideal, in practice liberal governing elites are never going to allow anything other than a liberal system of law to operate in a liberal state. What does multi-culturalism actually mean if it does not enable every community to live by its values and beliefs?

In a liberal multi-cultural society all are free to live as they wish provided they do not say or do anything to offend liberals. Clearly, liberals do not feel restrained in that way because they vigorously promote their ideology regardless of the offence or harm it causes others.

National Communities and Memory

Without memory, it is very difficult to engage in conversation. Without memory, there is no past and without a past it is impossible to understand the present or contemplate the future. A person without memory experiences things as they happen but has nothing to compare those experiences with; there is no context. A community without memory is similarly handicapped. Indeed, memory is such an important part of community that it is impossible for a community to exist without it. Perhaps that is why those who wish to destroy a nation, first set about destroying its memory.

The memory of an oral community is held in the minds of its members. It is often expressed in the form of verse, song, and playlets, and is added to as it passes from generation to generation. Core communal memories are of shared experiences, including victory or defeat in war, festivals, mourning, and famine. An oral community is, in a sense, more democratic than a literate community in that all can participate in retaining, recalling, adding to and passing on shared memories. There is no single approved memory, but its overall shape and unity is maintained by poets and bards, and sometimes priests. The powerful are better placed than others to influence what is recorded but in the long term, the record of events and deeds is subject to popular approval.

The memory of literate communities is mostly recorded in writing and images. The governing elite nearly always controls the formal recording and recollection of memory. The elite is better able to manipulate memory to suit its own purposes when there is much formal memory and little or no folk memory. Modern states with control of the education system are in a powerful position to write and rewrite history in ways that suit their needs. Thus, an inclusive British history is taught in English schools instead of English history, and the English are made invisible.

The education system is used to feed children *false* memories that bolster a particular view of history. Some memories are ignored and others emphasised, or even invented, to suit the ideological needs of those who control the system. Liberals are well practised in manipulating history and regard it as their duty to do so. The aim is always to ignore or downplay the English and their achievements so that the English have a negative view of their communal history and feel alienated from their national identity.

A recorded history is of little use to a community if it is written down but never read or widely known. It must be remembered and passed on as a continuous thread. Memories are kept alive by being revisited; recalling something re-enforces it.

Communal memories help people to work together in pursuit of a common goal. Memories of trials, triumphs and heroes can inspire a nation and help it overcome periods of hardship. Memories are essential to a sense of identity and the continuous process of communal regeneration.

No single person can know the whole history of their nation but all should know its outline and have access to more detailed information. It is the task of nationalists to ensure that a wide and long collective memory is passed on and that as much of it as possible is known to ordinary folk. Nationalists must prevent their nation's history being controlled and monopolised by outsiders or a governing elite that serves outside interests. History is a battlefield and there is no such thing as a neutral participant. Everyone has an axe to grind, and that is particularly true of academics, who usually claim to be above the fray.

Memory and Immortality

Every member of a community can become part of the communal memory by:

1. doing deeds that win fame and honour;
2. having children;
3. keeping alive the history, culture and identity of their community.

Our deeds enable us to live on in the memory of our community. Our physical existence and that of our ancestors lives on in the genetic memory of our community. By immersing ourselves in our community's culture and playing a part in its preservation and evolution we add to it and leave our mark. In doing any or all of these things we become part of something that has a life greater than our own.

1. Deeds and the Heroic Ideal

Heroism is a cultural ideal which encourages behaviour that benefits individuals and their community. It promotes a mental strength and comradeship that helps individuals overcome fear. Faced with a large and aggressive enemy, the instinct of a warrior to run away (*flight*) might be stronger than the instinct to stand firm and fight. The heroic ideal encourages warriors to place group interests above self-interest in as far as it is possible to separate the two. It is better to stand shoulder to shoulder with your comrades and win fame in fighting to the death, if need be, that to run away and face a lonely life of disgrace. This is not to suggest that a culture can turn anyone into a brave warrior. It is more a matter of enhancing innate qualities and enabling individuals to work as a group. Those qualities can be revealed and used in different ways.

The deeds that win respect and fame are those that give effect to the traditional virtues of hospitality, boldness, loyalty, honesty and courage.[203] Unlike some codes of behaviour, the traditional virtues promote a positive attitude to life. To behave in an honourable way is to observe the virtues in a manner that in some way benefits the communal good. All the virtues can be displayed in everyday life and all add to the good name of an individual and that of his or her community.

The heroic winning of fame usually requires a display of courage, which nearly all of us are given the opportunity to show in coping with the hardships of life. Some

---

[203] Hospitality is a form of generosity.

are courageous in their stoicism, while others display it in their determination to struggle and fight for a just cause. The heroic ideal was ingrained in the culture and lived on into the Christian period. Some of the English saints went abroad to do the work of their Heavenly Lord and if necessary to face death in that cause. In the Old English verse *Dream of the Rood*, Christ is portrayed as a warrior bravely and defiantly mounting the cross in the face of certain death. He is certainly not the wimpish effeminate hippie of modern times. The clergy were made of sterner stuff then and portrayed Christ in their own image, as indeed they do now.

Many people are heroic in the way they face tragedy and hardship in their lives but most do not seek out a test of their courage or rise to an avoidable challenge. It is not necessary to be a warrior to act heroically but great acts of heroism are not usually passive, they are sought out. Heroes generally go out and do things; they try to make things happen; they test themselves and the limits of what is possible. The heroic ideal is a product of a culture that is concerned primarily with the continuation of life in this world but in a different form. Heroism can transform a flesh-and-blood person into a legend and in that way they live for as long as their name is remembered.

The heroic ideal was an important feature of early English and other similar Northern Europe cultures but it is not restricted to any particular place, time or culture. The deeds of warriors, such as Beowulf, were recorded in verse so that their fame and heroism could live on and serve as a model for others. A willingness to risk life and limb in order to honour the traditional virtues and communal interests was seen as heroic, whereas performing the same deeds in pursuit of self-interest and material gain was unlikely to be seen in the same way.

Heroes were not motivated by the desire to win material wealth. Their inspiration was often the upholding of a bond of loyalty, perhaps to an individual or their community. Objects of material value were merely a form of currency, symbols of loyalty and gratitude that were given and received; a gift for a gift. Honour and fame were the rewards; material wealth merely one means of giving recognition. Thus, the heroic ideal and the triumph of the individual was encouraged within a communal framework.

It is not necessary to sympathise with the ideology of a person, or to like them, in order to recognise and praise their acts of heroism. Only the mean-minded and those lacking any appreciation of the heroic ideal would deny recognition to those deserving it. Heroism is seeking out and confronting powerful forces in the knowledge that the price might be personal hardship, suffering or death. Heroism involves courage and honour but a hero need not be a saint. Che Guevara, Malcolm X and Martin Luther King were heroic but none were without fault. Their imperfections do not detract from their heroism, they only add to it because they show that all of us, whatever our faults, can redeem ourselves by seeking out the point where what is within the power of individuals to change, meets what is hard and immovable.

Beowulf did not travel to a foreign land to seek out and fight Grendel for material reward. He fought Grendel, and later a dragon, in order to test himself, to challenge *Wyrd*, and to win fame. Most of us like to think that when a test comes we will respond in a courageous manner. A few do not wait for a challenge but set out to find one, and there is none greater than facing a powerful enemy and the prospect of one's own death in combat. When the time comes to fight, warriors of worth fight for their honour, their comrades, and their ideals

Heroism can be recognised, acknowledged and praised in friend and foe alike. The deeds of a hero can be an inspiration to all people, not just their own. None are truly dead until their name is forgotten.

The spirit of the heroic ideal can be seen in the following lines, which are adapted from *The Battle of Maldon*.

> Minds must be firmer, hearts the bolder,
> loyalty the greater, as our foes grow stronger.
> About us lie things that are dear to us.
> We shall see who has the courage to defend them.
> Stand proud and defiant; give no more ground.
> May he grieve forever who flees the fight.

2. Children

Only a generation or so ago people left school, started work, and became *old young people*. Childhood lasted longer than it does now but the change from child to adult was shorter. Individuals quickly assumed the responsibilities of marriage and raising children. Each new generation blended into the last. Biological and cultural instincts worked together in a way that renewed the life of the community and gave its members an interest in its survival and wellbeing. Cultural norms reflected an unstated belief that the primary purpose of life is to reproduce life. Those norms have been undermined and we are left with a deformed culture that deters rather than encourages reproduction. The instinct itself is encouraged but its purpose is discouraged and the genes of those susceptible to such cultural conditioning are lost. This weeding-out process is in the short-term like a plague but perhaps it is natural selection strengthening the community by purging its gene pool of damaging behavioural characteristics.

Some people choose, for one reason or another, not to have offspring, as is their unquestioned right. Others want children but are unfortunately not able to have them. Some spend their genetic inheritance on having *a good time* or pursuing a career. That is their unquestioned right but many of them regret it when they view their life from childless later-years. It is common to have a change of heart when

350

the attractions of self-indulgence wane but by then it is often too late. After many years of a me-me life it becomes difficult to get out of a comfortable routine and summon the energy that child rearing demands. Even by the age of 30, people have become set in their ways and are unable to change. Meanwhile, others have been getting on with the necessities of life and passed on physical and behavioural characteristics to the next generation. They have become complete adult people and survived the test of natural selection, which grinds on regardless of personal circumstances or ideological fashion.

Children demand a price in terms of wealth and freedom but there are many rewards, not the least of these being the personal satisfaction gained from creating and shaping another life. The experience also changes many of one's perceptions and attitudes, and is an essential stage in becoming a complete adult person. In addition, there is the comfort to be had when we are eventually compelled to face our own mortality, that part of us will live on. The older one gets the more apparent it becomes that liberal dogmatists greatly under-rate the benefits and satisfaction of family life.

3. A Communal Life

Only a few can attain great fame and some do not leave offspring but all become part of their national community simply by living as part of it. We can all in various ways help to nourish and preserve our community. It is for all of us to play our part by taking what is passed to us, adding to it, and in turn passing it on. It is sometimes those without children who do the most to actively further communal interests.

An important part of family and a wider communal life is to keep alive the memory of those who have gone before. In doing so we bind individual threads into the communal thread. Our community becomes part of our identity and we become part of its identity. It helps mould us and we help mould it. A community is a living and evolving memorial to those who have helped sustain and nurture it.

Community and Communication

An early way of illustrating the link between community and communication was to measure the flow of mail between the member states of the Postal Union. The flows can be shown as lines joining the main mail distribution centres. Web-like patterns of communication are revealed with the thickness of the lines reflecting the volume of mail traffic. The web image is a better one than that of the *friendship tree* because it reveals connected clusters of communication flow. If it were possible to refine the system, it would reveal in graphic form that the English have a high level of mail exchange with other Anglo-Saxons in Australia, New Zealand and North America. Pakistanis and Bengalis living in England have a high level of mail exchange with Pakistan and Bangladesh, Italians with Italy, Somalis with Somalia. The flow within states of personal post and other forms of communication similarly indicate the threads of communal webs. Areas with few links to a particular web might reveal low population density or places occupied by people belonging to a different community. There are many gaps in the English postal web indicating areas of foreign settlement. The communities in those districts are part of other webs having strong ties with places such as India, Ireland and the West Indies. As the English population of London continues its rapid decline, so the city becomes a smaller part of the English communal web.

In addition to mail, there are of course other forms of personal communication, including face-to-face conversation (which usually involves travel), email, and telephone calls. The threads and webs produced by these flows produce broadly similar webs. When many strands of the webs run together, they form strong cords. The more communication there is the easier it becomes and the more it is encouraged. Electronic communication can become *real* face-to-face communication through the increased demand and supply of cheap and easy transport.

Communal webs are flexible, strong and enduring. UK subjects/citizens may be deemed to be citizens of the European Union and the governing elite may want them to feel and act as if they are part of a European community but communication webs indicate otherwise. There is a trade web reaching out from the UK that has a high density of links with EU states, but there are also substantial trade links with North America. The strongest threads in the web of English communication are undoubtedly personal links with other Anglo-Saxons. It seems reasonable to suppose that most English people feel more comfortable with, and have greater empathy for, fellow Anglo-Saxons, wherever they might be in the world, than they do for, say, Greeks or Spaniards, wherever they may live. In other words, personal communication webs offer a better indication of real communities and loyalties than do either trade webs or geographical location.

The apparent disadvantages that foreign communities face in being immersed in an alien cultural environment actually helps bind them together, preserve their communal boundaries, and give them tight lines of internal communication. As outsiders they are able to see the host community in a way that insiders cannot and that enables them to recognise and seize opportunities for furthering their individual and communal interests. The political culture in the UK encourages non-European ethnic groups to adopt a racial identity, join a racial bloc, and pursue a racial political agenda. In other words, it encourages them to politicise race and use it as a political weapon. Race is the glue that holds a diverse alliance together and gives each small part the power of the whole. For instance, if organisations representing the interest of Nigerians living in the UK want to win a concession from the UK government, they have an incentive to couch their demand in terms of racial discrimination and the need to overcome it. That immediately puts them at an advantage because those to whom they make the demands wish at all costs to avoid the charge of racism. They believe that if they offend one part of a racial bloc they offend all parts.

Foreign communities benefit in many ways from being outsiders. They enjoy a high degree of internal face-to-face communication; a greater sense of communal identity and solidarity; a lack of any pressure or obligation for them to share their institutions and formal means of communication with those outside their community. These factors enable them to avoid many of the weakening effects of multi-culturalism. They are able to own and control their own institutions. Many have newspapers, journals, radio and television stations that are devoted exclusively to the needs of their community. They are able to enjoy privacy because unlike the host community they do not have to accommodate the views and interests of outsiders. Many of them also benefit from conducting their communal business in a language other than English. While enjoying those advantages, some members of some communities are able to infiltrate, manage and control the communications networks of the host community, which is made to bear the burden of representing Britishness and the diversity of a multi-cultural society.

The lack of an exclusively English network of media institutions denies the English communal privacy and hinders internal communication. It makes it difficult for the English to discuss the many matters that are of special concern to them, and to agree and pursue their communal interests. This handicap is made worse by the failure of the British state to recognise the English as a community with interests of its own. Discrimination is evident in the failure to recognise the English as an ethnic group in the gathering and presentation of official statistics, e.g. ethnic monitoring and census returns. Social-liberals not only ignore the English community but are scornful of the suggestion that it exists. They use arguments that in a roundabout way suggest that there is insufficient racial and cultural purity for the existence of an English ethnicity. Such arguments are not used against *minority* nations because they would rightly be condemned as insulting. So we have a situation where liberals refuse to recognise the English as a community but are prepared to accept that there is, for example, a Bangladeshi community in England that has interests, boundaries and a cultural identity. As a result of these discriminatory attitudes, and the policies they spawn, the English community is weakened to the point of being made defenceless and officially invisible in its own homeland.

This calculated policy deprives the English of an official right to participate in ethnic politics and thereby pursue their communal interests on an equal footing with other communities. While the English are treated like unwelcome ghosts that need to be exorcised, foreign communities are encouraged to be visible, to treat the place as their own and to create institutions for the purpose of furthering communal interests. Such institutions are often funded by the state but are otherwise independent and able to do as they see fit. Some are representative of only the half-dozen people running them but together they form a network that gives them strength and helps them to negotiate with and make demands of the state. Instances of this are campaigns for the state to provide services specifically for particular *ethnic* groups, such as sports and cultural centres, or separate accommodation and services for their elderly. It is inconceivable that state or local authority grants would be made available to fund a project that specifically served the English community.

As we have seen earlier, divided loyalties and interests within multi-nation states do not bode well for those societies because they become a battleground where competing communities strive to advance their interests and the governing elite becomes concerned with *buying off* communities in return for their electoral support. In England, those who suffer most as a result of this trading process are members of the English community whose institutions are weakened, undermined, made ineffective and sometimes destroyed by the policy of recruiting many of the institutions' managers and staff from foreign communities. The English have had their formal institutions, including those involved in public communication, taken from them and made to reflect and represent the interests of a multi-nation, multi-racial and multi-cultural British society. As a result, there are no institutions through which the English can communicate and organise as a politicised community. There is no means of effectively promoting the internal cohesion of the English community and representing its interests to the British government. This is an area where the English need to create and control new institutions, and fight for their interests in the same way that others do.

Life, Consciousness, Thought

According to the best information currently available and the best theory that incorporates it, the universe started about 15 billion years ago with a *big bang* which spewed out an expanding ball of energy and matter from what had been *the singularity*, the egg from which the universe hatched.[204] With the passing of time, the content and structure of the universe became increasingly varied and complex. From the matter came galaxies consisting of billions of stars, which processed simple elements like hydrogen into new substances of greater atomic complexity. In this way, it can be said that matter has evolved.

A big bang of a different kind occurred when a mix of chemicals in a sterile environment produced simple living things. Natural selection began its work and life became increasingly complex until a new level of evolutionary development gave rise to consciousness, self-consciousness, intelligence, thought and ideas.

---

[204] It is possible that the physical universe of which we are aware is but a small part of a much larger web of matter, energy and understanding about which we know nothing. The web of webs might be one where there is an overall balance between order and chaos with big bangs being common local occurrence. Perhaps 'the singularity' should be renamed 'a singularity'.

One of the stages in the evolution from energy and matter to abstract thought was the occurrence of communities – life forms co-operating for their common good.

Each new dimension of existence had its origins in the last and provided a new platform from which yet another layer of complexity could grow. Each layer is more wondrous than the last. From the non-living came the living, from the single came the communal, and from the concrete came the abstract. What will be the next stage that evolution gives birth to? Will it be the creation of man-made *artificial life* with intelligence and understanding beyond our comprehension?

Hardwiring and Softwiring: Evolutionary Psychology

For very many years there has been an often heated debate between those who believe that human behaviour is in the main determined by instincts, and those who believe it is determined by upbringing; in other words, *nature* versus *nurture*. This is similar to the determinism versus free will dispute. Are we merely acting out a script over which we have no control or are we able to make meaningful choices that affect the direction our lives take? The debate, which usually takes a polarised ideological either/or form, has recently focused on genes, the human brain, and the extent to which human behaviour and perceptions are determined by our evolutionary history. The discipline that deals with the evolution of behaviour is called, evolutionary psychology.

While many accept that our bodies are shaped by our genes, some are unwilling to accept that the brain is an organ that has been, and continues to be, shaped by natural selection. Our brain is pre-programmed (hardwired) with layers of survival strategies drawn from evolutionary experiences but it also has the ability to programme itself (soft-wiring) for the purpose of adapting to current conditions. This softwiring takes two forms. First, our brains are continually making connections and forming pathways in response to the input of information/experiences. Thus, each brain is unique in that it has been moulded by personal circumstances. Second, we have intelligence, which is an ability to organise information and solve problems. Each of us has a greater aptitude for solving some types of problems than others. Humans therefore have the ability to learn and make use of that learning for the purpose of adapting to their immediate environment. In other words, softwiring makes us more adaptable and our survival more likely, provided we use intelligence wisely.

Because softwiring is passed from generation to generation, it can be said to be hardwired into the brain. To put it another way, softwiring has been shown to offer humans an evolutionary advantage and, as a result, a softwiring capability has been hardwired into the human brain. An important point to grasp here is that evolution has produced a brain in which hard and soft wiring complement one another. They work together to further long-term and short-term interests. An imbalance in favour of softwiring encourages the pursuit of short-term interests to the detriment of long-term interests; which is a road to extinction. Too little softwiring reduces the ability of individuals and species to adapt to a rapidly changing environment, which is also a handicap. With an increasing ability to mould our cultural and physical environment comes the danger of pursuing short-term interests and failing to recognise long-term interests. This danger presents itself in the form of ideologues who try to suppress hardwired instincts for the purpose of achieving ideological goals.

The nature/nurture debate often focuses on the relative importance of the hard and soft wiring and the extent to which we are bound by our evolutionary history. There are, for example, some who believe that genes determine everything (the reductionism of the selfish gene) while others favour the view that we can, and should, free ourselves from the tyranny of hardwired instincts. The positions taken usually have more to do with political ideology than any understanding of the complex relationship between the many variables involved in their experiment. Those who think that social engineering and conditioning can overcome instincts, almost always underrate the sophistication of instinctive behaviour, and overrate the ability of social conditioning to suppress it.

Is it wise to suppress what we instinctively feel to be right in favour of what is ideologically correct? Probably not, yet we are being led by liberal ideologues who are unable to distinguish between what is possible and what is desirable. All would be well if they were marching alone to their extinction but they are taking our communities and cultures with them.

Culture: a Survival Strategy

Culture is a mediator between the instincts and interests of the individual, and the instincts and interests of the community to which they belong. Both individuals and communities are organisms; both have hard and soft wiring that enables them to adjust to their environment, and each is part of the environment of the other.

Cultures evolve. They become more complex and enable increasingly sophisticated forms of co-operation between individuals within a community. Cultures make it possible for the softwiring and hardwiring of individuals and their community to mesh together and run as one programme. The result is a mutually beneficial relationship.

Culture is shaped by the application of intelligence, and the test of natural selection. Most of the lessons that are learned and relearned generation after generation become hardwired into individual brains and the communal culture thus avoiding the need for each generation to make the same mistakes and learn the same hard-won lessons. It seems that it is not always an evolutionary advantage to pass on all lessons because it is apparent that each generation makes the same mistakes in personal relationships.

Communities are enveloped by and immersed in a culture that provides a framework for managing internal and external relationships. A successful culture provides insiders with a view of the outside world that enables them to survive as a community in a society of communities. It enables insiders to live by a set of rules that advances their common interests. Some of those rules are expressed in a formal moral code which promotes behaviour that is of benefit to the community, and discourages behaviour that is harmful.

Communal Morality and Law: Instinctive and Constructed Morality

If communities are to flourish, they need internal stability; insiders need to be able to co-operate and get along together with the minimum of misunderstanding and conflict. Natural selection has honed our individual and communal instincts so that we have a natural feel for what is fair and acceptable. It has also given us feelings of guilt and remorse that serve as a punishment and deterrent. The guiding rule is that we treat other members of our community as we would have them treat us. We therefore instinctively think it wrong for insiders to kill other insiders or steal from them or insult them or do any of many other things that cause conflict and ill feeling. This instinct, which can be called communal morality, is the root of *natural law* and *natural justice*. These notions reflect an individual and communal instinct for what is fair and reasonable; what is right and wrong. *Wrong* is what directly or indirectly harms us as individuals and as a community.

In traditional face-to-face communities wrongdoers are either punished within the community by various means indicating disapproval or they are driven out of the community or killed, which is a form of expulsion. These more drastic punishments are a form of communal natural selection in that those who are unsuited to communal living are expelled from it, thus making it difficult or impossible for them to have offspring within the community and pass on behavioural characteristics that are deemed damaging. The communal killing of murderers not only served as a punishment and deterrent but also as a means of removing from the breeding population those with a propensity to commit murder (unlawful killing).[205] This contrasts with the treatment accorded to those who, in times of war, are willing to risk their life and kill outsiders in defence of their community (lawful killing). This shows that there are different rules for insiders and outsiders.

Communal morality is, or should be, the foundation of formal conventions and laws. This additional codified law (*invented morality*) sets out guidelines for behaviour in situations where natural selection has not had the time or opportunity to produce appropriate instincts. Codified law often needs to be technically complex but the principles of communal morality can and should serve as a guide to the making of even the most sophisticated law codes. Any abandonment of the

---

[205] This is not meant to suggest that all or even most murderers have a genetic disposition to murder.

principles of natural law and natural justice have less to do with the difficulty of drawing an appropriate parallel as with a conflict between communal and elite interests. As governing elites rise above and become separate from the community, so the law they introduce tends to increasingly reflect their interests. Communal law is thus overlaid and submerged beneath a body of state law that is justified on ideological grounds and enforced by the state rather than the community. Even very powerful governing elites, including The *International Community*, feel the need to justify their deeds in terms of natural justice, hence their use of propaganda to create the illusion that their actions and goals are fair and reasonable. The problem for elites is that every now and then they pursue their interests in a way that stretches their justification so thin that a much larger number of people than usual are able to glimpse the elite's ugly nakedness. The illusion of selfless devotion to peace and goodwill is shattered.

An almost universal feature of recorded human history is that governing elites contain, and are sometimes dominated by, those who claim to know, either by personal revelation or the revelation of another, the will of a god or gods. The usual practice of these religious authorities is to claim a divine origin for communal morality, and to appoint themselves as its guardians. They also assume the right to interpret the divine will and on that basis they set about creating a body of *invented law*, which they mingle with the long-standing and accepted communal morality. Some of the additions are helpful to communal life and some are harmful. The helpful additions generally meet the needs of the community, and are based on principles drawn from and complementary to communal morality. They encourage behaviour and forms of organisation that reduce conflict within the community and promote the orderly, sufficient and sustained reproduction of the population. Such laws tend to be much the same throughout the world and are primarily concerned with: regulating sexual relationships; protecting the family unit and its individual members; establishing property rights; resolving disputes; enabling the victims of wrongdoing to be compensated by the wrongdoer; defending communal boundaries. Harmful invented laws have the opposite effect and are usually designed to either further elite interests or meet the requirements of a religious doctrine.

If the theology is stripped away, religions can be seen to be offering rules for the working of a community. Mullahs, Christian priests, Rabbis, Hindu holy men and all the rest have very much in common in that they seek peaceful, well-ordered, sustainable communities. They are what might be called *communal traditionalists*, which is what most nationalists are, whatever their religion or none.

Natural Law and Natural Justice

Natural law and *natural justice* are concepts that do not need to be taught; they are instinctive and at the heart of communal law. As law codes become more involved in the regulation of matters that are remote from the concerns of traditional communities, so the concepts of natural law and natural justice assume less importance. Law becomes a device for imposing elite values and perceptions, and pursuing elite interests. The making, administration and enforcement of law become a top-down process in which the guiding principals of natural law and justice are replaced by technical rules and ideological truths. The more detached the rules and truths become from notions of natural law and justice, the more determined the elite becomes to exclude the influence of communal (public) opinion. When those who are subject to a body of law do not regard it as fair, compliance is only likely to be gained by heavy policing and/or stiff penalties. Both of those things are expensive in financial terms, in wasted resources and a diminished quality of life.

There is little need to promote natural law within a traditional community because it is seen to serve the interests of all. Those who observe it gain good standing in the community while lawbreakers are known to all and suffer the penalty of bringing shame on themselves and their family. A good name brings advantages in a community; a bad name can make life far more difficult than it would otherwise be. Natural morality is more readily observed; natural law is more easily enforced and natural justice is more cheaply administered than are the *artificial* variants.

Communal law serves the interests of the community, and the community accepts and enforces it. Elite law serves elite interests and is enforced by agents of the governing elite.

Early English (pre-Norman) law was for the most part communal or common law. It was not perfect, none is, but it attempted to give expression to communal morality, natural law and natural justice. The people had confidence in the courts and a system of justice in which they took an active part. It was the king's duty to ensure that the system was properly administered and judgements enforced. An incentive to performing that duty was that part of the compensation paid by the offender went to the King. Another consideration was that the provision of cheap, reliable and accessible justice promoted confidence in the king and a greater willingness of the people, when necessary, to make sacrifices for the communal wellbeing.

The arrival of Christianity brought with it a centralised form of administration and the bureaucrats to run it. The Church recognised the king as God's earthly ruler and in return the king granted the Church land and freedom from the communal duties attached to it. The Church became very rich and powerful and kings no longer needed the approval of those they governed; they ruled because God rather than the people ordained it. The king's first loyalties were to God and the Church, thus the relationship between king and people was changed. He became the shepherd and they his flock.

359

The English did not rush out to be baptised into a new religion and culture. This was not because they were necessarily devoted followers of the old religion and its gods. The more likely reason was that the old religion was an expression of their communal values and culture; it was a backdrop to their way of life with which they felt comfortable. It provided a cultural framework for a scattered people with common origins. The old religion was adaptable to local needs and preferences because it was not uniform in belief or practice. In other words, it was not seen as a universal creed. It had natural boundaries and there was no imperative to go out and covert outsiders who had their own beliefs and way of life.

Unlike the old religion, the new religion did not spring from within the community but was divorced from it and imposed from above. Although Christianity rests on the foundations of an exclusive communal religion, it has no communal bounds. The imperative is to go out and convert others, and it was for that purpose Augustine was sent to England.

Christian sources report, as they were bound to, seemingly enthusiastic mass conversions of the English to Christianity. In some places there may have been mass baptisms but they probably took place on the instruction of members of a governing elite who saw a political advantage in being allied with the Church in Rome.

The ordinary English folk cannot be said to have enthusiastically embraced Christianity, they had it thrust upon them. The traditional law codes, which contained communal good sense, were modified and added to for the purpose of promoting and protecting the interests of the Church. Bans and punishments were introduced where none had existed before, most of them relating to communal religious and cultural practices. The gods of the English were condemned as devils and those who worshipped them became devil worshippers. The justification given by supporters of the new religion for attacking and seeking to destroy a way of life was, and is, that the bringers of the new universal religion had right on their side. They were the bearers of an eternal universal truth that would bring all nations enlightenment and salvation, whether they wanted it not. It all looks very relevant to today's ideological cleansing.

The view that the end justifies the means has been evident among empire builders in many parts for the world before and since. The bringers of universal creeds often suppress the communal identity and wreck the culture of those they claim to be saving. They first convert governing elites and though them set about creating societies that accord with the universal ideology. In modern times as in old, unbelievers are portrayed as devil worshippers. Condemnation and punishment serves as a warning to others who might dare resist. Rarely do the bringers of the new religion or ideology feel bound by the morality they vigorously impose on others. Theirs is a form of communal law that has different rules for insiders and outsiders. Hence the apparently absolute law, *though shall not kill* means in practice though shall not kill a fellow insider. It is often not only deemed acceptable to kill an outsider but a duty to do so, e.g. witches, heretics, the infidel.

Extracts from some of the early English law codes are reproduced below to provide an insight into the customs and superstitions of the early English and show how lawmakers are able to punish beliefs and actions that were formerly considered normal. Things can be made illegal and punishable not because they infringe natural justice or natural morality but because they are ideologically or theologically incorrect.

The Punishments section can be safely skipped over if it is of little interest.

Punishments for heathens and others
who turn from the Church of God. (c.690)

1. The Apostle says: 'Those who serve idols will not possess the kingdom of God.' Anyone who makes minor sacrifices to demons will do penance for one year; and for major sacrifices ten years.

2. If anyone, in ignorance, eats or drinks by a heathen shrine they are to promise never to do so again and to do forty days penance on bread and water. If it is deliberately done again, that is after a priest has declared that it is a sacrilege and the place a table of demons, the offender shall do penance on bread and water for thrice forty days. But if it is done to glorify the idol the penance shall be for three years.

3. If anyone sacrifices to demons for a second or third time they are to incur three years penance; then two years without any offering of communion. In the third five years, at the end of a five-year period the offender is capable of perfection.

4. Anyone who eats what has been sacrificed to idols and was under no compulsion to do so is to fast for twelve weeks on bread and water; if it was done of necessity they are to fast for six weeks.

5. Anyone who feasts in the abominable places of the heathen by taking and eating their food there, should be subject to penance for two years, and be offered on probation for full two years, and after that be accepted to perfection; when offered, test the spirit and discuss the life of each individual.

6. If any do sacrilege, that is summon diviners who practice divination by birds, or any divination with evil intent, let them do penance for three years, one of which is to be on bread and water.

7. Christians are not allowed to leave the Church of God and go to divination, or name angels or make assemblies which are known to be forbidden. If any be found following this occult idolatry, in that they abandon our Lord Jesus Christ, the Son of God, and gave themselves to idolatry . . .

8. Clerks or laymen are not permitted to be sorcerers or enchanters, or to make amulets which are proved to be fetters for their souls; those who act thus are to be driven from the Church.

9. Those who injure a person by black magic are to do penance for seven years, three of these on bread and water.

10. If any use love potions but hurt nobody; if he is a layman he is to do penance for half a year; if he is a clerk one year on bread and water; if he is a subdeacon he is to do penance for two years, one year of which is to be on bread and water; if he is a deacon, four years penance with two on bread and water; if he is a priest, five years with three on bread and water. If however by this means a woman is deceived about bringing forth, then he is to do a further three years penance on bread and water, lest he be accused of being a party to murder.

11. If any seek diviners whom they call prophets, or do any divinations, in that this is also diabolical, let them do penance for five years, three of these on bread and water.

12. If anyone takes lots, which are called contrary to the principals of the Saints, or takes any lots at all, or takes lots with evil intent, or makes divinations, let them do penance for three years, one of these on bread and water.

13. If any woman does divinations or diabolical incantations, let her do penance for one year, or thrice forty days, or forty days, according to the enormity of the crime of the penitent.

14. If any woman places her son or daughter on the roof for the sake of a cure or in an oven, let her do penance for seven years.

15. If any burn grain where a man has died for the sake of the living or of the house, let him do penance for five years on bread and water.

16. If any for the health of his young son should pass through a fissure in the ground and should close it after him with thorns, let him do penance for forty days on bread and water.

17. If any seek out divinations and pursue them in the manner of the heathen, or introduce men into their house for the purpose of finding something out by the evil arts or to make an expiation, let them be cast out if they be of the clergy; but if they are secular let them, after confession, be subject to five years penance, according to the rules ordained of old.

18. If any make or perform a vow at trees, or springs, or stones, or boundaries, or anywhere other than in the house of God, let him do penance for three years on bread and water. This is sacrilege or demonic. If any eat or drink there let him do penance for one year on bread and water.

19. If any go at the New Year as a young stag or cow, that is if he shares the habit of wild beasts and is dressed in the skins of cattle and puts on the heads of beasts, any who thus transform themselves into the likeness of beasts are to do three years penance.

20. Anyone who is an astrologer, that is someone who changes the mind of a man by invoking demons, is to do five years penance, one on bread and water.

21. Anyone who is a sender of storm, that is evil-doing, is to do seven years penance, three on bread and water.

22. Anyone who makes amulets, which is detestable, should do three years penance, one on bread and water.

23. Anyone who makes a habit of auguries and divinations is to do five years penance.

24. Anyone who observes soothsayers, or witchcrafts and devilish amulets and dreams and herbs, or who on the fifth day honours Jove [Thunor on Thursday] as do the heathen, is to do penance for five years if a clerk and three years if a layman.

25. Anyone who, when the moon is eclipsed, calls to her and practices witchcrafts to defend her in a sacrilegious manner, are to do penance for five years

26. Anyone who, in honour of the moon, goes hungry to bring about healing is to do penance for one year.

The Laws of Edward and Guthrum

OF WITCHES, DIVINERS, OATH-BREAKERS, &c.

1. If witches or diviners, oath-breakers or those who work secretly to destroy life, or foul, defiled, notorious adulteresses, be found anywhere within the land; let them be driven from the country and the people cleansed, or let them totally perish within the country, unless they desist, and very deeply atone.

The Laws of King Æthelstan (924–939)

OF WITCH-CRAFTS

4. And we have ordained respecting witchcrafts, and the giving of secret potions, and destruction-deeds: if any one should be thereby killed, and he who practised them could not deny it, that he be liable to his life. But if he will deny it, and at the threefold ordeal shall be guilty; that he be 120 days in prison: and after that let his kindred take him out, and give to the king 120 shillings, and pay compensation to the victims kindred, and stand surety for the murderer, that he evermore desist from the like.

The Laws of King Edmund (939–946)

OF OATH-BREAKERS AND SPELLWORKERS

5. Those who break oaths and work spells and make secret potions, let them be for ever cast out from all communion with God, unless they turn to right repentance.

Canons enacted under King Edgar (959–975)

16. And we enjoin, that every priest zealously promote Christianity, and totally extinguish every heathenism; and forbid well-worshipping, and spiritualism, and divinations, and enchantments, and idol-worshipping, and the vain practices which are carried on with various spells, and with peace-enclosures, and with elders, and also with various other trees, and with stones, and with many various delusions, with which men do much of what they should not.

18. And we enjoin, that on feast-days heathen songs and devil's games be abstained from.

The Laws of King Ethelred (978–1008)

6. And moreover we will beseech every friend, and all people who also diligently teach, that they, with inward heart, love one God, and carefully shun every heathenism.

7. And if witches or soothsayers, spellworkers or whores, or those who work secretly to destroy life or oathbreakers, be anywhere found in the country, let them diligently be driven out of this country, and this people be purified: or let them totally perish in the country, unless they desist, and the more deeply make atonement.

6. And it is the ordinance of the witan, that Christian men, and uncondemned persons, be not sold out of the country, at least not into a heathen nation; but let it be carefully guarded against, that those souls be not made to perish that Christ has brought with his own blood.

The Laws of King Cnut (1020–1023)

OF HEATHENISM

1. And we earnestly forbid every heathenism: heathenism is that men worship idols; that is, they worship heathen gods, and the sun or the moon, fire or rivers, water-wells or stones, or forest tree of any kind; or love witchcraft, or promote death-work in any wise; or by sacrifice, or by divination; or perform any thing pertaining to such illusions.

Laws for Northumbrian Priests (1020–1023)

47. We are all to worship and love one God, and zealously observe only Christianity, and every heathenship totally renounce.

48. If then anyone be found that shall henceforth practise any heathenship, either by sacrifice or by divination, or in any way love witchcraft, or worship idols, if he be a king's thane, let him pay 10 half-marks; half to Christ, half to the king.

54. If there be a peace-enclosure on any one's land, about a stone, or a tree, or a well, or any folly of such kind, then let him who made it pay a fine; half to Christ, half to the lord of the estate: and if the lord will not aid in levying the fine, then let Christ and the king have the compensation.

The codification of customary law tends to result in more importance being given to the *letter of the law* than the spirit of natural justice that may have inspired it. The lawcode itself and the rituals surrounding it assume a greater importance amongst lawyers than the justice that they are meant to be putting into effect. *The Law* and its words and procedures come between natural justice and those seeking it. Lawyers, politicians, and others involved in making and applying the law come to believe that the law is for specialists and that public opinion has no part to play in its making or interpretation.

The principles that underlie early English communal law were much the same as those found elsewhere in the world. The first aim was to compensate victims and make offenders pay for their wrongdoing. The presumption was that the wronged party had a natural right of retribution against the offender if the remedy offered by the *justice system* did not satisfy the victim and communal notions of natural justice. It was therefore necessary to provide sufficient compensation to the victim and sufficient punishment to the offender for the wronged party and the community to feel that justice had been done and that the right of retribution could be foregone.

Communal courts were open to all. A local person of repute or an appointee of the king took charge of proceedings and ensured that justice was done according to traditional rules that were widely accepted to be fair. Parties to a dispute were able to represent themselves and it was not until the arrival of the Norman ruling class that English men and woman had to pay French-speaking lawyers to represent them in proceedings conducted in a language they could not understand. Placing lawyers between the people and justice was similar to placing priests between man and God.

In traditional communities, those who abide by communal customs and laws are rewarded with esteem, while offenders incur shame. Such a system depends upon there being widespread acceptance of common values and a low level of communal privacy. Communal knowledge of communal deeds, good and bad, is essential to the proper working of communal morality, law and justice.

The anonymity of large modern societies prevents the proper working of communal justice. The remedy is perhaps to be found in modern communications technology which can be used by democratic communal institutions to make widely known the deeds, identity, and whereabouts of those who break the rules of natural law and justice. This would stand in place of direct knowledge gained from communal courts and word of mouth. Public humiliation through public information would, in appropriate cases, act as a better deterrent and a cheaper punishment than a prison sentence.

Democracy

Democracy is not just a system of government but a collective decision-making process that is subject to natural justice. Democracy is an arrangement that enables the members of a community to express their views freely and, by one means or another, to participate in and shape their cultural, economic and political way of life. Democracy is therefore much more than the occasional opportunity to vote in elections.

A democratic system of government is as local as possible and guided by the principle that sovereignty lies with the people. Those who govern must be constantly reminded and regularly made to acknowledge that the sovereign powers they exercise are not theirs to use or dispose of as they wish. They hold sovereign powers in trust from the people for the purpose of putting into effect the will of the people. The institutions of a democracy must give practical and formal recognition to that fact. Those who rule are the servants of the people and should not presume to have the right to instruct the people as to what they can and cannot discuss or demand.

A democratic form of government is one in which *the people* pool certain of their sovereign powers and elect an authority to exercise those powers on their behalf for the greater good of *the people* as individuals and as a community. It is for *the people* to collectively determine how and for what purpose their sovereign powers are exercised. It is for those who govern to consult *the people* and not presume the right to use the institutions of government to compel *the people* to do as the governors wish.

Selection procedures for democratic elections are subject to natural justice and include the right of all insiders, subject to minimal commonsense rules, to put themselves forward as candidates. All candidates should have an equal opportunity to make known their policies. If in practice it is necessary to be rich or have the support of those who are rich in order to be a successful candidate, the electoral procedure and the system of government is not democratic. Likewise, if it is necessary to acknowledge or denounce some dogma, in order to be a successful candidate or a candidate at all, the procedure is not a democratic one. It is for the people to decide the worth of the candidates.

Elite Democracy

Democracy is commonly said to be government by *the people*. In the USA it was long ago defined as government of the people, by the people, for the people. Some political systems and some governing elites take greater account of the wishes of *the people* than others but each frames democracy in a way that suits its interests. In the United Kingdom the electorate is considered sufficiently able to understand many complex issues for the purpose of electing a government every four or five years but between elections, individual issues are deemed far too complex for the public to grasp, unless of course it supports the government position. If the electorate fail to endorse particular government policies, it is deemed to be because they do not properly understand the issues and need to be educated. It is said that, *public opinion is not yet ready*. Which means that public opinion needs to be manipulated by whatever means possible until it is ready, and then the public is asked its opinion. The golden rule is to only ask a question when you know what the answer will be.

The great advantage to the governing elite of a manipulated referendum is that the public can be reminded that they made a *democratic choice*.

If it proves impossible to sway public opinion, we are told that some matters are far too important to be influenced by emotion and the unsophisticated, uninformed base instincts of the *mob*. The issues of capital punishment and immigration always fall in this category.

Another argument used to justify ignoring public opinion is that we live in a representative democracy. However, it is only representative in certain circumstances because MPs are not delegates and ultimately they are free to vote according to their conscience. In other words, MPs are not bound to represent the views of those who elected them.

The reality of liberal representative democracy is that if you are a liberal your views will be represented but if you are not your views will not be represented;

Representative democracy means a system where the elite initiates policies and pushes them forward and downward while public opinion is manipulated to accept and support what is being imposed on it. Democracy is deemed to prevail when a government puts into effect a manipulated public opinion. Michael Heseltine acknowledged this approach when he urged Prime Minister Blair to be better organised and to take a lead in preparing public opinion for the adoption of the Euro.[206]

Elite democracy involves the electorate being told what is good for it by an authority that assumes ownership of the people's sovereign powers. Any change

---

[206] House of Commons, February 1999

that comes about as the result of an election is marginal and more often a matter of style than substance. In the UK, that margin may become much greater and more meaningful if the very real crack in elite perception on the matter of the EU and a European currency gets wider. An election could actually determine something of great importance if the Conservative Party manages to withstand the vast resources deployed by those who are set on convincing the UK electorate that life outside the Euro zone and, worse still, outside the EU is an impossible fantasy. Key propaganda words and phrases are: – economic ruin; Little Englanders; need to be at the heart of Europe; must not get left behind; realities of the global economy; a Britain for the new millennium.

If any British government was to seek a more distant UK relationship with the EU, it is certain that the response from the EU Commission and member states would be fierce. Political and economic events would be manipulated to cause a crisis for the government and frighten it and the electorate back into the fold. If this can properly be called democracy, it is top-down democracy, which is a contradiction in terms.

A necessary condition of representative democracy is ideological diversity within the political system and the institutions of the state. In a totalitarian state, all institutions of the state and all who control them, are loyal to the state ideology. Liberals are near to achieving this goal in the UK. The educational and broadcasting institutions have for many years been completely dominated by liberals who use their power and influence to promote liberal dogma. That control has spread through almost the whole system and a mopping-up operation is now underway in which the armed forces and the police are being purged of anyone who resists. Is there, for example, a serving Chief Constable or Army General who is willing to express opposition to liberal dogma? Which of them does not repent of the sins of their organisations and declare not only their heartfelt support for liberal dogma but also their determination to impose it and root out those who resist? This is state-sponsored ideological cleansing on a grand scale. The most amazing thing about the brazen and ruthless imposition of ideological conformity is that it has been brought about in the name of freedom and democracy.

Communal Democracy

We may owe the name to the Greeks but they did not invent democracy. Democracy springs from community and thrives where individuals share certain common values, perceptions and interests. Democracy needs a cultural, political and economic environment in which individuals feel sufficiently secure and confident to willingly forego certain of their freedoms for the greater communal good. It requires a *we* sentiment and the trust that springs from sharing a common identity. Democracy gives expression to natural morality, natural justice, and natural law.

A community that is able to make its own laws and enforce them will, in all but exceptional circumstances, only lend those powers to fellow insiders. The reason is simply that fellow insiders are more likely than outsiders to be in tune with communal norms and can be better trusted to pursue communal interests. A community governed by outsiders and subject to the laws and policing of outsiders cannot be said to be a flourishing democracy or to be free. Such a situation is bound to create resentment and lead to rebellion. It is natural for a community to want to govern itself and it is a community's right to do so.

Communal institutions and democratic procedures should encourage popular participation in decision-making and ensure that those who are lent sovereign powers remain accountable to the community and its wishes. This means that they should listen to and do their best to put into effect what the community/electorate wants. In order to maintain that relationship it is prudent to ensure that those who lend their sovereignty are always collectively more powerful than those who borrow it. That power should be embedded in the constitution and be backed by practical measures for enforcing it. In some places it might be appropriate and practicable to ensure that *the people* are able to resist by force of arms the imposition on them of laws, cultural norms, and economic policies of which they disapproved. This is bottom-up democracy, truly government of the people, by the people, for the people.

The underlying grievance that unites most of the militia groups in the USA is that the Federal government has much more power, including armed force, than the people, and uses it to prevent *the people* from exercising their sovereign powers. The governing elite behaves as if it is sovereign and has the right to control the cultural, economic and political environment of *the people*. The aim of the militias is to weaken central government and decentralise power. They want more democracy not less but, as might be expected, they are portrayed as fools and cranks by those who favour centralisation. Some members of some militias open the whole movement to ridicule, and liberals are not slow to identify those people and publicise their views. In reality, the majority of those resisting *big government* are motivated by a genuine concern that they are losing control of their own lives and being made to live in an ugly society of which they want no part.

The principles and customs of communal democracy and natural justice are intertwined and readily acceptable to the vast majority of people because for much of human history they have provided the framework for free self-governing communities. The development of kingdoms and modern states brought with it the manipulation of communal sentiments to serve elite interests. States claimed as of right the power to exercise sovereign powers and demanded of their citizens the loyalty they naturally had for their community. In the society of states it became widely accepted that states have the right to defend their borders, population and system of government. States also deem that they have the right to call on their citizens to fight in defence of the state. For the most part, only citizens (insiders)

369

of a given state have the right to vote in elections, stand for office, make laws and enforce them. A crude model of communal loyalties and obligations is now being used to gain acceptance of and support for globalism and the further distancing of sovereign powers from they people to whom they belong. Decisions that effect individuals, communities and states are being taken by:

- distant corporations that are concerned only with money and markets;

- remote undemocratic organisations such as the EU Commission, World Bank, International Monetary Fund, World Trade Organisation and, if it eventually gets off the ground, the Multilateral Agreement on Investment (MAI).

The corporations are principally concerned with money and markets, while the other organisations are principally concerned with maintaining a broad economic and political environment that favours a liberal global society.

The problem for the Global Elite is that there is a limit to how far communal customs and loyalties can be stretched to suit the needs of their empire. More and more people will see that liberal representative democracy is nothing of the sort, and that they have little if any control over their lives, which are increasingly structured around the needs of those who control the global means of production and distribution. As the truth dawns, so the sentiments expressed by the US militias will become more widespread. The instinct for natural justice and communal democracy will reassert itself and serve as a guide for those who want to take back their sovereign powers and regain control of their lives.

Communal survival instincts come to the fore when a community is in a desperate struggle for survival. As with other living things, non-essential functions are shut down and resources are channelled into vital life-support systems. Many democratic procedures are suspended and emphasis is placed on internal unity. Communal interests are placed above concern for the interests of outsiders. A recent example is that of Fijians who found that they were becoming or had become a minority in their own country because the Indian settler population had grown more quickly than their own. A few years ago, the *CIA Fact Book* gave an estimated population for Fiji of 800,000, 51% of which were Fijians, 44% Indians, 5% Chinese and others. Estimates for the year 2000 give a population of 832,000, 49% Fijians, 46% Indians, 5% Chinese and others. Thus, Fijians form less than half of the population of Fiji, and in a few years, on present trends, they will be outnumbered by Indians. Fijians are naturally concerned at the prospect of being governed by outsiders, and being subject to the values and interests of those outsiders.

In October 1987, the government of Fiji, which was nominally led by a Fijian but controlled by members of the Indian community, was overthrown by a group of

Fijians. In 1990 a new constitution was introduced which guaranteed the political dominance of Fijians. Due to external pressure, principally from the Commonwealth, that constitution was amended to provide for a multiracial cabinet and a division of parliamentary seats (consociationalism) that made coalition government almost inevitable. The new constitution was approved in 1997 and came into effect in 1998. The General Election of May 1999 produced an Indian Prime Minister, Mahendra Chaudhry. The following May, Fijians led by George Speight rebelled. They were much criticised by Western liberals who thought the democratic institutions of the state and the principle of majority rule were of greater importance than the right of a nation to preserve control of its homeland and govern itself.[207] Nationalists around the world found the action understandable and natural, and saw that it accorded with the principles of natural justice and the belief that national communities have the right to govern themselves in their homeland. Why should Fijians hand their sovereign powers to foreigners?

If liberal states are deemed to have the right to defend themselves as they see fit, and suspend democracy in the name of self-defence, which is what they do in time of war, by what reasoning do they deny those rights to nations? No nation is obliged to put liberal notions of democracy and majority rule above its right to defend itself and survive.

Despite their proclaimed enthusiasm for a concept of democracy based on majority rule, liberals are strangely reluctant to apply that principle to their ideal of world government. The world government they seek is not founded on democracy and diversity but on the absorption of the whole world into their centralised, undemocratic, one-ideology Empire. When liberals find themselves in a minority, or their fundamental interests are threatened, they are no happier than any other group to submit to majority rule. If they really believed in majority rule they would advocate that the UN be run on those lines and would be willing to accept the will of a multi-cultural UN General Assembly. If liberals are unwilling to be bound by the principles of their own ideology why should anyone freely submit to them.

Various forms of democracy have existed in many different places and at different times. Democracy is not an invention of liberals and neither are parliaments. The early Greek democrats were not liberals.

When the Liberal Age passes, the parliamentary form of democracy will not necessarily pass with it. Hopefully it will become more democratic.

---

[207] It was particularly irksome that members of the New Zealand and Australian governments felt entitled to instruct Fijians as to how they should behave. Maoris and Australian Aborigines had a different view of the matter and sympathised with the Fijians.

Demagogue

A demagogue is a leader of the people; a popular political leader or speaker; a leader who gives voice to the concerns of the people. Governing elites are none too keen on demagogues and as a result the term tends to be used in a pejorative fashion and has taken on the meaning of a leader who appeals to the prejudices and passions of the mob. That the people are thought of as a mob when they challenge the values and perceptions of the governing elite gives an inkling of the contempt in which they are held by that elite.

Populist

A popularist trusts the commonsense political judgements of the people and believes that governments should take account of public opinion, and that the people should play an active part in governing themselves. Despite its democratic connotations, the term *popularist* is used as a term of abuse in much the same way as *demagogue*. Those politicians who use every trick in the book to override the democratic and communal instincts of those they govern, do not look favourably on the idea of asking people what they want instead of telling them what they must have.

Theory and Practice

Recap of Theory

Natural selection is a process that brings order to chaos but in so doing it creates complex systems and relationships that have within them new levels of chaos. From matter evolved life, consciousness, self-awareness, and thought. Other products of evolution include communities and the complementary behavioural/psychological instincts that enable communities to exist.

Communities are living things that are subject to natural selection, and as a result they instinctively behave and organise in a way that has been shown to enable them to survive. Communal culture also plays a part in shaping communities, and helps them generate, accumulate and pass on experiences and knowledge. Communities provide their members with a sense of security and trust that makes them willing to share knowledge and other valuable commodities. The exchange of information and ideas accelerates the rate of learning within a community and enables it to gain evolutionary advantages.[208]

Humans are instinctively communal beings. If we ask why and how humans first formed communities, we are starting in the wrong place. The ancestors of humans

---

[208] It has been found that young children playing together in groups develop their thinking and reasoning skills more quickly than those engaged in solitary play.

lived in communities and evolved communal skills that made the physical and mental evolution of humans possible. In other words, Homo sapiens came into existence as communal animals and community has always been part of their environment.

In addition to communalism, natural selection has produced self-awareness and an intelligence that makes it possible for our species to perceive problems, find solutions, and act on them. Humans are thus able to respond to stimuli in a way that is not solely determined by hardwired instinct. The ability to override some instincts in some circumstances is an opportunity provided by natural selection to shortcut the evolutionary process. Human intelligence can improve our ability to adapt and survive but it needs to be accompanied by caution and modesty because an apparently small and beneficial change in one place can produce a large and unexpected harmful change elsewhere. Cultures are tools for modifying *the natural state* but they are also part of *the natural state* in that they evolve by trial and error and are subject to the ruthless test of natural selection: mistakes are found out and punished. A way of life that does not take account of long-term survival will perish.

Men, Women and Children

Traditional communities work in harmony with instincts and build cultures around them. Liberal societies exploit gathering instincts while denying or suppressing the communal instincts that help restrain greed and maintain a balanced approach to life. The instincts of lust, consumption and pleasure-seeking are not ones to be ignored (life would be dull without them) but they need to be restrained and balanced by instincts for co-operation, natural justice and orderly behaviour. All of these instincts fit together within the wider instinct for individual and communal self-preservation.

An example of an attempt to suppress or ignore instincts that conflict with ideology is found in those extreme feminists who claim that the only unalterable difference between men and women is that of biological function and form.[209] All other differences are alleged to spring from male domination and socialisation.

Men and women have complementary characteristics that stem from a communal and biological division of labour. They have evolved the ability to perform specialised tasks and in doing so they have acquired complementary physical,

---

[209] This claim to *sameness* is often combined with contradictory supremacist tendencies. Some feminists are quick to point to activities where women perform better than men because they believe it suggests women are superior to men. For example, when it is shown that in the UK girls perform better than boys in school examinations it is treated as evidence that girls are more intelligent than boys but when boys perform better than girls in some other activity it is because girls are disadvantaged in some way. This *heads I win tails you lose* thinking is often used by those who adopt a *victim* approach to life.

behavioural and psychological characteristics. Women are better able than men to, among many other things, deal with several tasks at once. As might be expected they have aptitudes associated with caring and communication that include better language skills and the ability to empathise with others.[210] Women are communal peaceweavers.

Men have either never developed those kind of communal skills to the same level as women or have lost some of them in the process of gaining other aptitudes. A specialisation in hunting and building skills has resulted in men tending to be better than women at processing information about physical systems, and being generally better at the mental manipulation of three-dimensional images. These aptitudes are useful in, for example, engineering and architecture. Men also tend to have physical and psychological characteristics that are suited to fighting, not just individually but as a group. They tend to be more aggressive than women and more readily formed into orderly groups under a leader for the performance of dangerous tasks. It would be surprising if natural selection had not given men psychological dispositions and skills that matched their physical evolution and suited them to tasks so closely related to their primary communal role of providing food, shelter, and protection. War and hunting are communal activities requiring many similar skills. Both are dangerous activities and for that reason it is better that men undertake them. Women are more valuable to a community than men in that the communal birth-rate and communal survival are tied to the number of women of childbearing age.

Evolutionary specialisation does not mean that we should not attempt to modify *traditional* roles or refrain from encouraging some instincts and controlling others.[211] Nor does it mean accepting all cultural norms for all time; cultures evolve. We are moulded by our evolutionary history but we are not entirely bound by it. However, it is important that we try to understand our instincts and aptitudes before attempting to completely dismantle gender-related divisions of labour and open all tasks to competition. If we convince ourselves that men and women are equal and should be treated as such, we will be perplexed when one or the other is better able to succeed at particular tasks and activities because of an inherent physical or psychological advantage.

---

[210] Autism is a condition in which the *normal* balance between the world of the imagination and the real world is weighted towards the former. Autism affects language and social communication skills and can cause a person to be unfeeling for the plight of others. Men are much more susceptible to the condition than women. One explanation for this is that the internal communal disadvantages are the price paid for having people who are willing and able to fight ruthlessly in defence of their community.

[211] Traditional roles are not necessarily those ordained by natural selection. Some so-called traditional roles are specific to certain cultures and reflect cultural norms that have their roots in exploitation or privilege.

One of the most important areas in which the myth of equality has taken hold is that of sexual relationships. Men and women have different reproductive strategies and instinctively expect different things from sexual relationships. These differences are ignored by those who, in response to modern means of contraception and political fashion, promote sex as a recreational activity divorced from long-term relationships and reproduction. The obsession of social-liberals with sexual freedom has rightly been described as sexual incontinence. Their aim seems to be to free children as early as possible from parental guidance and encourage them to believe that community, be it family or nation, is a restraint on personal freedom. Fulfilment and happiness are not to be found in family and wider communal life but in consumption and image. They are being led to believe that they can be whatever they want to be; it is their right. Those who adopt this heavily-promoted view of life become sheep and are easily fleeced.

How do we correct the cultural imbalance between promoting what is easy in the short-term and what is necessary for long-term communal survival? It is not by trying to revert to cultural norms based on a distorted view of traditional roles and expectations. Instead, we must attempt to mould our culture and community in a way that meets the needs of the time while respecting our evolutionary experience. We need to bear in mind that whatever model we use, it must be able to withstand the examination of natural selection. Thus we need not necessarily be rigidly bound by traditional roles for men and women but should nonetheless make allowances for the fact that men and women have different skills and psychological dispositions that complement their different biological and communal functions. These factors need to be recognised and allowed for rather than being dismissed as things that can be overcome by social engineering. It may seem unfair that the onus is put on women to preserve communal life but they are at the heart of it. When women abandon their communal role many men tend to do the same. Liberals like to believe that their low-birth-rate societies are more accommodating of women and their interests but in reality they are cutthroat places where men's more aggressive and competitive instincts are freed from communal restraint. The more liberal a society becomes, the more aggressive, crude and sex-orientated it is likely to be. This can be seen in the low cultural horizons of the ever-growing number of lads and ladettes.

Marriage

Traditional communities and cultures are shaped by instincts for what is right and proper. Religions claim these instincts and customs as their own (God-given) and then add an invented morality which is sometimes helpful to communal life and sometimes harmful. Helpful moral codes serve the needs of a community by promoting behaviour and forms of organisation that reduce conflict within the community and promote the orderly, sufficient and sustained reproduction of the population and the communal way of life. Such codes tend to be much the same throughout the world and are primarily concerned with matters relating to the peaceful resolution of disputes; compensation for those wronged; punishment for those who harm others; and rewards for those who improve the lot of the community. Specific areas include sexual relationships, children and property. The thread that runs through the codes is a sense of what is fair and reasonable for the individual and the community. Marriage is one of the institutions that has been found to bring those things together within a formal framework. It gives formal recognition to the fact that the family and kinship are central to human communities, and links them with a body of law that has the purpose of maintaining an orderly and harmonious community. Marriage establishes who is responsible for the care and rearing of children, and it provides guidelines for property and other rights. A wedding ceremony is a public acceptance by both parties of their commitments, rights and duties.

In England, wedded couples have traditionally been seen as part of a self-sufficient family unit that is capable of, and responsible for, supporting its members, including children. It was, until recently, a custom that unmarried couples wed in the event of the woman becoming pregnant. This aimed to make the child part of a viable family unit and to remind everyone that they are responsibile for bringing up their children.

Instinct ensures the birth of children but the cultural invention called marriage, makes the circumstances that surround it more orderly and beneficial to the child and the community. This does not mean that things do not sometimes go wrong or that people do not make mistakes, but at least marriage provides a framework of rules and expectations for personal relationships and the care of children. It is an ideal to be aimed at because despite inconveniences and failures it has proved to be the best option available. Those who have experienced the breakdown of a marriage probably know better than most how important it is.

Individuals who live in traditional communities and keep to the rules but through misfortune fall on hard times generally receive sympathy and help. This comes first from their kin and then the wider community. Those who disregard communal rules are felt to deserve the *punishment* that befalls them. This sentiment carries through to modern times. For example, a young woman with insufficient means to support herself has *the right* to have a child but others have the right not to support her or the child. Likewise, a man has *the right* to father children but others have *the right* to demand that he care for his child.

Charity begins at home and it is for each community to care for its own. Charity is an expression of individual and communal self-interest, which is in effect a bargain or insurance policy – I help you when you need it, and you or another member of the community will help me when I need it. If parties to that bargain cheat, by taking unfair advantage of communal charity, they cause resentment and are punished in some way, perhaps by being excluded from the community. Worse still is the anger felt when outsiders, who by definition are not parties to the bargain, manage to benefit from the charity of a community to which they do not belong. Every community resents those who take but do not give.

Law and Enforcement

Some judges in the USA, such as Judge Ted Poe and Judge Whitfield, make use of shaming in the punishment of crime.[212] Simple measures like making those convicted of drunken driving stand by a busy road for several hours a day holding or wearing a sign that states, "I am a drunk driver. I am ashamed of what I did." Another example is to make a shoplifter stand outside a store with a sign, "I am a thief. I stole from this shop." When the alternative is six months in prison, shaming is usually the preferred option. It has the advantages that communal punishments usually have over imprisonment, it is far simpler, cheaper and more effective.

Other communal solutions include bringing the offender face-to-face with the victim, offering an acceptable apology and compensating the victim. Again, this is cheaper than prison and better than a fine that goes to the state rather than the victim.

Zero tolerance is another communal means of maintaining the habit of acceptable behaviour. It relies on every member of a community playing a part by, for example, tackling youngsters who test the limits of communal tolerance. The tweak of an offender's ear by a policeman and a word with his parents was often more effective than several *cautions*. Much of course depends on parents being ashamed when their children misbehave and accepting that others have the right to scold any child who breaks communal rules. Those parents who find this approach unacceptable could have the option of being personally liable for offences committed by their children and being punished in their place.

Curfews for children under sixteen years of age are one more innovation that has its origin in traditional communities and was revived in the US before being reintroduced to the UK. In England, innovation of this sort is usually met with expressions of concern for the civil liberties of offenders and the psychological damage done to them. This reaction is predictable because we have a very large number of people involved in caring for offenders who have both an ideological and economic vested interest in preserving and expanding the existing system. The solutions they offer are usually time-consuming, bureaucratic, costly and labour-intensive, e.g. counselling.

---

[212] Information from 1997

The simple communal ideas for maintaining order are mainly for use at the lower end of offending and are tempered by the underlying belief that everyone is subject to temptation and misjudgement. A first offence for a lesser crime should aim to compensate the victim and enable the offender to show genuine sorrow for their action and help them to avoid re-offending. Sympathy for those committing serious or second offences is much reduced and punishments more severe, although the aim is still to compensate the victims, or their kin. This approach is in keeping with the *three strikes and you are out* rule introduced in the US, a place usually considered by British liberals to have barbarian ideas on law and order. They find it hard to accept communal rules that start with the presumption that the offender is responsible for his deeds and must compensate those who suffer loss because of his misdeeds. The issue is simply did O do something improper that caused V loss? If so, O must compensate V. It is no concern of the injured party why the offender committed the offence. The victim should not be expected to go without compensation because the offender has experienced hard times or other misfortune.

When the victim or his kin have been properly compensated, the community may choose to look at the consequences for the offender. Perhaps the payment of compensation causes him and his kin greater hardship than natural justice deems appropriate. If that is so, and he is thought deserving of it, the community may decide to provide help. It can be seen that the good name or otherwise of the offender has a bearing on the amount of sympathy and help he receives.

Liberals see crime as a sickness of society for which they must find a cure. All parties to a crime are victims and all must be helped. It is not seen to be the responsibility of the state to ensure that the offender compensates the victim or that the victim has a natural-law right of retribution that the state must satisfy. The liberal frame of mind is geared to the offender. The state is deemed to have the right to forgive or be lenient to the offender without regard to the feelings of the victim.

Islamic law, as did early English communal law, recognises the natural-law right of the victim, or his kin, to decide between retribution in kind and monetary compensation. This has the merit of ensuring that the offer of compensation is high and is deemed a punishment in itself for those who must raise it, which is usually the offender or his kin. Joint liability of kin for the actions of one of their number encourages them to discourage wrongdoing and distance themselves from those they cannot trust. In early English times that meant not swearing to the innocence or good name of kin when it was not warranted.

As part of the judicial process surrounding a murder trial in Saudi Arabia during 1997, the offender and her kin were given a choice between offering to compensate the kin of the victim with a money payment or have the offender face rejecting it and thereby bringing about the execution of the offender. The principle involved is one of communal justice and serves a useful purpose but the principle was misrepresented. The term *blood money* was used in a sneering manner and the victim's kin were made to feel bad about the situation whether they insisted on the execution or accepted the compensation. According to liberals they should have done neither and just borne the loss. Better still, they should have publicly forgiven the offender and expressed pity for her. There was plenty of liberal condemnation of the Saudi legal system and Islamic principles of justice but no good reason was given as to why a murderer should not compensate the victim's kin. The reporting showed a lack of tolerance of other cultures and value systems. It was clearly thought that the only real justice is liberal justice, and that its principles should be accepted by all people of all cultures and countries. So much for the liberal commitment to multi-culturalism.

Despite the difficulties involved, it should be possible to make traditional communal solutions work in modern loosely-knit societies. It needs an understanding of the underlying principles and the will to apply them. Zero tolerance, compensation, curfews and loss of face for offenders are popular means of enforcing communal rules. Those who use them need an instinct for what is fair, workable and just. The problem is that professionals are encouraged to suppress their instincts and rely instead on a succession of fashionable theories. Perhaps the answer is to improve the jury system and place greater reliance on their sense of natural justice.

One of the characteristics of policemen and policewomen is a highly developed sense of natural justice and communal spirit. They generally have a liking for a well-ordered community and a dislike of inconsiderate behaviour. Communities need people like that to police them and the police need to be able to operate comfortably in the community. That way there is a flow of information and a feeling of common identity and purpose. There are of course a few among the many thousands of police who abuse their privileged position. Most, however, are doing their job well, driven on by a communal instinct to see peaceable behaviour and the punishment of those who do harm to others.

The great problem for policing in England is that many English policemen and policewomen feel hindered in their work by the breakdown of communal ties and the ideological hoops they are expected to jump through. They are not part of many of the communities that they have to police, and there is not the flow of communal information that they need to be effective. The members of many communities regard the police as outsiders and resent being policed by people with whom they have no communal bond or empathy. There are many English people who feel the same about being policed by outsiders.

Natural morality and the principles of natural justice accord with what we instinctively believe to be fair and reasonable. They usually produce an outcome that is widely accepted as fair and reasonable to the parties directly involved and to the community as a whole, which is what justice is all about.

Democracy and a Parliament for England

Natural justice and law form the basis of a democratic society where *the people* are able to play an important part in the shaping of their cultural, political and economic life. Unfortunately, modern globalism denies *the people* the ability or the right to shape their way of life. We are not experiencing the best of all possible forms of globalism but simply one dominant variant that is able to undermine and destroy its opponents.

Many claims are made for liberal globalism but democracy and natural justice do not come into any of them. Even the world government that liberals hold out as an ideal is at best a *top-down* democracy in which liberals are always in control and liberal values always prevail. Nowhere in this liberal global utopia is there room for the decentralisation and diversity that is essential to the working of communal democracy and natural justice. You can have any form of government you want as long as it is liberal. There is no recognition of the right of nations to defend and enjoy their sovereignty and way of life.

Today's globalism has its roots in World War II. If the Soviet Union had emerged from that war as the dominant economic and military power, it is almost certain that we would now be experiencing a different form of globalism. It was in fact the USA that came out of World War II much richer and more powerful than when it went in. That turn of events was not preordained, it was not part of an inevitable flow of history and neither is the globalisation that has flowed from it. Despite efforts to make us think so, we are not bound to accept as desirable the trend towards the Americanisation of the world. It is not an Americanisation that reflects the values and aspirations of Thomas Jefferson and the early Americans. Instead it is the Americanisation of a governing elite that cares little for the communal interests of the people it rules.

The US governing elite was offered, and it seized, the opportunity to build an empire and make the world in its own image. The great destruction of people and property during World War II and the later rapid collapse of the European empires and their currency zones left the USA as the dominant economic power and its dollar as, in effect, a world currency. That situation gave enormous trading and investment opportunities to the USA and its corporations. The collapse decades later of the USSR and its sphere of influence provided further opportunities for the US-led liberal empire to expand into new markets. It is an empire founded on the free flow of capital. Naturally, those who thrive on the system promote and preserve it by any means they can get away with.

Money is the powerhouse of what is called American culture. *Making a buck* drives everything, and it shows. When that outlook is combined with a *lets kick ass* mentality, we have the values that underlie a tacky global culture.

What can we do to gain control of our way of life and free ourselves from the imposition of this global dross? First, we must believe that we need not be helpless flotsam on a sea of global forces. Our aim must be to promote a communal bottom-up form of democracy. But how can that be done against such powerful opposition? Perhaps it will be necessary to wait for the present system to run out of steam or simply collapse, perhaps after a severe financial and economic crisis.[213] Other possibilities are failure due to some form of natural disaster such as disease or climate change. For instance, the rise in sea levels brought about by climate change will cause a new period of mass migration on a scale never seen before. The political, economic and cultural consequences will be great. Conflicts of all kinds will arise from the turmoil. Many perceptions will change, not least among liberals who will have to face the fact that it is impossible for Western states to take in and care for all the world's waifs and strays.

Whatever the turmoil ahead and however the current global system is brought down, we should start now to make use of the few opportunities that come our way to regain control of our lives. Despite the great power of the opposition, we should set about building organisations that preserve and promote communities and cultures. A start can be made with the creation of a parliament for England.

The British Labour Party was, for reasons of political expediency, converted to the cause of devolution within the UK. The devolution it offered was inspired by its need to tackle the growing strength of the Scottish National Party (SNP), which had been undermining support for the Labour Party and threatening the foundation of its UK power base. The Labour Party and the Labour government, both of which are dominated by Scots, saw the SNP as such a great threat that they set about undoing those parts of the constitution that held the UK together. It was calculated that the offer of a Scottish parliament with sufficient devolved powers to satisfy the demands of most Scots, would undermine the case for Scotland leaving the UK and becoming an EU member state. The expectation was that the Labour Party would win control of the Scottish Parliament and see a succession of Scottish Labour First Ministers (Prime Ministers). Such a happy situation for the Labour Party would strengthen its position in the UK and be a permanent source of weakness for the Conservative Party, especially if it managed to form a UK government.

---

[213] The big boom will be followed by a big bust despite the best intentions of the Chancellor of the Exchequer, Gordon Brown. The conspiracy to force down the price of gold and the massive speculation funded through gold leasing deals is likely to be seen as an important factor in sustaining the US boom and deepening the following global recession. See www.LeMetropoleCafe.com

Unlike their English counterparts, most of the Scots in the Cabinet have a strong sense of history and have been long-time supporters of some form of Scottish parliament. It was not therefore an entirely Machiavellian motive that led to the creation of a Scottish parliament. It was however the desire to gain a political advantage that led to the over-hasty cobbling together of a plan for devolved government in the UK. The plan, such as it was, sought to bring together the desire for a Scottish parliament with the need to comply with EU regionalisation plans, which have the aim of dividing the larger member states into regions and thereby weakening state governments. Certain powers will be devolved down to the regions (e.g. health and education) while social, economic, defence and foreign policy matters will be passed upwards from the member states to the EU. The parliaments and governments of member states will find themselves redundant. Evidence for this strategy is found in the forging of links between the EU and the regions that bypass state governments. There is also the creation of regional groupings that cross member state boundaries. For example, parts of the Southeast of England are in a group that includes parts of Northwest France. None of this constitutional and administrative change has what could properly be called democratic approval. Most people do not even know what is going on.

The commitment of the Labour Party to create a Scottish Parliament, subject to approval in a referendum, fitted in with the planned Northern Ireland Assembly, which is part of an arrangement by which Northern Ireland will be transferred to the Republic of Ireland. The creation of a Welsh Assembly was a necessary part of the overall scheme and, it was hoped, would secure Labour's position against the Welsh nationalists of Plaid Cymru. The plans for devolution within England and reform of the House of Lords were meant to look like part of a well-thought-out package of constitutional reform for the UK but, as with the other reforms, they actually had more to do with pursuing medium-term Labour Party interests. For example, reform of the House of Lords was inspired by the need to remove as quickly as possible an inbuilt, and unfair, Conservative advantage. That objective was pursued before any coherent plan had been put forward for something to replace the Lords. Justification for the haste is said to be opposition to an archaic institution founded on the hereditary principle. If that is so, why didn't the government set about abolishing the monarchy? Instead, Prime Minister Tony Blair was keen to make known his ardent support for the monarchy, which was probably due to the fact that a large majority of the UK population favours keeping it.

Given the importance of the US constitution in the moulding of an American civic identity, many Americans will find it amazing that a government can chop and change the constitution to suit its own purposes. It is like a US President with majority support in Congress and the Senate rewriting the US constitution in a way that suits the President's Party. Worse still, what if the president and the leading members of his government came from California and rigged the constitution so that California was given special powers to govern itself and was provided with substantial annual payments of Federal money to spend on the provision of health, education and other services? Why are the English so feeble in spirit and action that they allow others to treat them with such contempt? Do we English really want a Scottish government that treats England like a Scottish colony? That these things can happen adds weight to the allegation that the UK government, of whatever party, is an elected dictatorship.

The unravelling of the UK began with little thought being given to what the population of England wanted. Citizens in Scotland, and Wales were given the opportunity in referendums to decide whether they wanted their country to have a parliament/assembly but the people of England were not extended that courtesy. Instead, they were offered regional government on a take it or leave it basis. When that injustice is pointed out, it is said that the General Election of 1997 was a referendum. What is meant is that the Labour Party included an outline for English regional assemblies and city mayors in their 1997 election manifesto. It is a weak argument but there are some, like the Labour MP Tony Wright, who think it a very clever answer. If general elections, in which the entire UK electorate is able to vote, really count as referenda, why weren't the manifesto commitments to introduce a Scottish Parliament and Welsh Assembly deemed sufficient authority? Why was it felt necessary to incur the cost of specifically asking the electorate of Scotland and Wales if they wanted elected political institutions for those countries?

News releases from the Campaign for an English Parliament have pointed to problems and contradictions implicit in the policies of the main UK political parties.[214]

Reasons for rejecting the government's devolution plans for England

1. England, like Scotland, is one country and its people should be given the same opportunity as the people of Scotland to opt for a parliament of their own. At its simplest, it is a matter of fairness and equality of opportunity.

2. It is sometimes suggested that the 1997 General Election was a referendum on the issue of English devolution. It was not. Referenda are held on one issue and the people they affect determine them. Are the people of England really expected to be bound by the result of a so-called referendum in which the whole UK electorate was able to vote? That device was not considered

---

[214] The following, down to the heading *The Liberal Democrats and Devolution*, is for the most part from a News Release issued by the Campaign for an English Parliament, on 9th June 2000. Campaign for an English Parliament, 1 Providence Street, King's Lynn, Norfolk PE30 5ET email cep@englishpm.demon.co.uk, website www.englishpm.demon.co.uk

good enough for Northern Ireland, Scotland or Wales so why should the people of England accept it?

3. The creation of nine English Regions will not answer the West Lothian Question because it will leave the UK parliament unchanged.

4. It is for the people of England not the UK government to determine the way power is devolved within England. The current quango-based regional arrangements are being offered on a take it or leave it basis. That is neither fair nor in keeping with the proclaimed aims of devolution. When we have an English Parliament the people of England will be able to carefully examine all of the many options for devolution within England and adopt something that meets their wishes and best interests.

5. The imposition of nine Regions is a denial of a rare opportunity to build on English democratic tradition. We should be given the option to create an English Parliament suited to modern conditions:

   - a parliament that strengthens democratic control and makes governments more accountable to the electorate;

   - a parliament that is able to find English solutions to English problems;

   - a parliament that is able to consider the interests of the whole country and thus avoid the selfishness and squabbling that the current regional plans encourage.

6. A major selling point for the Nine-Region System is that those living in them will be better off as a result of attracting more investment and funding. Where is the additional money to come from?

   - Not from the EU because spending priorities are being switched to Eastern Europe.

   - Not from corporations because each Region will be competing with the others. Each will try to outbid the others with the offer of grants and concessions. In the end, all will be worse off.

   - Not through the Barnett Formula because if one Region gets more the others will get less. Some regions will be worse off because they will not only get less but also be expected to pay more.[215]

---

[215] *The Barnett Formula* is used to calculate the size of UK government funds allocated to Scotl and Wales each year. The figures for 1995–6 show that expenditure per person in Scotland was 2 higher than in England, and the amount for Wales 17% higher. The cost of the additional transfer resources to Scotland is about £7 billion each year, which is far higher than government revenue fr North Sea oil. This transfer explains why class sizes and hospital waiting lists can be smaller Scotland than in England. It also explains why treatment is available in Scottish and Welsh hospi that is deemed too expensive for England. If this unfair distribution of resources is to be rectif

7. If devolution is merely the division of the UK into regions, there is no good reason for not treating them equally. The nine English Regional Assemblies will not have the same powers as the Scottish Parliament, and the Regional *governments* will not have the same powers as the Scottish Executive. For instance, they will not have the same rights of representation with the UK government and the EU.

8. The drawing of lines on a map and the failure to recognise England as a natural political entity points to England being treated as if it were the last colony of the British Empire. The policy of divide and rule lives on.

9. *England is too big and an English Parliament will unbalance the Union.* That objection smacks of desperation and is based on an arbitrary rule concerning size. It can equally be argued that Scotland and Wales are too small and that the creation of the Scottish Parliament and Welsh Assembly has unbalanced the Union. The people of England should not be expected to bear the cost of preserving something that treats them less favourably than it treats other citizens of the UK. An English Parliament does not require the creation of a federal constitution. It can be set up in the same way as was the Scottish Parliament. The alternative is a renegotiated Union that meets the needs of all its parts.

10. *The Barnett Formula system for distributing funds within the UK means that England must be treated differently because what happens in England affects expenditure in other parts of the UK.* This argument is putting the cart before the horse. The simple remedy is to find a new system of funding that suits a new United Kingdom. The Barnett Formula is outdated and results in public spending per head being substantially higher in Scotland and Wales than in England. There is no good reason why England should continue to be treated as a milch cow for the rest of the UK.

Reasons for rejecting the "English votes on English Laws" *solution* **offered by the Conservative Party.**

1. The proposal is a step in the right direction because it recognises that the people of England are being treated unfairly under the present constitutional arrangement. However, it is a minimalist answer to the West Lothian Question that will not give England parity with Scotland.

2. It will not provide England with a First Minister and an Executive that are able to initiate and pursue policies specifically concerned with English problems and priorities. In other words, MPs representing English

---

England will need to negotiate a different arrangement. That will not be possible if England is divided into competing regions.

constituencies will only be able to react to proposals put forward by the UK government.

3. Even if the MPs representing English constituencies were able to initiate policy for English matters, they do not have the electoral mandate to do so.

4. It will not provide an English equivalent to the system whereby Scottish interests are formally represented within the European Union and the UK government.

5. It does not address the unfair system of funding which makes it possible for public spending per head to be significantly higher in Scotland and Wales than in England.

6. Gladstone considered a similar policy in 1886 and rejected it as unworkable in practice.[216]

7. England needs a well-thought-out constitutional arrangement that is designed to serve the long-term interests of the people of England. A fresh start needs to be made and the job done properly. We do not need a cobbled together arrangement suited to short-term needs.

8. The people of England should be given the opportunity to vote in a referendum for an English Parliament. We want equality with Scotland. Nothing more; nothing less.

The Liberal Democrats and Devolution

The word *England* is not in the political vocabulary of Liberal Democrats. Curiously, *democrat* and *democracy* clearly have different meanings on each side of the border. In Scotland, the Liberal Democrats are enthusiastic supporters of a Scottish Parliament, which is seen as an expression of democracy and national identity. However, in England they see the demand for a Parliament as something negative; the work of *dark forces*.[217] Part of the reason for Liberals supporting the regionalisation of England is that they believe it is better for their electoral chances.

The Party Positions

Unfortunately, all three of the main political parties are guilty of the double standard that recognises Scotland and Wales as countries and natural political entities but sees England as a constitutional inconvenience that needs to be dismembered, patronised or ignored. All three are determined to keep the Union

---

[216] *Devolution in the United Kingdom*, Vernon Bogdanor

[217] The Liberal Democratic Party usually gets better results in local elections on local issues than does in General Elections. They see Regional elections as suiting them better than England-wide elections. There is also the fact that Scots have a disproportionately large amount of power within the party.

together and all are willing to see England bear the cost of it. The Labour Party and the Liberal Democrats are particularly concerned not to offend the Scottish and Welsh electorate by changing a system that benefits them financially. The Conservatives do not make too much of the financial and democratic anomalies because they do not want to turn the English against the Union. Those who run the Conservative Party are first and foremost British civic-nationalists. Their first loyalty is to their British identity and the UK. If preservation of the UK demands that the English be treated unfairly, so be it.

The policy of ignoring the problem and hoping it will go away can only last so long. Eventually a constitutional crisis will come about as a result of a serious conflict between the sovereignty of the Scottish and UK parliaments. It is likely to cause an infectious ill-will and resentment in Scotland that will spread to England. The Scottish National Party is waiting for such a conflict because it will enable the party to push for Scottish independence.

If the Union is to survive, it will have to be re-invented. The old model is a relic of a bygone age. Things have changed and a new relationship needs be negotiated that is acceptable to all parties. Better to do that now before bitterness sets in and the task is made impossible.

Regionalism: Divide and Rule

An English Parliament should not be seen as a bar to decentralisation and greater democracy but as the means of bringing it about. Better to devolve power down from an institution that recognises England as a country, and serves the interests of all its parts, than to see England broken into competing regions, which is a divide-and-rule policy that serves EU interests. Better to let the people of England shape their democracy than have outsiders impose a structure. Better to devolve power through a modified version of the existing system of local government based on counties, towns, and cities to which the English feel some loyalty, than to force them into regions invented by bureaucrats. A sure way of improving turnout in local elections would be to give the electorate something important to vote on, which means giving local authorities greater power to tackle problems as local conditions demand.

The power of the EU and its allies in the UK to project EU and regional identities should not be underestimated. The introduction of vehicle registration number plates that carry the EU emblem and an EU regional identity are part of that scheme. So too was the year 2000 legislation which in effect recognised the EU flag as a state flag and made it possible for it to be flown from UK public buildings. If there is no intention to make the EU a state, why is it being given the powers and symbols of a state?

The ploy is to encourage the English Regions to compete with one another and it is already showing success. Ken Livingstone MP, the Mayor of London, who is outspokenly keen on supporting Irish nationalism and a united Ireland, is hostile to English nationalism and a united England.[218] A tactic he used during the London mayoral elections, and since, was to complain that London subsidises the rest of the UK. That claim is untrue because if all forms of public funding are taken into account it is evident that London receives disproportionately higher central funding than the rest of England. For example, what spending in any other Region matches that for the Millennium Dome and the Jubilee Line extension? It is high government spending, including higher wages (*London Weighting*), in London that gives a massive boost to the London economy and generates higher tax revenue.

England has been fobbed off with regions but left whole for the purpose of subsiding Scotland, Wales and Northern Ireland through the outdated and unfair Barnett Formula. It is not in the interest of either the Labour Party or the Liberal Democrats to change a system which ensures that public spending per head in Scotland, Wales, and Northern Ireland is much higher than in England. Neither the sanctimonious Scottish leader of the Liberal Democrats, Charles Kennedy, or the Scottish UK Prime Minister, Tony Blair, wishes to incur unpopularity in Scotland by stopping the drain of wealth from England to Scotland.[219]

In addition to Ken Livingstone attempting to stir a sense of regional identity, we have the well-entrenched Labour Party establishment in the North East of England which sees the opportunity for empire building. Their claims that a Regional Assembly would bring grants and an increase in public spending to the area are fantasy. Just where do they think the money will come from? The claim is often made that they will get EU grants but that particular source, which served the Republic of Ireland so well, is drying up. In future EU grants will be directed towards the new Eastern European members of the EU. From what other source will the North-East Region get its extra funding? Does it expect that other competing regions of England will hand it money? Why should they? The problem is made worse by the way it is suggested that all the Regions of England will benefit from devolution and a redistribution of resources? Will any of them be worse off? If not, it will be a miracle.

---

[218] Shortly before the year 2000 London mayoral elections, it was reported in the *Evening Standard* that Ken Livingstone wanted to have a St Patrick's Day parade in London that would be the largest outside Ireland and the USA. He is keen to promote a St Patrick's Day parade in the capital city of England yet mocks expressions of English national identity. Why does he lack enthusiasm for a George's Day parade? The reason is that he is a good example of a modern liberal.

[219] For reasons of political expediency, Tony Blair, a Scot, took to suggesting that he is English. If that is so, why did he choose to show support for the Scottish football team by visiting them and making a public display of his support for them during the 1998 World Cup competition in France?

It is sad indeed that England is being changed from a historically rich country to one where the leaders of regional governments will be traipsing around begging for handouts, mostly from foreigners.

Devolution in the UK is being introduced in a way that is blatantly unfair to the people of England. A government elected by all the people of the UK is able to control policy in England for:

- the National Health Service;
- schools and teacher training;
- further and higher education;
- local government finance and taxation;
- land-use planning and building control;
- the environment;
- passenger and road transport;
- economic development and financial assistance to industry;
- civil and criminal courts;
- much of criminal and civil law;
- prisons;
- police and fire services;
- food standards;
- certain areas of agriculture and fisheries;
- the arts;
- sport.

In Scotland, all of these matters are dealt with by the Scottish Executive (i.e. Scottish government) and the Scottish Parliament, the members of which were specifically elected by the people of Scotland for that purpose. They are therefore able to set their own priorities and tailor policies to suit the people of Scotland. This opportunity is denied to the people of England. This insulting treatment of the people of England will add to the already large numbers of English who feel no loyalty whatsoever to a state and system of government that does not represent their interests. Those who are trying to suppress English interests and an English identity in the name of preserving the Union are creating the conditions for its break up. Or, are the English the only people who lack the will and the guts to assert their right to govern themselves?

Campaign for an English Parliament

The Campaign for an English Parliament (CEP) is independent of political parties. Its purpose is to campaign for an English Parliament with the same powers as the Scottish Parliament: nothing more, nothing less. Devolution offers the people of

England the opportunity to improve their system of government and build on the English democratic tradition. It will help free them from a system that discriminates against them politically and economically.

The CEP has been successful in attracting support from individuals with very different political views and social backgrounds, few of whom claim to be English nationalists. Whatever their political affiliations, those running the CEP are mature enough to be able to work with others with whom they disagree on many other issues. Such a situation is rare and refreshing.

On many occasions the CEP has had to make it clear that it has nothing at all to say about who is and who is not English. That issue is completely irrelevant to the Campaign because an English Parliament will benefit all the people of England. We are all being denied the rights and opportunities that have been given to the electorate in other parts of the UK. We are all being fleeced by an arrangement that unfairly allocates less public spending per head to England than other parts of the UK.

The term *English Parliament* is used in the same way as are *Scottish Parliament* and *Welsh Assembly*. An English Parliament will not be restricted in the same way as is the Moslem Parliament of Great Britain. It will be a Parliament for all the people of England, whatever their ethnicity/nationality/origins/religion. Everyone on the electoral Register for Parliamentary Constituencies in England will be entitled to vote and stand as a candidate. This has to be stressed because people like Yasmin Alibhai-Brown seem to find the concept hard to grasp.[220] When the issue of an English Parliament was raised during a television studio discussion, she said something to the effect that *you* can have the rest of the country but *we* will take the cities.[221] *You* seemed to mean the English; *we* seemed to mean Asians and Blacks. Her unguarded remark gave a glimpse of how these people think and what the future holds.

The greatest hostility to the creation of an English Parliament comes from supporters of the Labour Party, although things are improving. The reaction of delegates to the 1998 Labour Party Conference was mainly one of scoffing. The problem was not with Scottish and Welsh delegates but with the English. The Scots and Welsh have some understanding of the arguments and were more often than not friendly and supportive. Many of the English delegates seemed to believe the idea of an English Parliament too absurd to take seriously. Two years later most delegates were willing to accept a CEP leaflet and many of the English among them expressed support. The type that remains particularly irritating is the person who retorts with overbearing pride, "I'm from Yorkshire!" It is difficult

---

[220] To her credit, Yasmin Alibhai-Brown recognises the English as a distinct group and does not claim that an English identity is acquired simply by living in England.
[221] *Channel 4* studio discussion following the Darcus Howe, *White Tribe* programme.

know if one is supposed to congratulate them and be envious or struck dumb with awe.

The delegates to Conservative Party Conferences are different in that the English are mostly very supportive, while the Scots and Welsh oppose an English Parliament because they see it as a threat to the Union. They are completely unconcerned about the unfairness of the present system and think it more important to preserve the Union than ask the people of England what they want. Their concern for preserving the Union has much to do with their fear of being forever a Conservative minority in Scotland and Wales.

There is a widespread belief in all three of the main UK political parties that an English Parliament will lead inevitably to the break-up of the Union, which is taken to be a bad thing. The CEP has no view on the matter but it is probable that most members of the CEP wish to preserve the Union, even if in a modified form. After all, it makes sense for people with so many links and common interests to co-operate. However, it must be a relationship freely entered into that benefits all parties.

The UK constitution is in a muddle because it has been unravelled before any coherent alternative has been put forward. The guiding rule seems to be to make up alterations as and when necessary but always with an eye to party political advantage. The changes will inevitably cause political and constitutional friction that will lead to declining support for the Union, the very thing the main political parties are so anxious to avoid. For those who want to preserve a Union of some kind, the best plan is to treat England, Scotland and Wales in an equal fashion, the model for all being the Scottish Parliament.[222]

---

[222] It is widely accepted that Northern Ireland is a special case that may need to be treated differently from other parts of the UK.

Part Four   The Great Upheaval

Liberalism and Multi-Culturalism in England

The orthodoxy of our age is that multi-national, multi-racial, multi-cultural societies are *a good thing*. That article of faith appears to be based on the belief that it is desirable to create societies where people of all religions, races and cultures can live together in peace and harmony. It completely ignores the fact that there is overwhelming evidence to show that multi-cultural, multi-racial societies tend to be unstable due to an incompatibility of perceptions, values, and aspirations. Multi-cultural societies generally only hold together when a dominant group is able, through its control of the state, to impose its values on the whole society. Western liberals see themselves as the natural dominant group and believe they can use that position to convert all the other groups to liberalism. The assumption that underlies liberal social engineering is that identities and loyalties can be moulded to suit ideological requirements. Racial identities are promoted in place of other identities. Thus the English are given a *White* or *White European* label. English culture is replaced with *British* or *European culture*. We no longer have our own language but merely speak a variant of global English, which is labelled *UK English*. England is no longer the homeland of the English nation but a piece of land inhabited by people of many cultures who are all English because they live in England. Overlaying that is an even more inclusive British and European civic identity. Ultimately we become Earthlings.

Liberals will be surprised to learn that their fantasy politics is giving rise to growing English resentment and an increasing hostility to liberal attitudes. One only had to be in an English gathering shortly after publication in 2000 of the *Report from the Commission on the Future of Multi-Ethnic Britain* to appreciate that resistance is hardening among even the most easygoing, tolerant, open-minded, and generous of individuals.[223] The Report's findings, which many regard as a declaration of war, were unsurprising given that those responsible for its recommendations were the usual collection of committee liberals and self-appointed representatives of racial and ethnic groups – the usual suspects with the usual prejudices. Among other things, they called for the redefining of British and English identities because *ethnic minorities* believe those terms have imperialistic and racial overtones.

> It is widely understood that Englishness, and therefore by extension Britishness, is racially coded ... unless these deep-rooted antagonisms to racial and cultural differences can be defeated in practice, as well as

---

223 Known as *The Parekh Report*

symbolically written out of the national story, the idea of a multi-cultural post-nation remains an empty promise.

It seems that there is an implication that to be English is to be White, which is not inclusive – a cardinal sin. No mention of course of the need to redefine Scottishness because of the implication that to be Scottish is to be White. No mention either of what the English feel about the whole business, which is unsurprising since hardly any of the members of the *think-tank* were English. That was all the more reason to regard it as impertinent of them to demand that the English redefine themselves. It really is none of their business.

Whether or not the siege mentality fostered in the English by this and other absurd reports will actually produce effective resistance is hard to say. A promising sign is that there has been a marked increase in the willingness of English people to openly express hostility to liberal policies. Many, who not long ago thought of themselves as liberal, are questioning the whole rambling liberal structure. *Liberal* is widely becoming a term of abuse and derision.

Liberals are being cut off from their English roots and becoming increasingly dependent upon the support of various groups of settlers. The more they are seen to be tools of these groups, the less relevant they and their ideology become to the interests of the English. Disillusionment is to be seen in the declining confidence many have in the political and electoral system. Liberals seem unaware of the shift and seem confident that they and their allies can continue to roll forward on a wide front crushing opposition at will. Somewhere there is a Stalingrad awaiting their arrival. The sooner they get there the better.

Immigration

Immigration is a sensitive issue but an attempt will be made here to address it in a way that represents the views of the many English people who feel their interests and wishes are ignored by elected politicians. This is a difficult task because liberals are unwilling to discuss the matter and try to prevent others from doing so. Perhaps their irrational and hostile reaction is due to fear of change or a dread of ideological strangers. Whatever problem liberals may have, the English have a right and duty to openly discuss a matter that is of proper concern to them or any other nation living in its homeland. Whatever the intent of those who promote mass immigration, its effect is to weaken the English nation. A nation can survive many setbacks but the loss of its homeland causes irreparable damage and raises the prospect of eventual extinction.

Here is as good a place as any to stress that the vast majority of people who settle in England do not come to scrounge or live a life of crime. They come because they believe the move will give them and their families a better way of life. They are what can be called *ordinary decent people* who deserve courtesy and consideration. However, the other side of this is a recognition that the vast majority of English people are also *ordinary decent people* who deserve courtesy and consideration. They too must do what they think is best for themselves and their families. They have a right to speak and be listened to.

It is an essential condition of democracy that the members of a community are able to speak freely about the issues that concern them. It is also essential that those who govern in the name of the people should respond to the concerns of the people. It is not for *representatives* in a *representative democracy* to dismiss, condemn or suppress opinions they find ideologically inconvenient. If indigenous people are concerned about high levels of immigration and object to changes being made to their way of life, they have a right to say so and it is the duty of the government to listen to and address those concerns. By what principle of democracy are *the people* obliged to remain silent on matters of such importance to this and future generations?

The governing elite is aware of the widespread opposition to their immigration policy but instead of addressing the issue directly and making it a subject for open public debate, they use their power to present immigration as something inherently good that is only resisted by thoroughly nasty people. In other words, they subject the English to unending propaganda which suggests that only racists, bigots and the ill-informed are concerned about immigration and opposed to it. The clear message is that decent sensible people are *proud of our long tradition of accepting refugees* and we all benefit from the *skills and enterprise immigrants bring with them*. Each new group of immigrants is deemed to be merely the latest in a continuous flow of immigrants. According to Darcus Howe:

> The truth is that this is a mongrel nation made up of waves upon waves upon waves of immigrants who have been coming here without interruption for more than 1500 years.[224]

A statement like that shows either a lack of knowledge of English history or a deliberate attempt to falsify it. For much of the history of England there has been very strict control over who entered England, where visitors went and what they did. It was common to place a limit on their stay and they could be expelled at any time. Much the same rules applied in most other countries and in many places they still do, as for example in Singapore and Saudi Arabia. But what chance is there for the true history of England and migration to be known when there has been wave upon wave upon wave upon wave of uninterrupted liberal propaganda for more than thirty years.

What happens when the self-proclaimed experts on English history are asked to give details of the waves of immigration since Norman times? "Well – um – there

---

224 *White Tribe*, Channel 4, January 2000

were the Huguenots and the Irish." Yes that's true but is that all? "No – there were Jews" Yes, but do these groups make up the waves upon waves upon waves of immigrants that have arrived during the past 900 years? "Well no – of course there were others - it's a well known fact. It's just that I can't recall the exact details."

Indeed there were others but the groups were small, insignificant, and easily absorbed. For the most part they disappeared without trace. The largest groups of immigrants and the most commonly named are as follows.

- The Huguenots (French Protestants – mainly Calvinists) migrated from France after Louis XIV revoked the Edict of Nantes in 1685 and opened the way to their forcible conversion to Catholicism. Of the 400,000 who emigrated, about 40,000 went to Britain.

- The potato famine in Ireland during the period 1846–51 led to 1·5 million people emigrating. The vast majority of them went to the USA, but some went to England and Scotland (figures not known).

- There was some migration of Jews from Russia and Eastern Europe to Great Britain towards the end of the nineteenth century but the numbers were not large. By the early 1920s there were estimated to be about 250,000 Jews in Great Britain.[225] The population of Great Britain at that time was about 43 million; England & Wales about 38 million.

These examples hardly amount to evidence for continuous waves of immigrants arriving in England in the period from the twelfth to the nineteenth century but that does not stop the mantra being chanted.

Despite the alleged handicap of very low immigration, the English created a great Empire, started the industrial revolution, become a world power, and were responsible for many inventions and the creation of much new knowledge. The English and the wider Anglo-Saxon diaspora have made an impact on world history that is equal to that of the Greeks and Romans. Yet where is the acknowledgement of that? Why are so many of those who come to England so keen to berate the English and try to belittle them? Is it jealousy or an inferiority complex that sparks such ill-mannered behaviour?

It was not until after World War II that immigration became a continuous flow with wave upon wave upon wave of immigration. Great numbers of people arrived who were and still are very different from the English in practically every way. The outer geographical boundary of the English community was breached and large numbers of individuals who had no historical, cultural, religious or linguistic connection with England, were allowed to enter the country. No proper reason was or is given for admitting them and the English were not consulted on the matter or asked for their approval. Most English people bitterly resented that policy, and still

---

[225] A.J.P. Taylor, *English History 1914–1945*, OUP 1965

do, but public expression of opposition to it is stifled. Politicians who mention the issue of immigration, especially during an election campaign, are accused of *playing the race card*. In other words, they are raising a matter about which many English people are concerned but which the governing elite have deemed to be outside the bounds of polite political debate. It is difficult to reconcile the much-proclaimed liberal concern for democracy, free expression, self-determination and human rights with their resolve to ignore and suppress views they find unacceptable.

Even a television programme ostensibly made to answer the question *Who are the English?* managed to almost completely ignore the English.[226] Nearly a third of the programme was devoted to the Romans, who came to and left Britain before the English conquest and settlement of lowland Britain began. The fascination and admiration that many liberals have for the Romans and their Empire is that they admire the way a comparatively small group were able to impose their will on so many. Liberals also see the opportunity to make a link between multi-culturalism and a great civilisation.[227] Sure enough, the programme presenter seized the opportunity, when talking of the Empire, to use the key liberal propaganda words – cosmopolitan, multi-culturalism, tolerance, and inclusiveness. No mention was made of the imperialistic nature of the Empire, and no parallel was drawn between the Nazis and Romans, both of whom invaded the homelands of their neighbours, built long straight roads, put up grand buildings and used a stiff arm salute. No mention that Julius Caesar and those like him were dictators who committed what are now commonly regarded as war crimes and crimes against humanity. Instead, liberals prefer to see the Empire's bureaucratic institutions imposing common standards and a common currency on a cosmopolitan population for the good of all. Perhaps we are supposed to see similarities between the Roman Empire and the new liberal European Union, where nations and national identities are things to overcome and destroy for the greater good of an inclusive and greater civic identity. Fortunately, many people do see the similarities and view the whole thing with alarm.

Having painted a glowing picture of the Roman Empire and the benefits it brought to one and all, the programme presenter, Brian McNerny, moved on, mentioning in passing that the Angles were the people from whom the name England came. With that he quickly passed over a thousand years of history to what he seemed to regard as the far more important migration of people from Holland to East Anglia. Next came the employment of Italians in the Bedfordshire brick-making industry. And then the Asians who like other migrants before them did useful work in the

---

226 *Think of England*, BBC 2, Eastern Region, 19th October 2000.

227 It should not be forgotten that the Roman Empire came about as the result of conquest. The people they conquered resisted and many died. Roman sources claim that one million Gauls were killed and two million captured during the Gallic Wars. It was common in those times to sell captives as slaves. Bids were put in for as many as 50,000 at a time.

multi-cultural society they joined. The message was clear, the enriching process of migration had produced a land full of people of many different nationalities, none of which was specifically English. Thus, the English are not seen as a distinct nation or ethnic group but as a collection of ethnic groups.

This liberal misrepresentation of English history is an essential part of the propaganda they have peddled for the past thirty years. It has been repeated so many times that it is widely accepted as being true. Or is it? There must be more than a few English people who have a niggling feeling that there is something not quite right about the claim that England has always been a multi-cultural and multi-racial society teeming with people from the four corners of the earth. Those who have seen early films from county film archives will have noticed an almost complete lack of African and Asian faces. Many of these films are street scenes of ordinary people going about their business or attending festivals. Some show large groups of city children going on their first trip to the countryside or seaside. The impression given is not one of a multi-cultural, multi-racial society but of a mono-cultural, mono-racial nation. Perhaps you have visited the Public Records Office in London to research your family history. If so you will have noticed an almost complete absence of Black and Asian people struggling to find desk space for the volumes of births deaths and marriages. Are they uninterested in their family history or is it that their family history is not to be found in those records but in anther country on another continent. Look at the names in the records and on the census returns and see how many Patels, Singhs, Mohammeds and other exotic names you can find. Likewise, old telephone directories, trade directories, and newspaper libraries tell a tale that conflicts with the multi-cultural fairy story we are told.

The reality is that the first large inflow of Black people occurred when American servicemen were posted to England during World War II. Most English people had never seen a Black person before. Yes, some English had visited parts of the British Empire and seen Black and Asian indigenous peoples but when they returned they saw, with rare exception, only the White indigenous people of England. Neither of my parents, who lived in the suburbs of London, saw a Black person until 1953. Prior to that, my father had been told that some were to be seen around the London docks but they mostly came and went as seamen, as did many more Chinese. Shortly before World War II there was a Chinese restaurant (New Friends?) in Lime House, near the West India docks. It was one of only two Chinese restaurants in London at that time.

When, as a child, I travelled with my parents by car from our home in Wembley Park to Central London we went along the Harrow Road, passing through Kensal Town. It was there, just before Great Western Road that we made a point of looking for Black people and were disappointed when we failed to see any. They were a curiosity. That was in 1958, a time when I knew a Sikh boy, whose father was a silk merchant. The Sikh family and two Irish boys at school were the only foreigners I was aware of. I also knew some Jewish children but I cannot recall thinking of them as foreign in the same way that the Sikh and Irish children were. I knew a Jewish girl, Christine Berger, and another Maureen Dreyfus. Christine was so named because members of her family had been killed by the Nazis during the war and her mother, who came to England from the Continent, did not want her daughter to have a name that identified her as Jewish. I must have been aware of a sense of Englishness because I wondered then about names and thought that while Christine was not a Jewish name, Berger probably was because it was not English. As for Maureen, who had long fair hair, I thought nothing of her surname. She looked English, sounded English and I thought of her as being English. Those observations are just that, and they certainly did not make me feel dislike of any of the children or hostility towards them.

It was not until 1962 that I saw a Black person regularly and at close quarters. On the last day of the summer term, the headmaster of my school announced that after the holiday a Black girl would be attending the school and we were all to be particularly kind to her and make her feel comfortable. She duly arrived and after the novelty wore off no one took any particular notice of her. As the terms went by, more Black children arrived and more Black people were to be seen in the streets around the school. Then, in my last term, a few Asian children started at the school. A year or two later I went with friends to a recently opened *Indian Restaurant* by Wembley Triangle. It was the first I had seen, and visiting it was an interesting experience. Unfortunately, the curry was very hot and I didn't eat another for many years.

By the late 1970's over 50% of the pupils at my former school were Black and Asian. By 1990 the proportion had risen to over 90%. Wembley High Road, which had been a thriving shopping centre, was by the 1980s very run down. Part of the reason for that decline was heavy traffic and the development of nearby shopping centres. Another important factor was the dramatic change in the makeup of the population in the surrounding area. The mainly Asian residents did not want to shop at Marks & Spencer or British Home Stores. Trade dwindled and the stores closed. Sari and other *Asian* shops opened and the whole nature of the area changed. When I returned there, about ten years after leaving school, I felt a stranger. A place that I had known well and felt comfortable in no longer seemed familiar. It didn't even feel like England. I can clearly recall feeling an unease that led me to question and soon after abandon my liberal views.

Later, I married and went to live in Harrow, which was further from Central London than Wembley, and still very English. Then in the 1970s Asians were expelled from Uganda and allowed to settle in England. Some also came from Kenya. One such family moved into the house next door. They were friendly, pleasant people with whom we got on very well. They introduced me to the custom of drinking condensed milk in tea – not something I recommend. It was apparently the only reliable milk available to them in Kenya. The local school, which had been almost exclusively English when my first child went there, began to gain more and more Asian pupils, as did all the state and private schools in that part of Harrow.

Several years later we sold our house to a Black family and my wife, children and I moved to the outer edges of suburbia. The situation there regarding schools was a repeat of the earlier experience. For educational reasons, my first son attended a secondary school in the area from which we had moved some years before, the pupils were mostly Asian and he formed part of a small English minority. I cannot recall seeing a single Black or Asian teacher at the school but I can recall that the teachers I met seemed fervently liberal. The school was clearly geared to the needs of Asian pupils and a celebration of their culture. It was at that school I saw the poster declaring *We British are a rich mixture*. It was also the school where my son was coached in writing an essay in which a White boy and a Black boy jointly commit a criminal offence. When they appear in court the White boy is let off but the Black boy is punished, because he is Black. The theme did not spring from my son's imagination but was planted there, as it had been in the minds of all the pupils in his class; Black, Asian and English. The teacher had written at the bottom of the short and poorly written story, "Well done. We will have to develop this further."

It was difficult after that to see my son's teacher and others like her as merely naive but well-meaning. It came home to me as never before that teachers are in a position where they are able to influence the perceptions of children by peddling a political dogma under the guise of truth and decency. Worse still, they do it with the approval and encouragement of the state and the teacher-training system through which they have passed. Some trainee teachers resist the indoctrination but others emerge like grinning Stepford Wives, keen to get on and do the bidding of those who have programmed them. The worst examples are the smiling, earnest, often childless women who do not understand the destructive historical and political consequences of what they are doing. These simple people think they are in touch with the needs of a new and wonderful multi-cultural society. Their reality is the world painted for them by *The Guardian*, *The Independent*, and other liberal newspapers.

Much of my experience is probably similar to that of many other English men and women of my generation. They too have known an England where there was a feeling of community, where people had a sense of identity, belonging, politeness, and relaxed oneness. It was not perfect but there was not the tension, aggression, and disunity of today.

Most of my contemporaries have experienced in education, the workplace, and elsewhere the reality of mass migration and multi-culturalism. Their lives have been dramatically changed by it. Many have gradually moved with their families to the outer suburbs of cities, often leaving behind elderly relatives who had set up home and put down roots before mass migration began. In their old age they have found themselves surrounded by an alien population and in a situation unimaginable to them in their youth. When, in the early days of the upheaval, they saw with their own eyes evidence of how things were changing they could not believe that it would be allowed to go on. It was felt that *the government* must be aware of what was happening and doing something to stop it. People disliked what they saw but thought they could one day move away from it. It was something that was just happening in their district. In other places things must be unchanged; surely the whole of England was not being changed in this way.

Some moved further out into the suburbs, while others moved beyond to the small but rapidly growing towns mostly occupied by English people. The migration of the English out of London and other cities began in a big way during the 1980s and is still going on. Many of those migrants commute back into the cities to work, and during the day, Central London still looks like an English city.

Not everyone who wanted to move out was able to do so. It is not easy to disentangle families from jobs, schools, friends and relations. Some were further restricted by their dependency on local authority housing. That tie had much to do with the survival of English working-class communities in inner city areas. In the outer suburbs there are still districts consisting mainly of English middle-class people but those areas are shrinking. Eventually they will reach a size that is not sustainable and, like other districts before them, will suddenly implode and vanish. Always the English are retreating, handicapped by an ever-declining population. Few are the family gatherings so common only forty years ago where several generations mixed and felt comfortable with a shared identity. There were always babies and old people, and a sense of renewal and continuity. Now we have disappointed wannabe grandparents who played their part in raising a family but nonetheless see their branch of the family tree coming to an end.

When a laissez-faire attitude is applied to human relationships, it gives rise to a society with a large number of mothers who are not in a long-term relationship with the fathers of their children. Most but not all of these mothers have neither the ability nor the will to support themselves and their children. They live their lives in a reckless way that is underpinned by the mistaken belief that *society*, *the Benefit* and *them at the Council* have an obligation to look after those who bring misfortune on themselves.

Just as damaging to a community is the high proportion of capable women who are physically able to have children but do not do so because from an early age they have been subject to liberal cultural conditioning which suggest that children are a hindrance to self-fulfilment. This is not to condemn women who choose not to have children. What is being condemned is a culture that encourages women to suppress their maternal instincts and lead them to believe that greater happiness and personal satisfaction can be found in a career and material consumption. For some, that is the best option and they are entitled to take it. However, it should not be presented as the way to be preferred by all. In other words, there are different ways of achieving success and happiness. A family life should not be seen as a sign of failure and a wasted life.

Beyond the cities there are still places that are predominantly English and have a strong sense of English identity. A new generation is growing up there and attending schools where they feel comfortable and at home. Unlike earlier generations of English children they live among adults who have had their lives changed by immigration. They know what it is like to be uprooted by force of circumstance and they are reluctant to let it happen again because they realise that there is nowhere else to go. Will the attitudes of those people be passed on to the new generation or will English children, subject as they are to indoctrination from the education and broadcasting systems, accept the new situation as normal? Will they too be overcome by change, and lament when they are older the passing of a time when they enjoyed a relaxed feeling of community and belonging.

It is probable that the vast majority of the English are aware of what is happening to them as a nation but feel powerless to stop it continuing. As new settlers arrive and more children are born to them, so more English move out of the cities. The houses, gardens, schools, libraries, shops and other things that were part of the English community become part of another community that feels no need to preserve anything of another community's past. They want to impose their identity and mark their presence on the land they have settled. None of that is surprising because it has happened throughout history during periods of migration and settlement. What is so very different about this migration and settlement is that members of the indigenous nation have rushed forward falling over themselves to welcome the newcomers. "Please take this." "What can we do to make you feel at home?" "How would you like us to re-arrange things so that you feel more comfortable?" Always a concern for the *rights* of others and always contempt for the English. The greater the vandalism the more they revel in the excitement of it all. The queue is never ending but however many come, they always want more. Never is the destruction enough to lift their burden of guilt and self-loathing.

Among the liberals forming the welcoming throng are the Church of England clergy who gaze heavenward as they chant, "Lord we have sinned but we will redeem ourselves by taking in all who wish to come here. They are our brothers and sisters, and it is our duty to welcome and befriend them. It is our duty as Christians to share all we have with the needy of the world." With gleaming eyes they urge their flock to show commitment to the teaching of the Lord. Such is their missionary zeal that they fail to notice a lack of enthusiasm among those they would lead.

There, with the rest, are the politicians who feel compelled to always be seen to be enthusiastic about the great upheaval. It is a wonderful thing; a great economic and cultural blessing, or so they say despite thinking it a great tragedy. They feel the guilt of collaborators but fear that if they say what they mean the sky will fall in on them.

Always the television programmes telling how unfortunate, genuine, and deserving of help the new arrivals are. Never a programme telling how the English feel about what is happening, unless of course it is to ridicule them. There can be few who have not noted the crude propaganda that compares decent, intelligent asylum seekers with English youths on the streets after the pubs have closed on a Saturday night. The more crude and badly expressed the views of the English the better they are suited to comparison with the heartfelt tales of woe from the asylum seekers.

The views expressed in the pubs and other meeting place of the English are markedly different from those broadcast each day by radio and television journalists. The English find a partial release from their frustration by grumbling to each other but they are unable to voice their views as a community, and this is the source of their weakness. Expressions of discontent remain isolated and ineffectual because the means for uniting the English are in the hands of those who are either actively involved in suppressing dissent or are scared to be seen supporting it. Occasionally someone manages in some way to make the feelings of the English widely known. Most know that they will be harshly judged and punished, and their views will be twisted and misrepresented, but better that than bearing the shame of remaining silent and accepting the fate others wish for them.

The inquisition of dissidents often begins when a witch-finder brings the offence to public attention. Accusers then flock around the victim striving to outdo each other in their condemnation and outrage. How brave these liberal warriors are, always risking all they have in such a noble cause against such powerful enemies. Always on the side of truth and decency, and always in favour of free expression. Well not always, "There really must be limits." They act with valour to deny freedom in the name of preserving it. "No of course it is not a denial of freedom to prevent dissidents from making their views known, it is merely a matter of upholding the law and civilised standards. The law is neutral." Were the laws of the Third Reich and the Soviet Union neutral? Was the punishment of dissent in those states just a mater of upholding civilised standards? Do those who make the law determine civilised standards? Can any law be neutral when politicians make it? Can laws that prevent the free expression of political views be lacking in political intent?

The Young English

Liberals use any means possible to sell their goods and their values. Youth culture is one of their most successful marketing devices. The selling technique is to pick and mix elements from different cultures and present them as a life-style – a popular or global youth culture. Above all, the life-style must seem an exciting and easy one to attain – just say the right things and buy the right products. For the past decade or so, one of the most important ingredients in the cultural cocktail has been Black-American urban youth culture, which is a fast, consumerist street culture with anti-authority overtones. It provides a means of promoting values and attitudes relating to consumption and family life that liberals and corporations favour. There is an emphasis on image and status derived from clothes and words, and no room for a formal family life. Relationships, like food, are taken on the hoof. We do what we want, when we want and see where it takes us. Self-indulgence and a disregard for wider communal interests are the norm. It is the culture of outsiders but it has been adopted by insiders and become part of modern global youth culture.

Such is the desire of young people to conform to the constraints of youth culture, that many Asian and White youths feel the need to talk, dress and as far as possible conform to the portrayed image of inner-city Black-Americans. Being Black seems more exiting and rebellious than being Asian or White. An association with Black people is thought daring in itself, and the feeling is enhanced if it provokes disapproval. Some Black youths, especially males, are also drawn to the entertainment industry's image of what it means to be Black. The more they adopt the stereotypical lifestyle the more successful and respected they think they are.

There are many in the Black community, especially among religious groups, who want to prevent their children looking to role models manufactured by outsiders and reinforced by insiders. They believe their children are being tempted into a crude and violent life-style that offers them no hope for the future. It also helps promote a stereotypical image of Black youths and Black culture that is very different from how most Blacks live and how most aspire to live.

Tony Sewell has pointed to the anti-intellectual nature of a culture that "authenticates everything by street machismo." It is a way of life "which mindlessly defies authority and doesn't take advantage of educational opportunity." "Too many black boys cannot free themselves from an anti-school, anti-conformity peer grouping, a credo which itself demands absolute conformity."[228]

---

[228] From an article in *The Daily Telegraph* 12th December 2000, reproduced there with permission of *The Voice*.

For more than twenty years those very same attitudes have existed among children in schools where there are no Black pupils. Tony Sewell could equally be describing a very large number of English boys. All of our communities are facing much the same problem. The various Asian groups in England find that their children are also attracted to a hybrid street culture, and pick up the attitudes, values, and way of life that goes with it. Those Asian parents who feel uncomfortable about their children being absorbed into an alien culture are not necessarily racists. They simply have a natural desire to pass on to their children cultural values and attitudes that are part of their family history and identity. Asian cultures, like successful cultures everywhere, provide an identity and a viable way of life that links all age groups from birth to death.

John Lovejoy sees the break-up of rounded birth-to-death cultures as part of a process called *deculturalisation.* [229]

> Deculturalisation ... leaves individual men and women in a conceptual wilderness and in an unresolvable crisis of identity.
>
> The individual can no longer answer such basic questions as:
>
> "Who am I?" "What are our beliefs?"
> "What do I believe?" 'What are our origins?"
> "Where do I belong?" "What is our destiny?"
> "Who am I loyal to?"

In the US during the 1960's Black people set about bringing their people together and creating a strong communal identity. The English need to follow that lead. If English identity and culture were similarly promoted, English youngsters would have something of their own to turn to. That does not mean that they should not enjoy things from other cultures, it simply means that a rooted sense of English identity and belonging would enable them to appreciate the many fine things their own culture has to offer. Equally important, it would encourage them to build on past cultural achievements and keep them alive. All communities would benefit from resisting the globalisation of culture, and striving to retain and build on greater cultural diversity.

The Right to Speak and Resist

One of the odd things about this period of upheaval is that while English liberals show total hostility to those who complain about what is going on, many, and perhaps the majority, of the non-English population of England understand and even sympathise with the frustrations felt by the English. The settlers can imagine how they would feel in similar circumstances. For instance, what if Indian

---

[229] The following quote is from *The Deculturalisation of the English People*, John Lovejoy, Athelney, 2000.

governments were to allow, and even encourage, large numbers of Black and White immigrants to settle in Indian towns and cites? How would they feel if the settlers demanded that Indian society change in order to accommodate the immigrants' needs? What if the indigenous population were told that within 60 years they would become a minority in their own land? It is probable that Indians would make their opposition known and do their best to prevent such things happening. What if instead of India it happened in Ghana or Ireland or anywhere else?

Although many commiserate with the English, there are some within the settler population who lack any sympathy whatsoever. Like many of those writing articles for liberal newspapers, they revel in the discomfort of the English and smirk at the thought of the English nation withering away. Some settlers have been given the status of experts on Englishness and Britishness, despite them displaying little evidence of expertise on those matters. They have nothing particularly original, interesting or intelligent to say but are nevertheless given space in newspapers and time in the broadcast media to say it. Media fame gets them invited on to committees where they are able to play a part in shaping reports and recommendations which criticise and make demands of the English. Have any of these reports ever been critical of settler communities? Do they lambaste anyone but the English for their discriminatory communal practices? What of the institutionalised discrimination that always assumes the worst of the English and the best of settlers? Why the discriminatory practice which ensures that investigatory bodies consist almost exclusively of liberals and a disproportionately high proportion of ethnic minority members? Is it not obvious that the findings and recommendations of such bodies will be hopelessly biased and worthless? What makes these people think that they have the right to sit in judgement of the English? The positive thing that comes from their hostility and snide remarks is that it gives the English a glimpse of what the future might hold for them.

The fault for the Great Upheaval lies not with the settlers but with the short-sighted people who have engineered it. Some have an obsession with profit and economic growth. Others are driven by naive idealism. The more lacking in worldly wisdom these people are, the more brightly their idealism burns. As it becomes increasingly obvious that their scheme cannot work, so they become more determined to suppress opposition and push it through at any cost.

The English have a right to resist the liberal onslaught and demand an end to destructive policies that they have neither called for nor approved. But rights cannot always undo what has been unjustly done. The damage is already so deep and the consequences so great that even if the problem is immediately tackled, future generations of the English nation will look back on this period as a time of national tragedy. They will be haunted by the question – why did our ancestors allow it to happen? What collective insanity made it possible for the English to meekly abandon what other nations sacrifice so much to attain and preserve?

The New Immigration Deal

Liberal governing elites are faced with the consequences of decades of liberalism. Their societies are unsustainable because, among other things, they destroy the bonds that hold communities and societies together. They fail to recognise that families consisting of mother, father and children in a stable relationship are an essential part of a healthy society, as indeed are the communal customs and institutions that surround family life. Children are not just an option for those who lack the ability to do something more worthwhile and fulfilling.[230]

We are now seeing the result of many years of liberal propaganda and policies. So many people are *fulfilling themselves* in an introverted way that there are not enough families and children to keep liberal societies going. There is a shortage of young people to fill positions as teachers, policemen, nurses, soldiers and one-hundred-and-one other jobs. Having done so much to deter people from having children and finding happiness in family life, social-liberals see no other option but to import people and make a virtue of it. The crutches of a deformed society are transformed into moral obligations. We must take in waifs and strays because of our humanity and the brotherhood of mankind. Such kindness and generosity brings us the reward of social and economic rejuvenation. Thus, a policy born of desperation is promoted as if it is something inherently good and natural – something that all decent folk will applaud and benefit from.

Economic-liberals are more blunt in presenting the issue as one of economic necessity. Again the deformity is ignored and the dependency is made to seem natural and desirable. People have been bringing their skills and enterprise to Britain since time immemorial. The only difference now is that we need more of them so that we can better compete and succeed in the global economy. Immigrants are seen as a commodity, importing more labour will enable us to export more goods and services, and of course, that will create jobs. Economic-liberals always show a touching concern for jobs. They are not advocating a policy because it suits them but because it will benefit us.

Liberals have become so dependent on immigration in both an ideological and practical sense that they would find it difficult to stop it even if they wanted to. Since World War II, Conservative and Labour governments, with the support of Liberals, oversaw large increases in the rate of immigration into the UK but always denied that they encouraged it. Each new wave was described as a one-off moral or legal obligation. Governments were always on the defensive, seeking to calm the fears of the indigenous population that they and their way of life would be submerged beneath continuous waves of immigration. Labour governments

---

[230] Government Ministers have declared that families are at the heart of peaceful and well-ordered societies. However, their policies and attitudes do nothing to encourage family life, unless a family is seen as little more than a group of people living together in a household, whether or not they are kindred – i.e. related by blood or marriage. Liberal *family life* is a microcosm of liberal society.

were the worst offenders but the allegation that the Labour Party was the party of immigration was dismissed as ludicrous.

In the late 1990s there was yet another wave of immigration overlaying an already high annual inflow. This time it was disguised as asylum seeking. Familiar clichés were trotted out, including the moral obligation that is said to flow from *our tradition of tolerance and understanding* and our historical willingness to take in refugees and those fleeing from oppressive regimes. The rhetoric has an American ring to it and that is no accident because the people spouting it want to make the UK an immigrant society like the USA.

This latest wave of immigration, which seems likely to continue indefinitely, compelled the Labour Party and the government of Tony Blair to change strategy. Both became officially in favour of immigration. No longer the defensive posture but a bold promotion of immigration as a necessity and a benefit to the wellbeing of one and all – it seems we just cannot manage without these people and their skills and vitality. Not only that, but we have always had waves of immigration and benefited greatly from it. Hence the renewed efforts of the education and broadcasting systems to promote a rewriting of history.

A campaign to justify the new approach was launched in September 2000 by Barbara Roche, the Home Office minister. She called for a debate on the need to permit the entry of economic migrants into the UK. There was little need for a debate because a new immigration policy had already been drawn up and was to be launched a few weeks later. What she meant by *a debate* was the opportunity for the launch to be preceded by several weeks of a media artillery barrage designed to soften up public opinion. Strong support came from the social-liberal press (e.g. *The Guardian, The Independent, The Mirror, The Observer*), which deems immigration to be *a good thing*. Economic-liberals (e.g. *The Daily Telegraph*[231]) also saw the need to import each year up to 100,000 skilled workers, including computer programmers and staff for *ethnic restaurants*. By the time the announcement was actually made its details had been so widely trailed they were well known. As might be expected the debate was one-sided and support for increased immigration overwhelming. Well, support was overwhelming among those journalists who expressed an opinion but it was not overwhelming among the electorate. (See *Readers Digest* poll below)

An official statement duly followed. The Home Office would set a maximum quota of 100,000 economic migrants per year. That would be new immigration, i.e. in addition to the existing level of immigration. The reason given was labour shortages due to low levels of unemployment and the difficulty (impossibility) of retraining poorly educated, unskilled jobless for jobs in information technology, engineering and teaching. Foreigners would be given permission to enter the UK if

---

[231] Article, *For the good of the country, let's have more immigrants*, by Matt Ridley, The Daily Telegraph 24th July 2000

they had qualifications that would enable them to find jobs that would boost the economy. A point system similar to that used in Canada was suggested.

Did this proposal appear in an election manifesto or was it otherwise approved by the electorate? Was any consideration given to cultural considerations or the need to preserve social cohesion? Was it suggested that the long-term problem of labour shortage might be solved by encouraging family life and a higher birth-rate among the indigenous population? Was it pointed out that the current rate of immigration plus births is already increasing the predominately young settler population at a rate exceeding 300,000 per year? Will the UK government be able to stop millions of people from Eastern Europe migrating to England when the EU is expanded Eastwards?[232] The answer in each case is *no*.

Another consideration is that a decline in population size would be a good thing because England is an overpopulated country. A reduction from about 50 million to 30 million would make England a more pleasant place in which to live.[233] For one thing, *urban sprawl* could be reversed. One of the problems liberals have with this approach is that they are locked into a quest for economic growth and the greater power and influence they believe it brings. An increasing population will in itself increase Gross Domestic Product if only because more people will be involved in economic activity. A smaller population generates a smaller *surplus*, which means less tax revenue with which to finance those things powerful states are said to need. The governing elites of civic-states therefore see no problem in importing up to another 100,000 people plus dependants each year – the more the merrier.

With fortuitous timing for Barbara Roche's *debate* came the publication of the results of an opinion poll commissioned and published by *Readers Digest* (October 2000).[234] The poll showed that 66 per cent of those asked believe that there are too many immigrants in Britain; 80 per cent believe that *refugees* come to Britain because they think it a "soft touch"; 63 per cent believe that too much help is given to immigrants.

Opinion is continually being polled and politicians are well aware that a large majority of the British population is opposed to more immigration and resents the way many would-be economic migrants falsely claim to be refugees. In England,

---

[232] When the EU is expanded eastwards, there will be large-scale migration to the west. Included in that will be the big *Gypsy* population, many or most of which will migrate to England. The free movement of people within the EU means it is impossible for the UK government to stop the migration. The same thing will happen if/when Turkey becomes a member of the EU. Yet most of the English population is completely unaware of the implications of EU enlargement. When the time comes, the UK government will simply say that they are powerless to do anything about it. In doing so they will admit that democracy is dead and they are redundant.

[233] 1999: England 50 mill; Scotland 5 mill; Wales 3 mill; N Ireland 1½ mill. www.statistics.gov.uk

[234] MORI interviewed 2,118 adults (aged 15 plus) face-to-face in their homes between 20th and 24th July 2000.

the part of Britain in which most immigrants settle, the percentage opposed to immigration is far higher. The results of these polls are not usually published, so, why was this particular poll, which was published under the headline "Are We a Tolerant Nation?" given such prominence in the media? The simple answer is that it was used as a device to attack the views of the majority and alleged they are based on ignorance and prejudice. That line was taken in a BBC *Newsnight* programme where Prof. Stuart Hall, an experienced broadcaster and commentator, was pitted against an inarticulate person who had been publicly complaining about the number of Eastern European immigrants in Dover. The Scottish programme presenter had no shame about revealing her liberal views (no surprise) and took the stance that the problem was not the inflow of immigrants and refugees but how to get more than 50% of the population to change its mind and adopt a welcoming liberal perspective. No concern whatsoever was shown for the fact that the views of 80% of the population were not being represented by MPs and the government. The presentation of the issue was entirely predictable but Prof. Hall made a telling remark when he told the campaigner from Dover that she was responsible for the Kosovan refugees in Dover because "you bombed Kosovo." The meaning seemed to be that she being British was responsible for the actions of the British government while he, being Black, was not. This after we have been told for many years that Black, White or Asian, we are all equally British.

The *Readers Digest* article claimed that the poll revealed widespread ignorance about the number of immigrants in Britain. Those polled gave an average figure of 20% whereas "the real figure" was given as 4%. In a similar way, it was believed that 26% of the population belongs to an ethnic minority whereas, "Actually it is around 7%."

Without knowing the way the question was framed it is difficult to interpret the answers. From what is known, those polled were expected to be able to distinguish between members of *the ethnic minorities* born in Britain and those born abroad. Most of the indigenous British population regards those people who are not English, Scottish or Welsh as immigrants, wherever they were born. Estimates of numbers are based on personal experience – what they have seen on their travels – and what their friends and relatives have seen. Those unofficial estimates are probably a lot nearer *the real figure* than the official estimates.

What is to be made of the statement that 7% of the population belong to ethnic minorities when it is clear that the total number of Irish, Scots and Welsh living in Britain greatly exceed 7% of the total? If these groups are excluded from the definition of an *ethnic minority* why are they excluded? How is an ethnic minority defined and who makes the definition? If the people conducting and publishing the poll use *ethnic minority* but mean Black and Asian why not say so?

How can it be claimed that immigrants make up 4% of the population when there are no figures for illegal immigrants or people from the EU? The claimed facts are not facts at all – they are only estimates. There are no *real* or *actual figures* as claimed in the *Readers Digest* article because nobody really knows how many immigrants there are in Britain or how many of them belong to ethnic minorities. Yet these so-called *facts* were quoted in the *Newsnight* programme.

What is known is that official figures always understate the number of foreigners living in Britain and every few years the official figure increases. In the early 1970s we were told that the number of people from the New Commonwealth (i.e. Black and Asian) made up less than 2% of the British population. This was regarded as an insignificant percentage. In the 1980s 4% belonged to ethnic minorities (i.e. Black and Asian); in 1996 5·6%; in 1999 7%. The census in 2001 is sure to push the official figure higher. Whether they be under-estimates or not, the official figures show an accelerating growth in the non-indigenous population of Great Britain. What percentage figure does the government think is significant? At what point is the indigenous population entitled to feel concern and express an opinion?

Attention is often directed at the official immigration and settlement figures for the ethnic minority population, which in effect means Black and Asian. Those figures even if correct understate the problem because there is also immigration from the EU (for which there seem to be no figures) which adds to the non-English population of England. In addition to lawful immigration from the EU, there is a steady flow of immigrants who gain entry as of right from other parts of the world because they are related to settlers who are already in the UK. On top of that, there are asylum seekers/economic migrants and well-organised criminal activity that brings in substantial numbers of illegal immigrants. When, in December 2000, P&O introduced checks on trucks using their ferries from the continent to England, they found 43 illegal immigrants on the first day. That is a yearly rate of over 15,000. What about all the other ferry operators and other means of entry? What also of the *marriages of convenience* that take place each year. The estimate for the number of these *false marriages* in London during the year 2000 is 10,000.[235]

The official figure for net immigration to Britain in 1999 is 185,000, which does not include illegal immigration and immigration from the EU. In future, we are to have up to 100,000 more immigrants per year plus dependants. The total inflow is likely to exceed 350,000 per year and will probably be much higher. There are many past and present members of the Immigration Services who believe that the official figures greatly underestimate the size of the non-indigenous population and the yearly inflow.

When mass migration began, liberals argued that the numbers were insignificant and that immigrants would be *integrated* into British society. When it was pointed

---

[235] *BBC News 24*

out that certain groups of immigrants had very high fertility rates, liberals argued that it was due to a history of economic hardship and high infant mortality rates. They went on to suggest that when the new arrivals become absorbed into British society their birth-rate would decline and come into line with that of the indigenous British population. Current figures show that immigration is not insignificant and that the assurances were worthless. Fertility rates declined but remained high because they were driven by culture. Communities that encourage and value large families will have a higher birth-rate than those where children are seen as a liability in the struggle for material wealth and self-gratification. Increasingly large numbers of settlers said no to liberalism and no to integration. Thus, liberals had little choice but to abandon their formerly heavily-defended lines and set up new ones. At the end of the transition, *integration*, which had once been at the centre of liberal immigration policy, was condemned as a racist concept. The new line on mass immigration became, "What does it matter? We are all British citizens in a British multi-cultural civic society – what does it matter where anyone comes from or who produces the children we all need?" They would say that wouldn't they but even liberals must be able to see that it does matter. Or are they in deep space and completely and hopelessly out of touch with reality on Earth?

Fertility Rates Determine Future Populations

The English birth-rate is not as popularly supposed an average of 2·4 children per couple. It is no more than 1·8 at most and probably about 1·6 or less. It is certainly well below the 2·1 rate needed to maintain the English population at its present level. An indication of the seriousness of the problem was given in a study by the Family Policy Studies Centre.

> The average number of children being born has fallen to 1·73 per woman, which although higher than in most European Union countries is still below the 2·1 birth-rate needed for the long-term replacement of the population.[236]

The oft-quoted but long out of date figure of 2·4 for the average size of a British family tells us little about the English birth-rate unless we also know how many Englishwomen there are and how many of them are having children. A better measure of whether a nation is growing in number or shrinking is the *total period fertility rate*. TPFR indicates the average number of births for all women during the whole of their reproductive life. The Office of Population and Census gives fertility rates for many foreign national groups living in Britain but it does not give figures for the English, Scottish or Welsh, perhaps because it does not recognise them as ethnic groups or because it is thought that such figures would cause alarm.

---

[236] Richard Eden in *The Daily Telegraph* 27th March 2000. The figures appear to be for the UK.

However, it is not difficult to see that the average TPFR for non-European ethnic groups is far higher than replacement level, while the average TPFR for the remainder of the female UK population is well below replacement level. In other words, the size of the English population is falling. The size of the Asian population (in particular the Moslem Asian population) is likely to continue to grow and will at least double during the next 25 years if its TPFR remains at the current level.

Because no figures are collected for the English fertility rate we have no way of telling just how low it is. What we do know is that it is below the 1·73 average. Fertility rates for ethnic minority groups are not only well above the average but also above replacement levels. Some ethnic minority groups, such as Bangladeshis, have fertility rates higher than 6, which means that there is a rapid growth in the size of the Bangladeshi population in the UK.

The English population is ageing. There are no official figures for the English but 17% of the White population in Britain is over 65, while the figure for the non-White population is 3%.[237] A large part of the English population is made up of those born in the baby boom after Word War II. As they die over the next thirty years, there will be a dramatic reduction in the size of the English population. If, as is likely, the immigrant population continues to expand, even if at a slower rate than before, it will form a very large proportion of the population. 33% of the ethnic minority population is under 16 while the figure for the White population is 20%. Look at the ethnic mix in schools and you have a view of the future. Ethnic minorities form 41% of the schoolchildren in Birmingham and 45% in Leicester. The proportion in both places is increasing and growth is likely to accelerate because a large part of the population in both places is Indian, Pakistani and Bangladeshi, three groups with high fertility rates. How many years will pass before liberals are able to welcome and celebrate yet another great achievement, an *English* city with an ethnic-minority majority. Perhaps that marker has already been passed because it is probable that less than half the population of London is English. We have the odd situation where we have figures for how many Chinese and Bangladeshis live in London and Great Britain but we do not have a figure for the number of English.[238]

---

[237] In England, as in many other places, life expectancy is increasing. That increase reduces the death rate and masks to some extent a declining birth-rate and a trend towards a long-term decrease in population.

[238] Due to institutionalised discrimination, no figures are gathered for any of the indigenous nations. In the 2001 census, 'Scottish' will be included in the list of ethnic groups in Scotland, and 'Irish' will be an option in Northern Ireland. The English and Welsh are to be ignored in their own countries.

Population Change by Ethnic Group 1981–1991 (Great Britain)

M4 Source 1991 Census as published in the Daily Telegraph 2nd March 1999

Group	1981 (000s)	1991 (000s)	% change
Total White	52,600	53,062	0·9
Black – Caribbean	422·5	522·2	23·6
Black-African	141·4	219·2	55·0
Black-Other	143·8	188·2	30·9
Total Black	707·7	929·6	31·4
Indian	627·8	877	39·6
Pakistani	344·5	500·3	45·2
Bangladeshi	87·8	171·5	95·4
Total	1,060·1	1,548·8	46·1
Chinese	111·5	160·8	44·2
Other-Asian	110·4	202·3	83·2
Other-Other	214·0	302·2	41·2
Total other	435·9	665·3	52·6
Total all ethnic minorities	2,203·7	3,143·7	42·7

The table above shows the percentage increase for the White population over the decade 1981–1991 as 0·9%. That figure does not represent English population growth because, as we have seen, the study by the Family Policy Studies Centre indicates that the English fertility rate is well below replacement level and the size of the English population is falling. The overall increase in the White population is due mainly to immigration from the EU and Eastern Europe. The size of the English population in England is probably about 40 million.

For the purpose of projecting forward population trends for 1981–1991 (see below), the steady fall in the English population has been ignored. For the sake of simplicity, the 0·9% growth figure for Whites has been used. It can be seen in the table below that if current trends continue, the White population of Great Britain will be in a minority about the year 2073. In England, where a disproportionately high number of non-White settlers live, Whites will be in a minority earlier. [239] The English will be a minority in England earlier still. Scots will probably remain in a majority in Scotland well beyond the end of the twenty-first century but they should not gloat because they too have a low fertility rate and they may be subject to English migration.

Forward projection of 1981–1991 population growth trends

Year to	White		Non-White	
	increase at 0·9% per decade	total population	increase at 42·7% per decade	total population
2001	477,560	53,539,860	1,342359	4,486,059
2011	481,858	54,021,719	1,915547	6,401,607
2021	486,195	54,507,914	2,733486	9,135,093
2031	490,571	54,998,486	3,900685	13,053,778
2041	494,986	55,493,472	5,566277	18,602,056
2051	499,441	55,992,913	7,943078	26,545,134
2061	503,936	56,496,850	11,334772	37,879,907
2071	508,471	57,005,321	16,174720	54,054,627
2081	513,047	57,518,369	23,081326	77,135,953
2091	517,665	58,036,034	32,937052	110,073,005

It can rightly be argued that trends can be misleading. For example, the growth rate attributed to the non-White population may be thought too high. Perhaps the rate of growth will reduce. Unfortunately, there is no evidence to support that view. On the other side it can be argued that the figures for the White population hide the rapid fall that is likely to occur in the English population during the period 2010–2030 when most of the post World War II baby boomers die. There is likely to be a further fall in the thirty years after that, as a generation dies which has fallen far short of replacing itself. Also, the figures do not reflect the fact that a disproportionately high number of settlers of all races live in England. Neither does it allow for illegal immigration and the consequent under-reporting of ethnic minority numbers in census returns and other sources of information. The official

---

[239] It is unfortunate that the discussion has to centre on the White – Non-White balance. English nationalists would prefer to use English – Non-English, thus avoiding the issue of race. Settlers are settlers whatever their race. However, the English are lumped together with others in a White category and that is what we have to work with.

starting figures for the non-White population, on which the projection is based, are almost certainly an underestimate, and by a large margin. There can be few people who believe official figures or government forecasts when the evidence of their own eyes suggests they are hopelessly wrong.

Another alarming aspect of the projection is that England looks likely to have Third World population growth and a population of about 200 million by the end of the century. If that does not come about it will be because something will have happened to change current trends.

Even if the rough and ready projection used above is rejected, it surely has to be conceded that the non-English population of England is increasing at a rapid rate while the English population is falling. Even if all immigration stopped tomorrow, the non-English population will on current trends continue to grow and the English will become a minority in England. The point at issue is not whether these changes are taking place but the rate at which they are happening. That in itself makes it a proper topic for discussion.

Those who think all of this is alarmist should consider the following information drawn from an article, *The last days of a white world*, by Anthony Browne in *The Observer*, 3rd September 2000.

> Due to immigration and higher fertility rates, the Asian and Latino populations of California have risen by about 30% since 1990. In the same period, due to low immigration and low fertility rates, the population of non-Hispanic Whites has fallen by 3 per cent.

> In 1970, 80% of Californians were White.
> By 2040, Hispanics are expected to form the majority in California.

> Trends in California are often followed in the rest of the USA. In the year 2000, about 72 per cent of the whole US population is non-Hispanic Whites. By 2060, non-Hispanic Whites will form a minority.[240]

> "Where America goes, Europe follows 30 years later. There is a potential for Whites to become a minority in some European countries."

> "At the moment ethnic minorities are about 40 per cent in London. The demographics show that White people in London will become a minority by 2010" "We could have a majority black Britain by the turn of the century." The quotations are those of Lee Jasper, race relations adviser to Ken Livingstone, Mayor of London.

> Due to higher fertility rates and immigration, the ethnic minority population in Britain is growing by 2 to 3 per cent a year.

---

[240] US Census Bureau

One demographer, who didn't want to be named for fear of being called racist, said: "It's a matter of pure arithmetic that, if nothing else happens, non-Europeans will become a majority and Whites a minority in the UK. That would probably be the first time an indigenous population has voluntarily become a minority in its historic homeland."[241]

What cultural, communal, economic, social and political problems are likely to arise as the result of such demographic changes? There is scope for endless speculation and projections of trends and interpretation of figures. The proper way to deal with the issue is to collect, publish and discuss information that throws light on the matter. A start can be made with an official recognition by the state that the English exist. The census and other fact-gathering projects should collect information about the English, Scots and Welsh, and give separate figures for England, Scotland and Wales. We need open sensible discussion that recognises English interests and concerns. We cannot continue to rely on liberal platitudes and unsubstantiated official statements that prove to be misleading and wildly inaccurate. What is needed is frank and open discussion, and the opportunity for the English to make known their views about the sort of future they want. We are entitled to that and demand nothing less.

The nationalist view on immigration is that if the English, or any other nation, are faced with the prospect of becoming a minority in their own homeland they have a right to discuss the issue among themselves and to take whatever action they deem appropriate. Commonsense suggests that an anticipated problem should be discussed and a reasonable solution sought at an early stage because that is when the options available, and the ability to act, are greatest. It is not for the people of other countries and states to pontificate and lecture an indigenous people on such important matters. Frankly, it is none of their business.

Some view with glee the prospect of the English becoming a minority in their own country. Does it really matter if it happens? Perhaps the English should stop complaining because to talk about it feeds racism? Anyway, they deserve what they are going to get. According to Yasmin Alibhai-Brown, it is the Empire striking back.[242] It seems from this that the children should pay for the sins of their fathers. The colonisation of England can go ahead without the settlers feeling any guilt because the ancestors of those colonisers had their homeland colonised by the British. But wait, didn't Indians play a part in the colonisation of Uganda? 'Ah yes

---

[241] It is misleading to suggest that the English are voluntarily becoming a minority in their homeland. They are having it imposed on them. The vast majority of English people want these flows stopped whatever the numbers involved but in our liberal *democracy* the views of *the people* count for nothing.

[242] *The last days of a white world*, by Anthony Browne in *The Observer*, 3rd September 2000

but that was the fault of the British who encouraged them to go there and many other places.' But it can be clearly seen that Indians were willing accomplices who went to various parts of the British Empire because it was in their interest to do so. Africans were no more pleased to have Indians in their countries than they were to have the British. In the end, the Indians were more disliked and resented than the British. The expulsion of Indians from Uganda had the overwhelming support of the indigenous people. The Indians were outsiders who had much closer links with Indians in India and other parts of the world than with Black Ugandans. Social contact and intermarriage between the two groups was minimal. The only real relationship was an economic one, with Indians controlling trade and commerce. The Indians were seen as colonisers and settlers in much the same way that Europeans are seen as colonisers and settlers in Zimbabwe and other African states. They are outsiders; they do not naturally belong there; the indigenous people resent their presence.

When the Indians left Uganda they went to the UK, primarily to England, where they again became settlers and outsiders. One consequence of that and other settlement is that we English have people in England re-writing our history, questioning who we are and lecturing us as if we are naughty children.

What of that other part of the Indian diaspora which colonised Fiji? Well, once again there are Indians who claim they were innocent participants. It was of course all the fault of the British, which in large part it was. But how very convenient it is for those who are colonising England to claim to be the victims of colonisation.

Indeed the British governing elite inflicted great and lasting harm on Fiji and Fijians, and many other indigenous people. Their concern then as now was primarily with trade, profit and economic growth. Indians were willing accomplices throughout. Since that time, the Empire has gone and there is no English settlement of Fiji. What crime did their ancestors commit against Indians to make Fijians so deserving of Indian settlement? It must have been very wicked because Fijians are suffering greatly. Does Yasmin Alibhai-Brown have any sympathy for Fijians or are they suffering for the sins of their ancestors? Perhaps the wickedness lingers on in the great resentment the overwhelming majority of Fijians feel towards Indian settlers. Most Fijians simply want to govern themselves and preserve their way of life, as do indigenous people everywhere, and that includes the English.

A fitting end is an eloquent appeal from a Fijian. Liberals will probably find it difficult to understand her sadness at what is happening to her homeland but others will sympathise.

Speech by Taina Woodward, a Fijian

Presented to a conference of women at the United Nations,
New York City, 8 June 2000

Published by Te Karere Ipurangi – Maori News Online http://go.to/karere
The Fijian Coupe Supplement http://maorinews.com/karere/fiji/

Good afternoon Ladies and perhaps a few Gentlemen.

By now most of you have heard of the coup in Fiji. About 30 of our people are being held hostage. The President has been forced to resign and the Constitution put in place in 1997 has been revoked. The army has taken over and for the most part law and order has been restored. Most of the World thinks that little is being done to resolve the crisis. They are wrong.

I have been invited to this meeting as a Fijian, a housewife, and mother of three. In addition, with my husband I look after my Mother and a nephew. I was born and raised in Fiji, I am a Fiji Citizen, and I intend to die and be buried in Fiji.

I do not represent any government or organization. I speak only as a Fijian, which in Fiji is understood to mean- "Indigenous Fijian". Other ethnic groups are called "Fiji Citizens", but not "Fijians". When I say "Fijian" in what follows, I mean "indigenous Fijian".

I want to speak to you from the bottom of my heart and try to explain certain things about the Fijian values, customs, ways of communicating, mode of leadership, and sensitivities. I want to speak to you about the Soul of Fijians. I hope that I can touch the souls of indigenous people everywhere.

We are a people who have occupied what is now the Fiji Islands for thousands of years. When we came, as far as anyone knows, no one else occupied the land. Our traditional oral history tells how we came and how we settled. Fiji is our "Promised Land", the land of our forefathers. Our language and customs are at one with our people and our land and our genealogy.

In 1870 our land was "ceded to Great Britain" under Queen Victoria. We were under attack by our neighbours, the "Friendly" Islands of Tonga. In addition, our dominant Chief Cakobau was being blackmailed by the local American Consul and had no means of paying the extortionate payment demanded by this man for having accidentally burnt his own house down during a drunken 4th of July celebration. American warships were on the way. Queen Victoria rescued us from these situations at the invitation of our paramount chief and we "voluntarily", if you can call it that, became a colony under a Deed of Cession.

There were certain understandings at the time of Cession to Great Britain and there were many things left unsaid. One was that we would continue to be led by our own chiefs with our own style of government, a style that is called "consensus".

But Queen Victoria also became our Queen. Another understanding was that while others were allowed to use our land, there was no such thing as the permanent alienation of our land, called "sale" in English. In times of war, some Chiefs sold islands out from under their people, but the intent here was to destroy or enslave the people, to detach them from their roots and their livelihood, to publicly humiliate them. If there is a meaning, this is the meaning of "sale of land" in Fiji. Land is a sensitive issue in Fiji.

In fact there is no word in the Fijian language to describe the "sale" of land, as the Western world knows it. It is not even a concept. If you were to sell your land, you at the same time sell your forefathers. The term "sale" is sometimes used, but it really means "lease", "rent", or "use" of land. This concept is familiar to many indigenous societies around the world, and it has been a source of great misunderstanding for people from around the world who have sought to acquire and settle land, and agony for those who thought it was perpetually theirs. We let people use our land and were surprised when they built fences and chased us away with weapons.

The British sent an expert to assess the economic potential of Fiji. This was around the time of the American Civil War and cotton was in great demand, so cotton was grown for a time. Later it was discovered that sugar cane was a more economic crop. Sugar became our major industry.

The sugar industry, like the cotton industry, required labour. We Fijians were self-sufficient nutritionally and economically with our abundance of sea and land resources. We were not interested in plantation labour. The British brought many workers from another of their colonies, India, to fill this need. These people worked hard, multiplied, and were allowed by the British Colonial Government to stay in Fiji.

At the time our chiefs ceded Fiji to Great Britain, we understood that other people would come and use our abundant land, but we did not foresee an open immigration policy or massive immigration. We did not know that we would come to be outnumbered in Our Sacred Homeland by people from another culture, many of whom did not wish to join our Family culturally.

We Fijians pride ourselves on our friendliness and hospitality. We welcome visitors and we try to make them feel at home. We invite them into our homes. But we do not expect them to take over our homes, even if they arrive in great numbers. This has confused people from other cultures who do not understand Fijians.

Fijians live in a communal lifestyle, which survives by sharing. We give and we receive. When the missionaries came and told us it was more blessed to give than to receive, this was nothing new to us. Most Fijians adopted Christianity readily. We found the values consistent with our own. Fijians are very generous people, but within our own system, there are also obligations. Some people from other cultures do not understand this. They think that when someone gives you something, it is a "good deal", a "bargain", and you should take more, and more, and more.

The British brought non-indigenous people to Fiji for their colonial economic purposes. They came in great numbers. They were of a different culture with different customs from our own; they married young and multiplied rapidly. For the most part they rigidly clung to their native cultures, religions, and value systems. Only a few joined ours. When the British left us Independent in 1970, they also left us with a majority non-indigenous, not-very-well-integrated population. The British did this in a smaller way all over the World. Perhaps they did not see the problems it would create. Perhaps they did and slyly washed their hands of it. In some cases in Africa, people and their descendants uprooted by the Colonial Government were offered citizenship in Britain. So many wanted to go to Britain that they had to create two classes of Citizenship. Not everyone who became a British Citizen in the Colonies was then entitled to settle in Britain.

Now Fijians welcome all kinds of people into their families. We especially like people who learn our language and customs. We have many instances of intermarriage and there are no taboos in this regard. But like all human beings, we tend to like people who like us. If people do not respect us, do not learn our customs, do not learn our language, do not learn to pronounce the names of places in Fiji correctly, after multiple generations living in Fiji, we tend to be suspicious of them. We especially don't like it if we perceive that such people try to take over our land and our government, and use fast economic growth, foreign aid, their concept of "democracy", and "strictly legal" means to justify it. This is not our way.

We do not like confrontation. When our people disagree, they remain silent. As you can well imagine, this is often misinterpreted by people who demand or expect that we tell them to their faces what we do not want. We want them to be sensitive enough to "feel" that we don't agree. This is part of our culture.

Economically, Fijians like to do things in their own good time. This is not always fast enough for other people. We have no objection if they move quickly or move on as long as they do not "step on".

Politically, we like to make sure everyone agrees before we move forward. We don't like to dominate minorities with majority rule. We like people to feel good about any decision. We are a small place, everybody knows most everybody, and people who try to push their own way get nowhere in the long run. Our value system has much to offer the World. We intend to preserve it and offer it to others. But we are only 350,000 people in a very large World. Size does not bother us. Our rugby teams are among the best in the World and beat countries 500 times our size. We are known as Peacekeepers with UNIFIL. The world needs to learn more harmonious ways of living and we have some good tips. But harmony usually requires the setting of and understanding boundaries of all kinds. We have our limits.

The current situation in Fiji is complex. There are many forces at work. The outside World sees primarily a racial issue. Fijians know that there is also a reconfiguration of power amongst the Fijians. There is a struggle between traditional Fijian Confederacies, there is a call for a new Confederacy, there is a struggle between the new middle class and the older traditions, and we women have also recently come into the political limelight. Reconfiguration of the Fijians is definitely our problem and no one else's. We will deal with it in our own good time. We welcome your views and un-tied assistance, but we will deal with it.

It is our relationship with our non-indigenous population that has attracted the interest of the World. The World media loves to talk about, exaggerate, and exacerbate the problems of "race". It provides prime time coverage and makes people not directly involved feel superior, no matter what they have inside them.

For more than 100 years, Fijians have lived side by side with our non-indigenous neighbours. We did not invite them, but we nevertheless welcomed them. We help them, they help us. We sometimes go to their houses and they often come to ours. We respect each other. We work together. We often drink and eat together. But for the most part, our cultures, and to a large extent our values, remain distinct. We believe that the vast majority of this population just wants to live and work peacefully in Fiji. We welcome this. We even allow them to get rich in Fiji, when few of us Fijians, because of our communal sharing-oriented society, can ever aspire to this. Many of them, when they can afford it or have the opportunity, move on to more developed countries with greater opportunities. Some choose to stay and live in harmony with us.

But we have our limits. We have our land, our people, our leaders, our customs, and our Souls. We want to be led by our own people who understand us and respect our customs. We cannot alienate any of our land any more than we can alienate our forefathers. Whatever the economic situation, the political situation, there is a boundary behind which we must fight for our survival as a people. No economic threats, bribery, media hype, or international organization will step across this line. Some people call this "indigenous rights". It is the "right to survive", have self-determination and ownership of our resources as an indigenous people in our homeland. This is in spite of TV, soap operas, The Simpson's, X-Files, global immigration and trade, all of which we enjoy in moderation just like you.

Recently, perhaps though the influence of TV, broader and better education, and general awareness, our people have become more vocal, and some even more belligerent. The emergence of previously quiet unspoken, usually smiling Fijians in our land is not unlike the emergence of women worldwide. We were not quite like this at the time Great Britain left us with a legacy of parliamentary government and a multi-racial population. We listened to our chiefs and our chiefs listened to the Queen of England.

The recent coup in Fiji was conducted at gunpoint by a handful of Fijians and their spokesman, George Speight. Some guns were fired; these people shot no one, although they did put a hole in the roof of our new Parliament building. They took some 40 parliamentarians hostage and some 10 have been released because they were either ill, or willing to sign away their positions in the former government. One was allowed to go home to her mother's funeral, and then return. Even in crisis, we practice the Fijian way.

The verbal manifesto of these rebels included revocation of the 1997 Constitution, resignation of the President, and installation of their own group of people to run the Government.

Some self-appointed "supporters" of the coup went on the rampage burning, smashing, and looting the capital city of Suva. Some even stooped to racial violence, which was totally unnecessary and uncalled for. This is what happens when things get out of control. Every society has its hooligans with a grudge against the World. Our police were caught by surprise. Fortunately, there was surprisingly little violence. A few days later, the first real casualty was a policeman whose car was shot at by some of the rebel supporters when he ventured into an insecure area. Our ordinary policemen do not, and never have, carried guns.

Why then, didn't the police and/or the army march in and stop this? Why do the Fijians allow a small band of armed rebels to take over their government? Why did security limit itself to restoring law and order in the streets and not the Parliament?

The answer is simple. While most people were disgusted with the violence, the causes espoused by the rebels had a considerable amount of mass support, some of which was out in the open – thousands of people marched – some of which was implicit – refusal to act against the rebels. Strong feelings of resentment have been suppressed by Fijians for decades. To this day, the degree of support for the rebel cause is unknown because no one on the outside really knows what lies at the bottom of the heart and soul of every Fijian. The police force was divided on the basic issues as was the army. One can assume that the whole of the Fijian population is divided or uncertain on the issues involved. We need time to self-examine, time to discuss, time to let our traditional leaders know in our traditional way. The answer is not obvious.

Fortunately, outside nations did not step in. They are watching anxiously, but they are waiting to see if Fijians can solve their own problems. This is good. Bloodshed has been largely avoided, even while the threat and potential exists. Fijians need to be left to solve their considerable problems in their own way and on their own schedule. It takes time to reach a consensus. Interference can make matters much worse and not solve the underlying problem.

The news media is impatient. Every Fijian knows that the whole of Fiji is a hive of talk and activity. Formal and informal meetings are being held. The pubs are alive. The village kava bowls are flowing. The telephones domestically and internationally are a-buzz. Gradually the chiefs will learn how their people really feel on the main issues. This is not a time for telling people what they want to hear, spouting religious moralisms, or pushing conventional wisdom. This is a time for searching out ones deepest beliefs and communicating them. Are we going to allow ourselves to be absorbed into the mediocrity of the modern world, or be dominated politically and economically by a foreign culture numbering nearly 1 billion people worldwide, or are we going to remain self-reliant and proud of our own culture of some 350,000 people? Are we going to claim our "indigenous rights", or are we going to join the soap operas of the world.

There are numerous examples of indigenous peoples who have either disappeared from the face of the earth or have been marginalized in their own land. We can look around the Pacific Rim at New Zealand, Australia, the United States, and Canada at countries where the indigenous people are found mainly on welfare rolls and in the prisons. They are an "endangered species". Why? Because they had different customs and traditions that did not stand up well to the onslaught and pace of colonialism and capitalism. Their souls were broken by their captors. They were, and still are, human, not material oriented, communalistic, but slower and less acquisitive. They had no powerful weapons. In addition, open or selective migration was promoted by the ruling cultures, so that the majority rule of democracy finished off the political marginalization process.

This will not happen to Fijians. We are drawing the line. Some are openly fighting for our beliefs. We do not know yet how many will join in non-violent support. We will wait and see because we do not want a blood bath and we trust our people and our traditional leaders.

What about our adopted non-indigenous brothers and sisters? They are part of Fiji. They have helped us as they helped themselves over the years and we sincerely hope they will continue to do so. We are basically a very peaceful and hospitable people. We espouse Christian values and we respect all religions. But we have learned the hard way that there is such a thing as giving away too much. We will not give away our sovereignty, our nation, or our souls. We will not allow our culture to be dismissed, absorbed, or outpaced. We will do things in our own way and in ways we choose to adopt, because these are the ways we know best and the way we will not be tricked into something we don't want. We reserve the right to bicker amongst ourselves and move slowly without fear of being taken over by a united non-indigenous majority. This has been a problem with our electoral system. This is why many feel that we need a Constitution that while offering

424

everyone some participation guarantees us our land, our leaders, and our ability to live and operate within our own cultural modalities. Such a Constitution would have to recognize and protect, in perception as well as in legalese, the indigenous rights of Fijians. We will have affirmative action in our Constitution, not in our welfare roles.

I repeat, we welcome and sympathise with our non-indigenous neighbours. We invite and want them to stay, in spite of the current turmoil. They are our friends and they have contributed much to the development of Fiji. They contribute in a major way to our economy. But they must accept our inalienable ground rules. Our own people will lead our own country as long as we have people to lead. And we will not divide our country. We are a difficult people to understand and especially to lead because our customs and traditions are different, and we tend to protect them. We would not wish this difficult task on anyone who is not fully accepted by our people.

As always, we want people who respect our culture, traditions, and language to join us and remain with us. We welcome everyone to our house, but please don't get the idea you own or should be the head of our house. As long as everyone understands these fundamental ground rules, Fijians will be at peace and continue to help bring peace to the rest of the world.

As this is a meeting for women, let me assure you that in Fiji we still believe very much in family values and we have roles for all ages, genders, and relationships. While we have only recently risen to political prominence, political participation and women chiefs and other leaders have always been with us. There is more work to do. At this critical time, let me just say that I am moved by my heart to join my Fijian brothers, uncles, and fathers in support, no matter which side they are on, as we go through this Identity Crisis as a culture and a nation. Fiji is all we have and we will keep it and maintain our God-given right to share it with whomever we want to when we decide to, without pressure from anyone.

Thank you all and I hope that I have stimulated some thought in you concerning us so-called "indigenous people". While it sounds like some kind of species, we are really the same as all of you. We will protect and share our culture with you. We have our roots and our Ancestral Homeland. You are all invited to come to Fiji and share our hospitality and friendship. We will welcome you into our homes, our hearts, and our hotels. This is part of being Fijian. We are proud of it and we will cherish and protect it always.

Vinaka vaka levu and thank you

Afterword

The need to write this book was fired by the school poster *We British are a rich mixture*. Just as the book was being completed a new poster came to my attention. It was seen in Westminster Hall, which adjoins the House of Common, and combined the words, *The Electorate of the Future*, with a picture of eleven children, only four of whom were White. Who produced the poster? What message is it giving? Who is the message aimed at?

What is happening in England today is not a game or the plot of a film or soap opera; although if it were it is likely that more people would take it seriously. It is actually happening, it is reality, and those who have eyes to see are witnessing something of immense historical importance.

The English need to quickly learn ethnic and diaspora politics because if we do not, and existing trends continue, we will perish. Essential to success is a widespread and celebrated sense of origins and identity. We have to defend and promote our communal culture. Our chance of success will be improved if we join with other members of the Anglo-Saxon diaspora, all of whom, to varying degrees, are faced with threats to their identity and way of life. Each part of the diaspora can learn from the experience of the others. In addition to that we should support and learn from all nations that are struggling to govern themselves in their homelands. We are all suffering at the hands of an aggressive globalism that is vandalising our physical, economic, political, and cultural environment. We all need to seek a form of democracy that gives us control over those aspects of our lives.

Those responsible for denying us the power to manage our lives want us to feel despair and resign ourselves to the inevitability of it all. It is for each of us to rise to the task in ways that suit our aptitudes, abilities and the opportunities that present themselves. It is a big task but a start has to be made somewhere. The first step takes place in your head; you must stop being afraid. They use fear to control you. It is fear, of what others may think, say, or do, that prevents you confronting those who wish to control your thoughts and actions. You have to be able to say to yourself each day, *I am not afraid of them and I will not be intimidated*. When you can say that and mean it you will be free. When they have lost the ability to control your mind, they will be afraid of you.

This is an opportunity to play a part in an heroic struggle. May he grieve forever who flees the fight.

Waes pa hael

Steadfast

An English Awakening

The aim of Steadfast is to encourage the English people to revive and embrace their communal identity, and thereby acquire the national self-respect and confidence that many of them lack. To challenge prejudice against the English; to expose misrepresentation of the English; to fight injustice and discrimination that disadvantages the English; without fear or favour wherever it arises.

For further details, please write, enclosing SAE to:

Steadfast, 27 Old Gloucester Street, London WC1N 3XX

Other titles

The Deculturalisation of the English People

John Lovejoy

In Australia the author witnessed the sad fate of Aborigines who have had their culture and communal life shattered. He saw how, despite immense difficulties, the Aborigines cling to a shared identity and struggle to recover and breathe new life into a set of values and a way of life known to their ancestors.

On his return to England, he saw the English facing a similar process of deculturalisation but lacking the will to resist or reverse it. The young have no sense of who they are or where they are from.

The English are not doing those things that are necessary to maintain a distinct culture and way of life. English identity is neglected and being left to crumble. Worse still, Englishness is actively discouraged and in its place we are offered the glitter of an easy one-size-fits-all Western identity.

Deculturalisation is revealed in the inability of many, and especially the young, to be able to answer the questions, Who am I? What do I believe? Where do I belong? Who am I loyal to? Everywhere we see the loss of communal values and perceptions.

John Lovejoy gives reasons for the deculturalisation of the English and points to the remedy.

£9·95   80 pages   paperback   A5   ISBN 1-903313-00-7

The English Dragon

T. P. Bragg

The English Dragon is a political novel with a small *p*. It is a story of loss of innocence; a search for identity; of what it means to be English.

Modern England is observed through the eyes of a baby. The narrative gives the flavour of a culture obsessed with image and dogma. There is a juxtaposition of the new and often violent urban society with the rural, traditional community.

The author does not shy away from difficult subjects - the treatment and housing of asylum-seekers being crucial to the novel's structure. A few will find it uncomfortable but most will recognise the England portrayed.

£9·95   256 pages paperback   A5   ISBN 1-903313-02-3

You can order from your bookshop or direct from Athelney.
Please enclose a cheque or postal order payable to Athelney.

UK – no charge for delivery
Europe – including **Republic of Ireland** – add 10%
North America add 10% surface delivery, 30% airmail
Elsewhere add 10% surface delivery, 40% airmail
Overseas surface delivery 6 – 10 weeks; airmail 6 – 14 days

Athelney
1 Providence Street
King's Lynn
Norfolk PE30 5ET